C0-AMU-846

DATE DUE

Demco, Inc. 38-293

A REVIEWER'S ABC

introduced by Rufus A. Blanshard

Collected Criticism of

CONRAD AIKEN

from 1916 to the present

WITHDRAWN
FAIRFIELD UNIVERSITY
LIBRARY

FAIRFIELD UNIV. LIBRARY

JAN 1 1996

a reviewer's

W. H. ALLEN   LONDON   1961

ACKNOWLEDGMENT: *I wish to thank the American Philosophical Society for the grant in 1956 to find and obtain copies of Conrad Aiken's essays and reviews.*   R.A.B.

PERMISSIONS AND ACKNOWLEDGMENTS

Acknowledgments for material reprinted in this volume are detailed in the *Checklist of Conrad Aiken's Critical Writings* on page 395.

Articles which initially appeared in *The Atlantic Monthly* (1939-1942); *The New Yorker* (1935); *The New York Herald Tribune Book Review* (1951); *The New Republic* (1915-1949); *Poetry* (1919-1940); and *The Yale Review* (1934) are reprinted by permission of these publications.

Copyright © 1935, 1939, 1940, 1942, 1951, 1958 by Conrad Aiken

Originally published in the U.S.A., 1958

First British edition, 1961

Printed in Great Britain by
D. R. Hillman & Sons Ltd., Frome, for the publishers
W. H. Allen & Co. Ltd., Essex Street, London, W.C.2

CONTENTS

Preface by Conrad Aiken   9

Introduction by Rufus A. Blanshard   11

Part I: Views on Literature and Criticism

Apologia Pro Specie Sua (1919)   25
The Mechanism of Poetic Inspiration (1917)   34
Magic or Legerdemain? (1919)   41
A Letter from America (1921)   46
The Analysis of Poetry (1922)   49
A Basis for Criticism (1923)   53
American Literature and American Critics (1924)   68
Metaphysics and Art (1924)   71
A Scientific Approach to Criticism (1925)   75
The Future of Poetry (1931)   78
Literature in Massachusetts (1937)   82
Back to Poetry (1940)   93
American Writers Come of Age (1942)   104

Part II: A Reviewer's ABC

Adams, Brooks and Henry (1920)   115
Aiken, Conrad (1917)   120
Aiken, Conrad (1918)   122
Aiken, Conrad (1919)   126
Anderson, Sherwood (1927)   130
Bennett, Arnold (1928)   133
Bishop, John Peale (1949)   134
Bosschère, Jean de (1918)   136
Bridges, Robert (1930)   141
Cabell, James Branch (1919)   143
Chekhov, Anton (1921)   148
Doolittle, Hilda (*H. D.*) (1927)   153
Dickinson, Emily (1924)   156
Dostoevsky, Feodor (1921)   163
Eberhart, Richard (1945)   168

Eliot, T. S. (1916)	171
Eliot, T. S. (1921)	172
Eliot, T. S. (1923)	176
Eliot, T. S. (1927)	182
Eliot, T. S. (1929)	184
Eliot, T. S. (1934)	186
Eliot, T. S. (1934)	188
Eliot, T. S. (1935)	191
Eliot, T. S. (1936)	193
Eliot, T. S. (1949)	194
Faulkner, William (1927)	197
Faulkner, William (1939)	200
Fitzgerald, F. Scott (1926)	207
Fletcher, John Gould (1921)	210
Galsworthy, John (1928)	213
Gissing, George (1927)	217
Hardy, Thomas (1924)	219
Housman, A. E. (1936)	223
Huxley, Aldous (1925)	225
James, Henry (1925)	230
James, Henry (1935)	233
James, Henry (1935)	236
Keats, John (1925)	238
Keats, John (1927)	253
Lawrence, D. H. (1924)	256
Lawrence, D. H. (1924)	261
Lawrence, D. H. (1927)	263
Lawrence, D. H. (1929)	266
Lewis, Wyndham (1928)	268
Lewis, Wyndham (1928)	271
Lindsay, Vachel (1923)	274
Lorca, Federico García (1940)	276
MacLeish, Archibald (1927)	278
MacLeish, Archibald (1929)	280
MacLeish, Archibald (1934)	283
MacNeice, Louis (1941)	285

Mann, Thomas (1928) 288
Mansfield, Katherine (1921) 291
Mansfield, Katherine (1922) 293
Mansfield, Katherine (1927) 297
Masters, Edgar Lee (1918) 299
Mencken, H. L. (1934) 301
Moore, George (1919) 303
Moore, George (1927) 307
Moore, George (1937) 309
Murasaki, Lady (1928) 311
O'Neill, Eugene (1928) 315
Péguy, Charles (1943) 318
Perse, St. John (1945) 320
Pound, Ezra (1927) 323
Pound, Ezra (1934) 325
Powys, John Cowper (1929) 327
Richardson, Dorothy (1928) 329
Rilke, Rainer Maria (1942) 331
Robinson, Edwin Arlington (1921) 333
Robinson, Edwin Arlington (1922) 341
Robinson, Edwin Arlington (1927) 344
Romains, Jules (1925) 346
Sandburg, Carl (1926) 349
Santayana, George (1936) 352
Schwartz, Delmore (1940) 355
Shapiro, Karl (1944) 358
Shapiro, Karl (1945) 361
Stein, Gertrude (1934) 364
Stevenson, Robert Louis (1928) 367
Thomas, Dylan (1940) 370
Thomas, Dylan (1944) 371
Turgenev, Ivan (1927) 373
Waley, Arthur (1919) 377
Williams, William Carlos (1934) 380
Williams, William Carlos (1951) 383
Winters, Yvor (1941) 387

Woolf, Virginia (1927)   389

Woolf, Virginia (1929)   392

Checklist of Conrad Aiken's Critical Writings   395

Index of Authors Reviewed   409

NOTE: Some of the pieces in this book are composite reviews. The name at the head of a piece indicates a prominent, but not necessarily exclusive, place in the review. For full entries see the Checklist, and for a full list of authors see the Index.

When I began to reread last year, for the first time since its publication, the accumulated critical work of almost half a century, much of which I had forgotten and some of which I would have denied having written at all, I was perhaps not unnaturally somewhat apprehensive. That fellow, in his twenty-sixth year, who had begun reviewing books as far back as 1915, hadn't he been pretty alarmingly young? Would any of it stand this reexamination, in another time, another weather?

And let me admit it at once, a good deal of that early work obviously *is young*, but I think, on the whole, disarmingly so. One must be prepared to forgive if one can what Marianne Moore once accurately termed "the snare-drum rattle of the adverbs." But against this, it seems to me, looking back from this perspective of time and change, that some of this immaturity, whether of style or content, is at least partly redeemed, and even in the very earliest of the pieces, by what I quite enviously confess appears to have been an uncanny sort of farsightedness. It pleases and amuses me in about equal proportions to see now how clearly that young man seemed to know where he was going, or where he *wanted* to go, and where also he wanted poetry, fiction, and criticism to go. In the "Apologia Pro Specie Sua," for example, which was written in 1919 (during an attack of German measles), as the introduction to *Scepticisms*, we find him already calmly invoking Sigmund Freud and sociology; and explicitly adopting a "relativist" position, one which he was further to explore and elaborate, five years later, in "A Basis for Criticism," and which was in a sense to govern his critical approach for his entire career as a reviewer. In the light of the new psychology, he was then already looking into the roots of things, whether they were poetry's or his own or mankind's, and adumbrating a possible post-Darwinian *weltanschauung*, which he facetiously called "the yea-sayings of one who finds nothing to say yea to." He was positing that neither *vers libre* nor Imagism was a sufficient answer to the problem of poetic form, which had just then become a major issue, but rather something on the order of the free-rhyming, regular-irregular verse of that new young poet, T. S. Eliot, in *The Love Song of J. Alfred Prufrock*. And he was candid enough to admit happily that this was precisely the direction that he hoped poetry would take, since this was precisely what he himself most wanted to do.

In short, I would not now want the end-result, as it has willy-nilly shaped itself in this book, to have been otherwise. Considering its pretty respectable range, it has pursued its own characteristic *parti pris* consistently enough. Such inconsistencies of tact or taste as do appear, and as were to have been expected, are perhaps implicitly soluble in the demonstrable stance that is almost always discoverably present. As for alterations of taste, such as they are, I think they constitute rather a sharpening than any basic change: that young man's perceptions, I note with some alarm, were pretty sharp to begin with.

It remains to say that I owe this book, *in toto*, to my friend Rufus Blanshard, whose idea it was and who heroically undertook the immense labor of research and copying and organization which it has involved. His assistance, too, in making the final selection—the present compilation consists of about half of the total material—has been invaluable; and to him go my grateful thanks. As it now stands, *A Reviewer's ABC: Collected Criticism from 1916 to the Present* represents what I wish to preserve of the work done in those forty-odd years.

Brewster, Massachusetts, 1958

Introduction by RUFUS A. BLANSHARD

In an age of criticism, such as this one has often been called, it is natural that poets and novelists should write about each other. They are the ones who in the first place make it an age of criticism by creating new things to talk about, both new kinds of literature and new views of life. This creative activity seldom goes on in a critical vacuum. A few untutored geniuses may have broken new ground in the arts, but for the most part the pioneers have been very conscious of the territories they were abandoning and possessing and could give you reasons for doing so. This is the beginning of a new criticism, when the creative and the critical faculties are closely allied. In this sense, it is no disparagement to speak of our age as one of criticism—though when criticism outstrips creation, or pulls it along paths already worn, we might grow justifiably alarmed. If excessive refinement is the price of self-consciousness, we may be said to be paying that price today; but would we be less self-conscious if we could? And it is the artists of thirty or forty years ago, more than anyone else, who in what they made and what they said gave our age its stamp by extending our self-consciousness.

These reflections are occasioned by a reading of Conrad Aiken's criticism. One more of that amazing group of (now aging) poets who created new things to talk about—and perhaps the most self-conscious of them all—turns out to have talked about them himself. What is surprising is not that he should have done so, but that we should only now be rediscovering his remarks. It has been said from time to time, by historians of modern criticism, that Aiken is an acute critic, that his book *Scepticisms: Notes on Contemporary Poetry* (1919) was one of the best commentaries of its time, that his piece on *The Waste Land* was worth reading. But he is never discussed as a "force" in criticism, he is not anthologized (in an age, too, of anthologies), and few of those who know his creative work well know more than a dozen of the uncollected reviews and essays. That he has failed until now to collect them is a prominent reason for our ignorance. Another reason, paradoxically, is the very fact that he *did* gather his earliest pieces into a book, after which, it might have been assumed, he wrote little in that way. In fact, since that book appeared he has written about 170 critical pieces. It is enough in bulk and range to have made the reputation of a lesser figure. It is, furthermore,

everywhere informed with that natural but unassertive authority of the dedicated and engaged writer to whom the extra
reputation he might win as critic is not so important as the self-
rewards of the critical experience. As we might have expected,
if we knew *Scepticisms,* it is a body of criticism both perceptive
and self-revealing. As that book charted the currents of the most
turbulent period in modern English and American poetry,
and charted them by navigating them, so Aiken's subsequent
criticism records, still from the stream, the thirty-year issue.

The best introduction to this book is the whole of *Scepticisms,* from which only five pieces are here reprinted. And
the best gloss is Aiken's other writing. If such a judgment
seems to give too much weight to the inside view, the *parti pris,*
the objection is overruled by the subject's self-awareness. It is
not that his self-awareness has made him more objective than
the rest of us, but that it has laid bare, for his own and our observation, the nature and extent of his subjectivity. In this sense
the title of the first chapter of *Scepticisms,* "Apologia Pro Specie
Sua," fits everything he has written—if we acknowledge the
subtle permutations through which apologetics pass to become
highly-wrought works of art. It fits most immediately, though
not so obviously as we think at first, the criticism. Aiken there
confessed that the reviews and essays he had collected constituted "an ideograph of Aiken. . . . They represent my own
particular attempt to urge the poetic currents of the day in a
direction that might be favourable to me." Lest our job in making out the ideograph seem by this statement too simple,
Aiken warned in an Appendix ("A Note on Values") of the
"widespread, though unconscious, dishonesty in all criticism."

The poet-critic, it is true, likes the sort of thing in the work of
others that he himself is trying to do. But how often, and how
completely, does he find it? And might he not, even, having
found a single "scarcely apprehensible kinship" with another
poet whose work as a whole is different from his own, flatter
himself that in praising that poet he is being broad-minded,
nay self-defeating, when in fact he is only rationalizing the
small bond which he cannot define? This perception is one
light that Aiken, the critic of himself as critic, throws on the
convolutions of the "pathetic ego," to the terms of which, he
says, "all human judgments or tastes reduce themselves under
pressure." This is the way he would account for his attitude
toward John Gould Fletcher, and we must acknowledge the
force of the confession if we contemplate the relationship be-

tween those two poets who "learned" so much from each other. Another light, a particularly harsh one, we remember from the "Apologia" itself, where Aiken notes that although an Imagist poet is almost bound to feel "that the qualities of Spoon River will always be somewhat alien to him as an artist (though he may appreciate them as a reader)," he might, as a critic, *praise* it, "in the belief that the success of so different a type of work will hardly affect his own, . . . reserving his animosity for something a little more dangerously on his own ground." Such cynicism may appall us, until we recognize it as the honesty of one examining his own dishonesty. Just as, in reading Aiken's symphonies, we are witness to an elaborate confession through a series of deliberately fragmentary masks and subterfuges, so in the comparatively "straightforward" criticism we are to watch the man, so to speak, both disheveling and assembling himself. If it be asked how so self-regarding an operation can lay claim to catholicity, Aiken has the answer (in the Appendix):

It is precisely because, on the whole, the reflections of the human organism, or consciousness, in the work of any particular artist, are so tiny and so incomplete, that we are compelled, if we are to discover ourselves with anything like completeness or find ourselves mirrored at full length, to gather our reflections in splintered fragments, to assemble the portrait bit by bit. If the poet-critic, therefore, sets about composing a self-portrait which shall never employ a stroke in the first person singular, but employ only those aspects of himself which he finds in his contemporaries—an undertaking which may or may not be conscious, usually not—it should be perceived at once that the process will be laborious and confused, that it will lead him at many points far afield, and that if the resultant portrait is to attain anything like completeness it will necessarily be forced to draw, for some items, on sources which at first glimpse might appear unpromising. Confused it must, certainly, seem to the reader, provided that the reader has at all been let into the secret; provided that the poet-critic has at all confessed what he himself may not have realized, the essential self-portrayal of any kind of criticism.

Thus we may expect, from the splintered fragments that make up Aiken's estimates of his fellow-writers, a portrait both of himself and of his times.

Those years from 1912 to 1920 were his own period of creative experiment, as they were modern literature's. Looking back on those years in his autobiographical essay, *Ushant* (1952), Aiken remembers his simultaneous effort to preserve his independent self and be a part of his age: "If D. had retained his independence, venturing to voice his own skepticisms as to what he thought narrow or extreme or absurd in some of the new theories and experiments, nevertheless he was as much immersed in the thing as any." It was the skepticisms that came through loudest in the criticism, and it was right to style those early pieces by that name; and yet there is in all of them that sense of immersion, of engagement in the literary adventure, even of exuberance, which differentiates the participant from the negative (or academic) bystander. The fun of the thing is a part of the whole experience: A couple of *jeux d'esprit* on his own books in the Chicago *Daily News* (omitted from *Scepticisms*) show the kind of zest a young skeptic can have; one, published anonymously, was sufficiently caustic to disarm his detractors, the other sufficiently zany to confound them. In the various literary quarrels of the day, he likewise took stands that could endear him to no side, but perhaps least of all to the outside, to those who wanted to turn back to the days before the quarrels. Free verse and Imagism, for example, he considered unfavorably in his very earliest critical pieces, but in showing their limitations could scarcely have given comfort to the traditionalists. Like Eliot, who a little later said, more bluntly, "*Vers libre* does not exist," Aiken felt that, without being "taken in," he could learn something from the experiments in the way of clearer images and freer rhythms. In fact, Aiken commended Eliot's early poetry as a demonstration of the counterpoint that the vers librists were sacrificing in their abandonment of known patterns. Again, was Aiken—to resurrect the fighting words—a "radical" or a "conservative," a "realist" or a "romanticist," a "psychologist" or a "colorist"? Though he had his preferences (for psychology above all), and stated them, it was difficult to pin him down; and though he was fond of classifying others according to such categories, it was so that he might isolate and highlight what was essential in each and turn those bright fragments to his own use. In short, he was on both sides in the civil war, and on neither. And the somewhat ironic result for his reputation was that the more militant partisans of the "new poetry," and after them their more earnest heirs, labeled him "conservative."

To feel the irony of the label, one need only recall his early championship of Eliot and Stevens, or his long-drawn battle with Louis Untermeyer and the "fuglemen of the autochthonous" (as he called them). But it is only a partial irony, as these very instances imply. What he was looking for was

an art that should reflect the sensibility of modern man in a
modern world and yet still be *art*, art that might take its place
in richness beside that of the past, and perhaps even surpass
it in subtlety. The correspondence between his critical and
creative interests is here again manifest. Aiken was not a revolutionary poet. He grew up on Keats and Poe, and retained, if
he modified, what he learned from them—romantic "color," for
example, and formal elaboration and the musical line. He
"found" himself, poetically, not by rejecting these things, which
were in the first place there in him to be drawn out and per-
fected, but by pressing them into the service of themes peculiarly his own and compellingly modern: the ego adrift on the
sea of the unconscious, the erotic-neurotic dance of urban
life, the psychic defeats and rewards of civilized godlessness.
Street lamps and cigarettes are more relevant to these themes
than moonlight and roses, but one does not therefore forget
what moonlight and roses are; the juxtaposition itself can be
painfully suggestive.

Something new, then, growing out of something already
there: that is the sort of evolution, not revolution, for which
Aiken strove in his own work and looked in the work of
others. And it was a different enough goal from those of the
various modish radicalisms of the day, which were declaring
war indiscriminately on the useful and the outmoded in convention, and not always substituting what was durable for what
was swept away, to make him seem comparatively, at times,
the cranky defender of the faith. The retrospective view in
Ushant shows what he felt he must defend: "D." had through
all the movements and countermovements "kept firmly to his
own slightly conservative bias, in the persistent belief that form
must be form, that inventions of form must keep a basis in
order and tradition, that a mere surrender to the pleasure
(which was undoubtedly to be had) of chain-making in the
bright colors of the colloquial and the colloquial cadence was
not enough." The "bias" made him see what has since become
clearer—that most of the poetry of that period, like most poetry
in any period, was not very good. It made him see, to compound the heresy, that the newfangled was no better *per se*,
though it might be more exciting, than the old-fashioned. It
made him, to return to that happy but thankless designation, a
skeptic.

As we move on to Aiken's criticism as a whole, we note first
of all the continuity. The criticism keeps pace with the crea-

tion, showing similar changes in emphasis (to which we must return) and a similar growth in range, notably a branching out into fiction, but there are no startling conversions to new methods, no sweeping repudiations of old. The very provenance of this collection remains the same in kind as that of *Scepticisms*. The *Poetry Journal* of Boston (1912-1918), for which Aiken became a sort of critical editorialist, had been one step behind *Poetry* of Chicago, interested in the new but generally more "conservative" on the controversial issues. *The New Republic*, in which his other earliest pieces appeared and for which he was to write more than for any other magazine over the next forty years, has always been alert in the arts but not esoteric. The main source of *Scepticisms* was *The Dial*, of which Aiken was a contributing editor in 1917-1918 before it moved from Chicago to New York. He continued to write for *The Dial* until it ceased in 1929, through its change from a liberal organ of progressive thought to the most distinguished American critical review under the editorship of Schofield Thayer and Marianne Moore. Ezra Pound had once said that the dial was the part of the clock that didn't move. Even in its later form it was not sensational. But it published Pound himself, Eliot (*The Waste Land*), Marianne Moore, Cummings, Yeats, Aiken, Crane, and others who did move. Of Aiken's critical work for *The Dial*, Marianne Moore has written (in *Wake* 11, 1952) that he was "the perfect reviewer, Diogenes' one honest man, fearing only to displease himself." Even here, Aiken is not in a definable "school"; he is characteristically pursuing his own way. The other periodicals in which his reviews appeared were as widely different as *The Criterion* and *The New York Post*—not to count those "London Letters" in *The New Yorker* (1934-1936) under the pseudonym of Samuel Jeake, Jr., or the tennis articles in the same magazine. In these scattered pieces there is no perceptible raising or lowering of the brow to suit the "tone" of the audience. His criticism, like his style, is middle-high. Its orientation, furthermore, as the range suggests, is transatlantic. From his earliest travels in England, dictated by his New England sense of cultural heritage, and from his semipermanent residence in Rye (in the shadow of Henry James) during the twenties and thirties, he acquired the double perspective that informs so much of his writing. It was this that gave point to the constant comparisons, in *Scepticisms*, of English and American poetry, and this that continued to give an unprovincial authority to his judgments when he came to write "Letters from

America" to *The Athenaeum* and *The London Mercury,* and to introduce the English public to Emily Dickinson. The Anglo-American polarity of the criticism is as much a part of the continuity as the civilized skepticism, and of course intimately related with it.

But the skepticism has a theoretical basis, too, which can be traced back to Aiken's early preoccupation with the "new psychology." His most sustained formulations of a critical theory, besides the "Apologia," are the chapter on poetic inspiration in *Scepticisms,* the article "A Basis for Criticism" (1923), and the review of I. A. Richards' *Principles of Literary Criticism* (1925). What animates these pieces, and those many others in which the theory is either stated or merely implied, is the thoroughgoing relativism that we have already noted in the "Apologia." It is a sort of anti-theory which insists that the traditional notions of "beauty" stand corrected by what we now know about the psychology of creation and consumption. Since a work of art is rooted in the personality, conscious and unconscious, of its creator, criticism should deal as much with those roots as with the finished flower. And since the value of the work depends on the effect it has on the similarly complex mechanism of the observer, there is no absolute scheme of values by which the critic can judge it. (Here Aiken crossed swords with Richards, who answered his review in an Appendix to the second edition of *Principles.*) It follows that criticism must deal also, then, with the function of art—with its psycho- and sociotherapeutic uses.

If art is in any sense wish-fulfillment—and Aiken took over enough of Freudianism to say it is—then both artist and observer are proper subjects for a kind of critical psychoanalysis, which of course is complicated by the critic's own involvements as observer. This subjectivity of both art and response may be deplorable, but it is a fact which a critic cuts himself off from reality by ignoring. It is moreover an opportunity for criticism to extend our knowledge and appreciation of just those subtle associations and suggestions that often constitute the characteristic stamp of a poet, a stamp which no amount of "objective" analysis can define.

On the face of it, Aiken's espousal of psychology as the key to criticism—"Criticism is really a branch of psychology," he wrote in another review—would seem to make him a too-special pleader. It is easy to point out the narrowness of any system of psychology as a basis for aesthetics. It is even easier to point out the limitations of deliberately "Freudian" art. Aiken has suffered, as both poet and novelist, at the hands of critics who realized *how* easy it was to do the latter, without recognizing the difference between, say, Demarest or Andrew Cather and a case history. He is likely to suffer similarly in estimates of his criticism unless he is recognized to be, in practice, larger and more flexible than the associationist and Freudian mold of his theoretical formulations. Indeed, if we take into account the time of those formulations, which is to say their timeliness, we will see them not as a somewhat dated exploitation of a fad—with their airing of such terms as "fantasy," "psychic injury," and "neurosis"—but as an effort to enlarge the scope of criticism, to add rather than to subtract a dimension, even to open the way for other and untried methods.

That he was aware of the possibly stultifying effect of Freudian theory, as of any theory, is manifest in his satirical review of *The Erotic Motive in Literature* by Albert Mordell (1919): Mordell, he says, "has swallowed Freud a little too whole, and has temporary indigestion." One never feels this of Aiken's criticism. On the other hand, neither is the psychological interest to be deprecated. If there is one distinctive feature that modern literature shares with modern thought in general, it is self-exploration. Whether or not we trace this feature back to the Romantics, as Lionel Trilling has done, we find its scientific rationale in Freud and psychoanalysis. When Aiken insisted on the importance to criticism of the self-revealing and self-exploring feature of art, he was in one sense, it is true, expressing the central concern of his whole creative effort; but he was also telling us, before it became a truism, that psychology is here to stay.

To go from the theory to the practice is to see at once how significant and how unconstricting Aiken's psychological interest is. Unconstricting because it does not exclude other interests, as we have seen in his preference for form as opposed to uncontrolled "chain-making." The reviews and essays, furthermore, are not systematically psychoanalytical even when they use the available terms. If Aiken was struck by "the singular psychological change" that came over Emily Dickinson and wished he knew "the causes of the psychic injury which so sharply turned her in upon herself," he devoted most of his longest essay on her to a discussion of the relationship between her individualism and those unique qualities in her poetry which no such delving can fully explain. (Her "affair" with Charles Wadsworth had not been substantiated when Aiken wrote this essay, but it is not likely that he would have written a very different essay in the light of it.) In a discussion of Hardy's "philosophy," Aiken says that one of the important questions for criticism is the psychological one: "Why has Mr. Hardy . . . always been so enthralled by 'ideas'?" But he decides that the question, provocative enough simply in being stated, can be left "to a chartered psycho-analyst" to answer. It is up to the critic first to note Hardy's emotional skepticism, then to answer the extra-psychological question about the "ideas" he adopted: "to what aesthetic use has he put them?"

In the long review of Amy Lowell's biography of Keats, Aiken postulates "an unusually intense erotic relationship between the mother and son" and sees Keats's whole life as "a feverish search for luxury as a replacement of his mother." This piece is undoubtedly Aiken's most sustained effort at psychoanalysis; but it is so partly because he saw the need for correcting an over-"external" approach to Keats's life (it is a biography he is reviewing); and it concludes with a sensitive and unsensational application of these ideas to the themes, moods, and textures of Keats's poetry—an application which we might expect not from a professional psychologist but from a poet to whom Keats has "spoken." These examples show that even at its most pressing, the psychological interest does not diminish, but rather augments, the aesthetic.

One can put the matter more positively by saying that Aiken's criticism is nearly always engaged in directing our attention to the way in which a work of art reveals and signifies—like a signature itself—the psyche of the artist. "The deepest quality of a work of art," Henry James once wrote, "will always be the quality of the mind of the producer." The parallel is not wholly fortuitous, since Aiken called James, long before the vogue, "one of the very few men produced by America or England (in this case by both) who approximate greatness as critics." James has "fathered" so many modern critics, however, that a distinction must be made between Aiken and two other kinds of followers: those who moved from an initial "aesthetic" position toward a commitment to moral or theological values, and those who, by concentrating on the "document," ushered in a new kind of absolutism through formal analysis. Aiken's review of Eliot's *For Lancelot Andrewes* (1928) shows how important Eliot has been in both of these directions; it shows also

how uncongenial to Aiken's own convictions and interests were
these developments. What Aiken tries to capture is "the quality
of the mind of the producer." He is never a moralist, not having lost his impatience with the traditional American view of
the man of letters as a social and spiritual leader with a "message." ("The Puritan is a long time a-dying," he says in one
place. "His only question before a work of art is 'What does it
teach?' . . . Melville, Poe, Emily Dickinson, and Henry Adams
can go hang themselves. And Henry James can go to England.")
Nor is he ever a methodical formalist. He does not concern
himself with detailed analyses of poems or novels or stories; in
fact he rarely gives an account of any single work except to illustrate a general statement about the author's main characteristics. He is more interested in "style" than in what is now
called "structure." The separate elements of style he sees as
interdependent clues to a poet's or a novelist's self-projection;
so that for him the style is, ultimately, the man. It is impossible to read his essay on Faulkner's method without wish-
ing that Aiken had done more of this sort of stylistic criticism,
but what makes the essay so rewarding is the insight it provides
into the total working of Faulkner's mind. Aiken explains the
point in one of his pieces on Robinson, a piece that treats at
some length that poet's use of the "vague phrase." This is a
matter of diction and tone, and the treatment is a "technical"
one; but technique, says Aiken,

is perhaps merely a more inquisitive term for "style," by which, again,
I suppose we mean the explicit manifestation of an individual mode
of thought. At all events, technique and mode of thought are inseparable, are two aspects of one thing, and it is impossible to discuss any
artist's technique without being insensibly and inevitably led into a
discussion of his mode of thought.

By "individual mode of thought" Aiken means that which distinguishes one mind, or sensibility, from another; in a former age
it would have been called the artist's "genius." Obviously, technique in its narrowest sense is one indication of this essence;
just as obviously, Aiken implies, to try to isolate the technique
is to run the danger of missing the essence. That is why, in so
many of his reviews, Aiken employs the suggestive, metaphorical, tangential method of describing style. It is not with
the idea of writing "poetic" criticism, of going his author one
better; this we might expect from a non-poet. It is rather to
convey his "feeling" for the total solution of which the style is

an inseparable element. This, for example, of D. H. Lawrence's poetry: "He seizes the moment violently, and kills it outright with a powerful, and sometimes bloody, phrase." Or, in another review, of Lawrence's prose: "In his passion for the direct, for the naked and unashamed, he insists on drawing our attention to the very odd clothes he wears (stylistically speaking), and, not satisfied with this, flings them off in a kind of dance of the seven veils." Such characterizations give us an image of Lawrence himself, an image shaped and colored, for the perceptive eye, by his style. That the perceptive eye is Aiken's, and is not without a certain "color" of its own, does not detract from the aptness of the image. All images are two-way affairs. And we have been told already about "the essential self-portrayal of any kind of criticism." Allowing for this subjectivity, even being grateful for it in Aiken's case, we may be surprised that his portraits of others are such telling likenesses of *them*.

Taken altogether, then, Aiken's criticism is "an ideograph of Aiken" that manages to be also a composite portrait of an age. We see things from his angle and are more alive to them than we were before. He does not cease to be the poet and novelist who is finding or failing to find, in the work of his fellows, the qualities he prizes most. And because he does not stand still, the angle shifts a little. We notice, for example, that as he continued to explore "consciousness" in his novels and poems, and came to think of this exploration as the poet's characteristic contribution to man's ultimate achievement of godhead (by which he meant total awareness), he became more impatient with the small, the dry, and the "safe" in literature. During the period of the composition of his two books of *Preludes,* it is in keeping with his growing conviction, and his unique translation of it into art, that he should entrust "The Future of Poetry" (1931) to those who have "a complete honesty in seeing life as a kaleidoscopic series of incandescent instants." That is to say, who see life as he does. Where the emphasis was once on the need for more "art," it is, in the later criticism, on the need for a new "romanticism." We would not expect to find in *Scepticisms* this passage (written in 1940): "Is not poetry an affirmation, even when it is fullest of despair . . . ? We need more than ever that taproot sort of affirmation, a blood-filled affirmation deeply rooted in the world—we need it now more than ever." Or this (1941): "Discipline . . . tends to avoid the properly 'poetic' field, which it considers a little too vulgar and easy, and to employ rather the method of the . . . critical essay. Statement, analysis, conclusion—the method, it will be seen, is anti-orgastic in the extreme. The poet is wholly safe, he runs no risk of embarrassment." It is the strategy, long ago announced, of the poet-critic who is never satisfied with the vogue. It is still Aiken the skeptic telling us we are not so good as we think. In the early years what we had was energy, what we lacked was refinement. When refinement came, in art and criticism alike, it came with a vengeance. And it was then that Aiken called for energy, for daring, for the sort of risks that Dylan Thomas took with language and emotion. Throughout those later reviews, which are still charting the literary currents, though by then such different currents, we see Aiken maintaining the integrity of his whole career, both creative and critical, by being true to himself.

Views on Literature and Criticism

It has not been my intention, in the pages which compose this book, to deal comprehensively with contemporary poetry, nor even, for that matter, to deal exhaustively with that part of it which I have touched at all. That sort of study has seldom attracted me. It has been my aim rather to deal only with the most interesting aspects of contemporary poetry, and to do so in a manner which might provoke and stimulate not only the casual reader but, odd as it may seem, the unfortunate poet himself. Anybody must have been aware, as I point out repeatedly in the following pages, of the fact that the present poetic era is one of uncertainty, of confusion and conflict. New ground has been broken in a good many directions, or ground which, if not new, has been at any rate so long unused as to have that appearance, at least, and to inspire a certain amount of scepticism as to the resultant crops; and it has been engagingly natural, under these circumstances, that each poet should claim the most astounding properties for his own plot of soil, and become a little wilfully cynical as to the claims of his rivals. No one would expect much praise of Masefield or Abercrombie or Gibson at the hands of the Imagists, for example, nor on the other side should one hope for much gratuitous enthusiasm over the Imagists or Others from, let us say, Frost or Masters. Those poets who, like myself, are critics of poetry as well, have had an almost unfair advantage in this situation. They have been able to articulate their particular theories, to argue for them in the public forum. It was a perception of the advantages of this sort of propaganda which drew the Imagists together under a somewhat specious symbol and persuaded them to write prefaces in which the self-consciousness of the authors was just a trifle shrill, just a shade too *Noli me tangere;* it was a perception of the same thing that suggested to Alfred Kreymborg and others the uses of a periodical of their own in which the nimble word-jugglers and sensation-balancers of that group—if it can be called a group—might juggle to their hearts' content, careless of ceiling or sky and happily aware of a certain amount of audience; it was the same perception, finally, which has led Ezra Pound, Louis Untermeyer, John Gould Fletcher, Maxwell Bodenheim, Miss Harriet Monroe, Miss Amy Lowell, and myself—among others—to write, first and last, a good deal of criticism of poetry. We have all pretended pretty much, of course, in these cases, to write judicially. Our utterances are apt to sound authoritative and final. But do not be deceived! We are no surer of ourselves at bottom than anybody else is. We are, in fact, half the time, frightened to death.

II

Frightened to death, I mean, precisely of each other. . . . No one, I daresay, who is not himself in the game, would guess this. The usual opinion of us is that when we are not rolling our eyes toward heaven in fine frenzies we are rather a sanguinary lot, spoiling for fights in sheer love of bloodshed. When I am seen, for example, assailing Mr. Untermeyer, or Mr. Untermeyer is seen assailing Mr. Fletcher, or Miss Lowell is seen assailing me, the usual observation is simply to the effect that "poets are certainly a vain and contentious lot of cockatoos." Well, vain enough we are, in all conscience; but I do not think we are by nature contentious. The fact is that we are simply, as I said, afraid—mortally and secretly afraid.

The reasons for this should be clear enough to any one who will give his imagination to it for a moment. What we are afraid of is the competition: a factor which few people are apt to consider in connection with the success or failure of an artist, but one which is always in considerable degree present, and which at the moment, as at all other moments of artistic recrudescence, is extremely important. The competition among poets in this country just now is, as a matter of fact, severe to the point of deadliness. Not merely, I mean, in the effort to secure publishers and publicity, though few enough, truly, achieve even that much; but more importantly in the next stage, when, having secured a certain indispensable amount of recognition, the poet begins to exert himself in the most audacious and exhausting task of his life, namely, to convince himself, his public, and his fellow-poets that there is nothing accidental about his success, that his work has about it a certain uniqueness of distinction which should commend it for perpetuity, and even that it may have, somewhat, the qualities of greatness. I do not wish to maintain that this undertaking is wholly conscious: but if the poet is not wholly or at all times conscious of it, neither is he wholly unconscious of it. And it is precisely of the ghastly possibility that his impression of himself may be wrong, that his undertaking, and indeed his life,—since the two are nearly synonymous—may be only dust in the nostrils, that he is so secretly and so profoundly afraid.

In these circumstances, it is entirely natural that the poet, if he command a decent prose style, or is accustomed to the exactions of speech-making, should set about hunting converts. What he is going to say is largely predetermined. It will be, as it were, a slow distillation of his temperament through his reason. There will be moments of uncertainty at the outset, moments when his temperament goes too fast for him, and is not properly alembicated. At such moments his dicta will have a little too much, as he perceives later, the air of personal tastes and whims, and not sufficiently the carved serenity of, let us say, a poetic decalogue. But with time he achieves this stony solidity: his pronouncements increase in massiveness and weight. And many a young head is crushed beneath them.

III

It is not, however, the young heads which most attract his lithologues: it is rather the heads of an age with his own, and those a little older—those that are bobbing, so to speak, for the same crown—which most perturb him. This attitude is only human; though one would scarcely expect most poets to admit it with much candour. If our poet is, for example, an Imagist, who has been, let us say, pretty successful as a writer of short lyrics in free verse, conspicuous for their coruscations of color, their glittering edges, and conspicuous also, in a sense, for their lack of conceptual or emotional elements, he will be a trifle skeptic about poetry which is narrative, or philosophic, or realistic. Let us perceive his case with care: let us sympathize with him profoundly. He is, let us say, hyperaesthetic, and exquisitely balanced; extraordinarily acute in his perceptions of sensory mood, miraculously adept in recalling, without allowing a single minute jewel-article of color to escape, the most evanescently beautiful of the kaleidoscopic patterns of sensation which fall together, and fall apart again, in the coolness of the mind. This is his temperament, and, slightly dimmed, this is his poetry. What must he conclude when he encounters a *Spoon River Anthology?* He is, of course, shaken to his foundations. He has found, beside his dwarf Japanese garden, a footprint which looks colossal merely because it is human. It signifies, for him, a world which is only too bewilderingly huge, a world which in his secluded course of refinement on refinement he had altogether forgotten as perhaps containing the potentials of poetry. His first reaction is an almost stupefied realization of the minuteness and delicacy of his own work. His heart sinks: he surveys this new thing with a mixture of admiration and terror. "If the world likes this, what can it find in me?" But habit and determination come speedily enough to his rescue—he needn't have been afraid for himself. His vanity has been growing too long and too sturdily to be so easily overthrown. And his theory of art—which of course is antithetical to that behind the *Spoon River Anthology*—is complete.

IV

The stage, then, is nicely set for one of those little aesthetic altercations which give poets reputations as pugilists. Our poet writes an article on the *Spoon River Anthology*. Will it be an unbiased article? Hardly. Too many things are at stake for him. The article will be honest enough: there will be no pretense about it, he will not conceal the fact that he admires the book tremendously, or that he thinks it contains certain of the qualities of greatness. But it will not be unbiased. Directly or indirectly, from start to finish, no matter how far it may appear to be from the subject, it will be an impeachment of the artistic methods of *Spoon River Anthology* and a defense of the methods of the Imagist. The degree of intensity with which this will be done, and the degree of candor, will vary. Our poet is faced with alternatives. Perhaps his own convictions and course are slightly modified by the apparition. In this case he will admit the brilliance of it, but point out how much better it might have been had its qualities of vigor and incisiveness been more richly fused with the qualities of luminosity, delicacy, and precision. He has found a new ideal: a combination of divers new qualities with his own. This is a combination of which, as a matter of fact, he had always been capable; but, quite by accident, he has never till now perceived it . . . On the other hand, if our Imagist is a little more limited as to adaptability, if he feels that the qualities of *Spoon River* will always be somewhat alien to him as an artist (though he may appreciate them as a reader) two courses of action are open to him. The first will be to ignore *Spoon River* completely. It will be considered coarse and artless, its success temporary. He will be quite sincere in this opinion. Or, on the other hand, one can conceive him, just as sincerely, lifting his voice in praise of *Spoon River*, in the belief that the success of so different a type of work will hardly affect his own; and reserving his animosity for something a little more dangerously on his own ground.

V

It begins to be seen how complex is this life-and-death struggle among the poets. Our Imagist is only one imaginary case. When we recall that every poet is at bottom just as self-centered, just as determined to achieve and perpetuate a sort of pre-eminence for the poetic methods which his temperament, or sensibility, has forced upon him, we see into what a pandiabolorum we have strayed. We see also how much we must be prepared to discount anything that these amiable creatures start to tell us about art. Be they never so entertaining, be they never so grave and polite to their rivals, rest assured there will always be concealed somewhere a mortal sting. Some poets believe in employing the sting with candor and gusto—some advocate that literary executions should be performed with an exquisiteness of tact, that the lethal weapon should not so often be bullet or bludgeon, or even a moonlit blade, but rather the serpent in a bed of roses, a poisoned perfume. One should not necessarily, I think, accuse the latter class of poets of being hypocritical. The method they choose is no indication of any timidity, they have no fear of violence, nor would it displease them to see their enemies go down under good red blows; no, if they choose the subtler and more Machiavellian method it will be because they believe it to be the more efficient, simply. "See," they seem to say, "how essentially good-natured, how candid and sweet we are! Could any one, under the circumstances, believe what we say of X to be anything but the most dispassionate aesthetic truth?"—Yes, this method has its advantages, as I have found. I used to be fond of the good old-fashioned sandbag. Miss Lowell once rebuked me for this: she warned me that I might become known as a "knocker." I thought she was wrong; but since then she has published *Tendencies in Modern American Poetry*, and I see that she is right. The sandbag is too clumsy. And silence, as Ezra Pound can testify, is just as effective.

VI

The situation, then, reveals itself as one to curdle the blood. Who is to be trusted? Who will tell us what to like? Who will say "this is false, this is true, this is bad, this is good"? Who is there whom we can follow with soft-eyed confidence into the silences of the arcana? The answer, as should have been foreseen, is "No one." We are all unreliable, all grinding our own axes. About a good many things, things which do not too directly concern us, we can tell you the unvarnished truth. We may be pretty reliable on matters of aesthetic fact—most of us would probably tell you that too many sibilants in the same line are to be avoided, that vowel sounds can be combined so as to make a very pleasant harmony (an art which many poets neglect), that "The Man with a Hoe" contains a good idea but is a lifelessly written and mediocre poem. But the instant we go beyond simple universals, distrust us! You can be sure that consciously or unconsciously we are setting out to poison whatever springs we believe will flow down to posterity. We are determined to give those waters a tinge of our own. Every one of us is secretly afraid that unless we do this we are doomed to oblivion. Miss Lowell's *Tendencies in Modern American Poetry* says very little of "Men, Women, and Ghosts," or "Sword Blades and Poppy Seed," or "Can Grande's Castle": it is an opera in which the prima donna's voice is heard off-stage only and fleetingly. But it is nonetheless Miss Lowell who is the heroine of that book, and it is Miss' Lowell's poetry which that book ingenuously and richly praises. Mr. Untermeyer's book, in the same way, is an oblique panegyric of Untermeyer: a quite deliciously naïve glorification of the temperament with which he finds himself endowed. How could it be otherwise? We are not really surprised at discovering this—we should only be really surprised if we came across a case to the contrary, if we found Miss Lowell, in a fury of self-abasement, making an immolation of her own works before the altar of Ella Wheeler Wilcox, or Mr. Untermeyer forswearing poetry for ever after reading T. S. Eliot's *Sweeney Among the Nightingales*. I exaggerate the point for the sake of emphasis. I do not mean to suggest that both Miss Lowell and Mr. Untermeyer do not very often, momentarily, escape the prisons of their temperaments and pay their respects to strains in contemporary poetry which they feel to be inimical to their own. What I do mean is that if you examine carefully the writings of any poet-critic you will find, a trace here and a trace there, the gradual emergence of a self-portrait; and one which is only too apt to be heroic size.

VII

This relativism dogs us even into the lair of the professional critic, the critic of poetry who is not himself a poet. In the magic pool of art what is it but the flattering image of himself that the critic parts the leaves to see? What indeed else *can* he see? We only perceive those things to which we are attuned; and no matter therefore how fine we spin a logic in defense of our tastes, all we do is subtilize the net of our temperament, the snare of our imperious desires, from which we are never destined to escape. We face here a disheartening determinism, we look across the abyss that lies between one individual and another, an abyss over which it seems almost impossible to communicate, and it begins to seem as if we should have to take refuge in that sort of aesthetic solipsism which, rightly or wrongly, we associate with Benedetto Croce and Professor Spingarn. If our tastes are mathematically determined by the sensibilities and temperaments with which we are born, and if any logic of aesthetics which we construct must therefore be mathematically determined by our tastes, of what use is any such logic of aesthetics? Of what use is it to talk of aesthetic values? Where all is relative, who will dare assume for himself the rôle of the absolute? Who has the courage to say, in these circumstances, "My taste is better than yours, and I have these reasons for it—"?

To the last question the answer is simple: we all have. Our self-assurances are sublime. What is a trifle like aesthetic determinism? We know what we like, and we know that what we like is the best. What results from this, of course, is the feral competition among critics and poet-critics which I have been discussing: it is the almost total absence of standard weights and measures which makes it possible. Success will be gauged, of course, by the size of the audience which we are able to attract and hold, the number of books we are able to sell. If art is a form of community expression, a kind of glorified communication (to quote Mr. Untermeyer) then it is clear enough, is it not, that at the present moment the best poets we have are Robert W. Service and Ella Wheeler Wilcox. But I hear already injured cries from other quarters. There are poets, I dare say, who will have the audacity to tell us that the figures should be reversed (such is the ingenuity of human pride) and that the poet who sells one hundred and nineteen copies of his book is really more successful than the poet who sells one hundred thousand. The audience, they will say, should be an intelligent audience—not merely numerous—and it should show a disposition to be cumulative, in increasing ratio, after fifty years.

And perhaps they are right. Perhaps, after all, this is the only sort of aesthetic decision we can come to; this gradual and massive decision of the slow generations, this magnificently leisurely process of accretion and refinement, particle by particle, century by century.

VIII

But this fact contains a ray of hope for us. Such massive decisions as this are objective facts, and may well therefore be food for the behaviorist psychologist or the Freudian. If in the long run humanity prefers this or that sort of art, it should be possible to find the reasons for this, to say eventually just what chords of human vanity are thereby exquisitely and cajolingly played upon. Perhaps we shall be able to determine, in relation to great social masses, the law of aesthetic fatigue which precipitates those changes in taste which we call "literary movements" or "revolts." It may even become possible, at a given moment, to predict a new era of "realism" or "idealism." Or to predict, for that matter, if social changes go far enough, the legal proscription of certain forms of art—the romantic, for instance?—Or the death of art altogether.

IX

These speculations, however, are a little frightening, and I leave them to the psychologists, who, I do not doubt, will give those of us who are poets frights enough on this score before we die. For the present it will suffice to point out that since in the sphere of aesthetics all is relative—or for each new generation, at any rate, relatively relative—and since this is particularly true just now, when experiment and innovation are so common in the arts, and give us so often work which cannot in any completeness be compared with works given to us by the past; it will be plain enough that a large part of the success of any such innovator or experimenter will depend on his own skill and persistence in making himself heard. This, at any rate, right or wrong, is his fixed idea. It is the fixed idea of pretty nearly every poet now writing in this country. We may pretend, sometimes, to be indifferent to our destinies, but at bottom it is a matter of considerable concern to us whether we can get our books published by Z. rather than by Q., or whether, having been published, they are favorably reviewed by *The New York Times*, *The New Republic*, *The Dial*, or what not. Not that we value the opinions of these journals—how perfectly idiotic they can be we wisely perceive when, as not infrequently, they presume to tell us what bad poets we are, or even, in their incredible blindness, ignore us altogether. But they command audiences, and

we ourselves wish to command audiences. If we are condemned
to be among those gems of purest ray serene which the dark un-
fathomed caves of ocean bear, we shall know how to find, ingeniously, a proud solace for that solitude; but we prefer—do
not be deceived by us for a moment—a well-lighted shop-
window on Maiden Lane. And we make this preference sufficiently manifest, I think, by the dignified haste with which we
accept any invitation to read or lecture, and the apparent in-
exhaustibility with which we are able to review books, particularly those of our rivals. It is a cut-throat competition, a survival
of the fittest. We lose no opportunity to praise our own sort of
work or to condemn that sort which we consider dangerous.

x

The reader now perceives, I think, what he ought to expect
of me. I am no exception to the rule. My own book is, in sum,
just as clearly an ideograph of Aiken as *Tendencies in Modern
American Poetry* is of Amy Lowell or *The New Era in American
Poetry* is of Untermeyer. The papers that compose it were, almost all of them, reviews of books, and they stand pretty much
as they were originally written. They represent my own particular attempt to urge the poetic currents of the day in a direction
that might be favorable to me. I make no real apology for this:
I merely maintain that I only do what all poets do. If pressed by
someone seriously well-disposed towards me to admit some
however tiny element of disinterestedness or altruism, I would
probably—like every other poet-critic—confess that my sympathies are, perhaps, just a trifle broader and more generous than
the average. . . . By which I would mean, subconsciously, that
I merely carry my defense-reactions a little further afield.

I could, to be sure, have rewritten these papers in such a way
as to have made a plausibly integrated unit of them—. I could
have divided my book neatly into chapters on Realism, or
Romanticism, or Vers Libre, or The Holophrastic Method; and I
could have mentioned, for the sake of sales, every poet in the
Cumulative Book Index. But to cover, as it were, all the
ground, has never been my purpose as a reviewer, and I do not
see why it should be now. My intention, in these papers, is to
provoke and to stimulate: to single out for a certain careful
casualness of illumination, among so many and such varied
aspects, only those facets of the poetic tendencies of the day
which are, for one reason or another, suggestive. In that sense
the book will be found, perhaps, to compose a sort of unit, or

comprise a gamut. That it contains no studies of such poets as Robert Frost or Edwin Arlington Robinson, poets whom I highly esteem, and whom I often have occasion to mention, is partly accidental, and partly because the works of both poets are conspicuous, in the contemporary medley, for precision and finish, and lack the tentativeness and uncertainty which provide for the critic his most seductive problems. For these omissions, and for the inconsistencies which indicate like milestones the tortuous course of my growth, and which the shrewd reader will discover for himself, I, therefore, make no apology. The inconsistencies I could, indeed, have eradicated. They remain because it seems to me that in so relative a world they may have a kind of value. One is least sure of one's self, sometimes, when one is most positive.

THE MECHANISM OF POETIC
INSPIRATION   (1917)

There is a widespread notion in the public mind that poetic inspiration has something mysterious and translunar about it, something which altogether escapes human analysis, which it would be almost sacrilege for analysis to touch. The Romans spoke of the poet's divine afflatus, the Elizabethans of his fine frenzy. And even in our own day critics, and poets themselves, are not lacking who take the affair quite as seriously. Our critics and poets are themselves largely responsible for this—they are a sentimental lot, even when most discerning, and cannot help indulging, on the one hand, in a reverential attitude toward the art, and, on the other, in a reverential attitude toward themselves. Little of the scientific spirit which has begun to light the literary criticism of France, for example, has manifested itself in America. Our criticism is still a rather primitive parade of likes and dislikes: there is little inquiry into psychological causes.

Meanwhile, if the literary folk have been droning, the scientists have been busy. Most critics, at least, are familiar already with the theory of Sigmund Freud, that poetry, like the dream, is an outcome of suppression, a release of complexes. To the curious-minded this, however erratic or inadequate, was at any rate a step in the right direction. It started with the admirable predicate that after all poetry is a perfectly human product, and that therefore it must play a specific part in the human animal's functional needs. It at once opened to the psychologist (amateur as well as professional!) the entire field of literature, and in a new light: he was invited to behold here not merely certain works of art, but also a vast amount of documentary evidence, in the last analysis naïve, as to the functioning of the human mind—in other words, so many confessions.

In the beginning, ludicrous mistakes and exaggerations were made. This was to be expected. Freud himself has steadily modified his position, as was bound to happen in the early and necessarily empirical stage of a new psychological method. There have been others, too, who have gone forward with the method, in a purely objective way, by trial and error. And the most interesting of them from the literary viewpoint is Nicolas Kostyleff, whose book, *Le Mécanisme cérébrale de la pensée,* was published in Paris within a few years. In addition to much in this book which is of an interest purely psychological, there are also successive chapters dealing with poetic inspiration, the poetic methods of Victor Hugo, and the method of the novelist. M. Kostyleff does not pretend to have solved any of these questions. He is content with indicating a direction—he does not attempt to delimit. He offers suggestions and observations that should be of tremendous value to the literary critic.

M. Kostyleff, in the chapter devoted to poetic inspiration, takes as his starting-point a belief that Freud's explanation of it as due entirely to hidden complexes, largely erotic, is insufficient. Certain types of poetry, notably those that approximate wish-thinking, clearly indicate such an origin. But what are we to do with the vast amount of poetry which cannot so conveniently be fitted into this category—poetry, for example, which does not in any obvious sense appear to be the satisfaction of either erotic or merely aesthetic needs: poetry, indeed, which would appear to belong to a cerebral rather than a merely emotional plane? M. Kostyleff here concludes, it appears wisely, that after all the writing of poetry is, like speech itself, a purely cerebral affair: and that it is not the result of a discharge of an excess of emotion in the poet so much as a cerebral reaction to external stimuli. This conclusion he at once connects with a theory, developed in earlier chapters, of verbo-motor reactions: a theory that words, like other sensory impressions derived from contact with reality, are stored in the mind, not discretely, but in chains of association, where they become unconscious and appear to be forgotten; but that upon a given stimulus these chains of associated words begin automatically unravelling, become again conscious.

With this theory of poetic inspiration in mind, M. Kostyleff approached various contemporary French poets and asked them to divulge the secret of their methods of composition. Among these poets were Madame de Noailles, M. Robert de Montesquiou, M. Haracourt, M. Abel Bonnard, and M. Fernand Gregh. The explanations of these poets seemed at first sight to be rather divergent. Some wrote rapidly, some slowly. Some conceived their poems in terms of visual line and space, some aurally in terms of music. Some started with the final or key line and wrote up to or around it, and some sketched rapidly in a sort of improvisation, later filling in and altering. But one fact began to emerge which seemed to be true of all: the fact that the initial impulse was almost always due to an external stimulus of some sort which effected, in a purely cerebral way, an automatic discharge of verbal associations, not necessarily attended by an excess of emotion. It became also apparent that the poets themselves were to a considerable extent aware of this. They sought to document themselves on subjects which appealed to them, so as to enrich their associations; and, further, they endeavored to surround themselves with objects in some way related to the chosen theme, or to adopt, if possible, a suggestive environment.

This is already, it is clear, a sufficiently shrewd blow at the usual theory of poetic inspiration, that it is due to a tempest of emotion in the poet. But M. Kostyleff makes it even shrewder. On examining carefully the work of these various poets he found it to be almost invariably true that the emotional value of the completed poem far outweighed the emotional value of the original idea. The latter, in fact, frequently became quite insignificant. This would certainly indicate that the original impulse is merely a slight spring, which, once released, sets in motion a rather imposing engine. In fact, it was found in many cases that the original idea was either lost sight of entirely as the poem developed or actually contradicted. The explanation of this is simple, if the basic theory is correct. For if it is true that verbal reflexes function in associated chains, then we should expect the discharge of verbal reflexes to be self-generating, one set of associations to lead directly to another. No sooner does one flight of ideas come to an end than some overtone in it awakens further associations and another flight begins. And this was precisely what M. Kostyleff found to be true in his examination of many of these poems, particularly in the first drafts of them, with the many omissions, the many leaps to what at first glance might appear to be unrelated ideas. The completed poems, then, appeared to be not so much orderly developments of the original theme (which indeed in most instances could not alone offer the necessary amount of associations to account for the wealth or emotional power of the poem) as an accumulation of successive waves of verbo-motor discharge due to association, each rushing farther from the starting-point. In this manner we get a finished poem which far outruns, in emotional weight, the initial impulse. Of M. Bonnard's "Le Chant du coq à l'aurore," for example, M. Kostyleff remarks:

It is evident that this inspiration is due in part to a profound emotion before the beauties of nature, but the verbal discharge certainly surpasses it in extent, and can only be explained by the pleasure of renewing it. . . . And, everything considered, the emotion and the reaction to it are not equivalent. This explains also why in other cases the emotion can be slight, almost purely intellectual. In the preceding poem it is an emotion such as one feels, or can feel, after pleasure, which stimulates the imagination. . . . It is, before all, a play of cerebral reflexes . . . it is not an equivalent of emotion alone. It would never have become what it is if it had not had at its disposal great richnesses of memory, verbal and visual; which permit [the poet] to prolong the emotion, to renew it, and to communicate it to others.

Again, of "Douleur" by Comtesse de Noailles, he says:

The feeling is always tender, but it awakens sometimes an exalted thought, sometimes a pessimistic thought. This proves once more that inspiration is not to be confused with the emotion which causes it. We saw it, in Bonnard, outstrip the emotional stimulus, we see it now in contradiction with itself; and that alone can explain the sustained flight of literary creation. If poetry were only an emotional discharge, it would be very much less complex than it is. In reality the emotional shock finds in the poet preformed cerebral mechanisms: mechanisms preformed by study, by meditation, by life. These are chains of reflexes which are not themselves kept in the brain, but the paths of which are traced there and easily reproduced. In a poet these reproductions are particularly easy, and the chains very numerous. The cerebral reflexes, becoming linked at the will of the unforeseen connections, draw him along beyond the emotional stimulus. . . . Indeed, what matters the extent of the emotional power, since the principle does not lie there, but in the chains of cerebral reflexes, and since the latter can be set off by a stimulus wholly cerebral? . . .

This obliges us to admit at last that poetic inspiration has two sources: the sensibility of the poet, and the preformed mechanisms of verbal reactions. These last we understand in the widest sense of the term, with the images to which they attach themselves, as also with quite precise qualities of rhythm and vocal harmony. A great poet is recognized not only because he is sensitive and vibrant, but also by the wholly personal qualities of this mechanism. And that is not a word of simple meaning. The personal qualities consist in the evocation of impressions which are not banal, and in the expression of them in a rhythm and sonority peculiar to themselves. . . . This formula seems to be important, especially for our time, when there are so many good poets—and so few great ones. . . . It is time to establish clearly in the eyes of the literary critic that to be a true poet it is not sufficient to have emotivity, internal fever, nor even a certain richness of cerebral images; it is also necessary to have a gift of verbo-motor discharge which is *personal*. For objective psychology, this presents something quite precise, the mental images being the cerebral reflexes directly associated with those of hearing and speech. This association is not innate: it is formed little by little from the first years of life. What is innate in the poet is a certain refinement of the sensorial organs. Seeing and hearing much as other children do, he must retain more memories, and better selected impressions. Each of these traces the path of a reflex; the visual and auditory reflexes are associated with definite verbal reactions; and at the time when his nervous system becomes rich enough to produce sensorial discharges, he finds himself already gifted with what we have just called the preformed mechanism of verbal reactions.

In this connection M. Kostyleff points out that, as we should expect, poets are precocious as children, read omnivorously at an early age, and thus store up rich deposits of verbo-motor reactions, rich not only as regards sensorial impressions, but also as regards prosodic arrangement. And as evidence that the mature poet is not above enriching his vocabulary by conscious effort, he goes rather exhaustively into a survey of the methods by which Victor Hugo was accustomed to document himself for literary creation, and into the rather elaborate system of auto-suggestion (through choice of environment, books, mode of life) by which M. Robert de Montesquiou induces in himself the proper frame of mind for work. And at the end of his chapter he concludes:

To be a great poet it is not at all necessary to have a temperament as pronounced as that of a Musset or a Baudelaire. A delicate taste, if it be personal, may also serve as a basis for poetic inspiration. But it is the essential condition for this that the specific sensibility of the individual should determine for him the formation of an adequate mechanism of verbal reactions. . . . The number of parlour poets increases, and many of them lack neither emotion nor energy nor sonority of expression. In what do they fail of being true poets? The study we have just made directly answers this question. They lack a personal mechanism of verbal reactions. This mechanism is part of inspiration. It is formed long before the moment of discharge, from all that the poet reads or hears, and when the moment arrives, it begins to act without his being able to say whence the words come to him. Every one uses words, most words can be made into verses, but the more or less personal character of the latter distinguishes clearly those which are only an imitation, an echo of the poetic harmonies of the past, from the "sovereign verses" which leap from the mind of the poet as the product of a personal faculty for storing up and grouping verbal reactions. . . . Objective psychology finds here a very important contribution. To the factor revealed by Freud,—(the stimulus in the revival of psychic complexes,—) we see added another having an equally precise place in the organism,—an extraordinarily extended chain of verbal reactions.

M. Kostyleff does not presume, naturally, in reaching this conclusion, to have cleared up the entire problem—he is probably as aware as any one that he has made only a beginning. For at once further baffling questions arise. To begin with, though we can subscribe without reluctance to the main tenet of M. Kostyleff's thesis that once set in motion a flight of poetic creations is to some extent self-renewing, ramifying by association from one group of reflexes to another; and though we cannot help being struck by the plausibility of his conclusion that the sole difference between the imitative and the original poet is in the more personal quality of the latter's mechanism of verbal reactions, it is clear that in this matter of the "personal quality" lies something which, though of very great importance from the literary viewpoint, is left rather vague. It will be recalled that M. Kostyleff makes a good deal of the fact that the poet, both instinctively in childhood and deliberately in maturity, seeks by reading to enlarge his vocabulary and the richness of his prosodic sense. But of course the imitative poet does this quite as much as the original one: if not more. His stores of verbo-motor reactions are acquired, presumably, in quite the same sort of way. Where, then, does the difference arise? In what manner does this store become, as M. Kostyleff says, more closely related in the one case than in the other to the poet's specific sensibility? It is at least questionable whether this distinction is not a false one. For, in a broad sense, no individual's store of verbo-motor reactions can be other than specifically personal to him. This would seem to force our search for a distinction backward one degree to the matter of sensibility itself. It would suggest a revision of M. Kostyleff's statement that imitative poets "lack a personal mechanism of verbal reactions" to a statement that, though fully equipped with such a mechanism, (many such poets have, even among literary folk, exceptional vocabularies) they lack any peculiarity of sensibility: they do not extend the field of our consciousness in any new direction. This would in turn indicate that M. Kostyleff puts undue emphasis on the merely linguistic aspect of the poet's function, with a faint, though perhaps unintentional, implication that language determines thought rather more than thought determines language. But may not a poet be great even if there be nothing remarkably original or bizarre about his work with respect to language or style—great by reason of the poetic content or thought rather than for verbal or prosodic brilliance? . . . This brings us to the fact that there are two great tendencies in poetry—two kinds of poetic value—and the classification seems to obtain for other arts as well. In one of them the emphasis is on the externals—on form, style, color, texture, with the intention of producing a sensorial effect as brilliant as possible; in the other the emphasis is on the content, and the style is made secondary, a transparent glass through which one may most perfectly see. Clearly, it is on poetry of the former rather than of the latter class that M. Kostyleff has based his conclusions: the lyric and decorative rather than the philosophical and narrative. For it is obvious at once that in poetry of the latter class the direction of the poem would not be dictated by the automatic unfolding of associated verbal chain reflexes, but, on the contrary, that the verbal mechanisms themselves would be directed throughout by the original poetic theme. . . .

If it is true, therefore, that M. Kostyleff has thrown an extremely interesting light on one mechanical aspect of literary creation, he clearly fails, indeed he does not attempt, to bring this aspect of it into relation with the aspect studied by Freud. We are shown parts of the machine, but not the machine in motion. What, after all, is the compelling power at the bottom of poetic creation? If it were merely a matter of mechanical reactions, on a verbal plane, blind and accidental, it is obvious that one experience quite as much as another would cause a poetic precipitate in the poet's mind. But we know this not to be true It is apparent that some selective principle is at work:

some affective principle, or pleasure principle, which vitally concerns the poet. He reacts more acutely and more richly to some stimuli than to others; and even among these reactions he exercises a rigid system of suppression and selection. To be sure this power is self-generating, once started—by accretion the affects intensify and perpetuate themselves, leaving always a richer deposit of associations, a greater capacity for prolonged cerebral response. But we must not forget that this selective principle has its beginning somewhere, that it is universal, that it arises in accordance with some need. Every man, as it has become commonplace to remark, is in some degree a poet. In consequence it is clear that in dealing with poetry we are dealing with something which plays some specific and organic part in the life of man. This, in default of any more plausible suggestion, brings us back to the theory of Freud. It is to some deep hunger, whether erotic or not, or to some analogous compulsion, that we must look for the source of the power that sets in motion the delicate mechanism, on another plane, which M. Kostyleff has begun to illuminate for us. It is clear that this is not merely a sexual hunger, nor an aesthetic hunger, nor an ethical hunger, though all may have their place in it. . . . Is it merely in general the hunger of the frustrate (which we all are) for richer experience?

However we answer that question, it is certain that such objective studies of literature as this of M. Kostyleff indicate for us a new method in literary criticism. With the clouds of myth and mystery blown away, we begin to see more clearly; we shall be better able to understand, to discriminate. And if we are thus made to see that literature plays a vital functional part in our lives, we must eventually begin to value our literature, *more consciously,* in the degree in which it fulfils that function.

MAGIC OR LEGERDEMAIN? (1919)

In every generation there are artists, men whose intentions are clearly enough honest, who tell us that in the act of artistic creation there is nothing mysterious or uncontrollable and that art is solely an affair of technique employed with a maximum of skill in accordance with aesthetic laws. At the beginning of a preceding chapter, that on the "Mechanism of Poetic Inspiration," I myself made statements which in this connection may, to some, appear confusing: I commented with some acerbity on the all too prevalent notion of critics and poets to the effect that there is something "mysterious" or "translunar" about poetic inspiration, something "which altogether escapes human analysis." These statements have indeed already proved misleading. I have even, as a result of them, been accused of maintaining, as Poe did, that a poem is a mathematically calculable product, a thing which can be constructed bit by bit, synthesized under the microscope in clearest view. That however is a theory which I have had no intention of maintaining. I maintain only that the *finished product* can and will profitably be submitted to analysis. The chemical contents of a substance may be fully known, and the scientist may none the less be unable to produce the same thing synthetically. A poem may be exhaustively analyzed, and its constituent motives noted on a relatively fine scale, and, for that matter, it should be so analyzed; but that with the knowledge thus acquired any individual could proceed to write a *Kubla Khan* or a *Divine Comedy* is—let us say—open to question.

For even if we agree in this regard with the fundamental (though not with some of the derived) principles of Freud and Kostyleff, and even though one therefore holds that the functional values of the arts in the life of man will be precisely understood, and defined (perhaps dangerously?), and the propulsive springs of the individual work of art with some clarity perceived; one does not on that account necessarily believe that the poet, who gives us a poem in which there is however small a grain of that sort of beauty which we call "magic," knows at every step in the course of composition precisely what he is doing. Quite, in fact, the contrary. I do not think I have ever believed or maintained anything but that it is usually during a poet's best moments that his medium is least consciously under his control. There are, I know, poets who argue, with their own cases in mind, that they know at every instant just what effect they wish to obtain and how to obtain it. One is permitted to doubt this statement, and to discredit it is not difficult. The most obvious answer is simply that it is nearly always the poet without "magic," the poet who does precisely control his medium at all moments, and who for that reason gives us a poetry of close approximations rather than of glittering achievement, who, naturally enough, denies the efficacy of the subconscious. But that retort is a trifle too recriminatory and easy. It is more profitable to assume for the sake of argument that such poets do, actually, strew their verses with the jewels for which we foolishly hunger, and, having made that assumption, to ask them whether after all they are so sure that the strewing of them was foreseen, calculated, and accomplished with conscious precision . . . or whether, for that matter, they know any too well how their jewels were originally come by.

The affair is really one of misunderstanding; to throw any light upon it, however feebly, compels us to shift our ground, and to inquire a little into the state of mind of the poet during actual composition and the preliminary soundings which precede it. There is, I suppose, no state of mind which to the poet is more exquisite, or which he would find harder to describe. It might by some be defined as merely a heightening of ordinary consciousness: but while that is perhaps partially true, it would be more completely true to say that it is a sort of dual consciousness, heightened no doubt on its ordinary plane, but conspicuously different from the usual state of mind in that the many passages which lead downward to the subconscious are thrown open, and the communications between the two planes, upper and lower, are free and full. The process by which this dualism is achieved may or may not be deliberate. It may be achieved by an effort, by the premeditated touching off, as it were, of an idea which, one knows, will explode downward with ramifying fires through the mine-chambers upon which by association one desires to draw, or, quite as often, the initial explosion may be accidental, the starting of the train of fire by the merest chance of phrase encountered or itself tossed up from the subconscious in response to some pressure from the world of sense. During this state of dual consciousness there is a sense in which it is true that the poet has his subconscious under control. Even when working at most rapid intensity, he is sagacious of his quarry, and although, if at any moment interrupted with the question—"What is it that you pursue with such delight—what is it that you hope to obtain by rejecting that word and taking this, what superiority is there in this rhythm to that?"—he might be totally at a loss for his answer, none the less he feels in the most intangible of ways that he knows to the minutest detail the value of the impalpabilities with which he is at battle. He is diversely and brilliantly conscious of all this, but conscious only in a peculiar way: he is aware of more than he precisely sees. His decisions themselves are largely conscious, but the logical train by which he reaches any such decision has undergone such a synhaeresis as to have been to all intents obliterated. Regarding his decision at such-and-such a point to break, for example his regular mode of rhythm and to introduce an interlude which shall act as a voice antiphonally heard, he can hardly be said to have foreseen in advance its effectiveness or, for that matter, even its existence. He has, let us say, just finished the last line of the preceding movement. It is quite open to him to proceed to a second movement growing logically and persuasively out of the first. But perhaps, for some unglimpsed reason, some twinkling signal from the depths of the subconscious which he searches with heaven knows what intensity, he is unsatisfied with this, he desires something else, it is something else which is needed if his hunger is to be appeased. What is this? And how shall he find it? Not, surely, by a reference to the many and so ludicrously simple rules he knows, nor even to the filed items of experience, which are useful but incomplete: at such a moment his salvation is only in an adamantine command to the whole conscious realm of his mind to be silent, and at once his entire attitude is that of one who listens. For his dissatisfaction with the fair enough coin tendered him by the upper plane of consciousness, the coin manufactured by labor and patience and skill, is itself an indication from the lower plane of consciousness that that consciousness has something finer to offer, something which it will gladly surrender if only the invitation have tact. The sensation of dissatisfaction is, it should be noted, not merely a negative affair. It relates sharply to the thing with which he is dissatisfied, hints at the specific incompleteness of that thing. And it is about this spark-point of dissatisfaction that he proceeds to generate, out of the fine air of expectancy, the combustible vapor which shall invite the explosion. It is then, if he is fortunate, that he does not merely find, but actually hears, the rhythm, the melody, the singular and unpremeditated tone of the next movement. Its superiority to what he had at first in mind is manifest. And his poem at this point takes on the glow and impetus of which perhaps he has hitherto not been able quite to guess the secret. It remains then only to take this tone-color, so charmingly a gift, and give it a precision of shape—to relate it organically, by employment of ideas akin to those in the preceding movement, with the general theme of the poem.

If something like this, therefore, is true of the method of poetic composition, it will be seen, when one considers its impalpability, how wide is the margin for error when one seeks with any exactness to define it, or, with regard to its use of conscious and subconscious, to delimit it. The poet, it is perceived, no matter how much he may call upon the subconscious and deliver himself over to it, is at all times pretty much aware of what he is doing, and why; though of the precise reward for it he may be singularly uncertain. It is with this fact in mind that some poets belittle the value of the subconscious, underestimate, perhaps, the frequency with which they call upon it. They do not remember, when the poem is finished, at what points, or how many, they called for this assistance; nor have they the modesty to admit that those things in the poem which have greatest magic and beauty are usually not the product of skill, merely, but the skillful use of a wealth for the most part subterranean, a natural resource, a wealth to which they have been given access occasionally, but a wealth in the deposit of which they have played as little conscious part as the surface of the earth plays in the crystallization of diamonds. One cannot be a poet without a fine sensibility; one's sensibility is hardly controllable; and the greater part of its deposit has been accumulated long before the poet is aware of its existence.

This is not to say that anybody can be a great poet by making drafts on his subconscious. One cannot dig up jewels from a commonplace sensibility, though quartz crystals may be plentiful. But in the case of the poet who is, however intermittently, a genuine poet, one may safely say, I think, that it is when he is most the craftsman that he is least magically the poet. Craftsmanship is the skill with which the poet turns his subconscious treasure to account. Without that application, no matter how deft it may be, mere skill, operating, as it were, in the air, will only approximate and imitate and endeavor to deceive. It is a thing done with hands, a legerdemain, not magic; one soon perceives the trick, and if one enjoys it one does so with the intellectual coolness of admiration, not with full emotional surrender, the uncontrolled surrender of one's own aroused subconscious. . . . When craftsmanship induces that surrender it proves itself to be more than craftsmanship. It discloses its essentially compulsory nature. And that the compulsions which give it color are often analyzable is not to say that the magic it achieves is a magic which the poet can altogether calculate.

South Yarmouth, August 1921

The recent publication of a study of *The American Novel,* by Mr. Carl Van Doren, editor of *The Nation* (N.Y.), affords an occasion for sober meditation on that subject—meditation, to be precise, not so much on the American novel as on the American critical attitude toward it. I have not read Mr. Van Doren's book: all I have read is Mr. Mencken's praise of it in *The Nation.* We are perhaps safe in taking Mr. Mencken's word that it is a pretty fair survey of the subject, if we except, to paraphrase Mr. Mencken, a slight bias in favor of Cooper. That is the only exception Mr. Mencken makes. He says nothing of Mr. Van Doren's treatment of Hawthorne, nor is there any mention of Herman Melville. Is Melville discussed by Mr. Van Doren, and, if so, is he placed, as he should be, with Hawthorne and James as one of our three "best"? Probably not; for Mr. Van Doren does not appear to be exceptionally enthusiastic over James, nor, for that matter, any more than Mr. Mencken, especially intelligent about him.

In fact, Mr. Mencken is delighted with Mr. Van Doren for his recognition of the "artificiality" and "superficiality" of "James, the man." With characteristic hyperbole Mr. Mencken touches off a handful of verbal fireworks of his own apropos of James's incessant and myopic preoccupation with a "furious study of the wings of butterflies: that there were also jackasses, hyenas, codfish, Congressmen, lice, cobras, and scorpions in the world apparently never occurred to him." It is appropriate, I think, to regard a statement of this sort, as also the concise indictment of James as "artificial" and "superficial," with the blankest astonishment. To be perfectly fair, I should add that in Mr. Mencken's opinion Mr. Van Doren does complete justice to James, the artist—"savors the least virtue." But how much does that mean? To see James as nothing but a biologist obsessed with a furious study of the wings of butterflies is to see him not at all. To indict him for artificiality and superficiality is to betray a total, a blinding lack of understanding. If it were necessary to refute so absurd a notion one could do so out of the very earliest and most immature work of James—out of the *Notes and Reviews,* contributed by him to the *North American Review* in his twenty-first and twenty-second years and now published by the Dunster Book House.

But it is not, of course, worth refuting. More engaging for the analyst is that other notion, that James wrote only of butterflies; with its implication that as James failed altogether to see life in true perspective or even, for that matter, to see it at all, he was therefore not a great novelist. What we encounter here is not merely a disastrous ignorance of the whole "idea" of James: it is, more importantly, a light on a critical attitude, common in America, toward the novel. I do not refer to the mere "best-seller," but to the so-called "serious" novel—it is so comparatively rare a phenomenon here that the adjective "serious" is almost invariably invoked, when it turns up, by the startled reviewer. Of late, however, it has taken to turning up with greater frequency: and that, whether in the case of Mr. Theodore Dreiser or Mrs. Wharton or Mr. Joseph Hergesheimer or Mr. Sinclair Lewis, the author of *Main Street* (now near the 300,000 mark), or Mr. Floyd Dell with *Moon Calf* or Mr. Sherwood Anderson with *Poor White,* has served to emphasize somewhat hideously the naive bewilderment of our critics. That they are naive does not make them any the less self-assured—Mr. Van Doren is precise, Mr. Mencken is trenchant; and they both represent fairly enough the contemporary cult, in American criticism, of the robustly emphatic. Nor does the fact that they are unaware of their bewilderment, whether they are journalistic or academic critics, render their bewilderment any the less dolorous.

This bewilderment is, in its essential nature, something, I think, peculiar to contemporary America. It results from the effort of our critics to see the novel simultaneously in two lights —to see it aesthetically, to begin with, but more importantly to see it as a document bearing on the spiritual, moral, psychological, and physiological welfare of these United States. It would be interesting to trace for a generation back the influence of the vogue for "muck-raking" on American fiction. That vogue was itself, no doubt, an aspect of a general social change, of which one of the most obvious characteristics was a sudden zeal for the true, the actual: a zeal for truth which was remarkably like a *nostalgie de la boue.* The zeal for the true, at all events, began early to manifest itself in the novel, and if one most naturally calls to mind Mr. Upton Sinclair's *Jungle* as the clearest "case" of muck-raking fiction, it is none the less in Mr. Theodore Dreiser's novels—*Jennie Gerhardt, Sister Carrie, The Financier, The Titan*—that one finds the impulse most nearly translated into the terms of art. However, for my present purpose it is fruitless to multiply instances of this influence. What I wish to emphasize is the habit formed by our critics—particularly our newspaper critics—in connection with this tendency of the novel, of examining every novel not so much as evidence of the author's artistic ability as evidence of his skill or courage as a sociological diagnostician. That part of the American "reading" public which takes a step beyond best-seller fiction takes its step naturally toward the diagnostic. Our present generation has a passion for the diagnostic. The appearance of Dr. Sigmund Freud was for this generation that of a *deus ex machina*—nothing could have been more profoundly satisfactory. But this has served only to stimulate our young appetites for the corrosively analytic. We see the influence of it even in our poetry—Mr. Masters has been profoundly affected by it, and his *Spoon River Anthology* is only surpassed in that regard by his own huge dredgings in *Domesday Book*.

What we see, then, in our critics is a kind of diplopia—they suffer from a doubling of vision by which they confuse the social value of the work of art with its aesthetic value. Mr. Mencken, when he expresses his annoyance with Henry James for his "furious study of the wings of butterflies," means by implication, of course, that he wants the diagnostic novel—something that sharply, painfully probes, it does not matter whether into the dark penetralia of the State or into the even darker subconsciousness of the individual. "Show us America—show us the American! Hold up your mirror to us, and the more singularly it distorts us the better." This is the kind of thing which our public is feeling, the kind of thing which our critics are formulating. Do we not see, in this light, a clearer reason for the prodigious success of *Main Street* than any afforded by its obvious but comparatively mild virtues as a work of art? Can we not see, in this light, the reason for the writing, and the success, of Mr. Floyd Dell's *Moon Calf*, a sharp enough psychoanalytic study of adolescence; or Mr. Sherwood Anderson's *Poor White*, with its clumsily poetic, vigorous but grotesque effort to "fix" a moment in the civilization of our Middle West? I do not think there can be any doubt of it, any more than there can be a doubt that we are in for a deluge now of *Main Streets* and *Moon Calves;* any more than there can be a doubt that the novel which is written primarily as a work of art will get, for a time, little of the attention it deserves.

This is all merely to say, in brief, that we have no critics, no criticism. In the meantime we take heart from the fact that as we have worried along in the past without criticism (except that

of Poe and James) we shall probably worry along in the future
and have, nonetheless, now and again a Whitman, a Hawthorne,
a Poe, a Melville, a James. We isolate, we exile our great men,
whether by ignoring them or by praising them stupidly. And
perhaps this isolation we offer them is our greatest gift.

THE ANALYSIS OF POETRY   (1922)

Nothing is more desirable than that the nature and function of
poetry should be analyzed, or the mind of the poet or fiction-
writer explored; nothing is so rare in criticism of poetry as the
discernment which knows how to operate without idolatry; but
if we are to have analysis and discernment of this sort, we must
insist that they should be exact. In this inquiry, we see clearly,
(it should always have been clear) that criticism is really a
branch of psychology. We have every right to insist that the inquiry, if it at all purports to be psychological, should be scientifically conducted; of mere vague happy speculation we have
had quite enough on this subject—from Plato to Sydney, from
Sydney to Shelley and Leigh Hunt and Arnold. This is a kind
of praise of poetry, a song in defense of song; it honors the religion; but it has added little to the total of our knowledge. Consequently, when Professor Prescott remarks in his book, *The Poetic
Mind,* that "poetry is itself a subject—the suggestion is clear—
which can only be treated poetically"—he must forgive us if we
begin to edge toward the door. There he lights garishly for us
the fault of his book—for, if we can pardon him, even sympathize with him, for his religious attitude toward poetry, we cannot at all pardon him for conducting his investigation so persistently and prayerfully in a dim religious light. What we want
is the dry light of science.

What we get, in *The Poetic Mind,* is an extraordinarily confused book which contains a few admirable pages and a great
deal of rubbish. Professor Prescott has read an amazing amount
of psychology—his preference appearing to be for James and Ribot, though he has also a reluctant respect for Freud—and cita-
tions from these and other psychologists play a large part in
his work. This, no doubt, will give some people the impression
that the book is a scientific one. Nothing could be further from
the truth. It is really a glorified Ph.D. thesis: an enormous accu-

mulation of quotations—poetic, critical, psychological, and religious,—which the author makes a heroic but wholly unsuccessful attempt to fuse into unity. One does not need to be much of
a psychologist to realize that one cannot without disaster compound the terms of Freud with those of James, or Ribot, or
Bergson; or, again, compound this compound with the terms of
Hunt and Keble; or lastly, compound this confusion with the
transcendentalisms of Emerson and Carlyle. One feels ultimately that it is the author's intention not so much to discover
dryly and accurately the "why" of poetry, with the aid of the
new psychology, as to show that even if reduced, by this dreadful psychology, to terms of "wish-thinking" or whatever, poetry
remains beautiful and mysterious, a mystic and prophetic expression of the "general mind," a throbbing vein which connects
man with the luminous infinite. Is Professor Prescott really engaged in a defense of his own somewhat sentimentally idolatrous attitude towards poetry and the poet? One notes his
luxuriation in such terms as the "poetic vision," the "poetic madness," and "inspiration" (with a suggestion of "influx" from the
"general mind"). For Professor Prescott, despite his delvings in
modern psychology, the soul appears still to remain a definite
reality, and one suspects that he identifies it with the "subconscious." What one feels that he is attempting is a sort of adjust-
ment between poetry as "revelation" and poetry as a product of
trauma or social pressure. His interest, in short, is a religious
interest, and focuses itself on that point at which the physical
becomes the metaphysical: even in the act of seeing poetry as
wish-fulfillment, he sees it also as a cooperation of the "indwell-
ing" and the "over-soul."

In other words, Professor Prescott's aim is not really a scientific aim, and his employment of the psychological method is
purely mediate, even when fairly precise. He has his moments
of precision—his chapters on imagination are, if not original,
suggestive, and he deals not too inadequately with the matter of
wish-fulfillment. But in general, his best pages are those in
which he himself contributes least—he has, for example, excellent things to say on symbolism, simply because he accepts
the Freudian lead. When he goes further than this, and attempts to develop an idea, or to relate it to other ideas, he is
immediately in difficulties. The amount of loose imaginative
generalization and of vague sentimental analogy which he employs is remarkable. The prolixity is unbearable. The book is at
least four times as long as it should have been, and in conse-

quence its good bits are simply lost in the enthusiastic profuse confusion. And everywhere is the platitudinous professorial drone. "How did God create the world? Not surely in six days— for the biblical myth must be interpreted—but by a gradual evolutionary process." How true: how extremely true.

It is difficult to pick out, from this extraordinarily uncorrelated welter, points for discussion; but the attempt must be made. We pass swiftly by when Professor Prescott argues that as Emerson's "over-soul" is so widely and eagerly read, there must therefore be truth in the doctrine of revelation as an influx from the "unique mind." We glide away with averted faces when he argues that "man must have 'innate ideas' (in some sense) and sentiments which cannot be explained as arising from his individual experience"—adducing as testimony Wordsworth's "Intimations." We merely wonder whether a man who believes in innate ideas, and who reasons in this fashion, can possibly be taken seriously as a psychologist. More interesting is it, perhaps, to quarrel with him over his view of the precise mechanism of "inspiration." This is an affair which he takes with religious seriousness—he appears to believe that the poet's "vision" is an intense and shattering thing, a violent seizure which transfigures the poet, whirls him out of time and space, and is accompanied by a profound emotional disturbance. This vision, it would appear, is purely visual—it has no verbal associations, and only when it is over does the poet then turn to the completely separate affair of "composition." Having recovered from the seizure, he sets about a laborious and inadequate translation of his extraordinary experience into metrical language . . . If, desiring to refute this absurd simplification, we were to employ Professor Prescott's method of simply quoting an opposite opinion, we might invoke M. Kostyleff, who in his *Mécanisme cérébrale de la pensée* (which remains the only reasonable piece of investigation on this subject) reduces the affair of inspiration to a matter largely of "verbal association":—brushing aside any possibility of "innate ideas" and ridiculing the usual myth of "emotional disturbance." M. Kostyleff maintains that some stimulus of experience sets in motion a train of associations which are *specifically verbal* and *prosodic*, positing that the poet is an individual in whom the variety of "verbal associations" is particularly large, and particularly related to the poet's own sensibility. This seems eminently more reasonable. For of course "inspiration" and "composition" cannot be separated: they are one and the same thing. Anyone can indulge in a daydream or vivid recollection or vivid anticipation (which is all there is to "vision") but not everybody is a poet. The poet is the individual in whom the process of daydreaming is inseparably bound up with what the behaviorists call the "language habit." What is more, by far the greater part of any given poem is generated in the act of composition: as M. Kostyleff remarks, the initial stimulus, the stimulus which first set the language habit to work, is soon lost sight of in the wealth of other language associations which are evoked from the subconscious, and the greater part of the poem may therefore have little or nothing to do with what Professor Prescott calls the "vision." It follows from this that even a bad poem is "inspired"—the badness is not caused, as Professor Prescott thinks, by the failure of the poet to evoke the subconscious: he may evoke his subconscious quite as much as the good poet does. The deficiency in such a case is primarily a deficiency of sensibility. This, in the case of the bad poet, was from the outset not sufficiently acute, and therefore the language associations which are evoked are neither rich nor individual. Thus the product of the "unconscious mind" is not, as Professor Prescott thinks, inevitably "original." It may be, and often is, as dull as ditchwater.

This appears to be a point of fundamental importance, and as Professor Prescott seems here to go seriously astray, so inevitably he is astray in much that follows from it. Only less serious, however, are some of his other errors. He seems, for example, to be somewhat confused by the matter of what he terms the "subjects of poetry." The subjects of poetry, he informs us, are in the realm of the "half-unknown" and "half-hidden": distance and dimness provide the charm. How can this doctrine be reconciled with that of wish-fulfillment or that "influx of the Unique Mind"? The connections are not obvious. The error here is the very old one of setting apart a particular class of phenomena as specifically and objectively "poetic." "The imagination starts only when the subject is more obscure, when it is a little more distant or dimly seen, when in consequence it begins to have color and shadow, when it begins to have mystery." But that, while true of certain kinds of poetry, offering a key to the cases of certain individual poets (Coleridge for example), can by no means afford a safe basis for sweeping generalization. What are we to do with Wordsworth's "And never lifted up a single stone," or Dante's "disiato riso" or Webster's "Cover her face. Mine eyes dazzle. She died young."—? The question is, after all, not so simple. To one poet it may be the distant and dim which are, by association, poetic, and to another it may be just as clearly the near and precise . . . It is perhaps another aspect of the same error that leads Professor Prescott to say that in poetry "a direct expression is improper or impossible; a veiled or 'poetical' one is the recourse. The motive impulse in poetry is supplied by the poet's desires. But these cannot give themselves free expression." What Professor Prescott does not see here is that poetry is *itself* the indirect expression, the substitute for action, but that *in* poetry the expression may be, and very often is, perfectly direct. Again, we encounter a distinction made between the "motive and inspiration" of poetry, which are traced to the desires of the "individual," and the form or "art," which are traced to "social" authority or convention. Is this distinction quite sound? It would appear that "motive and inspiration" are just as apt to show "social" influence, the influence of audience and tradition, as "form." This error we can follow back to Professor Prescott's artificial separation of "vision" and "composition." The two things cannot be parted, and social influence will be as conspicuous in the one as in the other, or as inconspicuous. The poet is one in whom feeling and thinking are inseparably associated with language and prosody; and the influence of traditions or taste will therefore operate on thought and language as if they were one.

These errors and confusions are characteristic of Professor Prescott's book. He has, as we have said, his good pages; he attempts an excellent thing; but the attempt is not enough, nor is it enough that in erudition Professor Prescott is a "miracle of nature, breathing libraries." What we want is a concise and accurate behavioristic study. And Professor Kostyleff's book remains the only one that is remotely of this nature.

A BASIS FOR CRITICISM   (1923)

It is not a bad thing, now and then, to explore anew, with lantern and pick, the foundations of the accepted. Contumacious such an undertaking will always appear to some; and often, to the explorer, fruitless. We may find, for all answers, a solid infinite masonry against which our lantern is the tiniest firefly, our pick as impotent as a reed. But there is always the chance, on the other hand, that we shall find the accepted singularly like a cloud or mirage, and as insubstantial. Thus, if we march with our lanterns and picks against the foundations of "criticism," literary criticism, it is with a singular and increasing sense that those majestic foundations, which we had thought to be among the solidest, most adamantine and enduring of things, evaporate as we proceed. We read some sort of criticism almost every day of our lives, and if it is adequately thought and expressed we accept it—accept it, that is, in the relative sense that leaves us free to agree or disagree. What we accept is the underlying hypothesis—implied as much by the fact that criticism is read as by the fact that it is written—that criticism has, as it were, a *point d'appui,* a support, a true center, and, in the upshot, knows what it is about. But *does* criticism know what it is about, or *has* it a true center? Or is it not rather, if we examine it with a just skepticism, a remarkably disorganized and empirical thing, in which ultimately it is always the personal note, the note of private like or dislike and of irresponsible theory, which is loudest? One critic talks to us of beauty, another of truth, another of the good, another of significant form, another of intuition. We read one day that beauty is an absolute thing, a thing which exists independently of ourselves, that its canons are as definite as if engraved in bronze, and that a work of art may be judged by these canons as coolly as we might judge the points of a horse. But the next day another critic informs us that there can be no canons, and that a work of art can only be judged in relation to its own ideal self. We go from aesthetic criticism to biographical, from biographical to historical . . . But is there no unity in all this effort? The critics, certainly, do not seem aware of any. "What is beauty?" Pilate might have asked, and the answer would have been no more forthcoming, one hazards, than to "What is truth?" Beauty, again, may be truth to the poet, and truth may be beauty to the scientist; but the poet and the scientist are two very different men, and for the former truth may as seldom be beauty as, for the latter, beauty is truth.

We cannot, in short, look very long or very hard at criticism, whether it be today's or that of the past, without noting that its most striking characteristic is its vagueness. That it is often, even generally, dogmatic, does not affect this fact in the slightest. It is natural to man to overstate that which he wishes to believe and wishes others to believe; he is never so unreasonable as when, with eyes as cloudily bright as the chimaeras they see, he gives himself up to the fine ecstasy of pure theory. For the merest phrase, the slightest shading of his theory, remote howsoever it may lie from the actual, he will lay down his life as if in defense of his very threshold. This devotion has its shining aspect, certainly, but rather because it supplies the energy for accomplishment than because it supplies any sort of precision. It speeds the poet but snares the scientist. And the more we examine criticism, from Plato and Aristotle to Coleridge and Arnold and Croce, the more we perceive it to be riddled with theory. Any sense of responsibility to the facts—and not to one fact, but to all the facts—is extraordinarily intermittent, and that critic seems to be a faint-hearted creature who has no grand solution to offer us, whether it be "emotion remembered in tranquillity," or "natural magic," or "intuition." What literature of criticism we have in English—and it is slight, for the Anglo-Saxon is not by nature a good critic—is littered with sham jewels of this sort, which have a pleasant gleam, but give little light. And this deplorable vagueness, this almost total lack of any system or scale of values, with its inevitably solipsistic outcome, is in a large measure the gift of what we call "aesthetic" criticism. Moral criticism of art makes no pretense to be anything but practical; biographical and historical criticism are constrained by facts; but aesthetic criticism—at any rate until the last few years, when it has been taken into the psychological laboratory—has been, for all its great brilliance and its accidental accuracies, for the most part an intense inane.

Its difficulty has of course been precisely its uncertainty as to what it is that is "beautiful." "Beauty," the concept or hypothesis on which the whole structure of aesthetic criticism rests, invoked on every page, in every paragraph, implicit in every slightest judgment, remains, despite our idolatry, singularly shadowy. Not that this is at all the impression which many of our critics give us—they talk of beauty as if they knew quite well what it was. That it "exists" they do not in the least question—they lift, for the far clear view of it, serious eyes, eyes perhaps a little proudly conscious that they see farther than most. It will be noted that there is something suggestive of the religious in this, and to that fact we shall return. For the moment, it is important to observe that these critics, every one of them, "assume" beauty as they might assume God, assume it as something detached, independent, not to say absolute, something which would exist whether or not there also existed any creature to give it praise. The error is ridiculous, elementary—elementary is the correction of it; but there is no correction which criticism so needs, just as there is nothing to which our critics so desperately cling as to their mythological lamia of a Beauty. "The unpardonable methods of a Nordau!" cries one; "The inexcusable methods of a Freud," cries another; as if, they go on to say, one could measure the spiritual with a foot rule! Any attempt at scientific psychological analysis is a horror to them. Analysis, to be officially "received" by them, must come with certain literary and aesthetic "references"—its terms must be beautiful, imaginative, analogical, rather than exact and dry; its analysis must be "literary" or philosophical or stylistic, that is, *of the document itself*, but not of the mind and body which produced the document in response to pressure. In short, the analyst will be tolerated only as long as he remains faithful to beauty, or, in other words, comparatively superficial, like Remy de Gourmont.

And meanwhile this beauty, in defense of which so much is said, cannot be presumed to have any existence whatever, in an objective sense. It is not an object, or a quality uniformly and universally identifiable, as one might identify, in any alloy, the presence of gold; it is the name we give to a pleasurable relationship which exists between ourselves and a given set of stimuli. It is, in short, if anything at all, a feeling—nothing more. We may and should attempt to analyze this feeling, to see what gives rise to it. Let us note at the outset, as confirmation of the absolute relativity of beauty, the very commonplace fact that what appears beautiful one year may appear empty or ugly the next. It is not the picture, the poem, which has changed, but ourselves. To that particular set of stimuli, or that particular arrangement of the set of stimuli, we no longer react. And thus we encounter at once the ancient question of form and content, that furious dialogue, sterile perhaps if we look to the adherents of either party for the whole truth, but certainly fruitful inasmuch as it has led by revolt and counterrevolt to countless new "movements" in art. Our out-and-out aesthetician will tell us that beauty lies in the "arrangement" of the stimuli, and that the precise nature of the stimuli themselves does not particularly matter; style is everything, and it is urged that *Hamlet* is a popular play not because it is a great work of art (which the critic questions) but because it is "the Mona Lisa of literature." What is implied here is that the emotional appeal of the content, the material, of a work of art is a spurious sort of thing which interferes equally with the aesthetic operations of creator and critic.

What is suggested is that art be purged of this kind of emotionalism, and the critic be left free for an enjoyment purely aesthetic.

This attempt of the aesthetician to eliminate from art all that he cannot comfortably call aesthetic is certainly interesting, as showing what is perhaps a tendency which increases with civilization; and to that aspect of it we shall return. But for the moment we must contradict the aesthetician. We have seen that his pleasure is in the "arrangement" of the material—but is arrangement, after all, quite enough? Why is it that a pattern of bricks cannot possibly delight us as much as a pattern of words? Simply, one presumes to think, because in the one case the material has meaning and in the other case it has not. What we come to is a perception of the fact that it is not mere material "blocks" which, in a work of art, are "arranged," but something infinitely more vital: we have referred to the material thus arranged as "stimuli," but we might now go a step further and recognize these stimuli as, precisely, the keys to associations. It is true that some of the arts are more independent of "associations" than others—architecture perhaps most conspicuously. But it is suggestive to notice that the arts are held in importance exactly in proportion as their freedom to play on association increases: painting is more esteemed than sculpture, music more than painting, literature more than music. It would appear, then, that quite apart from his pleasure in the aesthetic aspects of a work of art, the human being desires of the work of art primarily that it should thus play on his associations. When the work of art performs this office successfully for him, he has the feeling which he terms beauty, with its accompaniment of exaltation or euphoria . . . But this of course really explains nothing. Granted that man has the feeling called beauty when his associations are played on with the requisite skill; granted also, despite the aesthetician, that for any appraisal of a work of art it will be therefore as important to weigh the "associations" of which it is made as the skill with which the associations are woven together; granted all this, we still are left in ignorance of why it is that this curious process, this absurd serious tickling of the soul, should be held by him to be so important. Why is it, in short, that he holds so dear his mythological lamia of a beauty, and regards it so idolatrously? One suspects at once that it must be because beauty is useful to him, performs some vital function in his life. And if this is true, we may perhaps begin to glimpse a new basis for criticism which will be a trifle solider than our cloudy configurations of words about style, intuition, the ideal, the good . . . the beautiful.

II

But if our close scrutiny, first, of the relativeness of beauty, and, second, of the fact that beauty, when evoked by a work of art, is unexpectedly more dependent on "content" than on form, compels us to discard, for a critical basis, the purely aesthetic method, with its emphasis on "arrangement" or form; can we turn with any greater expectation to biographical criticism or historical criticism—will these methods afford us a basis any more solid and fixed? . . . Certainly, in the case of biographical criticism we feel ourselves to be at once on firmer ground. Here, if we sacrifice the privilege of finer flights and higher luminosities, of passages purple with a fine excess (usually of vagueness) we are rewarded at all events with a tangibility and a tough actuality that are unquestionable. We mean, by biographical criticism, the effort to see in an artist's life and personality the origins of his art. We have heard, we still hear, savage outcries against this method—it is by the idolators of art considered a despicable sort of espionage, this ruffianly pillaging of the great man's archives and arcana, this wholly unwarranted detective-work in his kitchen or sleeping-quarters. Does it matter what size his shoes were? Derision comes naturally to the tongues of the simple-minded—and "simple-minded" is perhaps the kindest term we can find for those zealots in every generation who ignore, resist or persecute any spirit of inquiry, any effort to extend the small horizon of man's self-understanding. Simple-minded certainly is the cry of these zealots today that the artist's "life" is not of the smallest importance, that his work is everything, and that if indeed there is any demonstrable relationship between the two—a fact considered by some extremely dubious—it at any rate sheds no light. It is not of the slightest consequence that Clare was mad, that Hearn was myopic, that Nietzsche was a paranoiac, that Wilde was homosexual, that Carlyle was sexually undeveloped, that Dostoevsky was an epileptic—only quite accidental is it that Clare's verse is mad, Hearn's prose full of descriptions microscopically exact, Nietzsche's philosophy a philosophy of aggrandizement, Wilde's verse and prose epicene, Carlyle's prose harsh to give an impression of exaggerated masculinity, Dostoevsky's novels vehement with the vehemence of the "epileptic equivalent," his famous "timelessness" and "mystic

terror" and passionate interest in pain and evil all precise symptoms of the epileptic . . . All these are accidents to be
shrugged away.

But, of course, they cannot be shrugged away, and if the relationship between life and work in these cases is specially
marked, it no less awaits discovery in every other case. Biographical criticism, in short, has proved itself indispensable to
any critic who is not content simply to accept art unquestion-
ingly as a blazing gift from God, a revelation of the "true" or
"beautiful," and to accept the artist as God's instrument. But
the method has the defect of all purely empirical method,
namely, that it does not go far enough. It has the clear virtues of
the "specific," but it must be observed that the "specific" only becomes wholly illuminating when that sort of larger pattern
which we call the "general" is the light by which we read
it. We begin to see the biographical method as a very useful ad-
junct, precisely as we must see also the historical method—the
latter attempting to do for the group, the era, the nation, the
whole world of art, what the former does for the individual
artist. The defect of the historical method is precisely that of
the biographical, that it gathers and arranges material, ex-
amines exhaustively the surface, but singularly, for the most part,
without a light. It "accepts" art as devotedly as the aesthetic
method and is therefore content to trace influences, to chart the
depths and shallows, to follow, as it were, the "stream"; but if
it attempts to find the origin of the stream it attempts to find it
rather in time than in cause. For the latter sort of exploration we
may seek in vain in the work of any critic—we must apply to the
psychologist, the anthropologist, the biologist.

And here we reach the real downward-ramifying mysterious
root of the matter. For if we look shrewdly at the enormous accumulation of so-called criticism during our two thousand five
hundred years of culture: this mountain of manuscripts, commentaries, biographies, histories, analyses of "style," classifica-
tions of art into kinds, attacks on art and defenses of art: we are
stupefied by the display of so multitudinous and ant-like an
energy, but we cannot help also being stupefied—may the
human race forgive us—by its stupidity. What feverish activity!
What a furious, troubled come-and-go, what laborious carryings
of grains of sand up the enormous grass-blade and down again.
What quarrelings over atoms and deaths in defense of the inde-
fensible! . . . For the truth is that all the critical energy of our
two thousand five hundred years has been a blind energy, en-

ergy operating without the control of fact: creative of the literary, the imaginative, the poetic, rather than of the wise and comprehensive. Arnold, no less than Shelley, beats his luminous wings in the void in vain (not altogether in vain, perhaps, for his wings are luminous, his flight often spectacular and of an unguessed precision) and his plight, it is scarcely an outrage to say, is that of every critic since Aristotle. Granted that the critic needs to be imaginative, poetic; that his criticism should be a pleasure to read—that is, well shaped; yet are these any reasons why criticism should not have a solid and permanent basis, or our beautiful ineffectual angels occasionally, from the bright void, come home? Come home, we mean, to the actual. Is there no conjuror's phrase which will cry them back? . . . Yes: there is. It is very simple, but, like David's pebble, it does the trick, it brings them down. It is a mere question. Let us ask them: What, in the life of civilized man, is the function of art— social, biological, psychological? . . .

The question has a certain absurdity; but its absurdity is conditional, and arises only because it is asked, by criticism, so late. It is the question that should have been asked at the beginning. And the implications of it are tremendous—its reverberations through the superb superstructure of "criticism" serve, like echoes, to reveal a hollowness. It means, put bluntly, that criticism is a mere chimaera, a happy indulgence of ingenuity and imagination, if it attempts to operate without a clear understanding of what it is, in the life of man, that art is for. If art has a function, as it must, then of what use is it to judge a work of art except in accordance as it fulfills that function? To do so is as ridiculous as it would be for an anatomist to value the human eye according to the color of the iris: it is to study the appearance but to ignore the use. And yet, is that not precisely what criticism has always been doing? Not always—we grant the exceptions. But the exceptions, we must notice, have been accidental, and in many cases have been rigorously excluded by the "critics" from any sort of standing: pulpit denunciations, for example, or the closing of the theaters in England in the seventeenth century, or the moral censorship to which English and American literature must submit today. These are acts of criticism which, for all their frequent stupidity, at any rate show an awareness of the fact that art is functionally and organically a part of man's life, and should, perhaps, be supervised with an understanding proportionate to its importance. Shall we recall also as an act of criticism which showed this awareness, awareness with disapproval, Plato's exclusion of poets from the Re‚ public? It will not be amiss to do so, if we complement it with the doctrine, which Platonists have brought forward from time to time, that the best art is that which leads us toward the "good life."

But the good, it can be objected, is as vague and relative a thing as the beautiful—it is perhaps another way of saying "moral beauty," which again is another way of saying "accommodation of the individual to the tribal law." Each particular race, with its own particular casually amassed conventions, will have its own conception of moral beauty and its own utilitarian standards for judging a work of art. If we seek therefore a functional explanation of art which will underlie not only these racial distinctions but also the distinctions between the good and the beautiful, our search will again take primarily the form of a question: namely, why is it that man so desperately craves the feeling we call beauty, or moral beauty, or aesthetic beauty, that he has developed, developed with religious zeal (as we said earlier) the activity known as art for the satisfaction of that craving? What is it that beauty does for him? Does it, as some of our intuitionists insist, constitute for him a sort of revelation, an apocalypse, a highest point of consciousness—a vein, as it were, between him and the infinite? That many critics insist on this view is certainly a testimonial to the religious seriousness with which man takes his art, but it offers him nothing in the way of explanation.

And the real explanation will not be metaphysical but psychological. Let us rashly posit that the pleasurable feeling we know as "beauty" is simply, in essence, the profound satisfaction we feel when, through the medium of fantasy, we escape from imposed limitations into an aggrandized personality and a harmonized universe. This kind of satisfaction not only can be said to give rise to the feeling "beauty"—it *is* beauty. Its very essence is illusion. And illusion is vital to us because of the restrictions, of every kind, that hem us in: we come into the world confident of omnipotence, and daily our power dwindles. Brightness falls from the air, pain teaches us that we are mortal, injury leaves us crippled, knowledge serves rather to show us our weakness than our strength. We look back to that earlier hour as to something infinitely bright and happy, we desire passionately and constantly to return to it, and we seek in daydream to do so. It has been urged that in the day-dream, or art, we do not really seek to escape from ourselves, but, precisely, to find ourselves. But what part of ourselves is it that we find? Is it not exactly that part of us which has been wounded and would be made whole: that part of us which desires wings and has none, longs for immortality and knows that it must die, craves unlimited power and has instead "common sense" and the small bitter "actual": that part of us, in short, which is imprisoned and would escape? . . . There can be little question about it, and it is precisely of the associations connected with these major psychic frustrations that we have evolved the universal language of healing which we call art. Let us not hastily condemn this view simply because it savors of the often-flouted "new" psychology. Freud is not, by two thousand two hundred years, the first to see art as primarily a process of wish-fulfillment. Let us recall Aristotle's theory of catharsis, and rub our eyes. The difference between catharsis and wish-fulfillment is slight to the point of disappearance.

III

We arrive, therefore, at our basis—we see art as fulfilling a definite and useful function in the life of man: feeding his vanity, fostering his illusions, aggrandizing his importance; exalting him (in the form called tragedy) particularly in his defeats; and from this basis we see a good deal more clearly and intelligently what is amiss in the tendency of modern criticism to concern itself only with the "aesthetic." We have already noted that what the aesthetician terms the "content" of art seemed to be perhaps more vital than "form"; and now, with a closer view of the psychological function of art, we are in a better position to emphasize that point, and also, perhaps, in the upshot, to challenge and somewhat further define the term aesthetic. The aesthetician, as we have seen, desires to eliminate all emotional accidents—which may creep in, with the material of which the work is made, like so many impurities—and, of course, all moral accidents, so that he may be left "free" for a comparatively pure contemplation of the "beauty" of style and form. But this, we see now, is a chimerical aim, for the material of art not only is, but must be, rich in emotional accidents, and it is possible to argue that the richer the better. To accept or reject a work of art solely in accordance with stylistic and formal neatness and control is palpably absurd: it is the method which exalts Dryden and scorns Shakespeare. Granted that criticism should deal exquisitely with the question of form: it should also deal profoundly with the question of material. What is more, if it is necessary to give a death blow to the notion of purely un-emotional aesthetic contemplation, it is possible to do so in quite another way. For if the material of a work of art is cunningly chosen so as to give us a sense of escape, of freedom for un-limited power and *experience*, may we not then go further and say that a quite parallel pleasure is afforded us by the *form* of the work of art, which is cunningly chosen so as to give us the feeling of unlimited power of *expression?* If that is true—and there appears to be no objection to it—we can perceive at once how natural it will be for the professional artist or critic to overestimate arrangement or form, or style, simply because of his own perhaps psychotic desire for skill of that kind. He is, in fact, a special case. And a sufficient degree of skill in a work of art will give him the same sort of illusion of transcendency that, to the layman, whose desire is for experience rather than for ex-pression, is given rather by the narrative in which the skill is employed.

In other words, there can be no *fundamental* distinction be-tween the sense of beauty as afforded by the content and the sense of beauty as afforded by the form: both are alike, in es-sence, the satisfaction due to a successful wish-fulfillment; and both, in the ideal work of art, are present. Again, further to re-inforce our view that the merely aesthetic method will not serve, we may argue that while content can be discussed apart from expression, expression cannot be thus isolated from content. Style and form are, after all, only aspects of the thing stylized or formed: they are the explicit manifestations of an implicit mode of thought and feeling. The poet, in short, when he chooses words and phrases and rhythms (or, to be more exact, is chosen by them) is not primarily choosing the mere word, phrase and rhythm—primarily, he is choosing the thought, feel-ing or emotion which they represent; if thereafter he rearranges his rhythms or word-order to make them more "effective," or "sharpens" a phrase by a substitution, it is not devotion to style that bids him do so, but a finer perception of his mood, a richer view of the happily exaggerative associations of which it is composed . . . This, it will be seen, puts more than ever, upon the aesthetic critic, the burden of psychological interpreta-tion. The aesthetic cannot be isolated as a mere matter of lin-guistics and prosody and syntax. If it deal with these things it must deal with them largely as evidence, as symptoms. It will be able to judge from them whether or not the artist thinks clearly, feels deeply and richly, and with what excesses or de-

fects of sensibility. It will be able to detect fraudulent emotion
or second-hand thought. This will be its nearest approach to the
merely "aesthetic," and this, clearly, is an inclined plane down
which it must inevitably slip, at last, to the "merely psychological." From praise of Dryden's neatness and precision of style,
his classical "elegance" and so on, the critic will find himself insensibly drawn into a discussion of the significance of these
things—their implication of a vigorous, logical, but unoriginal
mind which had, as its means of contact with the world, perhaps
the thinnest and poorest sensibility that has ever been given to
a famous poet; and had for that reason the minimum of emotional frustrations and the maximum of emotional shams. He
will see, our critic, if he is honest, Dryden as the most brilliant
example of that sort of artist whose triumph is a triumph of intelligence over poverty: he will also see the enduring reputation
of Dryden as one of the most striking cases of a reputation artificially got and artificially kept, a reputation purely "literary":
Dryden is an excellent example of that sort of artist whom the
public, finding in him no sustenance, no illusion, no escape,
would willingly let die. It is the public, in such cases, that
eventually wins. It cherishes its "heroic" literature—it clings to
its wild, rich, disorderly, emotional "Hamlet" despite all the
critics can do; and the insubstantial or jejune, no matter how
neat or clever, nor how much praised, it commemorates only in
stone.

And this is a fact that the critic cannot ignore: he cannot, with
a sneer, dismiss the tastes of the vulgar. Those tastes are important. They give us, in clearest view, the common denominator of art, the factor of wish-fulfillment without which art would
not exist. The dime novel or shilling shocker, the lurid melodrama and explosive farce, the cosmetic musical comedy and
the "movie"—these we have no right to designate simply as bad
or inferior art. They *are* the art of the people for whom they
were created; they give these people illusion, escape from themselves—and that is beauty; and if we wish to bring this sort of
art into relation with the sort of art we consider finer, the *The
Golden Bowl* or *The Brothers Karamazov*, we shall most accurately define the relationship by saying that the latter sort of
art, while in principle the same as the former, is designed for
people in whom credulity has been weakened by intelligence
or self-awareness: the desire for escape, for illusion, is as strong
in them as in those others, perhaps even stronger, but as they
are more conscious so they require more persuasion, that is,

a greater wealth of documentation. For these people a simple unqualified statement of a thing or action has no longer sufficient magic. It must be elaborated. They would scarcely be content, as their predecessors two thousand six hundred years ago were, with the plain Homeric statement that the lovers "embraced." Virgil, Horace, and Ovid, though they all felt it necessary to offer more detailed evidence, still leave something to be desired, and it is not till Dante is reached, with his *disiato riso* and *bocca tremante*, that the incredulous but still wistful modern can find full conviction. One is tempted to seek the explanation of this growing demand for *le mot juste* in the fact that as a people become more articulate, so the language loses force or virtue and requires, if it is to exert a magic, a freer use of the superlative and exaggerative. That, certainly, is an important aspect of the matter; it throws a light on the evolutions of style; but again, it is something which we ought to attempt to see, as it were, from underneath. For it is not the language that has weakened or been exhausted—language changes and grows, to be sure, but that is another matter. It is rather that man himself, in growing from simple to complex (which means also from less to more articulate), finds himself with a constantly diminishing responsiveness to the simple. This has been brought about, of course, by the fact that language and therefore art (which is language intensified) by enormously multiplying the frequency with which man can expose himself to emotional stimuli, have ended by wearing out, in these regards, the connections. Unfortunately, as the connections which first wear out, the ones most overworked, are precisely the most important and most vital to him, the ones at the very heart of his consciousness—the connections with such of his concepts as love, life, death, hope, faith, time, space; and as it is still to these concepts that he desires, above all, to respond, if he is to obtain illusion in art and an increased sense of his aliveness and awareness and grandeur, so it becomes necessary for art to discover, for these concepts, connections always more circuitous and elaborate. And it is exactly in this perpetual effort to recapture—by subtlety, by fine nets woven of association, by stealthy circumlocution or arrows of bright facts discharged in clouds—the first fine careless rapture; to be smitten again by the simple in experience with something of the hiss and clang and suffusion of rich color with which, in our infancy, that experience was attended; it is in this restless effort that we have enriched our prose with a sharper perceptiveness, a finer tactilism, a greater array, as it were, of sensory "evi-

dence," and our poetry with a symbolism always more exquisitely dim, a symbolism which, if it grows constantly more
peripheral, is thus outspread only that its current may sting, by
so many the more radii of association, that responsive center
which the single note will no longer arouse.

We come thus to see in another light the dichotomy between
the tastes of the vulgar and the refined. The former class, being
more primitive and less articulate, still responds to the simple,
the comparatively unarranged and unselective, the bare, bleak,
melodramatic tale, the unsupported statement, the crudely
suggested and imprecise emotion, the type instead of the
character: the latter, jaded by verbalism, finds the simple commonplace and flat, and must, in order to enjoy it, have it sub-
tilized. Thus far, there is no great difficulty for the critic. It is
in the perpetual warfare between the two classes that difficulty
arises, in the attempt of the refined minority to impose its
tastes on the simple majority, and vice versa. Here the critic,
who inevitably belongs with the minority and shares its virtues
and failings, must be on his guard. For in his passion for elaboration, the intensely articulate individual, whether layman or
artist, is prone to one singular error: he is prone to forget that
the essential aim of this elaboration is to re-create simple illusion, to restore color to the faded and actuality to the dull—to
provide, in effect, a magic carpet—and he makes the attempt
to isolate, for a special contemplation, his pleasure in *pure expression*. We have already dealt sufficiently with the inadequacy of this as a basis for criticism. But it remains to be noted
that within bounds the tendency is interesting enough and increases, as we have seen, with civilization. By all means let us
carry the doctrine of "beautiful elaboration" as far as we can—
but let us remember, as critics, that if we try to dispense with
"content" we shall almost certainly dispense, and dispense forever, with an audience. We shall have written, as it were, for
the delectation of a handful of verbalistic lunatics. The great
majority of mankind with less of our peculiar hunger for "speech
for its own sake" and more of the normal psychotic hunger for
imaginary experience, illusion, escape, will preserve of our
works only those that thus serve their needs, being rooted substantially in good human soil. The whole affair works out co-
operatively. The critics and artists drag the crowd into an ever-
brightening glare of self-awareness, a process permitted by the
crowd as long as the light is conceived to be flattering. What it
wants is revelation, and the illusion of transcending itself. But

those critics and artists who go in for the gesture: who, like deluded magicians, describe against the dark exquisite but un-
evocative curves of the sterile wand; these the crowd will bury
without a pang . . . The crowd will not forget that art is, after
all, human nature's daily food.

IV

The conclusion which we thus naturally reach, and which
will no doubt be horrifying to some, is that art exists primarily
for the fulfillment of an important social function, and that the
only sane, just, proportioned, and well-founded criticism of art
will be that which understands this, keeps this constantly in
mind, and judges the value of the work of art in proportion as it
performs its function. This sort of criticism will be essentially
"social." The biographical method, with its close study of the
nature of the particular artist, and how it happened that heredity and environment produced him; the historical method,
with its study of origins—religious and anthropological—and the
influence of the past on the present; the aesthetic, which will
become increasingly a psychological affair, a study of the precise nervous mechanism by which art achieves the desired
effect; these methods will be simply the adjutants of our profounder social view of the whole strange fact and function.
Criticism will, in short, go into the laboratory. It may well
make up its mind, eventually, what sorts of art to permit and
what sorts to proscribe. Nothing appears more likely than that
it will thus develop a new and terrifying "social" puritanism—
that it will put certain subjects, certain methods, under a ban,
preferring, for example, the less to the more "sublimated." It
may even, ultimately, abolish art altogether.

It is not suggested that all this can be done at once, or within
a hundred years. That would be fatuous. But it is clear that
criticism, if it is to escape from its present sterility and hopeless
solipsism, its individual wish-thinkings, its childish idolatries
and errantries, its mere baseless repetitions of likes and dislikes,
however discriminating and sensitive, its little pedantic displays of surface wisdoms, and its tireless empty reiterations of
unanalyzed concepts like "beauty," must resolutely begin afresh.
And its only sure ground will be the biological. Nor need this
inevitably dishearten artist and critic. The artist, better understood, both individually and functionally, will be better valued.
And the critic of tomorrow will not be wholly unlike the critic
of today. It will still be the critic of imagination, of delicate

emotional instability, the creature only less psychotic than the
artist himself, who will be the most valuable—he needs only to
place much of the existing machinery of criticism on its new
basis. A good deal of the method of criticism will be taken over
unchanged . . . If a Pater or Arnold might shrink from the
prospect, one feels tolerably sure that an Aristotle would go
forward to it with joy.

AMERICAN LITERATURE AND
AMERICAN CRITICS   (1924)

Of the abbreviated one-volume "popular" version of the *Cambridge History of American Literature* it is possible to mark
quickly and recite briefly the virtues. It is a useful short survey,
relatively complete, exact, arranged with proper chronological
care, and equipped with an excellent bibliography and an excellent index. Perhaps these, in a short history of literature, are
virtues enough. Nevertheless, one does look for something more.
American literature embraces only a century and a half; the
American "Hall of Fame" (to which Whitman, I believe, has not
yet been admitted) is not so crowded with names that approximate justice might not, in one good volume, be done to
them all; and in four hundred pages one would suppose that
Hawthorne, Poe, Whitman, Melville, James, Twain, Emerson,
Emily Dickinson, and Henry Adams might have been pretty
thoroughly "sounded."
   Unfortunately, the present *History* does not do this. To begin
with, the mistake was made of "dividing" the work, allotting
different authors to different critics. This need not have been a
bad thing if the "critics" had been well chosen, or if space had
been apportioned with some sense of an author's importance.
But instead, everything is on a dead, democratic level. Bryant
must have his fifteen fulsome pages—so must Longfellow and
Whittier and Lowell and Lanier; Poe gets no more, nor does
Whitman; and the only exceptions, astonishingly enough, are
Franklin and Lincoln. Much play is made with Franklin's Yankee astuteness as a diplomat, with his prowess as an inventor of
stoves and flyer of kites: and his moral aberrations are passed
quickly with averted eye. Mr. N. W. Stephenson devotes
eighteen pages to an exhaustive and exhausting analysis of the
"three manners" in Lincoln's prose, talking, by the way, a good

deal of high-falutin nonsense. He wants very badly to have us believe that Lincoln, though he did not go to church, was religious. But why Lincoln or Franklin at all? Why Jonathan Edwards, an eighteenth-century bigot, who, if he belongs anywhere, belongs to a history of American philosophy? Why drag in those admirable scholars Whitney, who knew a great deal about Sanscrit, and Ticknor, who wrote a history of Spanish literature? Or such preachers as Beecher and Brooks, good but ephemeral men, who have less claim even than the omitted Edward Everett Hale? What did any of these contribute to the world's letters? The answer is "Nothing." It looks suspiciously as if the editors had been trying, ignobly, to "pad" American literature.

This results not only in a waste of space, but also in a dishevelment of purpose. If a history of literature is to be anything more than a series of unconnected essays on individuals, it must show a unitary development in its subject, with the causes, external and internal, social and economic, of that development. This is a pretty conclusive argument for the one-man history. One's only doubt as to the advisability of this course, in America, arises from one's discovery that, of the score of critics who write the present book, only three appear to be conspicuously intelligent and discriminating, or to write with any distinction. Professor MacMechan is excellent on Thoreau. Professor Erskine contributes an admirable study of Hawthorne, which might have been better had it been longer. He "sees" Hawthorne in Transcendental New England with quite exceptional sharpness and justice. He emphasizes usefully—has it been so emphasized before?—Hawthorne's careful intellectual detachment, and his honesty in thinking out the moral and social problems which Emerson and Alcott had only stated and abandoned. Above all, he is fairer to the New England scene of Hawthorne's time than Henry James who, in his study of Hawthorne, perhaps desiring to exculpate himself for his own recent flight to Europe, quite shamelessly exaggerated the New England bleakness. The only other chapter as good is that by Mr. J. W. Beach on James, though it is too short by half. Mr. Beach has had insufficient space for any analysis (technical and aesthetic) of the "later" novels—an analysis indispensable in an essay on James. Nor is the criticism of James mentioned at all, though James is one of the very few men produced by America or England (in this case by both) who approximate greatness as critics.

For the rest, this book, racily informative as it is, sheds a light on American literature in a way which probably the editors did not intend. What strikes one, in this series of essays by different hands, is the uniformity and persistence with which American critics—most of them professors—weigh their subjects in the scales of moral and social *usefulness*. That explains the interloping presence here of Edwards, Franklin, and Lincoln —who have little importance in letters—and Beecher, Brooks, Whitney, and Ticknor—who have none. One is a little dismayed at the singleness with which all these critics expect a man of letters to be, first and last, a social and spiritual *leader*. His "message" is sought for with deep Teutonic earnestness. If he has it, well and good: it will not matter that he writes like a barbarian. The aesthetic question is seldom raised; the responsibility is declined. It appears to be assumed either (1) that all Americans write alike and like angels, or (2) that how they write does not, as long as they "have a message," matter in the least. Emerson's "ideas" are discussed—but not his prose or verse. Poe's bad habits are reprehended, his social and ethical deficiency marked with a red lantern; but his genius is left unmarked, unanalyzed, and unplaced. We are given no reason to suppose that Bryant was less important than Poe—the Bryant article is indeed a fine specimen of the "eloquent" style in American criticism; it positively yodels. It nowhere says that Bryant is thoroughly commonplace and dull. Nowhere is it said that Longfellow was a tenth-rate sentimentalist, a manufacturer of blancmange, who wrote two or three good poems; that Whittier was a jingling moralist; or that Howells was an honest novelist of manners with an appallingly undistinguished style. Some illuminating biographical facts are given about Whitman—it is interesting to learn that the famous poem about an unrequited love referred, not to a woman, as has usually been supposed, but to a young mechanic. There is also, however, in Whitman a profound critical problem—which is here ignored. Henry Adams is looked at askance because of his "*sense of futility*." No good American has a sense of futility. Herman Melville—perhaps because he, too, had a sense of futility—is fobbed off with four pages of tepid superficiality. *Moby Dick* is less important, apparently, than Beecher's *Seven Lectures to Young Men*.

What we come to is the fact that the short *History* lights in America an almost total lack of critical standards. It is unlikely that the editors intended to show this. They were perhaps not

altogether fortunate in their choice of critics. But they themselves must be responsible for the uncritical choice of subjects
and the indiscriminate apportioning of space. They must be
responsible for the glaring omission of Emily Dickinson—a poet
who rivals any American poet in importance, and who is unquestionably the finest woman poet who has used the English
language. And they are responsible for the omission of Stephen
Crane. . . . It is a thousand pities that the first "authoritative"
history of American letters should throw so remarkably little,
on the American literary scene, the light of a detached aesthetic
criticism, free from perfervid moral obsessions and free from
the aggressive consciousness of provincialism. The Puritan is a
long time a-dying. His only question before a work of art is,
"What does it teach?" And if it contains no good honest dogma,
no yea-sayings, no "urge" toward "higher things," then obviously it is of no consequence. Melville, Poe, Emily Dickinson,
and Henry Adams can go hang themselves. And Henry James
can go to England.

METAPHYSICS AND ART (1924)

It becomes increasingly difficult to be patient with Signor
Croce's books, whether they take the form of applied criticism
(as in the case of *European Literature in the Nineteenth
Century*) or critical theory. To some extent this is due to an
unfortunate tone, nowhere so apparent as in this latest book—a
tone somewhat truculent, somewhat peevish, as of an old pride
injured and angry, a tone alternately magisterial and patronizing, and not infrequently malicious. Have these things a place
in criticism, or need Signor Croce so often go out of his way to
throw derisive stones at other critics, his predecessors and
contemporaries? One is annoyed by his repeated habit of doing
so, and, passing beyond one's annoyance, one makes the unpleasant discovery of the large place which intellectual vanity
takes in Signor Croce's motive. Impossible, of course, to exorcise
this—every critic must have his secret share. But when, somehow injured, it begins to affect the critic's tone, to discolor
emotionally his perceptions and judgments, one loses that
comforting belief in his impartiality which one is so willing to
exert. It is only because Signor Croce is a very respectable

citizen of letters that one makes an effort, in this regard, to overcome one's distaste. And then one discovers that this is not the least difficulty which he presents.

One does not mean by this that there is anything abstruse or difficult in the book itself, which is a competent, if unexciting, survey of twenty-five rather capriciously selected nineteenth-century figures. One would even be glad if several of these chapters had been in this sense *more* difficult—one cannot feel that Signor Croce has adequately "seen" Scott or Stendhal or Manzoni or De Musset, to name but a few; and if he comes closest, in his treatment of Caballero and Monti and Baude-laire, and perhaps Leopardi, to enriching definitely our per-ceptions, he certainly does not enrich them very much. He has, too, his own quite emphatic sense of values, which prompts him to put Manzoni above Balzac and Byron, and to state that the works of Scott are not at all to be considered as "art or poetry" but as something else (?); and which, while it compels him (reluctantly) to diminish severely the stature of Leopardi, enables him to hail Carducci as perhaps the greatest poet of the century, "a poet-Vates, a heroic poet, an ultimate pure descendant from Homer," and the author of a poetry "suited to prepare and to comfort man in the battles of life with its potent, lofty, and virile tone." With this, which is simply a judgment, one sympathizes or not, according to one's taste. It is not in one's disagreement, here and there, that one feels a growing difficulty, a sense of obstruction and failure, but in something more profound.

This profounder something, which alienates one's sympathies, is in part Signor Croce's persistently metaphysical view of art, a view almost religious in intensity, hostile to all other views, and aimed primarily (so one feels) at a philosophical justifica-tion of art, not at a functional understanding of it. He begins with the hypothesis that art is something sublime, absolute, and autonomous; and his purpose seems not so much to attempt an analysis of its causes and roots in human nature as to assign it a metaphysical place. Perhaps one ought not to quarrel with this. What one has more right to resent is the fact that, while Signor Croce's view is so clearly a metaphysical one, neverthe-less he claims to be "scientific." Is it necessary to note that science does not always profitably build on large, loose, un-verified assumptions, and that a modestly empirical method of investigation is sometimes better? But Signor Croce's method is that of a generous hypothesis or two followed by an "argu-

ment," an elaborate logical structure, which as often as not is
pure verbalism, and often enough is not even good logic. In
"The Essence of the Aesthetic," for example, he says: "And if
it be asked why art cannot be a physical fact" (he has just
stated that it is not) "we must reply, in the first place, that
physical facts *do not possess reality*, and that art, to which so
many devote their whole lives, and which fills all with a divine
joy, is *supremely real;* thus it cannot be a physical fact, which
is something unreal." The reasoning, the assumptions, do not
seem flawless; nor, granting the idealist position, can one perceive precisely on what Signor Croce bases his discovery that
one's feeling (relation) toward a work of art is real, while one's
relation toward an apple (say) is not. One could multiply
instances of this sort of logistic thinking, a vague verbal juggling, which gets him again and again into terminological
difficulties from which the only escape is a quibble, and which
take him always farther from a genuinely scientific approach to
his subject. Art, in all this, is nowhere, is lost in the absolute, or
at best is glimpsed for a moment as "an aspiration enclosed in
the circle of a representation," or as something of which the
only "judgment . . . is philosophical."

This, of course, is not very helpful; and it is odd that Signor
Croce, who, in his preface, claims to be scientific, loses no opportunity of referring sarcastically to those who employ the
methods of biography or physiology or psychology, or (as he
likes to put it) "erotic psychopathology," in their effort to grasp
the nature of art or to understand its function. Why should this
irritate him so intensely? One suspects him of being half aware
of the hollowness of his position, and of its inadequacy; its inadequacy, that is, in providing him with a means of approach
to his subject. For, unhappily, his view of art as autonomous
and absolute; and his thence-deduced disbelief in categories,
"kinds" and "classes" of art; and his further deduction that
"form" and "material" cannot be isolated for study—these views
force him to make of his criticism very largely a sort of examination of souls, often conducted in a moral light, and with
apologetic reference to the influences of time or place or
history; apologetic, because these seem to suggest that there
is a part of art which is, in a sense, "external." And precisely
here one sees why it is that one always, in these critical notes,
feels a little cheated. It is because Signor Croce is himself
cheated. His "view" will not permit him, on the one hand, to
employ psychology and biography in his study of a poet's

"behavior" or development; nor, on the other hand, can he sufficiently admit the separability of form or literary class to devote himself to a minute testing of the principles there at work, and of the extent to which those principles control the writer or are controlled by him. We get from Signor Croce, therefore, neither a careful and precise analysis of style (from the linguistic or historical or prosodic or psychological viewpoint, coming to the aesthetic) nor an analogous study of motive, but an attempt, necessarily confused and incomplete, to give both at once in a somewhat sentimental, paraphrastic commentary on an author's character as revealed in his work. This Signor Croce sometimes does admirably, as in his study of Baudelaire; yet one wishes that he could free himself from his metaphysical and logical difficulties (which are unreal) and allow his perceptiveness and power of analysis a fuller play. "How does it come about" (he asks, after quoting a passage from Maupassant) "that these commonplace reflections, these poor words, move us to tears?" Well, how does it? Signor Croce does not answer his question, appearing to think that to have asked it is sufficient; it is a sort of question which he seldom raises, and answers almost never. And yet one is inclined to think that it is exactly here that criticism begins— where, unfortunately, Signor Croce leaves off.

In a sense a critic qualifies as intelligent more by his awareness of aesthetic problems than by his solution of them—the solution is apt to be temperamental, not logical, is not necessarily right or wrong, and one is free to agree or disagree, to sympathize or not, according to one's own temperament. It is when the perception of a problem is acute, rich in perspective and implications, that one honors a critic and profits by him. Signor Croce gives us, of this perceptive sort, little light; his theory of art as "intuition," and all the verbal paraphernalia dependent thereon, keep him, inevitably, close to mediocrity as a practical critic, since the intuitionist can only say "like" or "dislike," not pausing to say why. And as for the amazing metaphysical structure which he builds about art—dare one breathe the suggestion that it has, somewhat, the appearance of high-class intellectual fake?

A SCIENTIFIC APPROACH TO CRITICISM

(1925)

Some time ago, having occasion to outline a possible scientific approach to the problem of literary criticism, the present reviewer expressed a hope that a critic might appear who, possessed of both literary and scientific equipment, would attempt this task *in extenso*. Mr. Richards, in his *Principles of Literary Criticism*, if he does not entirely fulfill this hope, at any rate makes an extraordinarily interesting beginning. He is erudite and he is intelligent; he makes the courageous attempt to be at the same time scientific and psychological; and he has the great advantage of having at his disposal a knowledge of semantics. Many of the principles employed in *The Meaning of Meaning* (in which he collaborated with Mr. C. K. Ogden) he is able to apply with excellent effect in his search for a scientific approach to criticism. In fact, the present book is in some respects an amplification of certain chapters in the earlier one, notably those entitled "The Meaning of Beauty" and "Symbol Situations."

It will inevitably be objected by adherents of the purely "aesthetic" approach (which ought by now to be an exploded idea) that any such attempt must simply be an unwarrantable and fruitless substitution of one set of terms (psychological) for another set (literary). "He tickles this age"—one hears them quote—

> *who can*
> *Call Tullia's ape a marmosyte,*
> *And Leda's goose a swan.*

But no sensible person, who is not blinded by idolatry of the arts, will object to the substitution of a set of terms which is carefully defined for a set which—notoriously—is so vague as to be practically meaningless. In this regard, Mr. Richard's procedure is admirable. His terms are clear, useful, and conveniently few. Whether they would in all items be approved by all psychologists is perhaps immaterial. The lay or literary critic can find here no cause for complaint. His disagreements can profitably be only on matters more general.

Of these, unfortunately, it is possible to suggest, in a short review, only one or two. Mr. Richards' book is a crowded one —perhaps too crowded for wholly successful statement, or for what he would term "communicative efficacy." On a great many points, and at a good many levels, of his theme, he is illuminating. On the function of rhythm, on the distinction between symbolic and emotive statement, in his destructive analyses of the many divergent views of art which have been held in the past, in his analysis of the mode of thought and its relation to language and art, he is extremely helpful. His difficulty has been in giving, to material so complex and diverse, an arrangement. He has not succeeded in bringing it together in such a way that his thesis might stand forth: he leaves too much necessity to his reader for cross-reference and for disentanglement of the essential from the inessential. One has the feeling that, pondering too long, and using too many notes, he has lost his way a little. A summary, such as that used in *The Meaning of Meaning*, would have been useful. And instead of so many short chapters, all at one level of emphasis, fewer and longer ones would have been better, with subordinate divisions.

Briefly, Mr. Richards suggests that, having rid ourselves of the mythological concepts of "beauty" and "pure aesthetic contemplation," we must judge a work of art (1) according to the value of the mental experience it offers us; and (2) the efficacy with which that experience is communicated. A *good* work of art is that in which the experience is valuable and successfully communicated (symbolized). A *defective* work of art is that in which the experience is valuable, but the communication only partially successful. A *bad* work of art is that in which, no matter how skillful the communication, the experience offered is itself worthless. This appears fairly simple. It is when we discuss the nature of "value" and "communicative efficacy" that we begin to encounter serious difficulties and to murmur our provisos. Mr. Richards, in his definition of value, follows, a good deal more than he likes to admit, the Freudian lead. An experience, he says, is valuable in accordance as it organizes and uses without waste "conflicting impulses." The poet's experiences "represent conciliations of impulses which in most minds are still confused, intertrammelled, and conflicting." Again: "The poet makes unconsciously a selection which outwits the force of habit; the impulses he awakens are freed, through the very means by which they are aroused, from the inhibitions that ordinary circumstances encourage; the irrelevant and extraneous are excluded; and upon the resulting simplified but widened field of impulses he imposes an order . . ." With this definition of value we reach the turning-point of the discussion: we confront implications which are rather excitingly relativistic: and it is the most serious failure of Mr. Richards' book that it is exactly this point which he does not squarely meet. There being no universal of value (in an objective sense), then it follows that a poem in which *x* finds value (*i.e.*, a better organization of impulses than he can manage by himself) must be *good:* it arouses in *x* the feeling we loosely call beauty. To escape the staggering solipsism which must ensue here (and it is interesting to note that Mr. Richards *wants* to escape), he appears to assume (1) that *y* is a better judge than *x* if his mind is a finer (less wasteful) systematization of impulses; and (2) that as between two works of art that one is the better which is the more complex—is the resultant of an organization of a *greater number* of impulses. This is suspiciously like stating that a good critic is one who likes a good poem, and that a good poem is one which is liked by a good critic. It is an argument in a circle, and inevitably involves the surreptitious re-entrance of the "absolute" value which we had been at such pains to exclude. Mr. Richards even goes so far in this direction as to readmit "taste," which apparently he identifies with sensibility.

The reversal is tantamount to giving up the position as soon as won. Mr. Richards retreats from the purely social-psychological view of art because he dislikes the implication (which it leads to) that value in art must always be simply an equation between artist and audience. We have no right to assume—as he so devotedly wants to assume—that one level of art is "better" than another, or that *y* in liking it is necessarily possessed of a more "finely" organized mind. All we can say is that there *are* many levels in art, each suited to its audience (for which it *is* art, producing the desired effect); and then classify these, studying their history and laws, in terms of the simple-to-complex. Again, had Mr. Richards gone a little farther with Freud than he does, and posited a genesis for art partly or largely psychotic, he could not so lightly assume that the artist is one whose mind is "better organized," or whatever, than the average. A safer ground here, perhaps, is the assumption that the artist is one whose mind is *less* efficiently organized for a life of "action" than the average, and that his art is the process, analogous to the daydream, by which he seeks to maintain his balance. To those whose psychosis corresponds closely to his own, his work will be "good"—it becomes *their* successful daydream.

A purely functional view of this sort would, I think, prove

to be the soundest basis for criticism. It would find as interesting and valuable a place for Ella Wheeler Wilcox as for Henry James—at the same time noting their remarkable differences. It would correlate changes in art with changes in social temper and social organization. It might well predict the gradual decline of art, or, at any rate, of certain kinds, as society becomes less capriciously organized and individual aspirations are allowed greater freedom. At the present moment, for example, it would note, and attempt to analyze, the decline of "tragic" art and the corresponding increase in importance of the merely "amusing." In this fact it might see a decrease in the more profoundly psychotic elements in art—an interesting tendency which may or may not have far-reaching significance.

THE FUTURE OF POETRY   (1931)

Focus a little experience, give some scope and depth to your feeling, and it grows imaginative; give it more scope and more depth, focus all experience within it, make it a philosopher's vision of the world, and it will grow imaginative in a superlative degree, and be supremely poetical. The difficulty, after having the experience to symbolize, lies only in having enough imagination to hold and suspend it in a thought; and further to give this thought such verbal expression that others may be able to decipher it, and to be stirred by it as by a wind of suggestion sweeping the whole forest of their memories. . . . Poetry, then, is not poetical for being short-winded or incidental, but, on the contrary, for being comprehensive and having range. If too much matter renders it heavy, that is the fault of the poet's weak intellect, not of the outstretched world.

A middle-aged poet, invited to give his notions of what poetry should be, or may be, in the future, can think of no better exordium than this passage from Mr. Santayana's *Three Philosophical Poets*, which seems as valid and as suggestive, now, as when first heard in a lecture at Harvard twenty years ago. Everything pertinent to our question is implied here. There is no quarrel with the purely lyric poet; no quarrel with the witty poet, or the poet of marginal comment or observation; only a suggestion that this is the beginning of the matter, merely, and that the great province of the poet is farther on. I do not suppose that Mr. Santayana means to imply that a poet need have what is usually called a philosophical "system," or

that, if he has one, it need be provably "right" or even rationally
and schematically sound; the three poets whom he discusses at
length, and with brilliance—Lucretius, Dante and Goethe—are
all, in one sense or another, as regards datum or thesis or
detail of argument, out of date; but in the important sense as
great as ever. Each chose a lofty promontory from which to
view the world of his experience. Each had enough imagination
to hold and suspend this world "in a thought." The angle of
vision, in the light of modern physics or psychology, we may
find wrong; the altitude and magnitude remain.

And I do not think we can doubt that we should, and do,
look to poetry, now and in the future, for just such altitude and
magnitude. We have, and have had for two decades, an
abundance of good poetry about us; the number of books about
poetry and poets increases every day; the "new" psychology
seems increasingly to validate the function of poetry in the life
of civilized man—it is even suggested that in poetry man may
again find his religion. In fact, there are many signs that poetry
is once more in the ascendant. It is only the poets themselves
who, for the moment, seem to fall short of what might be expected of them: and for this perhaps they need not be blamed.

For the inheritance—sociologically speaking—of the contemporary poet is a very mixed one. At the beginning of this
century, if not indeed during the yellow 'nineties, the poet had
lost caste. Into the causes for this it is not my purpose here to
go; suffice it to observe that the poet had, in the eye of the
public, become synonymous with all that is effeminate, affected,
effete, decadent, immoral, conceited and useless. That a poet
should incidentally be a man, or even the greatest and wisest
of men, or the bravest, was inconceivable; and, unfortunately,
inconceivable even by the poets. The War, surprisingly, did a
good deal to correct this: that poets and philosophers should
suffer themselves to be shot, like other mortals, or invite imprisonment and social ruin by refusing military service, came
as a shock to many people—perhaps even to many poets. Nevertheless, much of the tradition of the decorative longhaired
"poetic" poet has persisted; a tradition, needless to say, which
has had little force in the great ages of poetry, or outside the
English-speaking countries. And the poets themselves have
suffered from this. They have been brought up to think that
they must put on the secondary sexual characteristics of the
poet: live in garrets, wear queer neckties, and so forth, in an
effort to flout foolish conventions as foolish as the conventions

they flout. This has been true, in the last twenty years, of even very good poets: I will mention no names. And the vice has crept into their poetry. Crossed with the echoes of French symbolism, with rumors of de Nerval's lobster and equally submarine whispers of Rimbaud, it has given us in recent poetry many ambiguous saffrons and doubtful mauves; it has helped to spread the notion that poetry should be outrageous, morbid, unintelligible, paranoid; that it should dispense with wisdom, knowledge, grammar, even with language; that it should become perhaps pure "affect," and regress through the primitive holophrase to the initial grunt.

This has been extremely entertaining—I exaggerate somewhat the state of things—but it is out of such conditions that contemporary poetry is trying to grow, and is growing, to its rightful inheritance of greatness. It is once more, slowly and painfully, learning to think. There is nothing really surprising in this. Poetry has always kept easily abreast with the utmost man can do in extending the horizon of his consciousness, whether outward or inward. It has always been the most flexible, the most comprehensive, the most far-seeing, and hence the most successful, of the modes by which he has accepted the new in experience, realized it, and adjusted himself to it. Whether it is a change in his conception of the heavens, or of the law of gravity, or of mortality, or of the nature of consciousness, it has always at last been in poetry that man has given his thought its supreme expression—which is to say that most of all, in this, he succeeds in making real for himself the profound myth of personal existence and experience.

II

But if poetry is to accomplish this, in any age, it must think: it must embody the full consciousness of man at that given moment. It can not afford to lag behind the explorations of knowledge, whether of the inner or outer worlds: these it is its business to absorb and transmute. What made Elizabethan poetry great, above all, was the fearlessness with which it plunged into the problem of consciousness itself. No item of man's awareness was too trivial to be noted, too terrifying to be plumbed. Shakespeare's poetry is everywhere vascular with this rich consciousness of self, thought being carried boldly into the realm of feeling, and feeling as boldly carried into the realm of thought. This was no mere decorative toy, no amusement or anodyne for women: it was the advance guard in man's conquest of the knowable. It was a portrait of man with the sweat on his brow, the blood on his hands, the agony in his heart; with his gayeties, his absurdities, his obscenities; his beliefs and his doubts. No poetry since has been so great, for none has been either so comprehensive or so truthful. The fashions changed, the "idea" of poetry changed, the novel absorbed a part of its province—one could multiply indefinitely the reasons for it. But today, as I have suggested, the signs are not wanting that poetry may again occupy its own province, may again speak with full-voiced gusto of the horrors and subtleties and magnificences of the great myth in which we find ourselves the bewildered actors.

The signs of this are rather, however, thus far, in the changed attitude of the people toward poetry than in the poetry itself. Poetry has certainly been more vigorous during the past decade or so, but its vigor has been more in color than in consciousness. There have been hints of what we want in Meredith and Hardy —more recently, also, but less conspicuously, in some of the work of Mr. Robinson, Mr. Eliot, and Mr. Stevens. But if, here and there, we come across passages of tough thinking to which has been given the rich timbre of emotion, or emotion which has been suspended "in a thought," we nowhere find it sustainedly, nor with that wise balance of the emotional and the intellectual (psychologists will pardon me for these loose terms) which is the characteristic of the best. In all this I am not so much suggesting that poets should be philosophers as that—in the sense of being questioners and understanders—they should be philosophic. The good poet must have not merely the clearest and subtlest of sensibilities; he must have also the boldest and subtlest of minds. The poet who is a mere drifting sensorium in a world of sense is of no more use to us than the most word-chopping of logicians. Each of them can afford us pleasure at particular moments only.

Perhaps the time is past for such complete philosophic "systems" as the philosophers used to think necessary. May it not be one of the superiorities of Shakespeare—to Dante, Lucretius, and Goethe—that he realized precisely the impossibility of dealing with the world, or experience, as a whole, and the necessity for dealing with it as a terrible complex of incompatibles? He examined it in detail: he examined it, one sometimes thinks, in almost *every* detail. Whatever else he found in it—and he found pretty nearly all that we know—he seems to have found no unity. Psychological unity—in the history of the individual human being, or group of interacting human beings—he does give us. For moral or spiritual unity we may search him in vain.

And what we get instead is perhaps exactly what I think the poetry of the future can most valuably give us: a complete intellectual integrity. We are complex creatures living in a kind of chaos. We live and die by question. What certainties we are born with do not survive us; our faiths are doubtful, our doubts are almost of necessity faiths. If we are good animals, we are courageous in this world of flux, and immensely enjoy it: we can learn, if we are intelligent and sensitive, to enjoy even our suffering. And it is the poet, in this situation, from whom we can learn most. It is he who is equipped to dive with full consciousness into this splendid Gehenna. We do not want him any longer to prettify, whether it be a sunset or a flower or a man's sense of evil. What we want from him is intensity, both in the analytic and *aff*ective parts of language; a complete honesty in seeing life as a kaleidoscopic series of incandescent instants—sometimes apparently meaningless, sometimes profound; that he should be religious, without religion; skeptic, without dogma; and should have tasted truth in all its inconsistencies of form. "It is the acme of life"—to quote again from Mr. Santayana— "to understand life. The height of poetry is to speak the language of the gods." . . . Or perhaps better—dare I suggest?—to speak the full language of man.

LITERATURE IN MASSACHUSETTS   (1937)

It must have been with some astonishment, to put it mildly, that the first settlers of Boston—who of course actually, to begin with, had planted themselves in Charlestown—found Boston itself to be already an English city, with a population of exactly one soul. This city, to be precise, consisted of William Blackstone or Blaxton, B.A., a graduate of Cambridge University, and one of the most curious and suggestive figures in the whole early history of the colonization of America. A member of the ill-starred Gorges expedition of 1625, Blackstone had spent two years in Wessagussett, now Weymouth. It appears that he had cast in his lot with Gorges not much more for reasons of Puritan conscience than because he simply wanted to be alone. At any rate, in what is now Boston, in the year 1630, "William Blackstone, a solitary, bookish recluse, in his thirty-fifth year, had a dwelling somewhere on the west slope of Beacon Hill, not far from what are now Beacon and Spruce Streets, from which he commanded the mouth of the Charles. Here he had lived ever since his removal from Wessagussett, in 1625 or 1626, trading with the savages, cultivating his garden, and watching the growth of some apple trees." Further, it is known that in 1634, reserving only six acres of land for himself—a parcel bounded roughly by Beacon, Charles, Mount Vernon, and Spruce Streets —he sold to the colonists the whole of Boston peninsula, which he himself had previously bought from the Indians; and "being tired of the 'lord brethren,' as he had before his emigration been wearied of the 'lord bishops,'" he then removed himself to an estate in Rhode Island, of which he was thus the first white inhabitant. This estate—to which he had presumably brought his books, as well as seeds and cuttings from his garden—he called Study Hill, and here he was destined to spend the rest of his life. Just once did he reappear in Boston, a good many years later, and then only for long enough to acquire a wife. He took this lady off to the wilderness with him, and Bostonians saw him no more.

It is an arresting and delightful figure, this young Cambridge graduate with his books and his apple trees, his conscience, and his passionate desire for privacy; and one cannot think of his perpetual centrifugal retreat from civilization, whenever it managed to catch up with him, without visualizing him as a symbol, or a charming figurehead, of the individualism which was to be so striking a characteristic of New England in the centuries to come. It was not that he was a misanthrope—not in the least. For it was at his own express invitation and because of his real concern for their plight that the wretched half-starved settlers of Charlestown were first brought across the river to the healthier slopes and the better springs on his own land. No, he was simply the first exemplar, the prototype of that profound individualism which has so deeply marked the American character ever since, and of which Massachusetts—especially in the field of letters—has been the most prodigal and brilliant source.

Of that fact, surely, there can be little question. In any summary, no matter how brief, of America's contribution to the world's literature, Massachusetts would be seen to have contributed most, not only in sheer quantity and quality but—and this is much more important—in that particular searching of the conscience and the soul, and of the soul's relationship to the infinite, which has almost invariably been the dominant feature of American literature at its best. Jonathan Edwards, Benjamin Franklin, Emerson, Thoreau, Hawthorne, Longfellow, Lowell, Melville, Holmes, Whittier, Emily Dickinson, Henry Adams, and the brothers Henry and William James—not to mention the historians Parkman, Prescott, and Motley—the mere recital of the names is quite enough to prove that without the Massachusetts authors American literature would amount to very little. It is a wonderful galaxy; and it is no exaggeration to say that the only absentees from it who are of comparable stature are Poe, Whitman, Mark Twain, and possibly Howells—and of these, Poe was himself at least a native of the State, for he was born in Boston.

The amazing outburst fell almost wholly within the confines of the nineteenth century; and in fact, within about a half of that, the years from 1830 to 1880. But if the quality of it is even more astonishing than the quantity and the range, what is more interesting, whether to the historian of morals and customs or to the psychological student of the origins and function of literature, is precisely the William Blackstone motif, which, as was mentioned above, has so persistently given it its character. New England individualism—and that is tantamount, of course, to saying Massachusetts individualism—has often enough been referred to, but one wonders whether it has ever been given quite its due as the real mainspring of New England letters. One reason for this has been the very widespread notion that it should simply be seen as the natural obverse of the excessive Puritanism and Calvinism from which it was in part a reaction; the individualists, in short, were nothing but small boys who had managed to escape from a very strict school. But this is a very superficial view of the individualist, and an equally superficial view of the Puritan. It might be fruitful to consider whether in point of fact the New England individualist was not just our old friend the Puritan writ large; and conversely, whether also the Puritan was not a good deal of an individualist.

The truth is, of course, that the two terms need not at all be mutually exclusive, and that we are facing here one of those charming but misleading over-simplifications with which the history books so constantly regale us. It is so much easier, and so much more flattering to the nineteenth century and all its works, to ascribe everything, *en bloc,* to the final overthrow of a sort of crippling Frankenstein monster, and to make out Puritanism as one of the most diabolical repressive hypocrisies with which a misguided mankind ever afflicted itself. Much can be said in support of this point of view, and much has been said; and it would be idle to deny that at its worst New England Puritanism became a dreadful thing; if the witch-hanging hysteria of the seventeenth century was the most violent culmination of it, it brought also in its train other forms of spiritual disaster which, if less conspicuous, were scarcely less terrible. The free Protestantism which the Pilgrims had brought with them from England had gradually hardened, under the influence of John Cotton and his descendants the Mathers, into a theocracy. "None should be electors nor elected, . . . except such as were visible subjects of our Lord Jesus Christ, personally confederated in our churches. In those and many other ways, he propounded unto them an endeavor after a *theocracy*, as near as might be, to that which was the glory of Israel." So remarks Cotton Mather of his grandfather, whose advice had been asked as to a revision of the "civil constitution" of the State.

But the fact is, that though the theocrats had their way a good deal, they did not have it entirely: and this for the very simple reason that the Protestantism of New England, as it had been based to begin with on the passionate belief of the individual in his right to believe and worship in his own way, still carried in itself these stubborn seeds of freedom. Roger Williams, "first rebel against the divine church-order in the wilderness" (again to quote Cotton Mather), submitted to a charge of heresy, and abandoned Salem, rather than surrender the tolerance which had outraged the church fathers. Another William Blackstone, he escaped to Rhode Island, and there wrote the first liberal document in American history, "The Bloody Tenet of Persecution for Cause of Conscience, discussed in a Conference between Truth and Peace." "A spiritual Crusoe, the most extreme and outcast soul in all America," he was, like Blackstone, though for very different reasons, a direct forebear of the great individualists of the nineteenth century. It is indeed essential that we should bear in mind this passionate belief in the freedom of conscience which underlay from the very beginning the foundations of New England culture. Its defeats and obscurities at the hands of the theocrats and zealots were at most only temporary; and there was never a time, even in the darkest passages of Massachusetts history, when it was not somewhere in evidence. It is evident in Jonathan Edwards's fierce conviction that the sacrament should be administered only to those who had had a radical experience of conversion—and who could properly judge of this save the individual himself?—as in the Northampton congregation which dismissed him, after twenty-three years, because it did not agree with him. And it is evident again in the calm fortitude with which Edwards accepted his exile, devoting the last six years of his life to a mission among the Indians of Stockbridge—the years, incidentally, during which he somehow managed to write his great philosophical treatise on the freedom of the will.

It was a period—the years from 1620 until the end of the Revolution—during which we must remember, in fact, that the congregation never surrendered its power both to choose and to dismiss its minister: it scrutinized his thought, and indeed his conduct, quite as closely as he scrutinized theirs. He might be tyrannical in his pursuit of his particular idea or ideal, but so, just as well, might they. Since God's grace was so arbitrarily bestowed, might it not fall upon Smith and Jones? Smith and Jones certainly thought so; and the result was a fierce co-operative and communal search for absolute truth, with a powerful clergy sometimes leading, but almost as often led by a powerful Church. The clergy might and did ally themselves and form a caste; but despite all their efforts, the Church remained essentially democratic, and essentially dictated—even when most misguided—by the original Puritan belief in freedom of conscience.

Meanwhile, during this period of nearly two hundred years it is scarcely an exaggeration to say that the liberal arts or anything even remotely like a literature simply did not exist in Massachusetts; and indeed it is difficult to conceive of their finding a place in a community so passionately surrendered to religious and moral preoccupations. But intellectual and spiritual and aesthetic sinews were there, none the less; the elements were ready; and it needed only the right catalyst, and the right moment, to release them in forms which probably nobody could have foreseen. The catalyst, or at any rate the most important of the catalysts, was the gradual rise of Unitarianism during the latter half of the eighteenth century, and then the phenomenal swiftness with which, early in the nineteenth, it effected an almost complete social conquest of Massachusetts. Here once more, but more clearly voiced than ever, was the Puritan insistence on freedom of conscience; but along with it also the revivifying force, almost impossible to gauge, of the Unitarian discovery that man's nature was not inevitably evil and inevitably doomed, but actually perhaps contained in itself the seeds of virtue. "How mournfully the human mind may misrepresent the Deity," wrote William Ellery Channing in 1809, in the course of a frontal assault on Calvinism, and, "We must start in religion from our own souls. In these is the fountain of all divine truth." What must have been the effect of this all-liberating doctrine on the subtle-minded New Englander, after his long winter of Calvinism? It was a blaze of sunlight, of course, and such a warming and thawing and freeing of locked energies as from this distance we perhaps cannot possibly conceive. And it was into this sudden summer, this sudden blossoming of New England into something almost like gaiety, with its wonderful discovery that virtue might go hand in hand with happiness, that the group of children were born who were destined to become the flower—and the end—of Massachusetts individualism. Prescott in 1796, Alcott in 1799, Emerson in 1803, Hawthorne in 1804, Longfellow and Whittier in 1807, Holmes in 1809, Motley in 1814, Dana in 1815, Thoreau in 1817, Melville in 1819, Emily Dickinson in 1830—these great-grandchildren of the New England genius were born by an inevitable conspiracy of time into just such an air as they needed for their purpose. What had shaped them—the ghost of William Blackstone, the proud and frontier-seeking independence of the Puritan conscience—they would themselves turn and shape to its final and beautiful mortal perfection.

The first quarter of the nineteenth century was for Massachusetts its period of greatest prosperity—nothing like it had been seen before, nothing like it has been seen since. The shipping trade was at its height, Boston and Salem had become great international ports, and in these and in New Bedford, where the whale trade had become a thriving industry, family fortunes were being founded almost overnight. Along miles of Cape Cod roadside, almost every cottage or house contained a blue-water sea captain, who knew St. Petersburg and Canton as well as he knew India Wharf in Boston. Everybody began to travel, Massachusetts had suddenly become cosmopolitan, and what for two centuries had been a queerly isolated and in many respects an extraordinarily innocent community on the way to nowhere, now began for the first time to feel itself in very close contact with the rest of the world. A new and infinitely richer sense of background became the common property of the people; the whole world was at Boston's door; new ideas were as common and as exciting as the exotic spices brought from Java and China.

An immense advantage, this, for the young Emerson and the

young Hawthorne, who, if they were caught willy-nilly in the new liberalism which was sweeping New England, were also caught in strange currents of rumor and echo from abroad. From England, from France, from Germany, came news of extraordinary developments in the literary world: the great secondary wave of romanticism, which followed by a generation the French Revolution, had begun to break in its thousand forms. What Channing's bold religious teaching had begun, the riotous brilliance and variety of the English romantic poets and the heady philosophy of Germany, at its most metaphysical, were to complete. The New England individualist who had first been a Puritan, and then a Unitarian, was now to reach his logical end in the lovely transparent butterfly hues of Transcendentalism.

When Emerson, who had been trained for the church and who preached for three years at the Second Church in Boston, resigned his pastorate in 1832 because he no longer believed in the communion and could not bring himself to administer it even in the abbreviated form then in use among the Unitarians —remarking characteristically that he simply "was not interested in it"—he was dedicating himself to the new wilderness and the new freedom, exactly as Roger Williams had done before him. Once more a frontier had been reached, but this one the most perilous of all—that frontier within man's consciousness where the soul turns and looks fearlessly into itself, where the individual, like a diver, plunges into his own depths to sound them, and in so doing believes himself effectually to have sounded the world. Man, according to Emerson, was to be self-sufficient, self-reliant, for his divinity was within himself. He must trust his instincts and his intuitions absolutely, for these were his direct communion with the Over-Soul, or God, with which he was in a sense identifiable. This direct knowledge of the divinity was not through the senses—not at all. It was a mode of apprehension that transcended one's sensory knowledge of the phenomenal world and all the experience of the senses, and it was this notion of a "transcendental" knowledge which gave its name to the little group which, after the publication of his first book *Nature* in 1836, formed itself about Emerson in Concord and Boston. "If the single man plant himself indomitably on his instincts, and there abide, the huge world will come round to him." "For solace, the perspective of your own infinite life."—this was almost or could easily be, the *reductio ad absurdum* of individualism, for it implied a negation of all authority, whether religious or social, and the complete autonomy of the individual soul.

Patently, this doctrine with its ancillary notions bore within itself the seeds of an intellectual and utopian anarchy; and it is interesting to notice, in this connection, how very flimsy and impractical, how absurdly and charmingly innocent, were such ideas of social awareness as this group entertained. It is hardly an exaggeration, in fact, to say that they were none of them concerned with society as such at all. The passionate search for a moral and religious center, a significance, a meaning, had led them steadily inward, never outward; and if they thought of the social problem at all, it was only to wave it away with the sublime assurance that, as man was essentially good, the social problem would quite nicely take care of itself. If the relationship of the Ego to God was satisfactory, then everything else would follow of course. The experiment at Brook Farm and Bronson Alcott's lesser adventure in a Utopia at Fruitlands were the natural, if humiliating, outcome of such beliefs, quite as much as Thoreau's attempt at a formal secession from society. Even the sole apparent exception to this indifference toward social problems, the antislavery agitation, in which practically without exception the transcendentalists joined, turns out on inspection to be not quite all that it purports to be. For here again the problem was looked at from the point of view, not of society, but of the individual; even the Negro should bow to no authority save God's, which was the authority within himself.

Emerson's influence, nevertheless, in spite of a good deal of misunderstanding, not to mention occasional downright derision, was immense and profoundly fructifying, both on his own generation and on that which followed. He was the real center of his time, and his mark is everywhere. Thoreau's *Walden,* both the experiment and the book, were but the carrying into practice of Emersonian self-sufficiency; and if they add a literary and speculative genius which is Thoreau's, the spirit of Emerson is indelibly in them. Not least, either, in the very conspicuous indifference, not to say contempt, for form. The method could hardly be more wayward; it is as wayward as Emerson's, who admittedly when he wanted an essay or a lecture just ransacked his copious notebooks, extracted a random selection of observations and gnomic sayings, and strung them together on a theme as best he could. And it is as well to observe in this connection that a comparative indifference to form was a perhaps inevitable attribute of vatic individualism—everything must be spontaneous, a direct and uncontrolled uprush from the divine well of the soul; one was merely a medium for the divine voice, and in consequence there could not logically be any such thing as a compromise with so external and strictly phenomenal an affair as form or style. Communication—yes, but only such as came naturally. Nor need one bother overmuch with consistency.

This individualist attitude to form is noticeable everywhere in the literature of the Massachusetts renaissance, as much in the work of the conservative Boston and Cambridge group—Longfellow, Holmes, and Lowell—as in that of the Concord radicals. To consider a poem or an essay or a novel as a work of art, was this not to yield oneself to a kind of outside authority, and to compromise or adulterate the pure necessity and virtue of revelation? Revelation was the thing; and everything depended on the swiftness with which one brought it up from the depths of one's awareness, so that not a spark of the light should be lost. The result was a kind of romantic mysticism which was at its most lucid in Emerson, at its sunniest and serenest in Thoreau, at its profoundest in Herman Melville, and at its most vapid and ridiculous in the orphic sayings of Bronson Alcott. And the result also was a pervading looseness and raggedness, a kind of rustic and innocent willfulness, whether in prose or verse, in practically all the work of the Massachusetts galaxy. It is evident in Emerson's crabbed and gnomic free verse and his homespun couplets quite as much as in his prose, where image follows image and idea idea with little or no regard for nexus or pattern, to say nothing of rhythm. It is evident again in that cryptic unintelligibility, the sibylline phrase, which, if it has a meaning, sometimes guards it all too well from the bewildered reader. The poor reader, indeed, was given no quarter, he must simply shift for himself; and presumably it was Emerson's idea, as it was Alcott's and Thoreau's, that it was a sufficient privilege for the reader that he thus overheard, as it were, the words of the oracle at all. The words were the words of the divinity, and must not be altered: all that was needed was that they should be received with an understanding equally instinctive and divine.

The truth is, the glorification of the individual and of individualism had reached such a pitch of egoism and self-absorption, accompanied by such an entire indifference to the external world, that had they not been geniuses, literary geniuses, none of these men would have escaped disaster. Only a genius can be artless with impunity, and of all this wonderful group only one was a genuine artist, Nathaniel Hawthorne. Hawthorne listened carefully to everything the others had to say, he was himself something of a transcendentalist, he even stayed for a while at Brook Farm; but he remained always a little detached, he was essentially both in his life and in his work a moral and social observer; and it was this carefully kept moral and aesthetic distance which enabled him alone of his group to understand the necessity for form and to achieve an individual mastery of it. Alone, too, was Hawthorne in having a quite definite social awareness, and in seeing precisely to what sort of bankruptcy the doctrine of uncontrolled individualism might lead. Emerson may not have realized it, but *The Scarlet Letter* was, among other things, a very grim comment on the doctrine of self-reliance; and *The Blithedale Romance* as well.

If in this sense Hawthorne was the only commentator on transcendental individualism, and the one analyst and chronicler of the final phases of the evolution of the Puritan passion for freedom of conscience, he was also the only link between the Concord group and the writer who carried farthest and deepest that perilous frontier of mystic consciousness which had always been the Puritan's fiercest concern: Herman Melville. *Moby Dick* was dedicated to Hawthorne, and it was written while Hawthorne and Melville were neighbors in Pittsfield. Without any question the greatest book which has come out of New England, and one of the very greatest works of prose fiction ever written in any language, it is also the final and perfect finial to the Puritan's desperate three-century-long struggle with the problem of evil. Hunted from consciousness into the unconscious, and in effect beyond space and time, magnificently sublimated so that it becomes not one issue but all issues, a superb and almost unanalyzable matrix of universal symbolism, the white whale is the Puritan's central dream of delight and terror, the all-hating and all-loving, all-creating and all-destroying implacable god, whose magnetism none can escape, and who must be faced and fought with on the frontier of awareness with the last shred of one's moral courage and one's moral despair. Man against God? Is the principle of things, at last, to be seen as essentially evil? And redeemable only by war *à l'outrance?* Impossible, at any rate, to surrender; one's freedom to feel toward it what one will, whether hatred or love, must be preciously preserved. One must grapple with it, and alone, and in darkness, no matter whether it lead to a death throe or to an all-consuming love.

Melville, writing to Hawthorne about this extraordinary book, which was destined for half a century to be considered just a good romance for boys, likened himself to one who strips off the layers of consciousness as one might strip off the layers of an onion, and added that he had come at last to the central core. And indeed to all intents he had; when a year later, at the age of thirty-three, he published *Pierre,* he had really finished his voyage. And he had carried William Blackstone with him to such strange borderlands as that bold explorer of Rhode Island never dreamed of. Perhaps it is worth noting that Melville himself denied that *Moby Dick* had any allegorical intention—if only to point out that the denial can really have no meaning. *Mardi* was quite obviously allegorical; allegory and parable came almost instinctively to the hands of a group so vitally concerned with moral and religious matters, and as a "form" it very likely seemed no more artificial or unusual to Hawthorne or Melville than that, say, of a poem: it was something which played with meaning and which gave out meanings on many different levels, and that was the end of it.

And indeed *Moby Dick* may be said to have been the great poem, the epic of the Puritan civilization, and to have marked a turning-point in its evolution, if not quite its end. There could not again be any such violent imaginative projection of the problem; the problem itself was beginning to dissipate and break up, to disappear in the dishevelment of analysis: individualism was to turn outward again. It could receive in the hands of Henry James a fine symphonic abstraction, or in the hands of William James a bold social and scientific externalization and analysis, but the creative poisons were all but drained from it. The worlds around were changing, new winds of doctrine brought new seeds and spores, and in *The Education of Henry Adams* one has almost the spectacle of a dead civilization performing an autopsy on itself. The note of retrospect, the backward-looking eye—this could have only one meaning, that the Puritan struggle was at last, in all important senses, over. One genius remained yet to be heard from, and this the most exquisitely characteristic of all—Emily Dickinson. In her life of hushed and mystic and self-absorbed sequestration, no less than her work, where we watch the lonely soul alembicating itself that it may test its own essence, we have the very mayflower of the Puritan passion for privacy and freedom. How strict was that soul with itself, when there was none to watch! Was it not her own epitaph that she wrote—or can we say that it was an epitaph for a whole phase of the human soul—in the lines:

Lay this laurel on the one
Too intrinsic for renown.
Laurel! veil your deathless tree—
Him you chasten, that is he!

This wonderful pride and immense strength in solitude which could give up as worth nothing any notion of fame or acclaim if only its soul's house be in order and its accounts straight with heaven—perfectly content, and serenely self-sufficient, so long as the windows which looked on the Eternal were kept clear—this was the final rededication of the spirit of William Blackstone, who had come to Boston when it was still a wilderness, was found there by the first settlers "watching the growth of some apple trees," and moved on to another wilderness and another privacy when the "lord brethren," his neighbors, came too close.

Emily Dickinson was the last of her line, the last of the great Massachusetts frontiersmen; and with her it may be said that the literature of Puritanism, as a purely local phenomenon, came to an end. Henceforth its heirs were to be sought farther afield, dispersed inconspicuously, but perhaps none the less indestructibly, in the consciousness of the country at large. Amy Lowell had little of this temper in her; and if in the contemporary scene it has any ambassadors, they are Robert Frost and T. S. Eliot. But the movement itself is complete and at an end.

BACK TO POETRY   (1940)

Has poetry become too theory-ridden? Has it fallen too much into the hands of social theorists and demagogues, on the one side, of snobs and pedants and schoolmasters on the other?

It is a curious and interesting and perhaps disturbing fact that for the past decade, during which there has been a revival of excitement about poetry comparable to that of the decade 1912-1922, so much of this excitement has been theoretic and critical, so little of it in any "good" sense popular, in any "popular" sense creative. The shadow of theory, of dogma, of debate, has hung over it; and if the poetry has certainly been there, it has been there, all too often, as the building, or the steeple, is there behind the scaffold: one takes the steeple for granted, perhaps, but what one actually sees is the scaffolding. And we may be pardoned, in that situation, if we tend to find the steeple impressive in inverse ratio to the scaffolding's elaborateness. Where there is so *much* supporting theory, so conspicuous and intricate an apparatus for care and repair, so much mere *critical* activity, in short, one not unnaturally begins to suspect there may be something wrong with the poetry.

Critical formulations, or crystallizations, tend to occur, it may be, at the *ends* of creative movements in the arts, rather than at their beginnings: with minor exceptions, they seem seldom to advance with them *pari passu;* and it might be argued that they almost invariably arise, therefore, when creative energies are low. The poem does not come out of the theory: the theory comes out of the poem. And the same *Zeitgeist* which has by degrees silenced or enfeebled the more vital and violent and generous elements in poetry, at a given moment, will afterwards govern, in the shape of dogma, the critical movement which follows. Common sense will probably be the cry—it almost always is. The theorist isn't a poet, or is at best a poet *manqué,* and what he wants, of course, is a poetry without nonsense, a poetry which can be achieved by formula, a poetry which can be guaranteed not to offend. The emphasis will all be on technique, on dexterity, on decorum, on good taste: in fact, on all the negative and more arid virtues; and the resulting poetry will naturally be a poetry made safe for the intelligent but unimaginative. It will be quite nice and dry, and comparatively free from sentimentality; but it will also probably be either dull, or precious, or both.

And we have been witnessing, I think, in the past decade, an attempt of this sort to dragoon poetry out of its freedom, its natural wildness (and let us not forget that it *has* a natural wildness) into a dead level of mere conventional excellence and suitability. These poor young poets of our time—what a wretched novitiate we have given them! For first of all, in the mass of theory with which they were confronted, was the sociological question, the sociological demand. What about that social contract, into which they had entered, poor devils, in the mere act of getting themselves born? Would they be willing to take sides? Would they choose the *right* side, and lend their art to it in the shape of propaganda? Had they at all considered the social *function* of the poet, or come to any conclusion as to its precise psychological nature, or necessity? Was the poet, for example, essential, anyway? Or was he in fact already outmoded, a mere social luxury? Had they read Marx, Freud, Pfister, Jung, Rank? . . .

The pressure was great, both in England and in America; it came from all sides; it was unremitting. Textbooks of literary history were suddenly written (to be almost as suddenly out of date) from the viewpoint of class warfare; anthologies of "proletarian" verse appeared; almost without exception, in the "left," and "little," and advanced magazines, the social problem was pushed forward, the aesthetic neglected or ignored. Small wonder, then, that these young poets were at first bewildered, and then hypnotized, by a social current so powerful and omnipresent, or that at last, fascinated by the reassuring pluralism of its motion, so many of them dived in. Besides, any motion or movement—according to Hegel—was simply a "manifestation of the dialectic," and dialectic was all the rage. All the bright critics, whether social or literary, were talking about it, weren't they? Well, then!—And so they became sociological poets, poets with a New Outlook, a social consciousness, poets with a burden. And good heavens, how they kept reminding us of that precious burden! And how they seemed to say, by the very *tone* of their poetry, that it was indeed a very great deal they were doing for us, a great deal they were giving up!

For observe, almost everywhere in the poetry of this group, from early Auden and Spender and Macneice and Day Lewis down to the least and latest of their American imitators, the weary valedictory and valetudinarian note, the seemingly offhand but careful flatness of the language—the voices are the voices of weary and excessively refined young men, anxious to avoid any overstatement, whether overt or implied; and anxious above all to avoid the "poetic," if only because to be poetic was somehow to be bourgeois. Says Mr. Auden:

It is later than you think; nearer that day
Far other than that distant afternoon
Amid rustle of frocks and stamping of feet
They gave the prizes to the ruined boys.
You cannot be away, then, no,
Not though you pack to leave within an hour,
Escaping humming down arterial roads.

Or again:

Hearing the arrival of his special train,
Hearing the fireworks, the saluting and the guns,
Bob and Miss Belmairs spooning in Spain,
Where is the trained eye? Under the sofa.
Where is Moxon? Dreaming of nuns.
Their day is over, they shall decorate the Zoo
With Professor Jeans and Bishop Barnes at 2d a
   view. . . .

Or again:—

The chairs are being brought in from the garden,
The summer talk stopped on that savage coast
Before the storms, after the guests and birds:
In sanatoriums they laugh less and less,
Less certain of cure; and the loud madman
Sinks now into a more terrible calm.

To which Mr. Macneice adds, as if in refrain:

But certainly it was fun while it lasted
   And I got my honours degree
And was stamped as a person of intelligence and
      culture
   For ever wherever two or three
Persons of intelligence and culture
   Are gathered together in talk
Writing definitions on invisible blackboards
   In non-existent chalk.

And further:

The country gentry cannot change, they will die in
      their shoes
From angry circumstance and moral self-abuse,
Dying with a paltry fizzle they will prove their lives
      to be
An ever-diluted drug, a spiritual tautology.
They cannot live once their idols are turned out,
None of them can endure, for how could they,
      possibly, without
The flotsam of private property, pekingese and
      poylanthus,
The good things which in the end turn to poison
      and pus. . . .

From the tired elegiac note of these English poets it is only
a step to Mr. John Crowe Ransom's

Autumn days in our section
Are the most used-up things on earth. . . .
Having no more color nor predilection
Than cornstalks too wet for the fire.

Or Mr. Robert Penn Warren's

Guns blaze in the autumn, and
The quail falls and
Empires collide with a bang
That shakes the pictures where they hang. . . .
But a good pointer holds the point
And is not gun-shy;
But I
Am gun-shy.

Or Mr. Allen Tate's

                                                      heredity

Proposes love, love exacts language, and we lack
Language. When shall we speak again? When shall
The sparrow dusting the gutter sing? When shall
This drift with silence meet the sun? When shall
I wake?

Or his

    We are the eyelids of defeated caves.

And once more, in the work of Miss Muriel Rukeyser, we find
the same elegiac note exactly:

As I went down to Rotten Lake I remembered
the wrecked season, haunted by plans of salvage,
snow, the closed door, footsteps and resurrections,
    machinery of sorrow.

And the same flat "social" cataloguing:—

                                    Truckdrivers
swing ungrazed trailers past, the woman in the fog
can never speak her poems of unemployment,
the brakeman slows the last freight round the curve.
And riveters in their hardshell fling short fiery
steel, and the servant groans in his narrow room,
and the girl limps away from the door of the shady
    doctor.

The unanimity of theme and tone, in fact, is astonishing; and
the instances could easily be multiplied. Anything to avoid the
poetic, anything to avoid the bourgeois! For these are really, one

would almost say, *frightened* young people: they have been frozen by fear into a kind of chattering abnegation of self, an abject abrogation of the rights of the individual. So fearful indeed have they become—it is hardly an exaggeration to say—of this shadow of social pressure, whether it take the form of war, revolution, change, order, or disorder, that they seem no longer to have either the will or the courage to look into themselves, calmly and steadily, in order that they may know and *separate* themselves; nor, conversely, have they the ability to see that social shadow any more clearly. Instead, alarmed, and as if electrolyzed by the powerful magnetic pluralisms that everywhere surround them, they appear only too hurriedly willing to give up, to give in, even to surrendering, in the interests of class and fashion, that passionate sense of identity which has always been the most preciously guarded possession of the poet—indeed, his birthright. For these poets no longer, alas, seem to have an "I" —that would be presuming too much. Instead, they have only, and with properly becoming modesty, the anonymously social and multicellular "we." It is no longer "I, the person, did this, saw this, felt this, knew this"; it is now "we the people." . . . Yeats alone, among contemporary poets, dared to retain the first-personal pronoun; alone continued to give it dignity and significance.

II

And of course, one must say at once, such an attitude is tantamount to poetic suicide. For surely the basis of *all* poetic activity, its *sine qua non*, its very essence, lies in the individual's ability, and need, to isolate for feeling and contemplation the relation "I: World." That, in fact, is the begin-all-end-all business of the poet's life. It is the most private and precious, as it is also the most primitive, of adventures, the adventure which underlies all others: for until he knows himself, and his twinned worlds, the inner and outer, how can he possibly know the worlds, inner or outer, of another? No: uncorrupted by temporal or social or fashionable or ephemeral distractions and disguises, he must first of all keep steady and intense and pure the essentially *lyric* nature of his relation to his own world and moment. It is unquestionably, but inevitably and rightly, the extreme of individualism; but it is the individualism from which ultimately all other human values are derived. Nor is there anything forced or self-conscious about it, or deliberate. The great poets are *naturally* shameless fellows. They go, without ostenta-

tion, even without awareness of it as anything in the least unusual, beyond, above, and below, moral or social fashions, and
are quite *simply* indifferent to them. They see the world perpetually as both old and new at once: in its complexity they
never forget its simplicity; they celebrate its universals, and
are therefore dateless; and precisely because they are themselves the most private and individualist of people, by articulat-
ing this extreme privacy of awareness they become themselves
universals. The proper logical sequence is not "we, the people"
—that is to invoke at once what Henry Adams called the "degradation of the democratic dogma": it is, on the contrary, and
dynamically, "*I*, the people."

And it is this virtue, this all-nourishing taproot integrity,
which the sociological poets, like all fashion-following poets,
have blindly thrown away. Their positions are honest enough;
and their statements are honest; but unfortunately neither position nor statement is *poetically* honest—they have compromised
where compromise is both unforgivable and fatal, namely with
poetry itself. The poet *cannot* write, of set purpose, for a group
or movement: he can only write for himself, and for that possible group in the future of which he is himself perhaps the
prototype. Otherwise, he finds himself, willy-nilly, confined to the
writing of what is rightly called a "poetry of exclusion." Certain
subjects will be taboo, certain others will be considered his
proper material. In the case of the sociological poet, this will in-
volve a rigid and sterile sentimentality about the "common" man
as against the bourgeois or privileged, with a natural selection
of the appropriate or correct properties—which are usually in
practice both dull and false. At all costs, he must avoid (I
quote Mr. Geoffrey Grigson, editor of *New Verse*) "that poetic
inflation, which follows when a poet mistakes the product of the
conflicts in himself for the gift, inspired in him, mysteriously, by
some outside agent." Was there ever so complete a psychological misunderstanding? Notice especially the emphasis on the
"outside agent": for these poets, nothing must come from inside—the subjective must be run from like the very devil; and
the poor ego, with its conflicts—that actual *fons et origo* of
everything, absolutely everything—is set up as a sort of anath-
ema or antichrist. No, the poet must be driven "outward on to
natural facts and forms"; he must be encouraged to "observe
well" and to be a "good reporter"; and above all, room must be
left for the "reason" and the "intellectual faculties." . . .

Obviously this insistence on the objective method, with the

Augustan virtues of reason and common sense, and "room for the intellectual faculties," would have pleased Dryden, as it would also have pleased Johnson. Obviously, too, the result, like the theory, is essentially antipoetic—for everywhere in this poetry the emphasis is on manipulatory dexterity, on ingenuity, on cerebral trick and clever word-play, on a *dry* manner, in short, which prefers the safer ambush of irony and satire to the more dangerous "open" warfare which is involved when the poet faces the world more directly, more instinctively, more emotionally. And perhaps not surprisingly, therefore, the word "poetic" has become, for these poets and critics, quite frankly a term of opprobrium. That a poem should be simple, sensuous, and passionate—*passionate*, above all things!—is for them not merely inconceivable, it is disgusting. To betray feelings in a poem, to run the risk of being charged with sentimentality—oh no, anything but that. And so a little cynicism must be injected; or a little irony, like so much precautionary iodine; and if the taste is bitter, that won't matter, for at all events we shall have avoided vulgarity.

However, to be quite fair, it is not the sociological poets alone who are to blame for this curious and regrettable reversal: the pedant-poets, the poet-critics—and there has been, significantly, an extraordinary number of these in the past decade—are just as much at fault. These earnest theoreticians of poetry—these scholiasts—subtle eyebrow-combers of style, calligraphic text-combers—have worked just as zealously to bring about a "poetry of exclusion"; and if not for the same reasons, at any rate in pretty much the same direction. These are the intellectuals, the aesthetes, for whom a poem "should not *mean*, but *be*." The poem, it would seem, must be conceived of as a detached aesthetic object, hung in the void, which has been shaped quite without feeling, exists by itself, and makes no statement: no statement, that is, but an aesthetic one. But just how it is supposed to work, this epistemological miracle, this process of poetic "being" without "meaning," and just how it is that the most supremely articulate statement of which man is capable (and that is what poetry is) can *exist* without meaning, are nowhere made clear. If poetry were a pure nonsense, or gibberish, that would be a different matter. But it is *not* a pure nonsense—though nonsense plays a valuable part in it, as Cammaerts and others have shown; it is, on the contrary, a supremely articulate statement; it is, in fact, and in essence, man's language; and therefore one is driven inescapably to the conclusion that a

poem cannot possibly be considered as a mere detached aesthetic object, but must, instead, be considered functionally and
vitally as a psychological and aesthetic *correlative*. In the last
analysis, it is nothing whatever but an objectification (by articulation) of feelings and beliefs. Its *only* being is in its meaning.
And meaning, we may therefore say (by which we intend *total*
meaning, with all the affective colorations and distortions), is
its function. . . . Exactly, of course, as it is the function of
language.

III

But if this is so; and if we can say, despite all these contemporary snobbisms, that the more meaning (affective as well as
conceptual) poetry has, the healthier it will be; and if we can
go still further and say that the greatest poetry has always been
that which, whether formally perfect or not, has been deepest
and widest, and most prodigal, in understanding: then it must
follow that our present poetry is badly in need of liberation.
What a juiceless and joyless and loveless thing it has become
—poetry, too, the most generous and lovely of the arts of mankind! How labored in its careful flatnesses, its dry avoidances,
its tuneless euphemisms, its frigid and gingerly decorums! How
false and affected even in its occasional violences! Good heavens,
what are we thinking of—are we going to let the critics bully
us into this, into leaving the world out of our poetry, in exchange
for a mere guarantee of good breeding, an assurance of good
taste? And who are these arbiters of taste, anyway, and who
gave them their yardsticks? Shall we listen to Mr. Cleanth
Brooks, for example, when he tells us, in *Modern Poetry and
the Tradition*, that the only poetry which achieves what Arnold called "high seriousness" is the poetry of wit? Or when he
tries to persuade us that in urging a deliberate return to the
seventeenth-century "meta-physical" style Messrs. Tate, Ransom, and others, have brought about the third, and greatest,
critical revolution in the history of English poetry? That is a
schoolmaster's vision, with a vengeance; and alas, it is all too
typical of the ungenerous, because emotionally undernourished,
theorizing of our school of scholiasts. And what it really represents—let us be bold enough to say it—is that sort of decay in
taste which accompanies a decline in poetic energies, and which
then organizes itself in defense, quite naturally, of the lesser
and more arid virtues of poetry: the jejune precisions of artifice
and formalism, the snug enclosures of wit and irony, the anti-

septic caustics of satire. Let them call it by whatever names they like, or disguise it as they will, it will bring about again, as it has brought about before, a withering of the poet's function; if only because the very concept of that function is so belittling.

The truth is that a wholehearted romantic revival is much overdue; and it is the poets who must themselves bring it to pass. They must throw the critics and schoolmasters out of the window, neck and crop, and the sociologists as well; and then themselves reëstablish poetry where it belongs—not in the margins of a textbook, but as coterminous with our awareness of the world. It is in the nature of English poetry to be romantic, —it has never at its best been anything else,—so let us again have it romantic. That need not prevent it from thinking— it never has. But for goodness' sake let us have back as well a few blistering sunrises and peculiar sunsets, a few fierce loves and melodramatic despairs—our private loves and terrors, like the grass blade, the sun, and the unexploded atom, will still be in fashion when the social cleavages and surfaces of our day, with all their ephemeral lumber, will have been forgotten. Let us be reckless, lavish, generous, afraid of no extremes and no simplicities—surely it is better to be fervidly baroque, a Swinburne, for example, than to be a snob: the cult of carefulness has gone far enough. Is not poetry an affirmation, even when it is fullest of despair, or apparently most nihilistic—and then most of all when it is tragic? We need more of that taproot sort of affirmation, a blood-filled affirmation deeply rooted in the world —we need it now more than ever. Let the poet therefore first of all *rediscover himself.* If he will do this, the rest will follow. Already there are signs of what may be to come, in the brilliantly imaginative poems of Mr. Dylan Thomas, a young Englishman with a genius for word-magic, a genuine and outrageous gift-of-the-gab, and in the richly framed psychological delvings and shapings of a young American, Mr. Delmore Schwartz. Mr. Thomas is violent and vivid, as a poet should be; he is a chameleon for colors, a word-spout, full of mad nonsense and humors, prodigal of *affects* (*sic*)—if his meanings too often escape us, nevertheless he can be read with joy for the shape and shine alone. Here he is, from his new book, *The World I Breathe:*

I make a weapon of an ass's skeleton
And walk the warring sands by the dead town,
Cudgel great air, wreck east, and topple sundown,
Storm her sped heart, hang with beheaded veins
In wringing shell, and let her eyelids fasten.

*Destruction, picked by birds, brays through the
      jawbone,
And for that murder's sake, dark with contagion
Like an approaching wave I sprawl to ruin.*

And again:

*The tombstone told when she died.
Her two surnames stopped me still.
A virgin married at rest.
She married in this pouring place,
That I struck one day by luck,
Before I heard in my mother's side
Or saw in the looking-glass shell
The rain through her cold heart speak
And the sun killed in her face.
More the thick stone cannot tell.*

And again:

*The hand that signed the paper felled a city;
Five sovereign fingers taxed the breath,
Doubled the globe of dead and halved a country;
These five kings did a king to death.
The mighty hand leads to a sloping shoulder,
The finger joints are cramped with chalk;
A goose's quill has put an end to murder
That put an end to talk.*

Mr. Schwartz is not so easy to quote from—he prefers to work in long form, he is a careful and accurate psychologist and makes perhaps fewer concessions to the more obviously sensuous graces of poetry than he need; but for subtlety, richness, and brilliance his *Coriolanus* (*In Dreams Begin Responsibilities*) is the most exciting long poem in more than a decade. One must go back to *The Waste Land,* or Wallace Stevens's *The Comedian as the Letter C,* for anything comparable to it either in scope or in virtuosity. These two poets are a promise, as much as a fulfillment—they take us back to poetry again, and that is something to be grateful for. But we need more than this, and we need it of every sort—if necessary we must break down the categories and invent new ones. In short, what we want to see is the poet once more standing, as he did in the Elizabethan age, naturally and vigorously at the centre of the world.

AMERICAN WRITERS COME OF AGE (1942)

It is solely due to the critics, who in our times still praise rude, savage, and, for us, meaningless works of the ancient Greeks: Sophocles, Euripides, Aeschylus, and especially Aristophanes; or, of modern writers, Dante, Tasso, Milton, Shakespeare; in painting, all of Raphael, all of Michelangelo, including his absurd "Last Judgment"; in music, the whole of Bach, and the whole of Beethoven, including his last period—thanks only to them have the Ibsens, the Maeterlincks, Verlaines, Mallarmés, Puvis de Chavannes, Klingers, Böcklins, Stucks, Schneiders; in music, the Wagners, Liszts, Berliozes, Brahmses, and Richard Strausses, etc., and all that immense mass of good-for-nothing imitators of these imitators, become possible in our day."

Many people will remember how Tolstoy, in that very interesting, very odd, and certainly very misguided book, *What Is Art?* bitterly attacked modern art and letters, practically all of it, as antisocial, immoral, and decadent; and then endeavored to formulate in its stead a quasi-religious doctrine of art of his own, based on the "brotherly union of man."

He was writing, of course, at a time which was later to be known, with some opprobrium, as *fin de siècle;* Russia, like the rest of the world, was beginning to react to the multiform ferment of French romanticism; and Russia, like the rest of the world, must at all costs be defended against this vile and insidious foreign infection. The notion of a "universal" art was not new, nor did Tolstoy himself succeed in making a more plausible program for it, either as religion or as psychology, than his predecessors. More diverting for us, if only as a cautionary tale for prophets and politicians and literary captains, at a moment when clearheadedness is at a premium, to look over the actual names of that era which were so unreasonably hated by so great a man—not, by any means, that he restricted himself to that era alone. It is a handsome list—indeed, it is magnificent. If it had been Tolstoy's intention to pick out, from among his contemporaries, those names which might *survive,* he could hardly have done better; it is doubtful if it was better done by anyone. And the list of contemporary painters with which he supplemented it was just as startlingly comprehensive. Monet, Renoir, Sisley, Redon, and Pissarro were condemned out of hand. Had Tolstoy know Cézanne and Van Gogh, we can be sure that they too would have been dismissed.

Taken altogether, this represents what is perhaps an all-time high, a *locus classicus*, of mistaken critical judgment; it remains, like a kind of wrecker's beacon, as a warning to those who would mix sociology and morals with their aesthetics *a priori*. Certainly, one can think of no pronouncement by a writer of comparable stature which contains so many confessions of blindness. But if we can recover from our astonishment at its sheer stupendousness, there is something we can learn from it, particularly at this precise moment in our and the world's history. That war renders a nation violently egoistic is a truism—Tolstoy himself had something to say about this, and we shall come to it later. Such egoism is inevitable; and it is necessary if a nation is to survive. But it is against its less desirable cultural by-products that we must learn to be on our guard; and it is already possible to see from what directions some of these might come.

One of these, for example, is our old friend, but now wearing a slightly different costume, the Cultural Protective Tariff. Never a very sound practice, but a comforting one, this took the form, during the lean years of our cultural adolescence, when the competition from abroad was too keen, of a kind of double standard in criticism. The critical tariff on imported works of art was kept high—was kept, as it were, up to international standards: an English poet or a French painter was to be judged and measured against the best of the whole present, the whole past. But of the domestic product the critics weren't quite so exacting. It was a little too much to expect, surely, of a nation still expanding, still thrusting forward its frontiers, whether geographical or psychological or industrial, that it should be as richly nourished on tradition or speak with as complex and formed a language (that is, literature) as those parent nations whose pioneering was long since done. And so, our good New England homespun, for instance, was unblushingly, if not indeed a little proudly, compared to foreign damask; and to be unostentatiously provincial was simply to continue those virtues of plain living and high thinking which had been common to the Puritans and—shall we say—the "better" of the Romans.

All of which was harmless enough, and perhaps in its season even useful, protecting as it did those tenderer shoots which a severer exposure might have killed. But one had thought, and hoped, that this was a thing of the past. Was it not, in fact, finished in 1919-1920? The famous mass migration of our literary expatriates to Europe at the end of the First World War has by some been taken to signify a lack or weakness in our own "scene"; and their mass return, a decade later, somewhat bedraggled, as a confession of that weakness in themselves, or an awakening to something in America which they had previously overlooked or ignored.

But this, I think, is to miss the point entirely—and it is a point of paramount importance. For it was precisely at the moment when the American *avant garde* artists were ready and willing to admit that Europe had something to teach them that, culturally, America grew up. This was the exact minute when the cultural protective tariff went down. From now on the American "scene" was confessedly and functionally to be no longer the isolated and provincial "independent" show it had always somewhat braggingly been, but a part of the world picture; it was ready for its natural inheritance of the whole tradition of man's past, no matter from what country or what century it might come. This humble migration in search of knowledge (it was our Grand Tour) marked our coming of age. And this modest preparation for a genuine internationalism of the arts was something precious which we must now—above all, now—try to remember and cherish.

Tolstoy's extraordinary blindness to what was excellent and life-giving in contemporary European art had two obvious causes. One of these was mere insularity—unacknowledged, to be sure, but insularity just the same. It was the age-old defensive suspicion of anything that was foreign. But even more blinding to him was his naive—*morally* naive—fear of anything that was new. No such good European as Turgenev (that great expatriate), and with no such ordered sense of historical and cultural perspective, Tolstoy was jealous, unconsciously, for Russia's backwardness. Inevitably irritated and perplexed by the rapidity, vehemence, and brilliance with which European art was advancing and changing, he was too fixed to be willing to understand it, too religious (in his own queer social sense) to have any longer the *capacity* for understanding it; and therefore it must be destroyed. To attack it merely because it was not Russian was impossible for him, even had he been aware that this was one of his motives; for this would have been to fly against his own theory of universal or international art. But he could and did attack it on the ground that it was meaningless, frivolous, and socially irresponsible—spiritually ugly and hyperaesthetic—in short for its decadence. Out it must go, every bit of it, lock, stock, and barrel. And not only the moderns, not only Mallarmé and Baudelaire, but Milton, Goethe, and Shakespeare as well. Only *Uncle Tom's Cabin*, like a sort of brave Noah's Ark, was permitted to survive the flood.

II

Two recent books by American critics make one wonder, with some uneasiness, whether we too are not to be treated to some such anachronistic purge: *The Opinions of Oliver Allston*, by Van Wyck Brooks, and *Intellectual America*, by Mr. Oscar Cargill. Mr. Brooks, as we know, and much as we admire him (and indeed we have long been greatly in his debt), is an implacable enemy of the American expatriate and all his works. Was it his own brief taste of the Lotus—at least, the English Lotus—that has embittered him? For one can have little doubt that his judgment of Henry James, and especially of those wonderful "late" novels, is more than Tolstoyan in its *parti pris* recklessness; nor that the opinions of Oliver Allston, his ventriloquist, on Ezra Pound, T. S. Eliot, and James Joyce, to mention only a few, will one day seem just as surprisingly wrongheaded. As Tolstoy sought his universal, misguidedly, in a kind of lowest common denominator of the arts which any peasant could grasp—sacrificing at one stroke both the great and the subtle—so Mr. Brooks and Mr. Cargill, with pretty much the same intention, might be described as Two Critics in Search of the Wholesome. Mr. Brooks makes the really startling admission that he prefers *Snow-Bound* to *The Waste Land;* and at this rate it cannot be long before some even bolder champion of the autochthonous will publicly prefer *Little Women* to James Joyce's *Ulysses*. Mr. Cargill, for his part, displays an almost Comstockian zeal in hunting out decadents—he finds decadents everywhere, and tears them to pieces with a relish which looks decidedly suspicious. Evidently, as Gypsy Rose Lee said of men, he "prefers them monstrous": he likes his decadence "high."

But what is interesting, and indeed disturbing, is that both critics, like Tolstoy, single out with a practically unerring eye the best, the most deeply creative writers of our time, not for praise, but for ridicule and dismissal. Mr. Brooks dismisses them as "escapists" and "coteries"; Mr. Cargill, with a handful of loose labels, bundles them together more or less indiscriminately and inaccurately as Freudians, Intelligentsia, or Decadents: he is a kind of grocer-critic, and weighs "content" as one might weigh sugar. Both critics betray a marked, though occasionally ambiguous, animus toward modern psychology—toward Freud and the notion of the unconscious in particular; and for both the idea of the "death-drive," Freud's *Beyond the Pleasure Principle* (which Santayana wittily called "a long way round to Nirvana"), is, at any rate as embodied in contemporary poetry and fiction, the very last word in defeatism, unwholesomeness, and decay.

Now what is really being proposed here, let us be in no doubt about it, is a moral, or social, intrusion into the world of letters: the world of letters, that is to say, has become a moral peril, and must be regenerated. And the step that is suggested, at any rate by implication, is that, if we are to recover that most price-less element in a work of art, the *will* (by which is no doubt meant the will to goodness, or the will to wholesomeness), we must begin, as Tolstoy began, by simply shutting the door to pretty much everything else. Above all, now that the world is at war, and when cultural interchange between the nations is so difficult (thus runs a common argument), now is the very time for a complete retreat, a return to our own inexhaustible inner resources, our own beautiful and inviolate regionalism and national purity. Let us therefore close the doors once again on these "foreign" ideas, these naughty, and alien, and for us so insoluble poisons. In short, let us now be good wholesome Americans and have a good wholesome American art. The time for decadence is past—and it was never really natural to us, any-way.

Leaving aside the somewhat frightening vision of what this "wholesomeness" would lead us to in literature—with its proto-typical Horatio Algers and Pollyannas, its rural innocence and regional Arcadias—it is perhaps more useful to take a good look at the notion of "decadence." First of all, let us note that deca-dence is always a relative thing: it is not an absolute, or defin-able as such, but merely and always a something which follows a something else—a something else to which it is assumed to be inferior. Nor is it quite as simple as that, either—for we must remember that if this decadence follows something, it also pre-cedes something. It is no more an end than it is a beginning: in fact, it is an organic and living part of a constantly changing and evolving continuum. And this continuum is nothing less, in turn, than the whole evolution of man's awareness. Literature, the plastic arts, the sciences—everything comprised in our cul-tural and intellectual evolution—are these not, insofar as they represent the steady advance in human awareness, completely identifiable with the evolution of man's "mind"—his capacity to feel, perceive, and understand?

And has this not been so from the very beginning? The inventors of the first words, the inventors of language—these were our first poets—were, like the inventors of the other arts and the sciences, biological "sports"; they were variants on the norm; it would not be amiss, perhaps, to say that they were our first decadents. As in every evolutionary process, the sieve of selective survival chose from among them those whose inventions were acceptable to the majority: these became leaders and priests, their teachings or discoveries being incorporated in the main stream of man's social growth; while those others, whose contributions were less generally suitable, were forgotten. In this trial-and-error evolution of consciousness, a new word meant, to all intents, a new feeling; a new cluster of words meant a new complex of feelings; and in each item it could perhaps properly be said that this new perception or feeling represented a splitting and refinement of the coarser and simpler perceptions which had preceded it. Practically, in short, refinement and decadence are the same thing. Parts were substituted for wholes, shades and discriminations for the more vigorous but less exact holophrases which they replaced. The evolution of form proceeded from the large to the small, from the single and simple to the comprehensive and complex; and analogously from the energetic to the subtle.

And in this evolution of language, which is also the evolution of literature and consciousness, it must be borne in mind that the process has always been a strictly individualist and minority affair, a game of follow-my-leader. There has never been, so far as we know, a "whole-society" art—the arrangement of society in the past has been just exactly as pyramidal, in its distribution of consciousness, as it is today. The very conscious have always been the very few: the comparatively unconscious the comparative majority. In any evolutionary process this condition must be inevitable. The artists, the poets, the scientists, these are the advance guard who explore or invent new mental hinterlands, which the rest of mankind adopts and validates as it can and will.

Thus man gets his "universal" in art, willy-nilly; but he gets it from the top, invariably, never from the bottom. And if we realize that this vital competitive hierarchy in levels of consciousness is indispensable to the continuation of a healthy and normal renewal and growth in man's awareness, then we can begin to see how mistaken was Tolstoy, for example, when he proposed to reduce all art to the level of understanding of the simplest peasant. At the drop of a hat, this would achieve that wholesale degradation of cultural energy (which Henry Adams foresaw) to a sterile uniformity. The creative principle of discrimination abandoned, all that marvelous process of exfoliation by which meaning has constantly given way to the more comprehensive on the one hand and the subtler on the other—the endless refinement of man's mind as externalized in his arts and sciences—all this would be at an end. For a faint notion of what it would lead to, one has only to consider the average total radio program of any given day. This is the field in which the Tolstoyan doctrine is most nearly applied.

And this, whether they know it or not, is exactly what the advocates of "nationalism," "wholesomeness," and "the closed door" are up to. They want to turn back the clock; and clearly they mean to do it if they can. At the very moment when America has reached her cultural majority, and when she is able to give the world artists and writers of the first rank, these critics propose once more to close America in, to make her once again provincial; and they begin with a threat of moral censorship on precisely those gifted writers who, in our time, have established themselves as "world" citizens, and are of international importance. We must have no decadence, they say, whether domestic or imported—no escapists, no coteries. Yet it was Baudelaire, a decadent on their own admission, who did most in the last century to restore to French poetry its greatness, giving it a power, a richness, and a beauty which it had never known before. And how few poets and artists in the history of mankind cannot be said to have been escapists, or members of a coterie! Is not art itself an escape, a sublimation —an escape *upward?*

Such mere name-calling will not stay the living forces of literature, nor reestablish outmoded customs barriers; nor can the complex, by a mere effort of the will, turn itself back into the simple, for those who fear it. At best, it will become the *faux bon,* the *faux naif;* at worst, the sentimental. The process of refinement—of "decadence"—has already gone too far. For every Henry James we get, every Proust or Eliot or Joyce (those dreadful fellows, who by some miracle of logic are "empty formalists" on the one hand and purveyors of ugliness and the "death-drive" on the other), the less likely are we ever again to have anything as genuinely naive as *Snowbound* or *Little Women;* and certainly the less likely are we to mistake an *Uncle Tom's Cabin* for a *Moby Dick.* Even in our much discussed "regionalism," what we are witnessing, one suspects, is the last stand of the naive, the final rear guard action of a "Little America" isolationism: for they too, the regional centers, are now fully and inescapably in the midstream of the one great human "thing," from which there is no longer any turning back.

It is no use fearing the complex or chaotic merely because we see all values so visibly and violently in the melting-pot— surely that is no reason for squeamishness, or timidity, or for not facing even the most disagreeable facts in human nature. Man has built himself churches in the past, and of humbler materials; he can build them again, and build them better. No, we must be open to all influences, all knowledge, all speculation, all the winds of doctrine. The arts must be free. For better or worse, American literature is henceforth a part of world literature; and to aim now at a self-conscious and limited "Americanism" would be nothing less than cowardice. The time for that sort of protective tariff, as for a limited-objective moral censorship, is past.

And we have a high responsibility. For if, at the moment, America is the arsenal of democracy, she is also the laboratory of the arts and sciences. Heir to all that is best in the history of mankind, let us hope that we can use our inheritance wisely, and that it can be said of us, as Sainte-Beuve said of Goethe, that he "assimilated not merely tradition, but all traditions, and that without ceasing to be a modern of moderns; he keeps watch for every new sail on the horizon, but from the height of a Sunium. He would use the larger background and perspective to round out and support his individual insight, and so make of the present what it should be—not a servile imitation, nor yet a blank denial, of the past, but its creative continuation. To the errors and aberrations of the hour"—he says—"we must oppose the masses of universal history." And as a salutary reminder, let us add to this Tolstoy's footnote to patriotism: "This disposition of preference for one nation over all others, like egoism, can in no wise be good."

A Reviewer's A B C

I do not know whether it is the custom in England, as it is here, to keep current statistics of the sales of books—to list, month by month, the "best-sellers"—and to compile from many sources a report on those books, fiction and nonfiction, "most in demand at the public libraries." It is an interesting institution, not without its value for the sociologist. Through its medium curious things come to light. Who would have predicted that *The Education of Henry Adams*, a five-dollar book, a work of biography, and of a fundamentally skeptical character, should for almost a year compete in sales with the most popular fiction, outlasting indeed, as a "best-seller," many books of that nature? Its success was phenomenal. The publishers stood a little bewildered in a glare of light from so unexpected a quarter. It is presumably to take advantage of this that almost simultaneously two new Adams books have been published: one of them by Brooks Adams, Henry Adams' brother; the other by Henry Adams himself, with a preface by Brooks Adams. It is highly doubtful whether either book will remotely rival *The Education* in saleability. In neither is the "human" element so conspicuous; in both the passion for theory, for the scientific attitude (particularly when it runs counter to the orthodox), is paramount. And of both, it goes without saying, the brilliance is manifest.

The book by Brooks Adams is not wholly new. It is *The Emancipation of Massachusetts*, and was, as a matter of fact, first published in 1887: a narrative, extraordinarily vivid and entertaining, of the bitter struggle by which Massachusetts, between 1650 and 1783, threw off a narrow ecclesiastical tyranny and obtained civil and religious liberty: a highly local historical document in point of fact, but in effect, also, a finely proportioned working model of a process which is universal. When first published it made a sensation. Later, it became a "classic," but one with which, somehow or other, few were acquainted. By the present generation, it is safe to say, it had never been heard of. It is now reissued with the addition of a preface which is a book in itself, and which relates to the *Emancipation* only in the most charmingly oblique and inferential of ways.

What connection there is, is disposed of in the very beginning. Mr. Adams, re-examining the book after a lapse of thirty years, finds it excellent as history, but, as concerns its philosophical implications, out of tune with his present convictions. When the book was written he still, by dint of inheritance and inertia, believed in the post-Darwinian doctrine of the evolutionary perfectibility, or "Ascent," of man. This doctrine now appears to him to be naively optimistic. He now sees the world as a chaos, guided by no simple primary law; a chaos in which man, an automatic criminal, doomed to follow forever the line of least resistance, is despite his idealisms "the victim of infinite conflicting forces." The motive of the whole preface is the conflict between flesh and spirit. Its conclusion is pessimistic in the extreme, a prophecy of gradual or rapid degradation for man—and likely to be rapid rather than gradual.

This note of "degradation," which is ultimately the key-note of the thought of both Brooks Adams and Henry Adams, and which was first clearly struck by Brooks Adams in his *Law of Civilization and Decay,* is not, however, stressed in this particular preface. What here concerns him is the essential dualism of man's nature—idealism as against physical necessity, self-interest as against the interest of the social organism. This is the recurring bitter theme, powerfully played upon. Our pessimist, self-possessed, undisturbed, humorous, gaily ironic, always gentle, runs the rich gamut of history from the time of the Exodus down to the departure of President Wilson from Paris. It is an extraordinary survey, amazingly complex in overtones; as a piece of special pleading it comes close to being overwhelming. Is the case so hopeless? That much, indeed, is open to question, and *will* be sharply questioned by historians and sociologists, not to say by Churchmen. But of the beauty of the preface as a literary document, or even as a vivification of history, there can be no possibility of doubt.

What emerges most in it is what also occupies the greater part of it in point of space—the study, the analysis, or rather the synthesis (since it is creative as much as critical), of the character and achievements of Moses. Mr. Adams seizes upon Moses as the supreme type of man, the "victim of infinite conflicting forces": the deluded optimist who believed that in his God he had discovered a source of primary moral power to which it was only necessary to connect his social engine to have it function to perfection; the idealist who attempted also to be practical; the practical idealist who believed that the end (the betterment of man) justified any means, and who became, therefore, as the active cooperation of God became less frequent and manifest, more and more of a politician, stooping more and more often to fraud and cruelty; eventually, the politician who had lost faith in his "motor," who succumbed to the chaotic physical forces about him, lost control of his people, and committed suicide, disillusioned.

It is a superb portrait, one that defies summary; a relentless, but singularly courteous, even poetic epitome of the nature of man as Brooks Adams sees him, and as, perhaps, he is. And the same principles, under his scrutiny, emerge, brilliantly magnified, in his salient turning-points of history between that time and this. One sees the horror of chaos which so delights Mr. Adams, one sees vividly also as a kind of counterpoint the perpetual accompaniment for man of certain grim physical laws, against which he struggles hopefully forever, only to be forever beaten down.

And it is more persistently, even exclusively, to these laws that we turn in the other new Adams book, *The Degradation of the Democratic Dogma*. It is a curious farrago—part history, part biography, part autobiography, part—and this perhaps conspicuously—science. The preface, which again is by Brooks Adams, occupies nearly half the book, and is entitled "The Heritage of Henry Adams." It is followed by three papers by Henry Adams: "The Tendency of History" (1894), "A Letter to American Teachers of History" (1910), and "The Rule of Phase applied to History" (1909). In his preface Brooks Adams faced a difficult task, one in which certain awkwardnesses were inherent. A biography of one who had written the *Education* would be superfluous. What was wanted was a survey of the important influences on Henry Adams, and as these were, in the opinion of his brother, his inheritance from his grandfather, John Quincy Adams, and the influence of himself, and as the latter was an influence which he no doubt preferred to leave, as far as possible, inferential, it was inevitable that the preface, while ostensibly a unit, would fall, without the author's clear admission, into two parts. In the earlier part the figure of John Quincy Adams rises before us, a figure, as his grandson presents him, curiously resembling in certain fundamentals the portrait of Moses: a speculative idealist, a believer in democracy (the eventual and essential goodness of man), a scientist, an optimist who died disillusioned. The portrait is vivid and unorthodox, the background is rich; in this, as in the analysis of Moses, Mr. Adams is at his happiest. In the later part he is perforce discursive, reminiscent, resorts almost inevitably to the "portmanteau" style, throwing in a little of everything. Here these two singular brothers converse before us, discuss the problems of human society, shape before us their projects. Brooks shows Henry the MS. of *The Law of Civilization and Decay;* and Henry, to our astonishment, tries to persuade him not to publish it, fearing the consequences. In the upshot he succumbed to the theory there first sketched, wrote a preface for the book, and from that time forth it was he who was to elaborate the theory scientifically, Brooks remaining content to have supplied Henry, in *The Law of Civilization and Decay,* and his work in general, with a sort of Prolegomena. It was on this foundation that Henry Adams built his *Mont St. Michel and Chartres,* projected his study of the Reformation. And the papers in this new book are, in the same direction, his parerga.

It is impossible to indicate adequately the wealth and scope of the two longer papers here published, to do justice to them as pieces of literature, or, for that matter, to exaggerate the skill, perceived in retrospect, with which Brooks Adams has traced, in his preface, the genealogy of the ideas there finally elaborated. The whole book, in this sense, is a genealogy of ideas: John Quincy Adams, Brooks Adams, and Henry Adams figure merely, perhaps, as successive "hosts," supplying each in turn what was necessary. John Quincy and Henry are, we here perceive, the extremes, the most "practical" and the most "speculative" respectively; Brooks is the mean, less "practical" than his grandfather, but on the other hand a good deal less a victim of the sort of volitional paralysis to which Henry's profound negativism at last led him. In the "Tendency of History" (1894) Henry speculated on what would happen if "some new Darwin" were to formulate the "laws of Historical evolution": "In whatever direction we look, we can see no possibility of converting history into a science without bringing it into hostility toward one or more of the most powerful organizations of the era . . . The mere fact that it overthrows social organizations cannot affect our attitude . . ." Plainly he foresaw a series of terrible disasters to society as it has for the last two hundred years been organized. And asking himself what course of action the teacher of history should pursue in this predicament, the teacher of history *as a science,* he remarks: "Beyond a doubt, silence is best."

Nevertheless he found it impossible to remain silent. And his "Letter to American Teachers of History" and "Rule of Phase applied to History" are his own rich contributions toward a demonstration of the laws of historical evolution. The first of these might better have been entitled "The Law of Degradation applied to the Social Organism." That, at all events, is the theme of it. It is an amazing panorama. The first chapter, "The Problem," asks and answers the question whether life should not be regarded as simply a form of energy, whether "vital" or mechanical, and whether, if so, it should not exactly be said to operate in accordance with the laws of thermodynamics, and in particular with the second law—the law that energy, once lost, is lost for ever. This question is elaborately and beautifully argued, and answered in the affirmative. And at once Henry Adams' magnificent engine of pessimism is on its way, carrying with it pretty nearly everything to which man attaches importance. The solar system is running down like a clock: man, of relatively late appearance in a world already well "degraded," himself low in the scale of life (considered in terms of energy), dwindles progressively before our eyes; brains are developed only in "impoverished" organisms; thought is a "degraded" Act; as man declines in energies, society does also, despite periodic "contractions" (as of the sun) or combustion of fresh races flung in (like so much fuel); the declension of the energies of society, of which man's intellectual development has only served to increase the rapidity, will end when a dead level, or rest, has been reached, in a chaos without coherence; and the so-called progress of man, in whatever sense, is illusory . . . The "impression of gain is derived from an impression of Order due to the levelling of energies; but . . . the impression of Order is an illusion consequent on the dissolution of the higher Order which had supplied, by lowering its inequalities, all the useful energies that caused progress. The reality behind the illusion is, therefore, absence of the power to do useful work—or what man knows in his finite sensibilities as death. . . ." This is sufficiently saddening: the conclusion is, therefore, that there is no excuse for history to be anything but a science, one which cannot truthfully teach anything but the gradual degradation of man. But in "The Rule of Phase" Henry Adams takes another step. Granted that history must be a science, that it will be basically a study of human society from the point of view of "degradation" (in the thermo-dynamic sense,) what principles will govern the direction and rate of degradation? . . . Once more the laws of physics and chemistry are called in—this time it is the Rule of Phase, as formulated by Willard Gibbs. Thought is the universal solvent, the index to the life of man: it is also a physical thing, will obey physical laws. Henry Adams proceeds, there-fore, to plot its phases, an astounding undertaking, which results in the tentative prediction, mathematically arrived at, that thought will reach its final or "ethereal" phase in 1921. This phase will last perhaps four years, perhaps fifty. After it will begin the long decline.

This meager summary may serve to indicate the engrossing character of the book: it cannot possibly give an idea, however, of its force and brilliance, of the charm of personality which constantly moves behind it. One puts the book down, as one does also *The Emancipation of Massachusetts,* with a great ad-miration, not wholly untinged with amusement. For it is a singular, delicious spectacle, that of these two Adams brothers, these pessimists, negativists, collaborators in the "bible of anarchy," who nevertheless inherit from their Puritan ancestry such love of order that, like a pair of melancholy Lucifers, they rise in starlight, and observe with fascinated horror the workings of an insensate law—which, they declare delightedly, is, from man's point of view, inimical and lethal.

AIKEN, CONRAD   (1917)

It is difficult to place Conrad Aiken in the poetic firmament, so difficult that one sometimes wonders whether he deserves a place there at all. Mr. Aiken himself seems to be somewhat un-certain as to his role—he comes to the rehearsal, to to speak, still fumbling in his pockets for his part. Sometimes the radicals please him and he plays with the radicals; sometimes he plays with the shell-backs. And even when apparently most single-minded he carries on clandestine flirtations.

This is a serious weakness. It points to a fundamental lack of conviction, in Mr. Aiken's mind, as to poetic values. If he is consistent as regards his material, sticking fairly closely to a preference for an objective psychological method in poetry, he is hopelessly confused as regards the problem of poetic form. In *Turns and the Movies* he willfully sacrificed his ability to write in smoothly involute curves for a dubious gain in matter-of-fact forcefulness. In *The Jig of Forslin* he recanted, and, with occasional sops to downright and rigid realism, abandoned himself to a luxuriation in romantic virtuosity. And now, in

Nocturne of Remembered Spring, he is more clearly than ever a schizophrenic.

For in the nocturnes and sonatas which compose the first part of this book, and which are Mr. Aiken's most recent work, one encounters a rather puzzling fusion of those two styles. These poems are half narrative, half lyric, half sentimental, half realistic. The musical symbolism, almost obsessionally pursued, develops a melodic line only to be broken in upon by a matter-of-factness which in the context appears only malicious. It is questionable whether this sort of counterpoint of ideas can ever be successful in verse. The unity of effect is jeopardized; the reader is more often perplexed than pleased. Furthermore, Mr. Aiken displays here a tendency to take refuge in an emotional symbolism which lies perilously close to the vague. This is particularly clear in the "Sonata in Pathos," where Mr. Aiken uses emotional symbols which are so idiosyncratic as to be almost meaningless. A certain musical continuity or flow is felt, on the technical side; but one cannot be certain of the precise cerebral values. This indicates a failure on Mr. Aiken's part to discriminate between these emotional symbols (the residue of his experience) which are merely peculiar to himself, and those which are common to mankind. He is carried away by successive trains of association which are of immediate and glowing value to himself, but which are frequently quite without pattern for his reader. It is dangerous, too, to develop psychological themes to such lengths as this without a more liberal use of narrative. One gets tired of psychological variations, no matter how contrapuntal or subtle, if no element of suspense is introduced.

After reading these studies in the stream of consciousness, shaped in a freely rhythmed and freely rhymed form which modulates itself in accordance with the thought, it is a little odd to come upon the two longer narratives, "Innocence" and "Dust in Starlight," which complete Mr. Aiken's volume—both in octosyllabic couplets. If the nocturnes and sonatas become tedious on the psychological side, these become tedious on the technical. One gets tired eventually of so many rhymes, so many reiterations of the iambic in the same tempo. In "Innocence" this is perhaps offset by the narrative speed and by the occasional flush of verbal magic. But "Dust in Starlight," in which the narrative is slower and the introspective passages are

longer, reminds one of Poe's dictum that there is no such thing
as a long poem. Many a stretch of desert must be crossed to gain
the occasional oases of color. Can anyone remain interested for
forty pages in the protagonist's vacillations between flesh and
sentiment—except the protagonist himself?

In general, it should be said that this volume shows a singularly limited range of material; a limitation which, if it extended
to all of Mr. Aiken's works, would be sufficient to pigeonhole
him. The dominant theme is erotic. In the "White Nocturne" it
is concerned with mutual disillusionment; in the "Nocturne of
Remembered Spring," with the recollection of a love affair of
youth; in the "Sonata in Pathos," with romantic frustration,
noia immortale, due to satiety and disenchantment; in the
"Meditation on a June Evening," with the backward yearnings
and rehearsals of a defeated lover; in "Innocence," with the
awakening of sensuous passion in the adolescent, and in "Dust
in Starlight," with conjugal infidelity. Isn't this going it a little
strong? Only two poems in the book deal with other material
—"Discord," which is too slight for consideration, and "The
Trenches; 1915"—which is not a poem.

AIKEN, CONRAD   (1918)

Boston, November 30, 1918.
Dear Henry: Excuse breathlessness of this letter. I have run all the
way from Cambridge.

You see, it was this way. Conrad and I were to have our third informal conference on midsummer housing at 1 o'clock. As I opened
the door I found him stuffing a manuscript into the fire. Knowing how
many masterpieces had already been sacrificed on the altar of his
modesty I seized it—and here it is. Oh, Henry, you wouldn't believe
how fast Conrad can run. But I have it. Henry. I have it.

Affectionately.

BOB

P.S. Be sure and send an issue in which this appears to every
member of the Poetry Society. If you haven't a list I will supply it.
It will stir them up.

Z-z-z-z-z

Dear Henry: The other night after you had asked me to review
The Charnel Rose, as I sat with a copy on my knee and
wondered how it was that I happened to write such a good

book, I must have fallen asleep, for on the parlor clock's striking sixteen I awoke from a very remarkable dream. As I recollected it I began to write it down, and it astonished me as I did so to perceive that the well-known personages of my dream were in many cases making remarks which I knew them actually to have made in real life. You will see that I have given the dream a dramatic form. This I did because such a form saved space, and seemed also to preserve best the singularly detached way in which everything, my own self not excluded, therein appeared. It might, indeed, have been merely my astral body which I saw in the obscurity approaching its fellow poets and offering for them the supreme sacrifice. The scene was somewhat vague. Was there a street lamp in the center? I think so, and I remember that in addition to the poets who actually talked there were others, such as Frost, Sandburg, and Lindsay, more remote and loftier, as if reclining on clouds, and watching with a kind of bored silence. The proceedings started a little disconcertingly with a remark, quite unwarranted, by—

KREYMBORG: Charnel houses no longer exist, do they? Perhaps, then, the nearest sewer would be the most suitable place for *The Charnel Rose*.

FIRKINS: But would the system be equal to it?

KREYMBORG: No: you are right. It would be indigestible. We had better tear it to pieces first, had we not?

CHORUS OF POETS (*joyously*): Ah, by all means!

MASTERS (*a little way off on a cloud*): Did some one mention immorality? Now, in my next poem, "The Afternoon of a Forn—" (*falls asleep*)

MISS LOWELL: The trouble with Aiken—

BODENHEIM: Is that he is an eclectic . . . The cloud delicately absorbs light. The wind peripatetically absorbs moisture . . . There are artists who, like pawnbrokers—

FIRKINS: Et hock genus omne—

BODENHEIM: Live on the borrowed faintly abraded trinkets of spirits wearily indigent. The cloud takes its shape from the many-hurrying jingles of the pilgrim winds.

KREYMBORG: Aiken is not a poet: he is a critic.

MISS MONROE: But is the subject really worth discussion? Now, Vachel—

FLETCHER: The trouble with Aiken is that he is a lyric poet and doesn't know it. He is obsessed with narrative, which he can't manage. He should write lyrics.

BRAITHWAITE: Aiken is a * great poet! Perhaps one of our
** greater poets! He may not be the *** very greatest, but
should we not put him among the *** greatest?

MISS LOWELL (*in mid-distance, on a cloud like a divan*):
Aiken should let himself go! His technique is superb, but he is
insincere. As for me—I sit on the dictionary and make poems
—big words and little ones, flat words and then soft ones, pale
words that writhe like vermicelli and round words with holes
in the middle like doughnuts. I sit on a dictionary and make
poems. What a pity that some words are pointed and blue like
new tacks!

MISS MONROE: I think the subject is hardly worth discussion.

WILLIAMS: The poems of Aiken are like split B.V.D.'s, basted.

BODENHEIM: The cloud absorbs light wearily: it has no soul
of its own **** Has Aiken any individuality? Does he exist?

MISS MONROE: He is an echo of Masefield and of Gibson.
The *Jig of Forslin* is like Owen Meredith's *Lucile. Turns and
Movies* is like *Hiawatha. The Charnel Rose* is like *The Old
Oaken Bucket.*

POUND (*wearily*):   Swinburne plus Fletcher minus Aiken
equals Aiken.

UNTERMEYER: Eliot plus Masters minus Aiken equals Aiken.

HERVEY: Baudelaire plus Evans plus De Nerval plus Verlaine plus Mallarmé plus Rimbaud minus Aiken equals Aiken.

KREYMBORG: Didn't you leave out somebody?

BRAITHWAITE: The subliminal is peculiarly unconscious. It
is evanescently through the impalpable that the immanent becomes imminent. In 1872 I prophesied that Aiken's true genius
was as a philosophical poet. Senlin carries one to breathless
heights of the ideal: it is a roseate apoplexy of Vision.

FIRKINS: A psychic hemorrhage!

PHELPS: Aiken was a poet once—in *Earth Triumphant.*
How he has changed!

FLETCHER: Aiken will be a poet—if he lives long enough.
Forslin contains passages which I would be glad to have
written myself. Aiken knows how to write, but his range is too
limited.

OPPENHEIM: His poems are merely monotonous.

FIRKINS: Immoral.

CLEMENT WOOD: Dish-rags and lace.

BRAITHWAITE: Trite.

MISS LOWELL: Artificial.

UNTERMEYER: Prematurely decadent.

MENCKEN: Long.

KREYMBORG: But we had forgotten *The Charnel Rose!*

ELIOT: Pound, who is Aiken? The name sounds familiar. Is he an Englishman?

BODENHEIM: He is a distillation of old hours, of leaves worn meekly smooth by the fingers of gently-stooping readers in the public library.

MISS LOWELL: Nonsense! He is a frog-hearted technician.

MISS MONROE: But is the subject vital? And besides in Chicago—

KREYMBORG: It is more delightful, verily, as in New York and the Zoo to search with delicate absorbed fingers through the long fur of our Me's. Why waste time on the trivial?

MISS LOWELL *(hurriedly drawing her cloud about her)*: My God, boys, here he comes!

KREYMBORG: Isn't he the quaint delicious long legged red headed whimsically melancholy smut-loving bird!

MISS MONROE: Good heavens, I have an appointment—excuse me if I hurry!

AIKEN *(approaching timidly)*: Hullo! Something important being discussed?

KREYMBORG: Well, no, not exactly—we were discussing *The Charnel Rose.* Perhaps, Conrad, you will tell us something about it—what it means, for example, and how you came to write it.

MISS LOWELL: I refuse flatly to listen. Aiken is still adolescent. As for me—I sit—

AIKEN: Well, you have all been very generous to me, and in consequence I think I will tell you my secret.

ALL: A secret!

AIKEN: Yes—you have been wiser than you knew. For I am not really a poet at all. I am a mathematician. I have discovered that poetry can be written by calculus—

ALL: *(delighted)*: Ah, that explains it!

AIKEN: And I have found a little machine which, if fed words from a dictionary at one end, turns out the finest metrical verse at the other, quite indistinguishable from the genuine article. Now, in *The Charnel Rose*—

ALL: Yes?

AIKEN: It simply happened that by mistake this little engine was fed a volume of Havelock Ellis—

BODENHEIM: Or Freud!

AIKEN: And in *Senlin*—

ALL: Yes! Yes!

AIKEN: (*bursting into tears*): I am ashamed to admit it—it was *Alice in Wonderland.*

MISS LOWELL   (*after a sympathetic silence*): Well, never mind, Conrad! Now that we KNOW you're not a poet, I think we're all going to like you much, much better. (She taps him playfully with her fan: he collapses. The poets step away one by one over his prostrate body.)

As you see, Henry, the dream is absurd, and you would not expect me to vouch for the veridity of all its details. Fancy O. W. Firkins descending to such trivial puns, for example, or Miss Lowell being so foolish as to talk polyphonic prose in her sleep! Then, too, Miss Monroe's attitude throughout! These things should not be permitted to pass without comment—though indeed, Henry, I could have trusted serenely that your native good sense would have made allowances for the irresponsibilities of a mere dreamer, who, as it happens, is yours ever,

CONRAD AIKEN

AIKEN, CONRAD   (1919)

By inviting me to review my own book for *Poetry,* Miss Monroe puts me in an awkward position. I suspect that a part of her reason for doing this is that she fancies the author can be severer with himself—or shall I say, more accurately severe?—than anyone else can be. She puts me, in a sense, on my honor to defeat myself. But one tires of shadow-boxing: there is no joy in it, for one's antagonist cannot retaliate. So I am going to be, for once, my own apologist. I do not mean by this that I am going to praise myself; any more, at least, than the artist who paints a self-portrait praises himself—which he does, in some degree, by the serious act of self-portraiture. What I do mean is that since, apart from any question of accomplishment, my aims in the writing of poetry interest me extraordinarily, and since I would like (naturally!) to see them more generally espoused, I shall discuss them naïvely and with candor.

Suppose I begin with one statement with which everyone will agree: that it is the aim of every work of art to evoke, or to suggest. There is no quarrel here. What artists will disagree on is as to how this shall be done. Some think it should be accomplished by methods mainly denotative—or realistic: they argue that the best way to imply is (in the correct degree) to state. Others believe the method should be mainly connotative: they argue that the best way to state is (in the correct degree) to imply. Both elements, of course, enter into every work of art, and the only real difference at the bottom is quantitative; yet it is sufficient to account for such wide areas as lie between the work of Masters, let us say, on the one hand, and that of Bodenheim on the other. The one is solid, the other diaphanous; and the difference in tactile quality may be followed even into the choice of language itself; for we see Masters preferring the precise, and as it were the square, and Bodenheim preferring the tenuous and the abstract; Masters employing the object or thing, and Bodenheim the quality of the thing. This is simple enough. But the affair becomes more complex when we observe that any individual artist is not to be confined to one region in this regard, but continually wanders up and down this gamut, striking now at the denotative and now at the connotative chords, never perfectly certain, in fact, which method is the more truly effective; and, of course, obeying not merely a theory but, quite as often, the dictates of compulsions more unconscious. It is going only a step further to note that the larger the medium in which a poet works, the wider and more frequent will be his rangings of this gamut.

It was to make more possible this delicious (and somewhat irresponsible?) ranging of the gamut that I evolved the symphonic form used in *The Jig of Forslin, The Charnel Rose,* and *Senlin.* I will not pretend that this was at the outset entirely conscious or clear. Theory always comes second in these cases. It was partly a natural enough ambition for more room, partly the working of some complex which has always given me a strong bias towards an architectural structure in poetry analogous to that of music. In the three parts of *Earth Triumphant,* anyone who cares to wade through fifteen hundred more or less impeccable octosyllabic couplets will find already a groping towards symphonic arrangement, though it is exceedingly rudimentary. In *Disenchantment,* which was given the subtitle *A Tone Poem,* the idea of variation of form was developed, though not far. In *The Charnel Rose* it was first consciously elaborated, though with errors in proportion. And finally in *Forslin* and *Senlin* it achieved something like a logical outcome.

What I had from the outset been somewhat doubtfully

hankering for was some way of getting contrapuntal effects in poetry—the effects of contrasting and conflicting tones and themes, a kind of underlying simultaneity in dissimilarity. It seemed to me that by using a large medium, dividing it into several main parts, and subdividing these parts into short movements in various veins and forms, this was rendered possible. I do not wish to press the musical analogies too closely. I am aware that the word symphony, as a musical term, has a very definite meaning, and I am aware that it is only with considerable license that I use the term for such poems as *Senlin* or *Forslin*, which have three and five parts respectively, and do not in any orthodox way develop their themes. But the effect obtained is, very roughly speaking, that of the symphony, or symphonic poem. Granted that one has chosen a theme—or been chosen by a theme!—which will permit rapid changes of tone, which will not insist on a tone too static, it will be seen that there is no limit to the variety of effects obtainable: for not only can one use all the simpler poetic tones (let us for convenience represent any five such simple poetic tones, each composing one separate movement to be used in a symphony, as *a, b, c, d, e*); but, since one is using them as parts of a larger design, one can also obtain novel effects by placing them in juxtaposition as consecutive movements: such as *ab, ac, cae*. For *a*, it is clear, if it is preceded by *c* and followed by *e*, is not quite the same as *a* standing alone. Something has happened to it. A peculiar light has been cast across it, which throws certain parts of it into stronger relief than others; and *a* itself reacts on *c* (retrospectively) and, a moment later, on *e*. In a sense, therefore, we have created a new poetic unit, *cae*, a unit of which the characteristic pleasure it affords us is really contrapuntal, since it works upon us through our sense of contrast. Each added movement further complicates the tone-effect, adds color to the hover of reverberations, creates a new composite unit. And we get finally a whole major section of the symphony so constructed of contrasts and harmonies; which in turn, if we are careful, will differ clearly in general tone from the next major part. And here the same principles apply. Part II, for example, following Part I, and preceding Part III, is by no means the same affair from the point of view of tone-effect, as Part II transferred so as to be Part IV. Thus Part IV of *The Jig of Forslin* (which deals with Forslin's religious debauch) owes much of its effect to its position following Part III, which deals with his caprices among lamias and vampires: an effect which originally, as Part II, it did not obtain. It was transferred for that reason.

All this, I must emphasize, is no less a matter of emotional tone than of form; the two things cannot well be separated. For such symphonic effects one employs what one might term emotion-mass with just as deliberate a regard for its position in the total design as one would employ a variation of form. One should regard this or that emotional theme as a musical unit having such-and-such a tone quality, and use it only when that particular tone-quality is wanted. Here I flatly give myself away as being in reality in quest of a sort of absolute poetry, a poetry in which the intention is not so much to arouse an emotion merely, or to persuade of a reality, as to employ such emotion or sense of reality (tangentially struck) with the same cool detachment with which a composer employs notes or chords. Not content to present emotions or things or sensations for their own sakes—as is the case with most poetry—this method takes only the most delicately evocative aspects of them, makes of them a keyboard, and plays upon them a music of which the chief characteristic is its elusiveness, its fleetingness, and its richness in the shimmering overtones of hint and suggestion. Such a poetry, in other words, will not so much present an idea as use its resonance. It is the apotheosis of the poetic method which we have called implication. It is a prestidigitation in which the juggler's bottles or balls are a little too apt, unfortunately, to be altogether invisible.

I have left myself little space for comment on *The Charnel Rose*, of which this paper is supposed to be a review. In the title poem the reader may observe, if he wishes, this method in process of ghostly evolution: it is, for example, working much more efficiently and consistently in the third and fourth parts than in the first and second, which seem indeed, by contrast, a trifle mawkish and archaic. Even so, the variation of tone has not been carried far enough: a little more statement and a little less implication would have been a good thing, for it verges on the invertebrate. If the poem is objected to for its decadence, however, it should be recalled that the decadence is, as it happens, implied in the conception, and that the conception has merely been permitted, and in my opinion rightly, to divulge itself. I should object to being called a decadent (as one or two have already called me) merely because of this poem, or because of a few passages in *Forslin*, equally compelled by the thesis. In *Senlin*, the other long poem in the volume, the conception is not decadent, and neither, therefore, is the treatment. The tone is acid, humorous, ironic. In general, too, I think the artistic problem has been a good deal better solved. It lacks here and there the opulence and gleam of parts of *The Charnel Rose*, but it makes up for it in precision, sharpness, and economy. (One always praises economy when one is running out of funds.) The theme is the problem of personal identity, the struggle of the individual for an awareness of what it is that constitutes his consciousness; an attempt to place himself, to relate himself to the world of which he feels himself to be at once an observer and an integral part. Reports that *Senlin* is—or was—a real person are erroneous. *Variations*, the remaining series of lyrics, was an experiment in modulation of emotion-tone. I do not feel that it was particularly successful. A theory should not be practiced in cold blood, and I am afraid that in this case the compulsion was not for all items sufficiently strong.

It remains, finally, to point out the profound danger of the method I have been outlining: the danger, I mean, that one's use of implication will go too far, and that one will cheat the natural human appetite for something solid and palpable. One cannot, truly, dine—at least every evening—on, as Eliot would remark, "smells of steaks in passageways." One must provide for one's symphony a sufficiently powerful and pervasive underlying idea—and, above all, make it sufficiently apparent. Whether the time will come when we shall be satisfied with implication for its own sake, no one, of course, can guess. In the meantime, one must compromise to the extent that one hopes for success. By which I'm not sure that I mean I compromise.

ANDERSON, SHERWOOD   (1927)

The writer of the jacket for this new book by Mr. Sherwood Anderson informs us that "we hesitate to call these new forms poetry; in doing so we lay them open to the microscope of the precisionist critic and the carping conservative." He adds, further, that *A New Testament* is the "testamentary doctrine (*sic*) of Sherwood Anderson; men and houses, moods and manners are considered—yet they are a definite whole, inasmuch as they portray each one some phase of the soul of

Anderson in relation to life; they represent in their entirety the revealed relation of the artist to the universe and eternity."

This sounds, to put it *pianissimo*, like a largish order; one must, after this fine fanfare of brasses, open Mr. Anderson's book with a mixture of fever and foreboding. It is not only that one invariably distrusts a publisher when he thus shares with us, confidentially, his awestruck admiration of an author who dares to grapple with those slippery angels, the universe and eternity. It is also because one has an *a priori* apprehensiveness when Mr. Anderson tries to "come the heavy." And in this book of free verse symbolism, or poetic prose, or parable, or whatever one wants to call it, it is unfortunately true that he comes his very heaviest.

Mr. Anderson has given us some admirable short stories, which are all the better for the strain of naive mysticism and childlike repetitive wonder which runs through them. When he is at his best, which is usually when he is also at his simplest, his air of newborn innocence is charming; it gives to his theme a lyric freshness that is all too rare in contemporary fiction. But, alas, some demon in Mr. Anderson's breast goads him perpetually toward deeper and more transcendental things, and these almost always play the very deuce with him. Like Mr. D. H. Lawrence, he has intermittently sought a kind of sex-mysticism, full of dark, esoteric currents and subliminal fevers, as the key to the universe; his novels are full of this. And it is, perhaps, also true that he shares with Mr. Lawrence a curious messianic preoccupation with the soul—the soul, be it understood, always envisaged as a thing essentially animal. Mr. Anderson's "dark laughter" and Mr. Lawrence's "lumbar ganglion" are merely their different ways of getting at this elusive phenomenon.

Mr. Lawrence entertains no doubts whatever as to his rightness about such affairs: he is emphatic, even savage, in his assertiveness. But Mr. Anderson, if he is just as dreadfully sure of himself, just as egotistically convinced of his vision and its value for humanity, and of the importance (as propaganda) of all the "phases of his soul" (again to paraphrase the writer of the blurb), proceeds to his assertiveness with his characteristic air of self-questioning. Here, in these curious parables, is once again that rather disarming manner of his, with its "What I mean is this" and its "Well, what I was trying to say—," and its "But I'll begin over again, and try to say it better." This manner has become a mannerism; one is too often reminded of the small boy desperately in earnest to say something that entirely transcends his powers of speech. And it has also, more is the pity, begun to seem, in Mr. Anderson, rather an affectation.

As for the parables themselves, or poems, or gnomic prose, in which we are to find Mr. Anderson's "doctrine" (*qui d'ailleurs n'existe pas*), the best one can say for it is that it is, unmistakably, imaginative. But beyond that one cannot go. For Mr. Anderson's symbolisms and parables are too wholesale to be effective, too amorphous to be clear, too structureless and humorless to be anything more than readable. Once or twice, when he condescends to be simple and forthright, as in "Young Man in a Room" or "In a Workingman's Rooming House," he gives us a vigorous and moving bit of poetic prose, succinct and real. But for the most part one feels that he is trying too hard, that he is a little overweening. His reach exceeds his grasp. The profuseness with which he empties his unconsciousness, the indiscriminateness with which he allows image to lead to image and one autistic chain of thought to bud another, defeats his own end, and in the upshot one has a mere welter of pictures, some bad and some good, but in the main meaningless.

One feels of Mr. Anderson that he has simply lost himself hopelessly in his own little poetic chaos, in the illusion that he has there discovered the ultimate truth. Might a sense of humor have saved him from this unreflecting verbalistic zeal? What can one say to an author who remarks, earnestly, "Sometimes as I walk in the streets, a look of intelligence comes into my eyes." To comment on that would be cruel. As for his explicit belief that "nothing is to be achieved by being smart and definite, and to be vague—they keep telling me—is to be insane, a little unbalanced," one can only retort that nothing is more dangerous in literature than the vague. Vagueness can only be used by a genius, and when it is so used it is usually, on analysis, found to be admirably precise. The terms may shimmer, but the mood and meaning are clear.

BENNETT, ARNOLD

The publishers describe this latest of Mr. Bennett's novels as a "playful and witty romance," as "gayly fantastic" and "shrewdly penetrating," and as being a novel that "will delight and thrill . . . Filled with chuckles and with wise commentaries on life and happiness."

With all due apologies to the gentleman who wrote the blurb, *The Vanguard* does, and is, nothing of the sort. It is one more evidence of the fact that in Mr. Bennett we have one of the most extraordinary instances of a kind of dual literary personality on record. There is the Mr. Bennett of *Clayhanger, The Old Wives' Tale*, and *Riceyman's Steps*, and there is the Mr. Bennett of *The Pretty Lady*, and never these twain shall meet.

In his "good" novels, which were good enough to figure in Henry James' dissection of the "new novel" a decade or so ago, Mr. Bennett has given us some pretty nearly first-rate fiction of the naturalistic school. One can subscribe somewhat to the objection of James, that in such novels as these we have all the circumstances of interest but not the "working out" of it—the saturation in the *donnée*, but no kind of evocation of its center. It is the slice of life for its own sake, and would no doubt have given the utmost satisfaction to the brothers Goncourt. And if one asks no more of the novel than that, then one must admit that Mr. Bennett is an admirable novelist and often a deeply moving one. He is solid and unsparing; he is an expert craftsman; he can be penetrating without being sentimental, and in his complete knowledge of English middle-class life he is the legitimate successor of Gissing, and rivaled, among his contemporaries, only by Mr. Maugham in his *Of Human Bondage*.

One does not go to Mr. Bennett, as one goes to the greater novelists, for the personality behind the book—there is no grandeur in Mr. Bennett, no nobility, no richness, no poetry. One does not bring away from him a spiritual fragrance, as one does from James or Turgenev, nor a tragic sense of life's greatness, as one does from Tolstoi or Hardy or Melville. Nor does one expect that from him. One expects, and one gets, a sober and meticulous and extremely convincing narrative, which deals with rather somber and dreary people, who, though intrinsi-

cally uninteresting, become interesting through Mr. Bennett's.
patient and level skill in portraiture.

The other Mr. Bennett is a different horse of another color.
He is the most conscienceless of potboilers. In *The Pretty Lady*,
it is true, there were indeed traces of skill; Mr. Bennett could
not entirely forget that there was a good novelist somewhere
in him, and the book had its flashes of brilliance. In *The Vanguard*, alas, Mr. Bennett seems to have succeeded wholly in his
task of forgetfulness. Surely never has a novelist of Mr. Bennett's reputation and ability produced so appalling a piece of
trash. The whole story is utterly unreal. One never for a minute believes in this millionaire and his yacht and his wife and
his financial machinations. The thing is as hollow as a cream
puff and not half so sustaining.

Nor, on the other hand, does Mr. Bennett succeed, as Mr.
Huxley might have done in similar circumstances, in making
an extravaganza of it. He leans a little in that direction, but
he leans timidly; and the result is a novel which is neither the
one thing nor the other. The humor is forced and vapid, the
satire is machine-made, the action is incredibly thin and unconvincing. One reads it only with the greatest difficulty; and
one gets from it only a renewal of one's astonishment that a man
who can, when he wants, write so well should stoop to the
production of a literary sham so shameless.

BISHOP, JOHN PEALE   (1949)

Edmund Wilson and Allen Tate and the publishers have done
American literature a genuine service in bringing together in
these two admirably edited volumes the best prose and verse
of John Peale Bishop. For Bishop belonged to a genus that is as
rare as it is precious in this country—he was the authentic
amateur of letters. This is meant in no pejorative sense: it is
the comparative absence of this kind of contribution to American literature, or the American literary scene, that enables
the forces of barbarism to re-emerge from one generation to
another, and keeps us—from a European viewpoint—uncivilized.

Bishop, like his more gifted predecessor and prototype,

Trumbull Stickney, was aware of this want in the scene, and aware also of the need in himself. He endeavored to make up for the deficiencies in the scene, so deplored earlier still by Henry James, by residence in France, by training in the classics and the deepening of his historical sense, and by a lifelong and severe discipline in technique. What he brought to this training and this discipline was not, I think, a truly outstanding talent— he had not the merely linguistic finality that Stickney began to achieve before his early death—but if it was a minor talent it was a real one, and he did not neglect it. It might even be argued, perhaps, that a *little* more neglect would have been a good thing.

For as one reads the poems in chronological order, beginning with those of Bishop's Princeton days and just after, one discovers a curious fact: in the early poems there is a quite surprising inventive and prosodic vigor, and not only this, but clear, if faint, indications of that elusive essential, *poetic character*. What became of it? It looks very much as if the tadpole lost his tail to get his legs. Excellent as much of the later poetry is, even to the point of brilliance on occasion, it is a poetry without personal aroma or idiom, or when, now and then, it *has* character or idiom, these seem oddly to have a sort of vintage mark on them, as of Pound 1922, or Eliot 1918. One begins therefore to suspect that the education, for so tender a talent, was too prolonged, too diverse and too severe. The classic file ended by filing away too much. The studious and ingenious search for a kind of classic amalgam of style (and let it be said emphatically in passing that here Bishop's taste was often extremely fine) found, not a style, but a virtuosity in styles, a kind of Alexandrianism. The poet, in the process of becoming accomplished, had somehow lost his private view.

Well, that has happened before to good poets, and will happen again no doubt, and we know that it is not necessarily fatal. The *Zeitgeist* can perform the oddest of chemical miracles in such matters as literary fashion and literary judgment; and it is entirely arguable that a later generation will not only admire, as we do, the accomplishment and variety of the best of Bishop's verse, but may actually discover in it a flavor—as of fashion not *quite* fashion—which we, too conditioned by the fashions, must inevitably miss. If so, it would be the best of poetic justice, for, in the essays and reviews which Wilson has brought together to make a surprisingly substantial and impressive volume, it becomes even clearer than in the poetry that something like this would be precisely what Bishop would have wanted.

Impressive not only for sheer quantity but for range as well—by no means a one-windowed ivory tower, Bishop's lookout was that of a many-sided and extremely human humanist, admirably perceptive and intelligent; and, if not often profound (perhaps he is weakest on the psychological side, and its effect culturally and socially), he is always individual and interesting, and often subtle. He is as good as anybody on Thomas Wolfe and Hemingway; better than most on Gertrude Stein (and very funny too); excellent on E. E. Cummings, Joyce, and Pound. But whether in these essays, or in the many good reviews of poetry, or in the delightful auto biographical flashbacks, or the informed and informative pages on Manet and Picasso, he is always, as at last explicitly in the essay called "The Discipline of Poetry," aiming consciously and persuasively at just one thing: the attainment of the classic balance, the classic attitude, in the trained awareness and judgment and "working" of tradition, whether esthetic or social.

To have attempted this at all in this country at this time was, or *should* have been, useful in the extreme; nothing could be more needed. And even if one now and then finds the prose somewhat irritating—it tends to rattle, and to be a little shapeless—one accepts this book with deep gratitude, and with a sense of great loss, and regret that it could not have been published in Bishop's lifetime. Let us hope that it may become the treasured *vade mecum* of every young writer and painter in this "barbarous" country.

BOSSCHERE, JEAN DE   (1918)

Who it was that started the current poetic fad for curio-collecting is a question not hard to answer: Ezra Pound is the man, let the Imagists and Others deny it as loudly as they will. Pound has from the outset, both as poet and as critic, been a curio-collector—a lover of trinkets, *bijoux* of phrase, ideographic *objets de vertu*, carved oddities from the pawn-shops of the past, aromatic grave-relics, bizarre importations from the Remote and Strange. There is no denying, either, that it is a delightful vein in verse. No great exertion is demanded of the reader; he is invited merely to pause before the display-window and to glance, if only for a moment, at the many intriguing minutiæ there arranged for him in trays. Is he tired of struggling with the toxic energies of a Rodin? Then let him rest in contemplation of a carved ushabti. Does a Strauss drag his spirit through too violent a progression of emotional projections? Does a Masters overburden him with relevant facts? A Fletcher fatigue him with aesthetic subtleties prolonged? Let him concentrate on a gargoyle.

This method in the writing of poetry is to be seen at its purest in the *Others* anthologies, the second of which Mr. Alfred Kreymborg has edited, apparently undeterred by the success of the first. Nevertheless it is a variegated band that Mr. Kreymborg has assembled, and if they have in common the one main tenet—that their poetic business is the expression of a sensation or mood as briefly and pungently (and oddly?) as possible, with or without the aids of rhyme, meter, syntax, or punctuation—they are by no means the slaves of a formula and present us with a variety that is amazing. There is much here, of course, that is merely trivial, and a measurable quantity of the proudly absurd and naively preposterous; but if there are no such outstandingly good things here as the *Portrait of a Lady* by T. S. Eliot in the earlier issue, or Wallace Stevens's "Peter Quince at the Clavier," or John Rodker's "Marionettes," we can pass lightly over the studiously cerebral obscurantism of Marianne Moore, the tentacular quiverings of Mina Loy, the prattling iterations of Alfred Kreymborg, the delicate but amorphous self-consciousness of Jeanne d'Orge, Helen Hoyt, and Orrick Johns, and pause with admiration and delight before the "Preludes" and "Rhapsody on a Windy Night" by T. S. Eliot, and "Thirteen Ways of Looking at a Blackbird" by Wallace Stevens. It is not that one is at all indifferent to the frequent charm and delicious originality (at least as regards sensibility) of the other poets, but that one finds in the two last mentioned not only this delicate originality of mind but also a clearer sense of symmetry as regards both form and ideas: their poems are more apparently, and more really, works of art. In comparison, most of the other work in this volume looks like happy or unhappy improvisation. It is significant in this connection that Mr. Eliot uses rhyme and meter, a telling demonstration that the use of these ingredients may add power and finish and speed to poetry without in any way dulling the poet's tactile organs or clouding his consciousness—provided he has the requisite skill. Mr. Eliot's "Preludes" and "Rhapsody" are, in a very minor way, masterpieces of black-and-white impressionism. Personality, time, and environment—three attributes of the dramatic—are set sharply before us by means of a rapid and concise report of the seemingly irrelevant and tangential, but really centrally significant, observations of a shadowy protagonist.

II

From Mr. Eliot to M. Jean de Bosschère, the Flemish poet whose volume *The Closed Door* has now been translated into English by Mr. F. S. Flint, is a natural and easy step. It would appear, indeed, that Mr. Eliot has learned much from M. de Bosschère; certainly he is, in English, the closest parallel to him that we have. It is a kind of praise to say that in all likelihood Mr. Eliot's *Love Song of J. Alfred Prufrock* would not have been the remarkable thing it is if it had not been for the work of Jean de Bosschère: in several respects de Bosschère seems like a maturer and more powerful Eliot. What then is the work of M. de Bosschère?

To begin with, and without regard to the matter of classification, it must be emphatically said that this book has the clear, unforced, and captivating originality of genius. Whether, as Miss Sinclair questions doubtfully in her introduction, we call him mystic or symbolist or decadent—and all these terms have a certain aptness—is after all a secondary matter. These poems, in a colloquial but rich and careful free verse, occasionally using rhyme and a regular ictus, very frequently employing a melodic line which borders on the prosodic, seem at first glance to be half-whimsical and half-cerebral, seem to be in a key which is at once naive and gaily precious, with overtones of caricature; in reality they are masterpieces of ironic understatement and reveal upon closer scrutiny a series of profound spiritual or mental tragedies. The method of M. de Bosschère might be called symbolism if one were careful not to impute to him any delving into the esoteric; his themes are invariably very simple. One might call him a mystic, also, if one could conceive a negative mysticism of disbelief and disenchantment, a mysticism without vagueness, a mysticism of brilliantly colored but unsustaining certainties. But perhaps it would be more exact to say that he is merely a poet who happens to be highly developed on the cerebral side, as well as on the tactile, a poet for whom the most terrible and most beautiful realities

are in the last analysis ideas, who sees that as in life the most
vivid expression of ideas is in action, so in speech the most
vivid expression of them is in parables. These poems, therefore, are parables. In "Ulysse bâtit son lit" we do not encounter merely the deliciously and fantastically matter-of-fact
comedy, naive as a fairy story, which appears on the surface;
we also hear in the midst of this gay cynicism the muffled
crash of a remote disaster, and that disaster arises from the
attitude of the animally selfish crowd towards the man of outstanding achievement. He refuses to be one of them, so they
kill him. "They roast Ulysses, for he is theirs." Likewise, in
"Gridale," we do not witness a merely personal tragedy; the
tragedy is universal. We see the crucifixion of the disillusioned
questioner by the unthinking idolaters. In "Doutes," under a
surface apparently idiosyncratic in its narration of the humor-
ously bitter discoveries and self-discoveries of a child, we have
really an autobiography of disillusionment which is cosmic in
its applicability.

And yet he still believes,
This burlesque of a man
Who has given himself a universe
And a god like an immense conflagration
Whose smoke he smells;
And indeed it is perhaps only a bonfire
Made with the green tops of potatoes.

Nevertheless he still believes,
Ax in hand, this burlesque of a man still believes;
He will cut his dream, four-square, in the hearts of
    men. . . .

There is nothing to laugh at, nothing to object to,
We are not animals
Living to feed our seed.
There is something to believe.
All men are not made of pig's flesh.
There is something to believe.

Who said that I am a poor wretch,
Mere flotsam
Separated from its imaginary god?

Again, in "Homer Marsh," we make the acquaintance of the
gentle recluse who loves and is loved by his house, his fire, his
kettle, his pipe and tobacco, his dog, his bees; but he goes away

to travel, and lends his house to his friend Peter; and on his return finds to his bewilderment and despair that all these beloved things have curiously turned their affections to Peter. The tone is lyric, seductively playful and simple; the overtone is tragic. It is a translation into action of the profound fact that ideas, no matter how personal, cannot be property; that they are as precious and peculiar and inevitable in one case as in another, a natural action of forces universally at work.

It would be rash, however, to carry too far this notion of parables. Some of the poems in *The Closed Door* are so sensitively subjective, so essentially lyrical, so naturally mystic—in the sense that they make a clear melody of the sadness of the finite in the presence of the infinite, of the conscious in the presence of the unconscious—that one shrinks from dropping such a chain upon them. All one can say is that they are beautiful, that for all their cool and precise and colloquial preciosity, their sophisticated primitivism, they conceal an emotional power that is frightful, not to say heartrending. What is the secret of this amazing magic? It is not verbal merely, nor rhythmic; for it remains in translation. It springs from the ideas themselves: it is a playing of ideas against one another like notes in a harmony, ideas presented always visually, cool images in a kind of solitude. It is not that M. de Bosschère is altogether idiosyncratic in what he does, that he sees qualities that others do not see; but rather that he combines them unexpectedly, that he felicitously marries the lyrical to the matter-of-fact, the sad to the ironic, the innocent to the secular —the tender to the outrageous. He sees that truth is more complex and less sustaining than it is supposed to be, and he finds new images for it, images with the dew still on them. If novelty sometimes contributes to the freshness of the effect, it is by no means novelty alone: these novelties have meanings, unlike many of those factitiously achieved by some members of the Others group. This is a poet whose quaintness and whim and fantasy are always thought-wrinkled: they are hints of a world which the poet has found to be overwhelming in its complexity. Song is broken in upon by a doubting voice; flowers conceal a pit; pleasure serves a perhaps vile purpose; beauty may not be a delusion, but is it a snare? And what do thought and memory lead to? . . .

Nevertheless he still believes,
Ax in hand, this burlesque of a man still believes. . . .

Ax in hand! It is precisely such bizarre but significant imaginings that constitute the charm of this poet. And it is a part of his genius that, although hyperaesthetic, he is able to keep clearly in mind the objective value of such images, and to contrast them deliciously with the sentimental, or the decorative, or the impassioned.

BRIDGES, ROBERT   (1930)

The poetry of Robert Bridges has never been particularly popular. It is probably less read than that of any other poet whose official standing is so high. Even now, when *The Testament of Beauty* has surprisingly taken the English public by storm, it is safe to predict that few people will trouble to read his four volumes or more of classic, or pseudo-classic, masques and plays; and if they do, it is almost as safe to predict that they will come away from that undertaking pretty empty-handed. The real reasons for the unpopularity of Bridges are clearest in these unfortunate experiments: they are cold, dull, precious, actionless, full of affectations and archaisms, primly formal, nigglingly florid. The characters are lifeless, the colors are dim; one feels no warmth in them, no rootedness in that rich life of consciousness which (for example and contrast) everywhere makes the Elizabethan drama so hotly vascular. An occasional song or ode of great beauty and delicacy does little to redeem them from the cardinal sin of deadness.

Even in the shorter poems—the "books" of lyrics—one encounters the same faults. These are the poems on which Bridges' reputation has hitherto chiefly rested, and among them are many lyrics which combine a kind of chilly loveliness with a high degree of technical and prosodic ingenuity. If one cannot agree with Mr. Brett Young (in his critical study of Bridges, 1914) that they have a "poetic richness and warmth of color unknown since Keats" or a technique "hardly approached since the golden age of Latin poetry," nevertheless one must do them homage. At their best, they tend to the elegiac. They are uniformly gentle, pensive, limpid; a deliberate pastoral note informs almost all of them; the language is prim, and touched here and there with archaisms of word and idiom; in short, they belong to a strain of English poetry which is very "consciously" English. One does not go to such poetry for the terrors or profundities of human experience: one goes to it rather for a mild and healing gospel of beauty, a gospel everywhere charming, but perhaps also a little bit epicene. And also one goes to it for a study of its curious and excellent technique.

The Testament of Beauty is in this respect—perhaps in every respect, but most interestingly in this—Bridges' finest achievement. The development of a quantitative hexameter for use in a long narrative or philosophic poem (with the aim of avoiding monotony) had already begun to concern Bridges even in his earliest work. Mr. Brett Young describes the matter admirably. "Bridges' method" (again to quote from his critical study)

is to avail himself of all the freedom which a stress-prosody allows, and at the same time to mitigate with every available device the anarchy to which it leads. Briefly, he abolishes syllabic strictness for the sake of introducing new and expressive speech-rhythms, and simultaneously restores the element of time, leaving their freshness unimpaired. The whole of his achievement in stress-prosody is to enforce the idea of regularity in line-length while avoiding suggestion of a recurrent bar-beat. It is impossible to find a principle which applies to the whole of his work in this manner. Every line shows its own device to escape from the double pitfall of stress-prosody, the dilemma whose horns are music and prose.

In that final clause, Mr. Brett Young adumbrated the whole problem, and anticipated practically everything that can be said, on this score, of *The Testament of Beauty*. It is perhaps no exaggeration to say that for the most part this poem moves closer to the "prose" end of the spectrum than any other quasi-successful poem (of similar length) which one can recall. And on the whole, this queer loose prosaic rhythm, with its oddities of inversion and its eccentricities of spelling, suits surprisingly well Bridges' semi-didactic, semi-allegorical purpose. The poem is difficult reading—the familiar faults are here again; here again are the archaisms, the frigidities, the primly florid uncouthnesses and heavy pseudo-classical asides; but they fit the method and the theme, and moreover there are many incidental passages of extraordinary beauty. In short, the poem achieves a queer kind of uniqueness—something analogous, perhaps, to "Mansoul," or "The Dawn in Britain," of Doughty, in which there is the same effort toward the formulation of a pure convention.

Of the content of the poem it is sufficient here to speak very briefly. It is a mildly philosophical essay, a good deal influenced by Santayana's "Sense of Beauty" and "Life of Reason"; very loosely assembled, not always very cogent in reasoning, suffused everywhere with an odd and almost medieval simplicity and old-fashionedness. It reminds one even a little of *The Anatomy of Melancholy;* it has the same air of amateurish charm, the same earnest sincerity. It is a gentle testament, and ingenuous—the gentle praise of a gentle ideal. There is no wrestling here with the dynamics of the soul, no probing of horrors or sounding of wonder; chaos has removed itself from the shores of Albion; everything is peaceful and detached and comfortable; and everything is as consciously and purely English as it can possibly be.

CABELL, JAMES BRANCH ·   (1919)

It is one of the anomalies of the present literary situation in America that although it has been called, in a sense, a renaissance, a period of flowering, which implies, of course, the presence upon the scene of many figures distinguished for great ability, if not, to use a favorite American word, for genius, few if any of these personages have been writers of fiction. Of history, of poetry, of criticism and theory of criticism, of biography, the last half-dozen years have given us volumes relatively brilliant. One thinks offhand of such books as *The Education of Henry Adams,* Spingarn's *Creative Criticism,* Mencken's *Book of Prefaces* and *The American Language, Spoon River Anthology,* by Masters, *North of Boston,* by Frost, *The Man against the Sky* and *Merlin,* by Robinson, *Irradiations* and *Goblins and Pagodas,* by Fletcher; one thinks, again, of such of the younger men as Kreymborg and Bodenheim and Wallace Stevens, who have, in a sort of accidental unison, unexpectedly restored a vitality, as yet uncertain, to a moribund art, the poetic drama; and beyond these, of the many small groups and isolated figures which have added color, even points of brilliance, to the somewhat kaleidoscopic background; but the names of novelists are singularly absent. Theodore Dreiser

· And Joseph Hergesheimer. For bibliographical details of this and other composite reviews, see the Checklist under the appropriate year.

there has been of course—a novelist to whom one cannot deny respect, whatever one thinks of him as an artist. More creator than artist, certainly—though *Jennie Gerhardt* is perhaps a book to demand a more cautious dictum; and, at all events, a writer extraordinarily characteristic of the era through which we are passing, an impersonation, on a scale as coarse as heroic, of the uncertainties which beset us—uncertainties moral, social, and aesthetic, above all aesthetic. Taken as a mass, we seem to have reached our maturity too late, we discover our powers at a moment when such powers are in the process of being savagely discounted. Values are destroyed before our eyes, we are compelled to work as it were in a vacuum—at any rate, in a chaos, and in the merest twinkling instant our young bright optimism has become, or is in danger of becoming, not a healthy but a morbid skepticism; the sense of futility is always with us, and in our work this is reflected as a kind of emotional sterility.

This is not to be taken as universally true, nor is it true necessarily that the tendency toward spiritual impotence is one that will not somehow be overcome. Perhaps, also, I am wrong in seeing as "cases" of this sort of paralysis the only two writers of fiction who have emerged here, within the last few years, into anything like prominence. These two novelists are Mr. Joseph Hergesheimer and Mr. James Branch Cabell. Mr. Hergesheimer is already known in England through the publication of *The Three Black Pennys* and *Java Head*. Mr. Cabell has had, I believe, no books published there, and has therefore probably not been heard of. Both authors have just brought out new novels—Mr. Hergesheimer his *Linda Condon*, and Mr. Cabell his *Jurgen*. And of both authors it is beginning to be said, as is customary here of an author who has reached a certain point, that "he is the great American novelist."

It is permissible, on this point, to remain skeptical. Yet these two novels are of great interest, and one of them at least, Mr. Hergesheimer's *Linda Condon*, is delightful. Perhaps it is a good deal more than that: one is tempted certainly to say of it things much more flattering, despite one's inevitable lack of perspective, since the book is necessarily so recent an acquaintance. If one hesitates it is because one has after reading it, none the less for one's extraordinary pleasure, no pressing desire to re-examine it, even a faint reluctance to do so—perhaps one remembers paragraphs, pages, episodes that are a little suspect, areas which a second inspection might prove too

thinly threadbare. At all events I should like to be a little rash
and say, with such reservations, that *Linda Condon* is one of
the most vivid and charming portraits of women which we
have had—lyric, colorful, accomplished in a minimum of space.
As a study in the coefficient of the forces of heredity and environment it is, in fact, brilliant; and it is also, in a sense, amazingly a complement to *What Maisie Knew,* by Henry James—
with the difference that the inheritance is not, in the case of
Linda, vicious on both sides, nor even where vicious, un-
mitigatedly vicious; and that Mr. Hergesheimer does not concern himself solely with the childhood of Linda, as James did
with Maisie, but in Linda's later life unfolds gradually, with a
fine contrapuntal sense of inevitability, the many deep implications of the prelude. Mr. Hergesheimer's analysis of character is acute. Linda, by a kind of miracle, like an exotic flower,
grows before our eyes, grows and yet seems not to change,
retains even after many disenchantments a singular, remote,
cool, childlikeness of mind. The conception is a finer one than
anything in *Java Head,* though it will be obvious that the
milieu is less charmingly ready to Mr. Hergesheimer's hand
than, in that book, Salem was. Perhaps it is this that gives one
a recurring sense of disappointment—one misses in *Linda Condon* the tranquillity, the slow grave beauty of style, for which
Salem gave, in the first fifty pages of *Java Head,* so happy an
opportunity. May one suspect also that the touch is not always
quite so sure? Mr. Hergesheimer is not, for example, at his best
when he describes the talk of artists. Or does he not take them
quite so seriously as he seems to? A minor point, no doubt,
and more than offset by the many occasions on which he reminds one richly that the novel is lineally descended from the
narrative poem.

I have not dwelt further, in the case of Mr. Hergesheimer, on
the presence in his work of what I defined earlier as the "emotional sterility" which blights so much contemporary American
work; if one feels this at all in *Java Head* and *Linda Condon,*
one feels it only a little, in retrospect, and less as if it were
something *in* these novels than as if it were something which
in the most impalpable of ways hung over them. It is a suspicion rather than a charge. To justify the latter, in its full
force, one must turn to Mr. Cabell's *Jurgen,* a book which is by
way of making far more of a sensation than *Linda Condon,*
which has already been called, by Mr. Burton Rascoe, of the
Chicago Tribune, "one of the finest products of creative imagi-

nation known to our literature," and which has recently moved Mr. Hergesheimer himself to a singular flight of panegyric in the pages of the *New York Sun*.

He may be seen [says Mr. Hergesheimer of Mr. Cabell, in his "Improvisations on Themes from 'Jurgen'"] a remotely composed being withdrawn into the shadows at the edge of actuality; and then he is lost in the vapor rising delicately from the golden vessel of his imagination . . . All the fabulous loveliness that has drugged men with rapture and death returns in the magic of Jurgen: Guenevere in a robe of flame-colored silk; the pallid charm of Queen Silvia Tereu vanishing at the cock's crow; Anaitis, in Cocaigne, drawing desire into shuddering ecstasies of sensation; a brown and dimpled Hamadryad; Dolores of Philistia, beautiful as a hawk, but tenderer in the cloak of night; Florimel—in a quiet cleft by the Sea of Blood—who knew what to do with small unchristened children; and Phyllis, Satan's wife, an enchanting slip of devilishness, with the wings of a bat . . . Jurgen, riding on a centaur into the past, is fantastic, yet compared with the journeyings of the mind, the dark corridors and lands and beasts of thought, it is all as ordinary as any street of the present.

And so forth and so forth.

It will be seen that *Jurgen* (it was to have been called *The Pawnbroker's Shirt*) is, as Mr. Rascoe terms it, a *roman de la vie cérébrale*—a novel to make one think of *Marius*, or *Sixtine*, or *A Night in the Luxembourg*, or *Penguin Island*, or Arthur Machen's *Hill of Dreams*. It is above all a novel to make one think of Anatole France, and of the monstrous debt that Mr. Cabell owes him . . . To which, one might mischievously ask, does he owe the more—to Machen or to France? For Mr. Cabell has drawn heavily on both—on Machen for his *Beyond Life*, which is little more than an elaboration of *Hieroglyphics*, more weightily, but less charmingly written, and for portions of *The Cream of the Jest*; on France for other portions of *The Cream of the Jest* and for *Jurgen*. I do not mean to say that Mr. Cabell is a plagiarist; but it is obvious that he battens rather on literature than on life, and takes in consequence a hue therefrom. His favorite, almost his only protagonist, has always been the man of letters, and Mr. Cabell's sport has been the observation, half tender, half derisive, of this creature's antics in pursuit of the unattainable. His favorite setting has been the country and period of the troubadours. And his style has become, almost automatically, an affair of hollow elaborate punctilios—full of mock romanticisms, courtly rhetoric, mincing and somewhat fatiguing circumlocutions.

These tastes have combined in one or two instances to produce work of some distinction. *The Soul of Melicent,* one of Mr. Cabell's earlier novels, is delicious—so delicate a fusion of romance and extravaganza, so adroitly woven of ethical inversions, that one is perpetually in a pleasant state of uncertainty as to the author's intention. To *The Cream of the Jest,* also, one must pay one's respects—a well-elaborated study of schizophrenia, of the dual life of a man of letters, partly real, partly imaginary—and which is imaginary? . . . One drifts imperceptibly over the threshold. But in these, as in all of Mr. Cabell's work, one finds oneself at the end, in possession of a considerable sense of irritation. This is due partly to the aggressive monotony of the style, for one wearies, and rightly, of so much studied affectation, of these so often repeated drylyornate conventions of speech. But the style is not wholly the cause of one's irritation . . . it is rather itself merely a symptom of the cause, which underlies and is responsible for it, as it is responsible also for the choice of theme. This cause is Mr. Cabell's bitter-bright temperament, a temperament which compels him at the same time to seek the "romantic" and to disclaim it: he marries his illusions, as it were, only to divorce them, and what wedlock there is, is brief and bitter. Incapable of surrendering to his own fictions, he must perpetually put in the cynical comment, the dry curl of the lip, mortally afraid lest anyone catch him taking things too seriously. This might be a virtue in a philosopher, but in a novelist it is an ailment. Consequently, Mr. Cabell is forever touching things only to see them wither, a sight which, unhappily, his readers are thus doomed to share. To his readers, I am afraid, Mr. Cabell's recent work has too invidiously the flavor of Dead Sea fruit.

This is particularly true of *Jurgen.* As soon as one has foreseen the plan of *Jurgen,* one is *parti pris*—one cannot help sympathizing with an author who, in this era of the sciolistically psychological novel, of shallow realisms and valetudinarian introspections, undertakes a novel on wider premises and with the attempt, at least, of a wider view. But one's sympathies are sharply chilled. Mr. Cabell's ambition is, if the point be permissible, an acquired rather than a natural one, and while his curiosity is possibly adequate to the undertaking, his intellect, his emotivity, his tastes, are not. He has had, unhappily, a bad attack of Anatole France. His attempts at light irony are clumsy and obvious, his attempts at wit are for the most part little more than boyish *double-entendres* dealing with sex.

Jurgen has its moments of charm, but in large measure it is merely a recital of the erotic exploits of its hero, each exploit precisely like the last, each reduced by the author to the lowest common denominators of animalism. Granted that Mr. Cabell wishes to show himself a cynic in this regard, to emphasize the motive power in human conduct of this impulse—a theme not wholly new—he has shown himself only the more, dealing with it thus, as lacking imagination and art. One perceives the force and adroitness of his curiosity, the wealth of his erudition on matters profane: if one were adolescent one might enjoy them. As it is, the book for all its ambitiousness comes very near to being repellent, no less for the pseudo-romantic smartness of the style than for its phosphorescent contents. It is, distinctly, a prize for the Freudians! . . . One hopes faintly that, having thus ingloriously purged himself, Mr. Cabell will turn to new work with a clearer temper.

CHEKHOV, ANTON   (1921)

You are traveling from New York to Chicago, and the stranger with whom you have been talking leans with restrained excitement towards the car window, as the train passes a small town, and says: "I lived in that town for three years." It looks like any other town. But you stare at it as if it concealed something amazing, had some secret; and when, after a pause, he begins telling you the story of something odd that happened to him there, a story not very remarkable in itself nor involving very remarkable people, nevertheless the story, the people, the town all seem to you very extraordinary: you listen with an intensity of pleasure that is almost painful, you strive desperately to hold in mind the picture of that town with its small brick shops, dingy fences, white wooden church, to penetrate it, to live in it; and when the narrative is finished you have suddenly an overwhelming desire to tell the stranger a similar narrative, something real, convincing. You have, maybe, no such story at your disposal. You might tell him of something that happened to your friend S., but that, you feel, would not be so satisfactory: the effect of it would not be so powerful. What you desire to say is: "That reminds me of something that occurred when I was living in a small town in Ver-

mont, two years ago . . ." You are silent, and wonder why it is
that the stranger's simple tale has so absorbed you.

Its charm, of course, is simply in the fact that it is actual,
that it really happened. This charm is intensified by the fact
that it is narrated by the protagonist himself, simply and art-
lessly, and by the fact that you have actually seen the town
that served as a setting, two things that combine to make the
reality overwhelming. You have been treated to a "slice of
life," a "human document" . . . It is in this kind of actuality
that we find, perhaps, a key to the work of Anton Chekhov,
possibly the greatest writer of the short story who has ever lived.
The stories of Chekhov have precisely this quality of natural,
seemingly artless, actuality—casual and random in appearance,
abrupt, discursive, alternately overcrowded and thin. Chekhov
is the stranger who sits in the train beside us, who suddenly
exclaims, "You see that town? I know a queer thing that happened there," and he tells us, in a normal, conversational tone,
of the real things that happened there to real people. Observe
his openings, taken in order from his volume, *The Schoolmistress, and Other Stories.*

At half-past eight they drove out of town.

A medical student named Mayer, and a pupil of the Moscow School
of Painting, Sculpture and Architecture, called Rybinikov, went one
evening to see their friend Vassilyev, a law student, and suggested
that he go with them to S Street.

The twilight of evening. Big flakes of wet snow are whirling lazily
about the street lamps, which have just been lighted.

In the year in which my story begins I had a job at a little station on
one of the south-western railways.

Nadia Zelenin had just come back with her mamma from the theatre,
where she had seen a performance of *Yevgeny Onyegin.*

In every instance the pitch is at once plausibly colloquial.
"I am not," Chekhov seems to say, "up to any literary tricks,
I have no artistic designs upon you—literature bores me, with
its exaggerations and flowerinesses. No, I simply happen to
know about this case, and this is how it was." This disarms us—
we are now ready to believe literally anything. The primitive
desire to listen to a story has been aroused in us, but that is not
all: we have been convinced *a priori* by the speaker's very tone
of voice, by his calm, and above all by the absence, on his part,

of any *desire* to convince, that what he is about to tell us is true. His audience is already half hypnotized with the first sentence.

In this regard, Chekhov is obviously in the tradition of the Goncourts, with their "human documents," and of Gogol: he was a contemporary of Maupassant in more than mere moment. The theory of the "slice of life" was, at that moment, the thing, and Chekhov, with Maupassant, remains as the chief exemplar, in the short story, of that theory. Yet that theory as it worked through Chekhov is not what it was as it worked through Maupassant: a world of difference sunders the two men. Basically, the difference lies in the fact that Maupassant was a logician of the short story, and Chekhov a poet. Maupassant's mere "mechanics" are superb; far better than Chekhov's. There is no waste, his items are well chosen and "clear"; he arranges them with precision and economy and in a sequence logically overwhelming; he makes his case with a miracle of cold dexterity. Grant his hypothesis, his Q. E. D. will punctually flower.

There is little of this in Chekhov. His stories have not this flat, swift trajectory, are not logically "rounded," do not move, as narratives, to an overwhelming provided conclusion, through an unalterable certainty which one has been permitted, or rather compelled, now and again terrifyingly to feel. Many of his stories do not, in this sense, conclude at all—they merely stop. In fact, the conclusion in itself did not interest Chekhov. He did not desire to emphasize, as Maupassant emphasized, the "final" event, nor, indeed, any single event; his method was more copious, and his concern was not so much with the possibility that in this copiousness a narrative current should be felt, as with the certainty that through it should be perceived a living being or group of beings, beings through whose rich consciousness, intense or palpable, we are enabled to live, backward and forward, in time, lives as appallingly genuine as our own.

Here we reach naturally the question of psychology, and must observe that while Maupassant's characters obey a logic in this regard, obey it mechanically, like marionettes, and have no life apart from it, Chekhov's characters are complex, indeterminate, diffuse a consciousness wider than the bounds of the particular event in which we see them participating: they come to it from "somewhere" (we know only vaguely where), and depart from it for somewhere else. This is due not merely to the fact that Chekhov is more concerned with the effect of

"actuality" than with "story," to the fact that, as was said
above, he was a poet. His sensibilities were rich and of an
immense range, had thrust their roots, one dares to think, almost as widely and deeply into life as Shakespeare's: his understanding was unsurpassed, and if he falls short of the greatest
of artists it is not for a lack of that faculty. No artist has known,
by introspection, more "states of mind," no artist has known
better, by observation, what shapes they assume in talk or be-
haviour. This, after all, is Chekhov's genius—he was a master
of mood. His stories offer not only an extraordinary panorama
of scenes, actions, situations but, more importantly, a range of
states of consciousness which is perhaps unparalleled. It was
this pluralism, this awareness of the many-sidedness of life,
that sent him to the short story rather than to the novel, and
made of his longer stories, as he himself says, mere accumulations. These accumulations—"A Dreary Story," "My Life," "The
Steppe"—do not disintegrate, as the short stories do not, simply
because, like the short stories, they depend for unity not on
the formal working of a theme, but on verisimilitude, on the
never-diminishing saturation of consciousness in the life to be
"given": their unity is a unity of tone.

If we evade for the moment the question of the precise
value, in fiction, of the "actual," and of the extent to which it
may be permitted to supplant all other values, and evade, also
for the moment, the question of the kind of actuality toward
which Chekhov felt a compulsion, it is perhaps profitable to
note how interesting are the aesthetic problems raised by the
effort to capture, in fiction, that tone. We have already observed
that Chekhov instinctively or consciously uses, at the outset of
a story and throughout, a colloquial tone—he is never better
than when he tells his story in the first person singular. He
wishes, in other words, to keep the pitch of the story down, to
diminish what is called "the psychic distance"; his picture is
to be frameless and immediate, so close to us that we can touch
it. He does not want us to be conscious of his style, nor of any
arrangement. He wants us to see his people and scenes just as
they are, neither larger nor smaller than life. Every trace of
sympathy must therefore be excluded: "When you depict sad
or unlucky people try to be colder—it gives their grief, as it
were, a background. . . . Yes, you must be cold. . . . Every
trace of stylization, of heightening, must be expunged. . . .
Beauty and expressiveness in Nature are attained only by
simplicity, by such simple phrases as 'The sun set,' 'It was

dark,' 'It began to rain,' and so on. . . ." In everything we see
the avoidance of the phrase, the detail, the attitude, the sense
of "frame" of "scheme," which might mitigate the effect of
immediacy. "But of the word 'art' I am terrified. . . ." No
wonder—by art he meant conscious art, and Chekhov was only
intermittently a conscious artist; he knew that he was at his
best when, on a theme out of memory—a face, an incident—he
gave himself up to rapid improvisation, an improvisation which
took the form of a complete surrender to that face, that incident, a submersion of the senses.

This, of course, *was* his art—an art, of its sort, perfect. Yet we
come back to question again the extent to which this effect of
overwhelming actuality may be permitted to supplant other
effects—the effects, for example, of an art more deliberate,
more conscious. The two sorts of art ("two" if we take merely
the extremes, say, Chekhov and Henry James) are not of course
mutually exclusive, there will be room for both; the generation,
like the individual, will make its natural choice and rationalize
its choice *ex post facto*. Yet if we need not necessarily at the
instant choose between them, it is none the less fruitful to
observe their distinguishing characteristics, and we can do no
better at the outset than to quote Henry James himself, speaking, in his essay on "The New Novel," of precisely this question of the degree in which mere immersion in the actual may
be sufficient.

Yes, yes—but is this all? These are the circumstances of the interest—
we see, we see; but where is the interest itself, where and what is its
center, and how are we to measure it in relation to that? . . . That
appreciation is . . . a mistake and a priggishness, being reflective
and thereby corrosive, is another of the fond dicta which we are
here concerned but to brush aside . . . appreciation, attentive and
reflective, inquisitive and conclusive, is in this connection absolutely
the golden *key* to our pleasure.

This is a statement of a theory of art so antithetical to that of
Chekhov (insofar as he consciously entertained one), that it
is reasonable to suppose that he simply would not have understood it. Here we have an artist who not only selects one from
among many themes because it is richest in possibilities of
being "worked," but also positively invites his reader to observe at every moment the "working" of it, to look, as it were,
at the back of the clock no less often than at its face, so that he
may know not merely what it says but how it says it. This is a

pleasure to which Chekhov does not invite us: to make that invitation is, in the same breath, to take a deliberate step away from the "actual."

Compare Chekhov's *In the Ravine* with Turgenev's *A Lear of the Steppes*. The themes have much in common. But whereas Chekhov has richly and beautifully improvised, always in the key of the actual, giving us an immense number of scenes, dialogues, persons, all of them palpitantly real and caught in an exquisite, quiet beauty of tone, Turgenev has gone more deliberately to work: he strikes sharply, even artificially, his "theme" in the opening, giving us thus in advance a glimpse of the whole, and then proceeds to the fine development of this theme through a series of delicate exaggerations— he aims not at the immediate but at the distant, slightly distorted by a trick of atmosphere; not at the actual, but at the larger than the actual. One feels the artificiality, certainly; but one enjoys it, and in retrospect it is the Turgenev story that one clearly remembers, not the Chekhov story. Harlov we still see, but we do not even recall the name of Chekhov's Lear, any more than we see him as a person. He was living as long as we read of him—more so perhaps than Harlov. That whole life, in which Chekhov drowned us, how beautiful, resonant, full of echoes it was, how aromatically it ended! But it is our joy in the tone of it that we recall, and not the things that created that tone.

We come back, therefore, to the point from which we started, to a clear realization that Chekhov was in essence a poet, a poet of the actual, an improviser in the vivid. His compulsions drove him to seek character, perhaps—more precisely, to seek mood, state of mind; he profoundly knew the quality, the light, the timbre, the fluctuations of mood, particularly those of a melancholy tinge; and if, in retrospect, we find that his characters have an odd way of evaporating, it is because so often our view of them was never permitted for a moment to be external—we saw them only as infinitely fine and truthful sequences of mood. Chekhov was great because his sensibilities were of sufficient range to enable him to apply this method almost universally. His sympathy, his pity, his tenderness, were inexhaustible. He lived, and thus permitted us to live, everywhere.

Despite one's very great respect for H.D.'s poetry—and respect is perhaps the word, for it is a poetry which never warms or excites, but at its best elicits (rather) a cool intense admiration in which feelings are suspended—one must admit that the extraordinary power and richness of her novel, if novel it can be called, came as a surprise. One is tempted to say that the world of Palimpsest and the world of poetry are two entirely different things. That would be convenient, but it is not quite exact; for it is, of course, easy enough to trace, in the prodigal and sometimes disheveled magnificence of the prose, the hard, and occasionally too neat, small objectiveness of the verse. Nevertheless, one cannot evade the feeling that in prose H.D. is a much more impressive and disturbing person than in verse: which is tantamount to saying that she has a great deal more to express than she found it remotely possible to express in the somewhat narrow, somewhat precious, poetic mode which she had invented for herself. One can only guess, idly, at the reasons for this—one supposes that she had some queer *idée fixe* as to what sort of thing poetry should or should not be; that it should not, for instance, be too candidly emotional, or too indulgently rhythmical, or too lavish of colored phrase; that it should be spare, and hint rather coldly at its ardors, and perhaps be also a little asymmetrical in design. Whatever the reasons for these odd inhibitions, it is obvious enough that she has inverted the usual procedure, and has found in the prose of *Palimpsest* a far deeper emotional release and escape, and therefore a more intimate mode of expression, than her verse has ever afforded her. She takes at last the plunge—she delivers herself at last completely to the whole range of intensities of feeling and perception, which, in her poetry (she had the air of saying) were things a little too frightening, things that had better be run from, and mentioned, if mentioned at all, a little breathlessly. And the result is a novel which invites comparison with the very best fiction which has been written, in any language, in this century.

Of H.D.'s debts and affinities one need not say too much, beyond noting that she owes a good deal to James (in the third part) and to Joyce (in the second part)—sometimes a shade too palpably echoing the styles of those two writers, especially James. Of her theme, one need only remark that it perhaps carries a little too far toward the esoteric, perhaps toward the mystic (in its suggestion of recurring personalities and situations, or even reincarnations), its elaborate analysis of the queer oppressiveness of the sense of the past. One would like to be surer than one is that H.D. does not take all this too seriously. If, in this regard, one gives her the benefit of the doubt, then one has little left but praise. The three long episodes of which the novel is made—one in ancient Rome, one in postwar London, one in modern Egypt—are given us with a richness and vividness, an unintermittent saturation of verisimilitude, and a balancing of the objectively beautiful with the psychologically true, which one would have to go far to match. There are stylistic oddities—elisions and abruptnesses—which pull one up, and occasionally carelessnesses (split infinitives, modern French phrases in the Roman section, and other small matters) in the midst of a prose so beautiful as to make such errors glaring; and one notes again, as one always notes of the "stream of consciousness" method, that one now and then founders a little in the fragmentary and chaotic and repetitive welter of the interior monologue. One would have preferred, in the second section, a little more stiffening—more of the direct narrative (retrospected or vatically projected), and less of the obsessed round-and-round of the heroine's mind, which sometimes, in its endless repetitions of certain leit-motifs, goes beyond the limits of the credible, as also of the aesthetically endurable. Nor need the first part have been quite so bristlingly and barbedly archaistic in order to attain a flavor as of the "classic." But these are minor objections, and so is one's feeling that H.D. overdoes a little the interpolative method, with its interjections, qualifications, parenthetic questions, parenthetic reminiscences—one feels, in the midst of this burning subjectivism, this consuming Narcissism, that it would be a relief to come oftener upon a simple narrative statement or a connected bit of dialogue. And one is sure that this need not have diminished in the slightest the extraordinary evocativeness of this prose, nor in the least have impeded H.D.'s remarkably subtle apprehension of mood and feeling, and the logical sequences of mood and feeling that we call character.

Emily Dickinson was born in Amherst, Massachusetts, on December 10th, 1830. She died there, after a life perfectly devoid of outward event, in 1886. She was thus an exact contemporary of Christina Rossetti, who was born five days earlier than she, and outlived her by eight years. Of her life we know little. Her father, Edward Dickinson, was a lawyer, and the Treasurer of Amherst College; and it is clear that what social or intellectual life was in that bleak era available, was available for her. That she did not choose to avail herself of it, except in very slight degree, is also clear; and that this choice, which was gradually to make of her life an almost inviolable solitude, was made early, is evident from her *Letters*. In a letter dated 1853, when she was twenty-three years old, she remarked, "I do not go from home." By the time she was thirty, the habit of sequestration had become distinct, a subject on which she was explicit and emphatic in her letters to T. W. Higginson—editor of the *Atlantic Monthly* at that time. She made it clear that if there was to be any question of a meeting between them, he would have to come to Amherst—she would not go to Boston. Higginson, as a matter of fact, saw her twice, and his record of the encounter is practically the only record we have of her from any "literary" personage of her lifetime. Even this is meager—Higginson saw her superficially, as was inevitable. Brave soldier, courtly gentleman, able editor, he was too much of the old school not to be a little puzzled by her poetry; and if he was fine enough to guess the fineness, he was not quite fine enough wholly to understand it. The brief correspondence between these two is an extraordinary document of unconscious irony—the urbanely academic editor reproaching his wayward pupil for her literary insubordination, her false quantities and reckless liberties with rhyme; the wayward pupil replying with a humility, beautiful and pathetic, but remaining singularly, with unmalleable obstinacy, herself. "I saw her," wrote Higginson, "but twice, face to face, and brought away the impression of something as unique and remote as Undine or Mignon or Thekla." When, thirty years after the acquaintance had begun, and four after Emily Dickinson's death, he was called upon to edit a selection from her poetry, practically none of which had been published during her lifetime, his scruples were less severe, and he spoke of her with generosity and insight. "After all," he then wrote, "when a thought takes one's breath away, a lesson on grammar seems an impertinence." Again, "In many cases these verses will seem to the reader like poetry torn up by the roots." And again, "a quality more suggestive of the poetry of Blake than of anything to be elsewhere found—flashes of wholly original and profound insight into nature and life."

Thus began and ended Emily Dickinson's only important connection with the literary life of her time. She knew, it is true, Helen Hunt Jackson, a poetess, for whose anthology, *A Masque of Poets*, she gave the poem "Success," one of the few poems she allowed publication during her life. And she knew the Bowles family, owners and editors of *The Springfield Republican*, at that time the *Manchester Guardian* of New England—which, as she put it mischievously, was one of "such papers . . . as have nothing carnal in them." But these she seldom saw; and aside from these she had few intimates outside of her family; the circle of her world grew steadily smaller. This is a point of cardinal importance, but unfortunately no light has been thrown upon it. It is apparent that Miss Dickinson became a hermit by deliberate and conscious choice. "A recluse," wrote Higginson, "by temperament and habit, literally spending years without setting her foot beyond the doorstep, and many more years during which her walks were strictly limited to her father's grounds, she habitually concealed her mind, like her person, from all but a very few friends; and it was with great difficulty that she was persuaded to print, during her lifetime, three or four poems." One of the co-editors of *Poems: Second Series* assures us that this voluntary hermitage was not due to any "love-disappointment," and that she was "not an invalid." "She had tried society and the world, and had found them lacking." But this, of course, tells us nothing. Her *Letters* show us convincingly that her girlhood was a normally "social" one—she was active, high-spirited, and endowed with a considerable gift for extravagant humor. As a young woman she had, so Mrs. Bianchi, a niece, informs us in the preface to *The Single Hound*, several love affairs. But we have no right, without other testimony, to assume here any ground for the singular psychological change that came over her. The only other clue we have, of any sort, is the hint from one of her girlhood friends, that perhaps *"she was longing for poetic sympathy."* Perhaps! But we must hope that her relatives and literary executives will eventually see fit to publish *all* her literary remains, verse and prose, and to give us thus, perhaps, a good deal more light on the nature of her life.

Anecdotes relating to her mischievousness, her wit, her way-
wardness, are not enough. It is amusing, if horrifying, to know
that once, being anxious to dispose of some kittens, she put
them on a shovel, carried them into the cellar, and dropped
them into the nearest jar—which, subsequently, on the occasion
of the visit of a distinguished judge, turned out to have been
the pickle-jar. We like to know too, that even when her solitude
was most remote she was in the habit of lowering from her window, by a string, small baskets of fruit or confectionery for
children. But there are other things we should like to know
much more.

There seems, however, little likelihood of our being told, by
her family, anything more; and if we seek for the causes of the
psychic injury which so sharply turned her in upon herself, we
can only speculate. Her letters, in this regard, give little light,
only showing us again and again that the injury was deep. Of
the fact that she suffered acutely from intellectual drought
there is evidence enough. One sees her vividly here—but one
sees her, as it were, perpetually in retreat; always discovering
anew, with dismay, the intellectual limitations of her correspondents; she is discreet, pathetic, baffled, a little humbled, and
draws in her horns; takes sometimes a perverse pleasure in indulging more than ever, on the occasion of such a disappointment, in her love of a cryptic style—a delicate bombardment of
parable and whim which she perfectly knows will stagger;
and then again retreats to the safe ground of the superficial.
It is perhaps for this reason that the letters give us so remarkably little information about her literary interests. The meager-
ness of literary allusion is astounding. The Brontes and the
Brownings are referred to—she thought Alexander Smith "not
very coherent"—Joaquin Miller she "could not care about." Of
her own work she speaks only in the brief unsatisfactory correspondence with Higginson. To him she wrote in 1863, "I
wrote no verse, but one or two, until this winter." Otherwise, no
scrap of her own literary history: she appears to have existed in a vacuum. Of the literary events, tremendous for America, which were taking place during her most impressionable
years, there is hardly a mention. Emerson was at the height of
his career, and living only sixty miles away: his poems came
out when she was seventeen. When she was twenty, Hawthorne
published *The Scarlet Letter*, and *The House of Seven Gables*
the year after. The same year, 1851, brought out Melville's
Moby Dick. The death of Poe took place in 1849—in 1850 was

published the first collected edition of his poems. When she was twenty-four, Thoreau's *Walden* appeared; when she was twenty-five, *Leaves of Grass*. One can say with justice that she came to full "consciousness" at the very moment when American literature came to flower. That she knew this, there cannot be any question; nor that she was stimulated and influenced by it. One must assume that she found in her immediate environment no one of her own stature, with whom she could admit or discuss such things; that she lacked the energy or effrontery to voyage out into the unknown in search of such companionship; and that, lacking this courage, and wanting this help, she became easily a prey to the then current Emersonian doctrine of mystical Individualism. In this connection it is permissible to suggest that her extreme self-seclusion and secrecy was both a protest and a display—a kind of vanity masquerading as modesty. She became increasingly precious, of her person as of her thought. Vanity is in her letters—at the last an unhealthy vanity. She believes that anything she says, however brief, will be of importance; however cryptic, will be deciphered. She enjoys being something of a mystery, and she sometimes deliberately and awkwardly exaggerates it. Even in notes of condolence—for which she had a morbid passion—she is vain enough to indulge in sententiousness: as when she wrote, to a friend whose father had died on her wedding-day, "Few daughters have the immortality of a father for a bridal gift."

When we come to Emily Dickinson's poetry, we find the Emersonian individualism clear enough, but perfectly Miss Dickinson's. Henry James observed of Emerson:

The doctrine of the supremacy of the individual to himself, of his originality and, as regards his own character, *unique* quality, must have had a great charm for people living in a society in which introspection, thanks to the want of other entertainment, played almost the part of a social resource. . . . There was . . . much relish for the utterances of a writer who would help one to take a picturesque view of one's internal possibilities, and to find in the landscape of the soul all sorts of fine sunrise and moonlight effects.

This sums up admirably the social "case" of Miss Dickinson—it gives us a shrewd picture of the causes of her singular introversion, and it suggests that we are perhaps justified in considering her the most perfect flower of New England Transcendentalism. In her mode of life she carried the doctrine of self-sufficient individualism farther than Thoreau carried it, or the naive zealots of Brook Farm. In her poetry she carried it, with its complement of passionate moral mysticism, farther than Emerson: which is to say that as a poet she had more genius than he. Like Emerson, whose essays must greatly have influenced her, and whose poetry, especially his gnomic poems, only a little less, she was from the outset, and remained all her life, a singular mixture of Puritan and freethinker. The problems of good and evil, of life and death, obsessed her; the nature and destiny of the human soul; and Emerson's theory of compensation. Toward God, as one of her earliest critics is reported to have said, "she exhibited an Emersonian self-possession." Indeed, she did not, and could not, accept the Puritan God at all. She was frankly irreverent, on occasion, a fact which seems to have made her editors a little uneasy—one hopes that it has not resulted in the suppression of any of her work. What she was irreverent to, of course, was the Puritan conception of God, the Puritan attitude toward him.

Heavenly father, take to thee
The supreme iniquity,
Fashioned by thy candid hand
In a moment contraband.
Though to trust us seems to us
More respectful,—we are dust.
We apologize to thee
For thine own Duplicity.

This, it must be repeated, is Emily Dickinson's opinion of the traditional and anthropomorphic "God," who was still, in her day, a portentous Victorian gentleman. Her real reverence, the reverence that made her a mystic poet of the finest sort, was reserved for Nature, which seemed to her a more manifest and more beautiful evidence of Divine Will than creeds and churches. This she saw, observed, loved, with a burning simplicity and passion which nevertheless did not exclude her very agile sense of humor. Her Nature poems, however, are not the most secretly revelatory or dramatically compulsive of her poems, nor on the whole, the best. They are often of extraordinary delicacy—nearly always give us, with deft brevity, the exact in terms of the quaint. But, also, they are often superficial, a mere affectionate playing with the smaller things that give her delight; and to see her at her best and most characteristic and most profound, one must turn to the remarkable range of metaphysical speculation and ironic introspection which is displayed in those sections of her posthumous books which her editors have captioned Life, and Time and Eternity. In the former sections are the greater number of her set "meditations" on the nature of things. For some critics they will always appear too bare, bleak, and fragmentary. They have no trappings, only here and there a shred of purple. It is as if Miss Dickinson, who in one of her letters uttered her contempt for the "obtrusive body," had wanted to make them, as nearly as possible, disembodied thought. The thought is there, at all events, hard, bright, and clear; and her symbols, her metaphors, of which she could be prodigal, have an analogous clarity and translucency. What is also there is a downright homeliness which is a perpetual surprise and delight. Emerson's gnomic style she tunes up to the epigrammatic—the epigrammatic she often carries to the point of the cryptic; she becomes what one might call an epigrammatic symbolist.

> *Lay this laurel on the one*
> *Too intrinsic for renown.*
> *Laurel! veil your deathless tree,—*
> *Him you chasten, that is he!*

This, from *Poems: Second Series*, verges perilously on the riddle. And if often happens that her passionate devotion to concise statement in terms of metaphor left for her readers a small rich emblem of which the colors tease, the thought entices, but the meaning escapes. Against this, however, should be set her capacity, when occasion came, for a granite simplicity, any parallel to which one must seek in the seventeenth century. This, for example, called "Parting."

> *My life closed twice before its close;*
> *It yet remains to see*
> *If Immortality unveil*
> *A third event to me,*
> *So huge, so hopeless to conceive,*
> *As these that twice befell.*
> *Parting is all we know of heaven*
> *And all we need of hell.*

Or this, from *The Single Hound:*

> *Not any sunny tone*
> *From any fervent zone*
> *Finds entrance there.*
> *Better a grave of Balm*

Toward human nature's home,
And Robins near,
Than a stupendous Tomb
Proclaiming to the gloom
How dead we are.

Both these poems, it will be noted, deal with death; and it must be observed that the number of poems by Miss Dickinson on this subject is one of the most remarkable things about her. Death, and the problem of life after death, obsessed her. She seems to have thought of it constantly—she died all her life, she probed death daily. "That bareheaded life under grass worries one like a wasp," she wrote. Ultimately, the obsession became morbid, and her eagerness for details, after the death of a friend —the hungry desire to know *how* she died—became almost vulture-like. But the preoccupation, with its horrible uncertainties —its doubts about immortality, its hatred of the flesh, and its many reversals of both positions—gave us her sharpest work. The theme was inexhaustible for her. If her poetry seldom became "lyrical," seldom departed from the colorless sobriety of its bare iambics and toneless assonance, it did so most of all when the subject was death. Death profoundly and cruelly invited her. It was most of all when she tried "to touch the smile," and dipped her "fingers in the frost," that she took full possession of her genius.

Her genius was, it remains to say, as erratic as it was brilliant. Her disregard for accepted forms or for regularities was incorrigible. Grammar, rhyme, meter—anything went by the board if it stood in the way of thought or freedom of utterance. Sometimes this arrogance was justified; sometimes not. She did not care in the least for variety of effect—of her six hundred-odd poems, practically all are in octosyllabic quatrains or couplets, sometimes with rhyme, sometimes with assonance, sometimes with neither. Everywhere, when one first comes to these poems, one seems to see nothing but a colorless dry monotony. How deceptive a monotony, concealing what reserves of depth and splendor; what subtleties of mood and tone! Once adjust oneself to the spinsterly angularity of the mode, its lack of eloquence or rhetorical speed, its naive and often prosaic directness, one discovers felicities of thought and phrase on every page. The magic is terse and sure. And ultimately one simply sighs at Miss Dickinson's singular perversity, her lapses and tyrannies, and accepts them as an inevitable part of the strange and original genius she was. The lapses and tyrannies become a positive charm—one even suspects they were deliberate. They satisfied her—therefore they satisfy us. This marks, of course, our complete surrender to her highly individual gift, and to the singular sharp beauty, present everywhere, of her personality. The two things cannot be separated; and together, one must suppose, they suffice to put her among the finest poets in the language.

DOSTOEVSKY, FEODOR   (1921)

The two novels which make up the twelfth volume in Mrs. Garnett's translation of Dostoevsky, *The Friend of the Family,* were published ten years apart—the title-story in 1859, the year in which Dostoevsky finally obtained permission to return from Siberia to St. Petersburg, and *Nyetochka Nyezvanov* in 1849, the year of his arrest and imprisonment. They are both remarkable productions; they have both been somewhat slighted by critics, simply, one supposes, because they are, naturally, less remarkable than *The Idiot* or *Crime and Punishment* or *The Brothers Karamazov.* They share, they show, nonetheless, their author's genius—they are, despite their "age," more sharply "modern"—a term by which one presumably means fine and searching in a psychological sense—than anything present-day American fiction can show, for all its advantage, in point of time, of seventy years. They have also, for those who are interested in the extraordinary literary case with which Dostoevsky presents us, their special points: *The Friend of the Family,* written about two years before *The Idiot,* contains the prototype of Myshkin, and adumbrates, faintly but clearly, that whole later series of novels in which one overhears the dialogue between good and evil, faith and cynicism, altruism and egotism. *Nyetochka Nyezvanov,* too, is important, among other reasons, if only because it shows us clearly a Dostoevsky who already, before his imprisonment, was conspicuously, for the eyes of a psychologist, marked; although of course, even before this, Bielinsky the Russian critic, had said, "What he needs is medical attention."

Critics of an academic cast, critics for whom literary values approximate the absolute, and for whom art is a kind of religion, profoundly distrust any attempt to trace aspects of a work of art to the psychic disequilibration of the artist. Dostoevsky has especially, at the hands of his admirers, come in for this kind of shielding. Again, this shielding is most conspicuous on the part of those, precisely, who see in Dostoevsky not merely an artist but also, and perhaps more importantly, a prophet, a seer. Thus, Mr. J. Middleton Murry, in his book on Dostoevsky, attacks the notion of ascribing to epilepsy any relevant effect on Dostoevsky's work, and ridicules it as not merely stooping to "the unpardonable methods of a Nordau" but also as confounding cause with effect: Mr. Murry prefers, despite all the evidence, to believe that it was exactly the strain of literary creation which brought on the active phase of the epilepsy.

The facts are, of course, that Dostoevsky inherited a tendency to hysteria; that the disorder manifested itself even in his boyhood; that even before he was sent to Siberia he was a confirmed hypochondriac, who reveled in searching medical books for "symptoms"; and finally that, whether or not in later life the worry and prolonged intellectual effort contributed to the increasing violence of his attacks, none the less he was already an epileptic, with all that fact, as we shall see, can imply. Writing at the age of twenty-seven, to his brother Michael, Dostoevsky, after mentioning a marked increase in his "nervous irritability" (a precise characteristic of the epileptic) went on to say: "Whenever formerly I had such nervous disturbances, I made use of them for writing; in such a state I could write much more and much better than usual." This gives us a Dostoevsky who is capable of exploiting his disease. Not for nothing was he a hypochondriac. His descriptions, again and again, of hysterical states of mind are of unparalleled exactitude and vividness.

Of the causes of epilepsy little is known; of its effects, which are obvious, let me quote Dr. J. F. Munson, in an article on epilepsy in the *Modern Treatment of Mental and Nervous Diseases* of Drs. White and Jelliffe:

The characteristic features of the disease influence the life of the afflicted individual in every particular. . . . There are practically no epileptics without some mental change. . . . [Epilepsies are] characterized by mental change and by certain traits of mind and character which exist independent of the seizure . . .

Aschaffenburg lays special stress on the variations of the physical condition (mood) which may occur independent of attacks. Grasset characterizes them more harshly, but with much truth, and indirectly points out the variability of the epileptic's psychic condition:

On the one hand, they are sombre, taciturn, defiant, suspicious, always ready to fly into a passion, to hurt people, to become enraged, and to strike; on the other hand, they are contrary, obsequious, obliging, wheedlesome, full of effusion and gentleness. In reality, epileptics are all, or nearly all, irritable, subject to attacks of sudden, violent and ferocious transports of rage, during which they do not, as it were, belong to themselves. This irritability is the keynote of their character. Many have, in addition, vices and perverse instincts. . . . They frequently have a tendency to a sickly piety or a sort of excessive religiousness, mixed with hypocrisy. . . .

Add to this that epileptics are further described as "full of contradictions and contrasts"; unstable; that ideas of religion are common during the seizure; that there is apt to be a complete disorientation of time and place; and that in the delirium "the ideas often assume a mystic character and are associated with a state of euphoria which may reach the intensity of ecstasy," and we have a fairly complete clinical picture of the epileptic.

What is more, we have a fairly recognizable portrait of the Feodor Dostoevsky who emerges for us in the novels and letters, so recognizable that it must be impossible for the intelligent critic to ignore it. Can we, in this light, follow such a critic as Mr. Murry, who would have us regard Dostoevsky as a seer, as a leader of thought, one who will take us beautifully into a new intellectual realm in which the truth is especially luminous? What we must have, in a leader of this sort, is sanity—it is no use begging the question, as Mr. Murry does, by endeavoring, as it were, to discredit "sanity" on the witness-stand. Sanity is a relative thing, true enough, it is the relative freedom of the sound mind in the sound body. In the case of Dostoevsky this freedom was impaired by a specific cause of which, happily, we know the specific effects. It is no use setting up, as Mr. Murry does, Dostoevsky's "timelessness" and "mystic terror" and excessive religious humanitarianism as absolute virtues, for we cannot help seeing them as products of a disease. Tuberculosis makes its victims optimistic, but we do not necessarily accept their views of life. Why, then, should we accept, as something *ex cathedra*, the turbid mysticism, the febrile hypochondria, of Dostoevsky? We might as well adore the disease that produced them.

No, we find it impossible to accept as a seer, as a thinker, one on whom the stigma of psychic compulsion is so plain. Dostoevsky is perhaps the supreme instance of the compulsive nature of the artist's ideas. But if that means that we cannot take too seriously his "ideas," it does not mean that we cannot take him seriously as an artist, as a creator, whether it is only to see in him, as Mr. Hueffer does, "a portentous writer of enormous detective stories," or to see in him, as many other critics have done, the greatest of all novelists. Granted that he was, as Mr. Murry says, the "most sensitive soul" which the modern world has produced, he was also an injured soul, and his novels are the profuse, extraordinary record of that injury, the bewildered confession of an acutely sensitive but grievously wounded sensorium. Seen in this light, especially, but indeed seen in any light, his novels are "dreams": confused, wandering, crowded; lighted everywhere with the red light of fever.

Dostoevsky himself admitted more than once that he had little "control" of his story—he chronicles, in one of his letters, his difficulties with *The Possessed,* in which a new hero, one who had originally been designed for a somewhat minor role, took possession of the novel; he speaks elsewhere of the "shapelessness" of his stories; he reproaches those who demand of a man in his circumstances, "lucid art, effortless and untroubled poetry"; but he comes no nearer to lucidity or to the untroubled in *The Brothers Karamazov,* the only one of his novels composed at leisure. His novels are, in fact, dreams in a Freudian sense, since they are the projection, again and again, of his own difficulties in life. His characters all verge on the hysterical or epileptic— some of them project, as it were, one phase of the disease, and some another.

It is possible to carry too far this theory of genesis, but one hardly hesitates in ascribing to epileptic mysticism and euphoria the origins of Myshkin, of Sonia, of Alyosha, as one also is prone to see, on the other hand, in the "evil" or perverse phases of epilepsy, the origins of Rogozhin, Raskolnikov, Svidrigailov. One need not simplify excessively—there are other factors to be considered. There is, for example, Dostoevsky's metaphysical preoccupation with the problem of good and evil, a problem which essentially provides the core of all his greatest work: the theme, if we see it in abstract, of *The Idiot, The Possessed, Crime and Punishment, The Brothers Karamazov;* the theme, for once explicitly, of *Notes from Underground.* But do we not see the stigma of disease, once more, precisely in this excessive morbid preoccupation? It was a problem with which Dostoevsky was obsessed; the sense of "evil" rode him like a demon, a protean demon which at one moment was the monstrous symbol of pain, at another the symbol of the sense of horror and futility which arises from too acute a consciousness of the blank, empty, and indifferent determinism in which the human consciousness finds itself enmeshed.

In his analysis of the latter sensation, Dostoevsky went extraordinarily far—has anyone been more conscious, as it were, of consciousness, or so singularly and persistently endeavored to shed the light inward on himself? The tissue of that analysis is a marvel of impalpability, the logical filaments are luminous and exquisite, and we only begin to see the fundamental error when we see that the logic is more often one of sensation or feeling than one of thought, and that the datum from which it all grows is the assumption, natural only to the injured and abnormal mind, that the measure of one's "awareness" is precisely the measure of one's "disgust."

But we need not subscribe to Dostoevsky's ideas to delight in his novels—we are wise if we accept them simply as amazing psychotic improvisations on a theme, psychological symphonies of unparalleled sensitiveness and richness; and if we are bound to wonder whether their characteristic extravagant vehemence is not a hint that the composition of them was often precisely an "epileptic equivalent," that need not lessen for us in the slightest our delight in abandoning ourselves to the torrent. What we come to is the fact that the later novels are not a transcription or representation of our actual world—they have their contact with it, obviously, their roots in it, but they flower, remotely and strangely, in another and translunar atmosphere. They approach, by this kind of singular abstraction and attenuated contact with the real, an "absoluteness" in fiction which we can perhaps only parallel, odd as the parallel seems, with the later novels of Henry James—*The Golden Bowl, The Wings of the Dove, The Awkward Age, What Maisie Knew, The Ambassadors.* I do not suggest any such absurdity as that these novels resemble, in any other remotest particular, *Crime and Punishment* or *The Brothers Karamazov.* Dostoevsky did not, as James did, calculate his effect; he was not even aware of it. He asked, in one of his letters, "Is not my fantastic *Idiot* the very dailiest truth?" Well, of course it is not; nor do we wish it to be. It is perhaps something better than the truth.

That much of contemporary poetry is written rather for the eye than for the ear—even, perhaps the greater part of it—has been often observed, and that it constitutes a grievous loss to the poetry itself cannot, one thinks, be seriously questioned. And the loss is not a simple one, either. It is not merely a matter of sacrificing a certain sensuous or decorative quality, or combination of qualities, for whatever compensating virtues of exactness, austerity, unsentimentality, easy colloquialism: it is not merely beauty of form, beauty of sound, that is flung out so ruthlessly in this passion for the antipoetic: it is, on the contrary, in a very important measure the sense, the *meaning*, which gets itself inadvertently flung out, like the baby with the bath. Poetry, alas, is not science, it is not statistics, it is not algebra or geometry, it is not philosophy, it is not music. It may and should incorporate elements of these, but it can never attain to the cold, pure abstractness which is the principle they have in common without *ipso facto* ceasing to be itself.

For the meaning of poetry, like the meaning of language itself, is double: it consists of both sense and sound: and paradoxically it might well be argued that the sense, the poetic sense, is more in the sound than in the so-called or obvious "meaning." It is precisely in the sound-effects, or more properly the sound-*aff*ects, and in its deliberate use of the feeling-tones and associations inherent in them, that poetry most characteristically takes its departure from prose. It is thus a perpetual renewal of language. It remembers that language is oral, that it must be whispered or spoken or shouted or sung, and that it is only in the knowing and ordering of these affective sound-values that language again becomes whole and our meaning complete. After science, or statistics, or algebra, or geometry, even after philosophy and music, poetry has the last word. In poetry, could it not be maintained? always comes man's final statement, at whatever point in the evolution of his awareness. It is the whole speech of the whole man. The feelings, the affects, are again reincorporated at a new level, no matter how complex the statement, and we speak once more as we should and must: not only of what we know, but also of

· Also reviewed here: Kenneth Rexroth, Ralph Gustafson, and John Malcolm Brinnin.

what we consciously, and even unconsciously, *feel* about what we know.

To neglect or despise sound-values, therefore, is, practically speaking, to use only one half of the poetic language, and to the poet's cost. Impatient he may be with certain *kinds* of effect, for there are changing fashions in these as in all matters of form; but if he discards he must also invent. Mr. Eberhart, for example, shows that he is very much aware of this necessity, and even concerned about it, but one is hardly convinced by anything in his new selection that he is any nearer to his private solution. His "Groundhog" remains one of the most remarkable of contemporary poems, its Blakian intensity and fierceness of vision unimpaired, if not actually enhanced, by the wanton roughness of form, the perverse metrics; and the variant of it which appears in "Triptych," recast in the key of Jacobean canting and ranting, is almost as good. But Mr. Eberhart, either because his ear is defective or because he is overanxious to avoid the merely smooth, makes the not uncommon mistake of establishing violence and perversity as his norm, with the inevitable result that where everything shrieks and clashes, the uproar at last cancels itself out, and it is as if nothing had been heard at all. This is a great pity, for he has a wonderful energy of vision, together with a fine gusto in phrase and an enviably muscular capacity for compressed statement: if he could only be severe with himself, and canalize his gifts, instead of simply going hell-for-leather at his Idea, with capitals, he could be one of the very best of contemporary poets, as he is already one of the most exciting.

Mr. Kenneth Rexroth, who began his poetic career as an Objectivist, is now, with his new book, *The Phoenix and the Tortoise*, a welcome addition to the very small company of poets who are not afraid of long-form. The title poem is a long philosophical meditation, scientific in temper, pagan in flavor, historical in method, devoted, along with the shorter poems which follow, "to the discovery of a basis for the recreation of a system of values in sacramental marriage," to quote from the author's preface. One need not follow this, or agree with it, and one feels occasionally that some of the "largeness" in Mr. Rexroth's poem is akin to that somewhat specious and stagey largeness which California so impartially visits upon trees, fruits and prophets alike; but this is an impressive piece of work, very much alive intellectually, as impressive for its obvious integrity as for its range: here is a poet to be reckoned with. One's chief complaint, as with Mr. Eberhart, is over the matter of form, of sound-effect: but whereas Mr. Eberhart surfeits us with too much violence and cacophony, Mr. Rexroth goes to the opposite extreme and gives us no sound at all: particularly in the title poem, this is the most entirely visual poetry that one could imagine—visual, that is, in the sense that it is meant for the eye, on the printed page, and not at all for the gratification of the ear. It is limpid, it flows, it is always agreeably readable, but of mnemonic or sensuous or formal device it is usually disdainful, and for that reason, despite its intellectual vitality, it slips out of memory as fast as it is read. That Mr. Rexroth can do better about this when he wants to, is shown in such admirable short pieces, of a more descriptive sort, as "Now on this day of the first hundred flowers."

Much that one says of Mr. Eberhart can be said as pertinently of Mr. Ralph Gustafson, a young Canadian poet. But with a difference. Mr. Gustafson has Hopkins a little too much on his mind, he is determined to make things very hard for himself, and here we have tortured syntax, tortured order, tortured everything—anything, almost, if only to avoid the merely straightforward and formal and simple. But Mr. Gustafson has an eye, and he loves words and the feel of language, and for all its strainings after effect, this is an unusual first book.

Mr. Brinnin is a pegasus of another color entirely. The exception in this quartet of poets, he is an extremely competent, sometimes brilliant, exponent of form and tone-color, and what worries one about this new book of his is something else: it is the fact that it falls so much into a contemporary poetic "fashion." Here is all that baggage of tired and disillusioned intellectualism with which we are so familiar—the so carefully negative and latinate epithets, the continuous watchfulness to mitigate, to abstract, to deprecate, as if to feel too strongly, or too obviously, or not in terms of the self-contradictorily intricate, were somehow to be poetically indecent:

The vision of an old cosmology
And all who in its service die
On rivieras of the intellect.

And the negative angels, and all the rest of it. This is a poetry that wants to be cosmic, but also to sneer at the cosmic, and itself; and what it adds up to is something very like decadence. But Mr. Brinnin often proves himself to be much better than the

fashion he follows, and one does not doubt that he will do so
again.

ELIOT, T. S. (1916)

As anthologies go nowadays, Mr. Pound's *Catholic Anthology*
is an interesting one. *Catholic,* to be sure, seems somewhat of a
misnomer for it—the selection is perhaps catholic as far as the
more radical modern poets are concerned (though even here
with signal omissions—the Imagists, for instance) but certainly
it makes no pretense at inclusion of the more conservative.
When Mr. Pound says Catholic, it appears that he means catholic
as regards the comparatively small group of radicals with whom,
for the moment, he is in sympathy—with the addition of two
conservatives who must be conciliated, Harold Monro and Harriet Monroe.

Within these limits the selection is an interesting one. Dull
things there are, of course—each critic will find his own—but
for the present critic the *Catholic Anthology* seems worth while
if only for the inclusion of *The Love Song of J. Alfred Prufrock,*
and the *Portrait of a Lady* by T. S. Eliot. These are remarkable. They are individual to a degree. Mr. Eliot uses free rhyme
very effectively, often musically; and with the minimum of
sacrifice to form conveys a maximum of atmosphere. Both
poems are psychological character-studies, subtle to the verge
of insoluble idiosyncrasy, introspective, self-gnawing. Those who
are constitutionally afraid to analyze themselves, who do not
think, who are not psychologically imaginative, will distrust
and perhaps dislike them. In this volume, they stand as the
crystallization of the efforts of the other contributors: one feels
that here, in some such form as this, is the logical outcome of
such unfinished, though often brilliant work, as that of Messrs.
Masters, Bodenheim, Pound, and Rodker. For the rest of the
book, the ten portraits taken from *Spoon River* are well selected: among them are some of the best. Mr. Pound's selections
from his own work are in his pleasantest aphoristic manner. For
these, and for one or two other interesting things here and there,
one accepts the remainder, and forgives the disordered and
Whitmaniac egotism of Orrick Johns, the truisms of Allen Up-

ward, the seductive dullness of *The Letter from Peking*, and the hysterical movie scenarios of John Rodker.

It is a pity, of course, that Mr. Pound's quarrel with the Imagists has prevented the inclusion of any of the works of the more romantic of the radicals—that the whole volume should be composed (unless one excepts Mr. Eliot?) of the realistic. But perhaps Mr. Pound would object to these terms—and perhaps the Imagists would too. It should be added that any anthology, which, like this, blows the horn of revolution in poetry, whether sound or unsound, is at the least certain to interest all poets, even the most conservative; and will, perhaps, be of value to them.

ELIOT, T. S.   (1921)

Mr. T. S. Eliot has, as we know, an eye for the odd, and yet that is not to do him complete justice: his eye is for what is significant in the odd; and thus it is that we find him quoting, opposite the first page of his small, delightful book of criticism, *The Sacred Wood*, the cryptic line: "I also like to dine on becaficas." Becaficas? If one is not expert in sixteenth- and seventeenth-century literature one learns from the dictionary that becaficas are "small birds" or "warblers" or "golden orioles": what the Italian peasant would indiscriminately term *uccellini*. Mr. Eliot, that is, likes to dine on song-birds; and he apprises us, with a gleaming and slightly sinister politeness, that he is about to do so. Would Mr. Eliot have us suppose that there is a trace of ferocity in this attitude? Does he wish to appear as something of a monster, perhaps in contrast to the sentimentality and idolatry which too often masquerade as criticism of poetry? One need not take the point too seriously. Yet it does afford, no doubt, a glimpse of motive. We are aware that Mr. Eliot intends, very deliberately intends, to be analytic and severe— severe even to the point of destructiveness. Nor is one, in this regard, disappointed. His book is severe and analytic, and one can think of no two qualities in criticism which are at the moment more desirable. We should like to see every one of the thousand poets in this country with a copy of *The Sacred Wood* in his hands. It would perhaps restore to some that wholesome sense of the responsibility of the poet which, in America, has been weakened throughout our entire literary history by our proneness, as a young nation, to a maternal tenderness toward the local product. Mr. Eliot insists upon the value of tradition: it is a value which can not, just now, be too much insisted upon. He insists, again, on the elimination, as far as possible, of irrelevant emotional factors which may interfere with the best judgment of art: there is no country, which pretends to any interest in art, where that doctrine is needed as America needs it.

But if to say these things is to praise Mr. Eliot's book on general grounds, is to praise, in a general sense, his temper and his attitude, it is not our intention to praise his temper and attitude unreservedly. It is, perhaps, rather what Mr. Eliot intends, in temper and attitude, than what he achieves, that we like. It is a good thing, at this moment, to have a young critic who so deliberately, even contemptuously, turns his back on the contemporary, and who endeavors to see afresh such poets as Massinger, Jonson, Blake, Dante, even Shakespeare. Mr. Eliot is not timid, nor is he without learning; he speaks with confidence. One admires also, if one be in sympathy with that sort of thing, his tendency toward what might properly be termed the scientific method in criticism. But it is precisely here that one begins to qualify praise; for although one may agree with Mr. Eliot that criticism might profitably be more scientific, one is by no means convinced that *The Sacred Wood* takes criticism very far in that direction, nor, indeed, that Mr. Eliot *sees* very far in that direction. It is clear enough that for scientific criticism a very definite *point d'appui* will be indispensable, even if the *point d'appui* be only that aesthetic values are relative. The critic should apprise us at the outset what his attitude will be, thus enabling us to discount it. He must, therefore, be clear as to his attitude, must know thoroughly and easily the world of values in which he moves, must decide in advance what terms he will use. His terms should be expressly defined. If he intends, for example, to use the word "feeling" in the modern psychological sense, as distinct from "emotion," he should say so in advance, lest his reader be confused; or else substitute for it the less equivocal word "affect."

Mr. Eliot is not, in these matters, precise. He has been infected by modern psychology, and he uses the terms of it not infrequently; but the basis from which he employs it shifts, and one is not sure that he is aware of the shift. Not with impunity can one mix the James-Lange set of terms with the terms of Freud: nor again the terms of de Gourmont (who was an amateur psychologist, and often a misleading one) with those of Kostyleff. Poetry, says Mr. Eliot on one occasion, "is not the expression of personality, but an escape from personality." On another occasion he says: "Massinger had not the personality to create great farce." Again, he quotes with approval de Gourmont ("Problème du style"): "*Le but de l'activité propre de l'homme est de nettoyer sa personnalité, de la laver de toutes les souillures qu'y déposa l'éducation . . .*" Of Massinger again: "His personality hardly exists." Now perhaps Mr. Eliot has something definite in mind when he speaks of personality, and perhaps he has some theory of the manner in which the personality of the poet relates to his work; but he fails to make either thing clear. To what extent, when he thinks of personality, is he thinking of sensibility? If sensibility be called *a* and experience *b*, then is personality *ab*? And would this make de Gourmont's advice meaningless? And, in the upshot, do we not make it clear that "personality" is so vague a word as to be useless, even dangerous, if it is our intention to be scientific?

Mr. Eliot perceives keenly the need for definition: love of definition is one of his most obvious characteristics. He performs an admirable service of this sort when, in his essay on "Poetic Drama," he opens a coroner's inquest on the word "rhetoric." But his sense of the definite is intermittent; it abandons him often at the most critical moment, and in consequence Mr. Eliot himself is forever abandoning *us* on the very doorstep of the illuminating. One has again and again the feeling that he is working, as it were, too close to the object. He is meticulous without being clear; he passes quickly from one detail of analysis to another; he is aggressively aware that he is "thinking," his brow is knit; but he appears to believe that mere fineness of analysis will constitute, in the sequence of his comments, a direction. What happens is that he achieves a kind of filigree without pattern. He does not always know in advance where he is going, and it often occurs, therefore, that he takes the wrong train of thought. That his talk continues to be of extraordinary interest does not avail: he is rapidly borne out of earshot. "*On pense mal quand on sait que l'on pense.*" Mr. Eliot is so intent on being intelligent at every point, in every sentence, in every syllable, that many of his pages become mere incoherences of cleverness; the evidence of thought is weighty, but the value of it is vague.

If Mr. Eliot is only intermittently and at times sciolistically a psychologist in his effort toward a scientific method, one must observe also that at the very basis of his attitude, where it is most explicit, in the essay called "The Perfect Critic," he is least scientific. The ignorant reader (I quote a passage in that essay) "is unable to distinguish the poetry from an emotional state aroused in himself by the poetry, a state which may be merely an indulgence of his own emotion. . . . The end of the enjoyment of poetry is a pure contemplation from which all the accidents of personal emotion are removed; thus we aim to see the object as it really is. . . ." Is this "pure contemplation" perhaps a chimera? Is poetry an object, or an experience, a relation to an object, a relation between ourselves and a set of stimuli which the artist has "arranged"? If the latter, which of the emotions aroused in us are the "accidental"? The artist alone can tell us. I do not know, here, whether I agree or disagree with Mr. Eliot: I wish merely to point out that in what is obviously meant to be an important passage he falls far short of being clear. Supplement, moreover, the passage just quoted with this, from the essay on *Hamlet* (a play which Mr. Eliot terms an artistic failure): "And probably more people have thought *Hamlet* a work of art because they found it interesting than have found it interesting because it is a work of art. It is the 'Mona Lisa' of literature." This statement is quite logical in its context. It is here significant because it arouses a suspicion that Mr. Eliot is distrustful of the artist who uses "interesting" material, that he prefers the work of art which is a triumph over material of which the direct "emotional" interest is less obvious (the plays of Massinger and Jonson, for example). But surely a work of art is no less a work of art for dealing with an emotional experience which interests or charms us than for dealing with one that repels or leaves us indifferent? Let us again have recourse to algebra: let x represent a theme which "interests" us, y a theme which does not, z the utmost possible skill of arrangement of the theme. It will be clear that xz will delight us more than yz. And it is proper, is it not, that this should be so? Mr. Eliot desires, of course, to make a distinction between the "emotional" appeal which a work of art may make, and the "aesthetic" appeal. The distinction is worth making, but not if it leads the critic to condemn the former in order to exalt the latter, or if it leads him to attempt to isolate the latter, for "pure contemplation."

All of this is confusing because it is part of an attempt to make a beginning of scientific criticism on what is really a secondary plane. It is useless, or nearly useless, to attempt an estimate of the "skill" of a work of art, because, as long as we do not know what the work of art is for, we can not hope to know precisely what will constitute skill. If criticism is to be a science, then we must begin with an attempt to understand what is the function of art, socially and psychologically. What is the function of art in the community? In the life of the artist? This must be the starting-point, and the inquiry will deal very largely, at the outset, precisely with the question of "theme" as distinguishable from "arrangement." Analysis of the "aesthetic" values will come later.

Mr. Eliot's perplexity and obscurity and lack of coherence result from the fact that he is on this secondary plane and does not know it. It would be extremely unjust, however, to leave it at that. His observations are acute, his temperateness is refreshing. It is a testimonial to the range and ingenuity of his mind that as one puts down his book one thinks of so many points about which one would like to quarrel with him, and quarrel, moreover, respectfully. *Is Hamlet* a failure as a work of art? *Does* Mr. Eliot find, in his essay on that play, the "objective correlative" of his conviction? *Was* a suitable mythological or philosophical framework, provided by tradition, lacking for Blake? With such questions as these Mr. Eliot invites us to a meditation prolonged and delicious. . . . Nor would one forget to abuse him for his clever but insufficient theory of the prose style of Mr. Arthur Symons.

ELIOT, T. S.   (1923)

Mr. T. S. Eliot is one of the most individual of contemporary poets, and at the same time, anomalously, one of the most "traditional." By individual I mean that he can be, and often is (distressingly, to some) aware in his own way; as when he observes of a woman (in "Rhapsody on a Windy Night") that the door "opens on her like a grin" and that the corner of her eye "Twists like a crooked pin." Everywhere, in the very small body of his work, is similar evidence of a delicate sensibility, somewhat shrinking, somewhat injured, and always sharply itself. But also, with this capacity or necessity for being aware in his own way, Mr. Eliot has a haunting, a tyrannous awareness that there have been many other awarenesses before; and that the extent of his own awareness, and perhaps even the nature of it, is a consequence of these. He is, more than most poets, conscious of his roots. If this consciousness had not become acute in *Prufrock* or the *Portrait of a Lady*, it was nevertheless probably there: and the roots were quite conspicuously French, and dated, say, 1870-1900. A little later, as his sense of the past had become more pressing, it seemed that he was positively redirecting his roots—urging them to draw a morbid dramatic sharpness from Webster and Donne, a faded dry gilt of cynicism and formality from the Restoration. This search of the tomb produced "Sweeney" and "Whispers of Immortality." And finally, in *The Waste Land*, Mr. Eliot's sense of the literary past has become so overmastering as almost to constitute the motive of the work. It is as if, in conjunction with the Mr. Pound of the *Cantos*, he wanted to make a "literature of literature"—a poetry actuated not more by life itself than by poetry; as if he had concluded that the characteristic awareness of a poet of the twentieth century must inevitably, or ideally, be a very complex and very literary awareness, able to speak only, or best, in terms of the literary past, the terms which had molded its tongue. This involves a kind of idolatry of literature with which it is a little difficult to sympathize. In positing, as it seems to, that there is nothing left for literature to do but become a kind of parasitic growth on literature, a sort of mistletoe, it involves, I think, a definite astigmatism—a distortion. But the theory is interesting if only because it has colored an important and brilliant piece of work.

The Waste Land is unquestionably important, unquestionably brilliant. It is important partly because its 433 lines summarize Mr. Eliot, for the moment, and demonstrate that he is an even better poet than most had thought; and partly because it embodies the theory just touched upon, the theory of the "allusive" method in poetry. *The Waste Land* is, indeed, a poem of allusion all compact. It purports to be symbolical; most of its symbols are drawn from literature or legend; and Mr. Eliot has thought it necessary to supply, in notes, a list of the many quotations, references, and translations with which it bristles. He observes candidly that the poem presents "difficulties," and requires "elucidation." This serves to raise at once, the question whether these difficulties, in which perhaps Mr. Eliot takes a little pride, are so much the result of complexity, a fine elaborateness, as of confusion. The poem has been compared, by one reviewer, to a "full-rigged ship built in a bottle," the suggestion being that it is a perfect piece of construction. But *is* it a perfect piece of construction? Is the complex material mastered, and made coherent? Or, if the poem is not successful in that way, in what way *is* it successful? Has it the formal and intellectual complex unity of a microscopic Divine Comedy; or is its unity—supposing it to have one—of another sort?

If we leave aside for the moment all other considerations, and read the poem solely with the intention of understanding, with the aid of the notes, the symbolism; of making out what it is that is symbolized, and how these symbolized feelings are brought into relation with each other and with the other matters in the poem; I think we must, with reservations, and with no invidiousness, conclude that the poem is not, in any formal sense, coherent. We cannot feel that all the symbolisms belong quite inevitably where they have been put; that the order of the parts is an inevitable order; that there is anything more than a rudimentary progress from one theme to another; nor that the relation between the more symbolic parts and the less is always as definite as it should be. What we feel is that Mr. Eliot has not wholly annealed the allusive matter, has left it unabsorbed, lodged in gleaming fragments amid material alien to it. Again, there is a distinct weakness consequent on the use of allusions which may have both intellectual and emotional value for Mr. Eliot, but (even with the notes) none for us. The "Waste Land" of the Grail Legend might be a good symbol, if it were something with which we were sufficiently familiar. But it can never, even when explained, be a good symbol, simply because it has no immediate associations for us. It might, of course, be a good *theme*. In that case it would be *given* us. But Mr. Eliot uses it for purposes of overtone; he refers to it; and as overtone it quite clearly fails. He gives us, superbly, a waste land—not *the* Waste Land. Why, then, refer to the latter at all—if he is not, in the poem, really going to use it? Hyacinth fails in the same way. So does the Fisher King. So does the Hanged Man, which Mr. Eliot tells us he associates with Frazer's Hanged God—we take his word for it. But if the precise association is worth anything, it is worth *putting into the poem;* otherwise there can be no purpose in mentioning it. Why, again, Datta, Dayadhvam, Damyata? Or Shantih? Do they not say a good deal less for us than "Give: sympathize: control" or "Peace"? Of course; but Mr. Eliot replies that he wants them not merely to mean those particular things, but also to mean them in a particular way—that is, to be remembered in connection with a Upanishad. Unfortunately, we have

none of us this memory, nor can he give it to us; and in the upshot he gives us only a series of agreeable sounds which might
as well have been nonsense. What we get at, and I think it is
important, is that in none of these particular cases does the
reference, the allusion, justify itself intrinsically, make itself
felt. When we are aware of these references at all (sometimes
they are unidentifiable) we are aware of them simply as something unintelligible but suggestive. When they have been explained, we are aware of the material referred to, the fact, (for
instance, a vegetation ceremony,) as something useless for our
enjoyment or understanding of the poem, something distinctly
"dragged in," and only, perhaps, of interest as having suggested
a pleasantly ambiguous line. For unless an allusion is made to
live identifiably, to flower where transplanted, it is otiose. We
admit the beauty of the implicational or allusive method; but
the key to an implication should be in the implication itself, not
outside of it. We admit the value of esoteric pattern: but the
pattern should disclose its secret, should not be dependent on a
cypher. Mr. Eliot assumes for his allusions, and for the fact that
they actually allude to something, an importance which the allusions themselves do not, as expressed, aesthetically command,
nor, as explained, logically command; which is pretentious. He
is a little pretentious, too, in his "plan"—*qui pourtant n'existe
pas*. If it is a plan, then its principle is oddly akin to planless-
ness. Here and there, in the wilderness, a broken finger-post.

I enumerate these objections not, I must, emphasize, in
derogation of the poem, but to dispel, if possible, an illusion
as to its nature. It is perhaps important to note that Mr. Eliot,
with his comment on the "plan," and several critics, with their
admiration of the poem's woven complexity, minister to the
idea that *The Waste Land* is, precisely, a kind of epic in a wal-
nut shell: elaborate, ordered, unfolded with a logic at every
joint discernible; but it is also important to note that this idea
is false. With or without the notes the poem belongs rather to
that symbolical order in which one may justly say that the
"meaning" is not explicitly, or exactly, worked out. Mr. Eliot's
net is wide, its meshes are small; and he catches a good
deal more—thank heaven—than he pretends to. If space permitted one could pick out many lines and passages and parodies
and quotations which do not demonstrably, in any "logical"
sense, carry forward the theme, passages which unjustifiably,
but happily, "expand" beyond its purpose. Thus the poem has
an emotional value far clearer and richer than its arbitrary and

rather unworkable logical value. One might assume that it originally consisted of a number of separate poems which have been telescoped—given a kind of forced unity. The Waste Land conception offered itself as a generous net which would, if not unify, at any rate contain these varied elements. We are aware of a superficial "binding"—we observe the anticipation and repetition of themes, motifs; "Fear death by water" anticipates the episode of Phlebas, the cry of the nightingale is repeated; but these are pretty flimsy links, and do not genuinely bind because they do not reappear naturally, but arbitrarily. This suggests, indeed, that Mr. Eliot is perhaps attempting a kind of program music in words, endeavoring to rule out "emotional accidents" by supplying his readers, in notes, with only those associations which are correct. He himself hints at the musical analogy when he observes that "In the first part of Part V three themes are employed."

I think, therefore, that the poem must be taken—most invitingly offers itself—as a brilliant and kaleidoscopic confusion; as a series of sharp, discrete, slightly related perceptions and feelings, dramatically and lyrically presented, and violently juxtaposed, (for effect of dissonance) so as to give us an impression of an intensely modern, intensely literary consciousness which perceives itself to be not a unit but a chance correlation or conglomerate of mutually discolorative fragments. We are invited into a mind, a world, which is a "broken bundle of mirrors"; a "heap of broken images." Isn't it that Mr. Eliot, finding it "impossible to say just what he means"—to recapitulate, to enumerate all the events and discoveries and memories that make a consciousness—has emulated the "magic lantern" that throws "the nerves in pattern on a screen"? If we perceive the poem in this light, as a series of brilliant, brief, unrelated or dimly related pictures by which a consciousness empties itself of its characteristic contents, then we also perceive that, anomalously, though the dropping out of any one picture would not in the least affect the logic or "meaning" of the whole, it would seriously detract from the value of the portrait. The "plan" of the poem would not greatly suffer, one makes bold to assert, by the elimination of "April is the cruelest month," or Phlebas, or the Thames daughters, or Sosostris or "You gave me hyacinths" or "A woman drew her long black hair out tight"; nor would it matter if it did. These things are not important parts of an important or careful intellectual pattern; but they are important parts of an important emotional ensemble. The relations between Tiresias (who is said to unify the poem, in a sense, as spectator) and the Waste Land, or Mr. Eugenides, or Hyacinth, or any other fragment, is a dim and tonal one, not exact. It will not bear analysis, it is not always operating, nor can one with assurance, at any given point, say how much it is operating. In this sense *The Waste Land* is a series of separate poems or passages, not perhaps all written at one time or with one aim, to which a spurious but happy sequence has been given. This spurious sequence has a value—it creates the necessary superficial formal unity; but it need not be stressed, as the Notes stress it. Could one not wholly rely for one's unity—as Mr. Eliot *has* largely relied— simply on the dim unity of "personality" which would underlie the retailed contents of a single consciousness? Unless one is going to carry unification very far, weave and interweave very closely, it would perhaps be as well not to unify at all; to dispense, for example, with arbitrary repetitions.

We reach thus the conclusion that the poem succeeds—as it brilliantly does—by virtue of its incoherence, not of its plan; by virtue of its ambiguities, not of its explanations. Its incoherence is a virtue because its *donnée* is incoherence. Its rich, vivid, crowded use of implication is a virtue, as implication is *always* a virtue—it shimmers, it suggests, it gives the desired strangeness. But when, as often, Mr. Eliot uses an implication beautifully—conveys by means of a picture-symbol or action-symbol a feeling—we do not require to be told that he had in mind a passage in the *Encyclopedia*, or the color of his nursery wall; the information is disquieting, has a sour air of pedantry. We "accept" the poem as we would accept a powerful, melancholy tone-poem. We do not want to be told what occurs; nor is it more than mildly amusing to know what passages are, in the Straussian manner, echoes or parodies. We cannot believe that every syllable has an algebraic inevitability, nor would we wish it so. We could dispense with the French, Italian, Latin, and Hindu phrases—they are irritating. But when our reservations have all been made, we accept *The Waste Land* as one of the most moving and original poems of our time. It captures us. And we sigh, with a dubious eye on the "notes" and "plan," our bewilderment that after so fine a performance Mr. Eliot should have thought it an occasion for calling "Tullia's ape a marmosyte." Tullia's ape is good enough.

It has been often enough, perhaps too often said, of late, that the almost fatal difficulty which confronts the poet nowadays is the difficulty of finding a theme which might be worth his power. If he be potentially a "major" poet, this difficulty is thought to be particularly formidable, if not actually crippling; but for even the "minor" poet (to use minor in no pejorative sense) it is considered serious. Mr. T. S. Eliot, whose *Poems* have been reprinted by Mr. Knopf, has himself contributed something to this theory. In his admirable note on Blake, in *The Sacred Wood,* he suggests that Blake was potentially a major poet who was robbed of his birthright by the mere accident of there not being, at the moment, a prepared or traditional cosmology or mythology of sufficient wealth to engage, or disengage, his great imaginative power. He was compelled, in the absence of such a frame, to invent a frame for himself; and in this was, perhaps inevitably, doomed to failure. Had he been born to a belief as rich and profound as that which Dante inherited, might he not have been as great a poet? . . .

This is an ingenious idea; but it is possible to take it too seriously. It is obvious enough that some sort of tradition is a very great help to a poet—it floats him and sustains him, it carries him more swiftly and easily than he could carry himself, and it indicates a direction for him. But a fact too often lost sight of, at the present time, is that the great poet may be, precisely, one who has a capacity to find, at *any* given moment, a theme sufficient for the proper exercise of his strength. There were contemporaries of Dante who were excellent poets, but for whom the cosmology which enchanted Dante was not evocative. If Blake scanned his horizon in vain for "huge cloudy symbols," Goethe, scanning the same horizon, was not so unsuccessful. It is true enough that, with the decay of religion as a force in human life, poetry must be robbed of that particular kind of conviction, as has been noted by Mr. I. A. Richards; but to assume from this that the poetry of the future must inevitably be a poetry of skepticism or negation is perhaps to oversimplify the issue. Poetry has always shown itself able to keep step easily and naturally with the utmost that man can do in extending his knowledge, no matter how destructive of existing beliefs that knowledge may be. Each accretion of knowledge becomes, by degrees, a part of man's emotional attitude to the world, takes on affective values or overtones, and is then ready for use in poetry. The universe does not become each year simpler or less disturbing: nor is there any reason to suppose that it ever will. The individual who is born into it will continue to be surprised and delighted by it, or surprised and injured; and in direct ratio with this surprise and delight or surprise and injury, he will continue to be a poet.

The wail of contemporary criticism, therefore, to the effect that poetry can find nothing to cling to, leaves one a little skeptical: though it is easy enough to sympathize with the individual poets who, suffering from that delusion, have for the moment lost themselves in self-distrust. Mr. Pound and Mr. Eliot are perhaps very typical victims of this kind. But whereas Mr. Pound has evaded the issue, seeking asylum in a sense of the past (rather half-heartedly held) Mr. Eliot has made a poetry of the predicament itself. His poetry has been from the outset a poetry of self-consciousness; of instinct at war with doubt, and sensibility at odds with reason; an air of precocious cynicism has hung over it; and his development as a poet has not been so much a widening of his field—though at first sight *The Waste Land* might suggest this—as a deepening of his awareness of it. Prufrock, who antedated by a decade the later poem, could not give himself to his emotions or his instincts because he could not bring himself, *sub specie aeternitatis,* quite to believe in them: he was inhibited, and preferred to remain a despairing spectator: but at the same time he wished that he might have been a simpler organism, "a pair of ragged claws." The theme of *Gerontion,* a good many years later, is the same: it is again the paralyzing effect of consciousness, the "after such knowledge, what forgiveness?" And *The Waste Land* is again a recapitulation, reaching once more the same point of acute agony of doubt, the same distrust of decision or action, with its "awful daring of a moment's surrender, which an age of prudence can never retract."

The reissue of *Poems* is not the occasion for a detailed review of Mr. Eliot's early work, however; for our present purpose it is sufficient to note that Mr. Eliot has conspicuously shared the contemporary feeling that there are no "large" themes for the poet, and that he has had the courage and the perspicacity to take as his theme precisely this themelessness. Why not—he says in effect—make a bitter sort of joke of one's nihilism and impotence? And in making his bitter joke, he has written some of the most searchingly unhappy and vivid and individual of contemporary poetry. One feels that his future is secure, by virtue of his honesty quite as much as by virtue of his genius.

ELIOT, T. S.   (1929)

If it is impossible to read Mr. T. S. Eliot's criticism without respect, it is also becoming increasingly impossible to read it without misgivings. In *The Sacred Wood*, and again in *Homage to John Dryden*, Mr. Eliot provided his immediate generation with a group of literary essays that were an admirable corrective for many of the intellectual and aesthetic disorders of the time. They were compact, precise, astringent; they brought the past to bear on the present, the present into a visible relation with the past; in short, they helped materially to restore, for a literary generation which had lost its bearings, a sense of tradition as a living and fruitful thing. If one had any complaint to make, with regard to these essays, it was not of their main tendency, which was wholesome; nor had one any fault to find with Mr. Eliot's intelligence and aesthetic tact, which were acute; it was rather with regard to the plane on which Mr. Eliot chose to conduct his analysis—and the tone which he adopted—that one might have caviled. In the matter of plane, one had to note that Mr. Eliot tended to be somewhat abstract, not to say academic. His analysis was more often analysis of the document itself than of the psychological dynamics of which the document was the sign; he seemed to regard literary forms as absolute and autonomous; and correspondingly, he seemed to minimize the merely functional, or social and psychological, elements in the creation of literature.

These restrictions made for simplicity and weight; but they also gave one an uncomfortable feeling that a great deal was being left out. In his very preoccupation with what was past and fixed, Mr. Eliot was perhaps already beginning to define himself, and his limitations, more candidly than he was quite aware. It was as if the immediate, the fluidly immediate, the here and now—whether it were to be seen in terms of personality and the relation of personality to the work of art, or in terms of the relation of the work of art to its social "moment"—were positively frightening to him. Again and again he took elaborate pains to evade or minimize the problem of personality: even going so far as to maintain that the work of art is an *escape* from personality; a very revelatory view. It may here be pertinently questioned whether it is not precisely in this curious *doctrine* that Mr. Eliot is seeking an "escape from personality." From the psychological chaos of the "I" and the "now," let us seek refuge in a world of canons, forms, and rituals.

But if one felt, now and then, a shiver from this quarter in *The Sacred Wood,* one is exposed to a merciless blast of it in Mr. Eliot's new book, *For Lancelot Andrewes.* In this, Mr. Eliot seems to be definitely and defeatedly in retreat from the present and all that it implies. A thin and vinegarish hostility toward the modern world is breathed from these pages. Seeking certainties, or at least a hope of certainties, Mr. Eliot sounds a quavering recall, and attempts to lead us back to classicism in literature, to royalism in politics, and to the Anglo-Catholic church in religion. Humanism he condemns as merely a "sporadic" ancillary of religion, a kind of parasite, unable to exist fruitfully in its own right. Reason is bankrupt. Of the human race, the less said the better. Of Machiavelli, he remarks in this new book: "He was no fanatic; he merely told the truth about humanity. The world of human motives which he depicts is true—that is to say, it is humanity without the addition of superhuman Grace. It is therefore tolerable only to persons who have also a definite religious belief; to the effort of the last three centuries to supply religious belief by belief in Humanity the creed of Machiavelli is insupportable. . . . What Machiavelli did not see about human nature is the myth of human goodness which for liberal thought replaces the belief in Divine Grace."

It is hard to describe this as anything but a complete abdication of intelligence. And *pari passu* with this abdication goes a striking change in Mr. Eliot's whole outlook and style. A note of withered dogmatism sounds repeatedly in these pages; the circle of Mr. Eliot's sympathies has narrowed and hardened; in his essays on Andrewes and Bramhall, he is even led, by his propagandist zeal, to write dully of dull subjects. Throughout the entire book—unless we except some excellent pages on Middleton and Baudelaire—we feel the presence of a spirit which is inimical to everything new or bold or generous. Cautiously, jejunely, with an air of puritan acerbity, it seeks a refuge from humanity in Grace, from personality in dogma, and from the present in the past. Turning its back on the living word, it retreats into a monastic chill; and denies the miracle and abun-

dance of life. But can the miracle and abundance be denied in
this fashion? Not, one suspects, so simply or so summarily. The
moment is still with us, it is a world to be explored, and there
are still intrepid explorers. Mr. Eliot might have been one of
these—as indeed in his verse at times he *has* been—and, but for
the Grace of God, he might be yet. It is to be hoped that he
will not continue to prefer a narrower and safer path.

ELIOT, T. S. [*]   (1934)

Mr. Eliot's new essays, which were delivered last year at Harvard from the Charles Eliot Norton chair, have all the virtues
of the first-rate lecture: they move easily, they are lucid and
orderly, they are informative without being too much weighted
with pedantry, and they do not forget to be entertaining. We
are given a survey, excellently planned and simplified (and, on
the whole, with very judicious omissions) of the linked progress,
or evolution, side by side, of English poetry and criticism, from
Elizabethan times to the present day. Mr. Eliot's method is that
of the inquirer—he makes few assumptions, he has little recourse to dogma. He asks questions, very pertinently and gently; and answers them, generally, with a careful tentativeness.
If at times he appears a little superficial, or sketchy, or if his
transitions are occasionally somewhat meager and hurried, it is
only fair to assume that at least a part of this arises from the
normal difficulty of the lecturer. A style too packed or dense
would have defeated his purpose.

What emerges from the book—of general "view," or conclusion—does so largely by implication: if Mr. Eliot lays down any
emphatic dogma at all, it is simply that poetry can, and does,
vary in its function at different times and in different places;
and that along with it, *pari passu*, criticism alters its pace and
direction. That criticism has gradually sharpened its technical
analysis, in objectivity, in its ability and willingness to keep
fresh a sense of the past, and in psychological and social awareness, Mr. Eliot seems to admit. This evolution he traces, very
neatly and illuminatingly, all the way from Sidney to Mr. I. A.
Richards. But that with this "progress" in the perceptiveness of
criticism has developed any clearer or more precise idea of what

[*] *The Use of Poetry and the Use of Criticism.*

poetry is, or what it is for, he does not appear altogether convinced. What his own views may be, of the nature and function
of poetry, or of the nature and function of criticism, emerges,
again, rather by implication or negation than by statement; and
these, of course, are of particular interest, as coming from one of
the most important poets of our time. Implied, to begin with, in
Mr. Eliot's whole attitude to his subject (the variability of poetry's social use or function) is a skepticism as to the existence
of any universal, or essence, or "permanent," in poetry—or, at
any rate, a doubt as to what it is. "The extreme of theorizing
about the nature of poetry," he says, "the essence of poetry if
there is any, belongs to the study of aesthetics." Perhaps he
might better have said, to psychology and to sociology—for
aesthetics, like poetry, changes its tone and temper with time
and place. If there is any "permanent" or universal in poetry, it
is its social function; and about this, modern psychologists have
already had a good deal to say, and will have more. Sooner or
later they will tell us what, at all times and in all places, poetry
does. It is my own opinion that Mr. Richards, in his *Principles of
Literary Criticism* especially, but in his other books as well, is
making a very important step in this direction.

From Mr. Eliot's view of poetry as a thing of variable and
indeterminate function to his suggestion that it is not so much
a "communication" as "itself a thing to be communicated" (a
separate entity) is a natural step. This is again to cut away the
psychological roots. It seems to me quite impossible to rule out
communication. If language is communication, poetry is simply
communication (or language) working at its highest pitch.
Poetry cannot communicate itself alone, any more than language can communicate itself alone—Miss Stein to the contrary.
What the writing of the poem does to the poet, the reading of
it does to the reader; and whether we call it "organization,"
with Mr. Richards, or revelation, with the mystics, it is *au fond*
a sharing, a making common, a communication. Criticism,
here, will simply say how successful the communication is, and
why, and of what; it will regard the poem not as an absolute but
as a dynamic: and will trace its references backward to the poet
and forward to the reader. A poem as a completely separate
entity would be a poem completely without reference, and
therefore without meaning: an impossibility. This is not to say
that criticism could not usefully discriminate between the thing
communicated (the world) and the communication (the
word). But analysis, pushed far enough, would discover them

(one suspects) to be the same thing. In this regard, Mr. Eliot's remark that "meaning" may be simply the chief method of keeping the reader diverted "while the poem does its work upon him" seems to be the result of confused thinking. Remove the logical statement from a poem, an important part of the "meaning" would still remain—the affective. And it is precisely in this way that poetry makes the highest use of language, as it perhaps also represents the highest degree of consciousness of which man is capable: the most complete. It combines the logical or factual with the affective.

As will seem natural enough from the foregoing, Mr. Eliot shies at the notion of poetry as "revelation," and equally at Mr. Richards' suggestion that in poetry we can find a "substitute" for religion: he must have them separate. Is this our old friend the Ivory Tower? Perhaps Mr. Eliot's private religious predicament is answerable for it—in any case, he is at some pains, and with considerable sophistical disingenuousness, to ridicule Mr. Richards' idea that mankind, having shed religious dogma and arbitrary faith, will find through poetry a sufficient communication with the world and sufficient source of "belief." I am myself in entire agreement with Mr. Richards about this—it seems to me not impossible that religion was simply a temporary form of poetry. And I cannot agree with Mr. Eliot that poetry cannot be philosophic, or can only *borrow* its thinking: poetry can think deeply and still be poetry; it has thought deeply in the past, and is learning to think again. Poetic "thinking" is a real thinking. What about Zarathustra?

ELIOT, T. S. (1934)

To read these two new books of Mr. Eliot's together is to be made more than ever uncomfortable about his present predicament, his present position and direction. It is unfair to examine a lecture as closely as one would an essay in criticism, and *After Strange Gods* consists, of course, of three lectures delivered at the University of Virginia. It is equally unfair to judge the printed text of a pageant, a pageant written in cooperation with others and for performance on a special occasion, as one would judge a new book of poems presented in the ordinary way. In other words, one must begin by discounting both books as not quite "pure" Eliot. Nevertheless, there they are, they must be fitted into the Eliot tradition, they fall into line, and Mr. Eliot himself invites the comparison by publishing them; and it must be confessed that they leave one with a feeling of dissatisfaction and uncertainty.

The lectures consist chiefly of an extension and elaboration of the now-famous essay in *The Sacred Wood*—"Tradition and the Individual Talent." It is difficult to see that they add much of importance, whether in refinement of perception, or in division or addition; if anything, they are a dilution of the earlier work, they seem a little thin. Of course, as we all know, Mr. Eliot has turned to religion in the interval of thirteen years between *The Sacred Wood* and *After Strange Gods,* and it is not without a melancholy interest to consider the later book in this special light. From "tradition" to "orthodoxy" was, in the circumstances, a natural semantic and mantic step to take; Mr. Eliot takes it, and is at no pains to conceal it. Everywhere here is the implication that not only is it of vital importance for the artist (as individual) to remain in a sort of conscious connection with the tradition from which he springs, but also that if this contact can be further or more deeply extended to include a connection with the Church he will be safer still. Leaving aside, as one must, the whole question of religious belief, or of orthodox religion, nevertheless one is at once aware that the change in Mr. Eliot's critical attitude is decidedly in the direction of limitation. Already, in "Tradition and the Individual Talent," his emphasis was not so much on the *freedom* offered the artist by tradition as on the *restrictions;* the use of tradition was rather to hold one back than to release one for a forward step of exploration; in short, the position was a cautious one. The effect of orthodoxy is not unnaturally to deepen this timidity. If little room was then left for the individual's "free play," there is now very much less. As a mother of the arts, Mr. Eliot's "tradition" would be a very anxious and possessive one indeed; and (one is afraid) very crippling. Individualism must go by the board—if such a program should become universal—and the creative renewal of the arts fall to so low a level as to lead inevitably to stagnation. With the death of the individual would come the death of tradition; and art would be simply a history.

A curious state of things, a curious attitude in one who has himself been one of the most pronouncedly and creatively "individual" of contemporary writers, and himself therefore a

pretty violent *creator* of tradition; and one immediately begins
to wonder what effect his doctrines will have on his own
poetry. *The Rock* alone cannot give us much of an answer, for
as observed above, it is not a "pure" offering, but an amalgam.
In conjunction, however, with the handful of poems which Mr.
Eliot has given us in the twelve years since he published *The
Waste Land*, it is enough to make one uneasy. Without in any
way detracting from the extraordinary beauty of *Ash Wednesday* or *Marina*, or from the occasional brilliance of other of the
later poems, one cannot fail to notice a contraction both of
interest and power in the recent work. *Ash Wednesday*, let
it be said at once, is perhaps the most beautiful of all Mr.
Eliot's poems: it seems not unlikely that its "value" will out-
last that of *The Waste Land*. It is purer and less violent; it
depends less on shock, though elements of shock are still
there, enough of them to give energy; in Mr. Eliot's own sense,
it is more absolutely a poem, has a new being and constitutes
a new experience, and is so much more without "reference,"
or conscious reference, and so much more heavily weighted with
*un*conscious reference (or *affect*) as to approach the kind of
heavenly meaninglessness which we call pure poetry. But,
though we can like it better than *The Waste Land*, or feel
it to be finer, we also feel it to mark the beginning of a diminution of vigor and variousness: the circle has narrowed, and
it has gone on narrowing.

We cannot, of course, argue that this change is due to the
change in Mr. Eliot's views, any more than we can argue that
some deeper diminution of energy led to the change of view;
all we can do is observe that the two things have gone together.
In *The Rock*, the choruses are not the very best Eliot, though
they are skillful and beautiful; they are admirably calculated
for declamation; they have an excellent hardness and plainness;
but at times one feels the cunning of the rhetoric and the
rhythm to be almost too glib and easy, and as if usurping the
place of what would formerly have been a richer and more
natural inventiveness.

Mr. Eliot remarks, in *After Strange Gods*, that to write
religious poetry is one of the most difficult of all things. *Orthodox* religious poetry, yes: for that is merely to state, or to state
by referring, or to argue: which is propaganda, or something
very like it, as long as it remains within that given frame of
traditional or taught conviction, as it must. It is this that makes

one uneasy about Mr. Eliot's future: this and his converse belief that poetry, or even the poetic genius, cannot be a substitute for religion. To many of us it must appear that "orthodox
religion," on the one hand, and "tradition," on the other, are
simply nothing but a temporary conservatism, or freezing in
formula, of the initial poetic impulse. Beyond a certain point,
or for more than a given time, it *cannot* be formalized: along
comes a poet who reaches through it to the thing itself. Perhaps
Mr. Eliot's experiment with dramatic form in *The Rock,* which
must have been as highly suggestive to himself as to his auditors
and readers, will release him once more in ways which neither
he nor ourselves can foresee.

ELIOT, T. S.

(1935)

We ought, of course, to have gone to Ascot to see the gray top
hats and lovely dresses (not to mention the umbrellas) and perhaps a horse or two; instead we joined a very different pilgrimage, and one with an even statelier history than Queen
Anne's Royal Ascot. In short, we went to Canterbury. It was the
week of Canterbury's annual Festival of Music and Drama, an
affair organized by the Friends of Canterbury Cathedral, its
admirable object being to raise funds for the upkeep and repair of the church. The program of entertainment was unusually good this year—first-class concerts in the Cloisters by the
B.B.C. Orchestra, and also in the Cathedral itself (the only regrettable feature of this being that for the moment one was
unable to see the newly restored tomb of the Black Prince,
now bright gold), with music by Bach, Ravel, Holst, Vaughan
Williams, Scarlatti, and so forth. No wonder the little town was
crowded, swarms of uniformed schoolgirls being especially conspicuous, but the strangest thing of all was the fact that this
year the chief attraction was actually the work of an American.
To be exact, an ex-American. T. S. Eliot had been invited by
the Friends of the Cathedral to write a play for the occasion—
no doubt because of his production of *The Rock* last year at
Sadler's Wells, in aid of the City churches—and he complied,
giving them *Murder in the Cathedral.* Thus, without any preliminary fuss or fanfare, without advertisements in the news-

papers, or any advance announcements except through Church channels, a poetic play was staged in the Chapter House which may well mark a turning point in English drama.

Making every allowance for the extreme impressiveness of the surroundings—the hall of the Chapter House is, of course, magnificent—and for the extraordinary associational aid in the fact that a play about Thomas à Becket's martyrdom was being performed on the very spot where the martyrdom itself had been enacted—a combination of circumstances which must remain unique—nevertheless, one hadn't listened five minutes before one felt that one was witnessing a play which had the quality of greatness. If one had become uneasy about the effect of Eliot's churchward leanings on his poetry, one forgot that at once. Performed in a barn, and before an audience of skeptics, *Murder in the Cathedral* would still be a profound and beautiful thing. It transcends the particular beliefs on which it has been built—or, rather, it creates its own beliefs out of its own sheer livingness—exactly as *Everyman* does, or *Oedipus Rex,* and, incidentally, with striking technical resemblances to both. The use of the chorus of ten women, and the choruses themselves, were superb. One's feeling was that here at last was the English language literally being *used,* itself becoming the stuff of drama, turning alive with its own natural poetry. And Eliot's formalization wasn't at all the sort of thing one has grown accustomed to expect of poetic drama—no trace of sham antique or artiness about it; nothing, in the "dead" sense, "poetic." No, the thing was directly and terribly real, the poetry of the choruses was as simple and immediate in its meaning as our own daily lives, and the transition into satirical modern prose at the end, when the four knights turned and addressed the audience, came without shock. It is a triumph of poetic genius that out of such actionless material—the mere conflict of a mind with itself—a play so deeply moving, and so exciting, should have been written; and so rich, moreover, in the various language of *humanity.* That is perhaps the greatest surprise about it—in the play Eliot has become human, and tender, with a tenderness and a humanity which have nowhere else in our time found such beauty of form.

The production by Martin Browne was perfect. The stage was of the simplest, the actors approaching it from the center aisle of the hall, through the audience; the chorus, when not speaking, sitting at the right and left in the niches between little columns, as if merely a part of the design. Robert Speaight, as

Becket, was superb. The other parts were taken by amateurs, the Cathedral Players, who gave a performance that professionals might envy. And the speaking of the choruses was so beautiful that one actually resented at moments the singing which served as a counterpoint for it, from the gallery at the other end of the hall; for once, the spoken word was all one wanted. Altogether, an event; and we shall be surprised if later this lovely thing isn't given a run in the West End of London, or even put on by the Theatre Guild in New York.

ELIOT, T. S. (1936)

Mr. Eliot is nothing if not thrifty. Of the ten essays in his new book, five appeared formerly in *For Lancelot Andrewes*—among them, the admirable little note on Baudelaire. Three other papers from that book have not, for whatever reasons, been retained: those on Middleton, Crashaw, and Machiavelli. One regrets their omission, if only because, in the religious aridity to which Mr. Eliot now so often leads us, they formed a refreshing oasis of color. And in the present volume their places have been taken by essays which on the whole are Mr. Eliot at his heaviest—"Religion and Literature," "Catholicism and International Order," "Modern Education and the Classics," "The Pensées of Pascal," and a brief note on Tennyson. Heaviest and, let us add frankly, dreariest: for Mr. Eliot is very much in earnest, he is very solemn and, alas, he is often very dull. The prose, in the religio-social essays, is tired and flaccid, the argument tedious and thin; and ultimately one finds oneself reflecting that one's interest is not at all in the ideas presented, which are nowhere very surprising, nor in the reasoning, which in its bland exclusions often strikes one as queerly *innocent*, but in the fact that these ideas and these reasons are Mr. Eliot's. The spectacle, in short, is that of one of the finest and most perceptive minds of the age, and one of the wittiest, occupied in a retrogression, or regression, which is as astonishing as it is melancholy.

The main features of Mr. Eliot's panacea for a barbarous and backsliding age are of course familiar enough—he would have us be good Christians, by which he means good Anglo-Catholics, and he would have us read the classics. For the understanding of the latter, and of literature in general, and for the proper judgment of values, both in letters and in life, he suggests that we must bring the touchstone of Christian ethics: a singular *dénouement* for the critic who, in "Tradition and the Individual Talent," sailed so close to the Siren shores of Abstract Art. With Mr. Eliot's feeling that the age is too much secularized, or too materialistic, and that we must rediscover our religious instincts or perish, it is impossible not to agree. What one *cannot* agree with is his notion that religion can exist only in a church, or in one kind of church. Any more than one can agree with him in his strange idea that regionalism, both national and international, is the only remaining political hope of mankind, or that the revival of monastic teaching offers the only hope for the study of Latin and Greek "in their proper place and for the right reasons." Shades of Erasmus! But this is Mr. Eliot at his most priggish, and it is pleasanter to record one's gratitude for the notes on Pascal, which are very good indeed, and the charitable act of restoration which he performs in so generously praising Tennyson. *Too* generously, perhaps. When he says that the poems of Thomas Hardy—among which one must remember *The Dynasts*—are "small work in comparison with 'In Memoriam'—it is greater than they and comprehends them," one feels that the gambit is a trifle risky. And one wonders whether Mr. Eliot doesn't admire Tennyson for the wrong reasons—and in the wrong places. Just the same, to reread Tennyson is a good idea.

ELIOT, T. S.   (1949)

Forty years ago Cambridge, Massachusetts, or that part of it adjacent to Harvard College, was not at all the ugly manufacturing city it has become: it was still in many senses a village. Lilacs and white picket fences under elms, horse-drawn watering-carts to lay the dust in the blindingly dusty streets of summer, board-walks put down on the pavements every winter and taken up again every spring, sleighs and pungs in the snow, and the dreadful college bell reverberant over all. Were we gayer as undergraduates than those of today? At all events we were gay, and my earliest single recollection of our sixty-year-old hero is of a singularly attractive, tall, and rather dapper young man, with a somewhat Lamian smile, who reeled out of the

door of the Lampoon on a spring evening, and, catching sight
of me, threw his arms about me—from the open windows above
came the unmistakable uproar of a punch in progress. "And
that," observed my astonished companion, "if Tom remembers
it tomorrow, will cause him to suffer agonies of shyness." And no
doubt it did: for he *was* shy. Not that this by any means kept
him out of social circulation. For if we met to begin with as
fellow editors of the Harvard Advocate (*diaboli Advocati*),
whether at board meetings on the top floor of the Union, or at
initiations, or punches, or even at tea (with rum in it), we also
met at Buckingham and Brattle Hall dances and at the Signet,
a club with vaguely literary pretensions and an excellent small
library, which was said to have been founded by a scion of the
Bonaparte family. He was early explicit, too, about the necessity, if one was shy, of disciplining oneself, lest one miss certain
varieties of experience which one did not naturally "take" to.
The dances, and the parties, were a part of this discipline, as
later on—after a year at the Sorbonne, at the end of which we
met in Paris for *sirop de fraises*—was his taking of boxing-les-
sons. He had returned to Cambridge and Harvard to work for
his doctorate in philosophy, returning already perceptibly Eu-
ropeanized: he made a point, for a while, a conspicuously un-
American point, of carrying a cane—was it a malacca?—a little
self-conscious about it, and complaining that its "nice conduct"
was no such easy matter. He had taken a room in Ash Street,
installing in it a small stove—"something to point the chairs at"
—and a Gaugin *Crucifixion,* brought from Paris. The suggestion
that the latter was a kind of sophisticated primitivism brought
the reply, with a waspishness that was characteristic, that there
"was nothing primitive about it." (A waspishness, let us say
parenthetically, that has now and then got him into trouble;
"Shelley was a fool," for example, or, of Chekhov, "I prefer my
Ibsen straight.") The boxing lessons, meanwhile, took place at
a toughish gymnasium in Boston's South End, where, under the
tutelage of an ex-pugilist with some such monicker as Steve
O'Donnell, he learned not only the rudiments of boxing but
also, as he put it, "how to swarm with passion up a rope"—his
delight in this attainment was manifest. Was Steve O'Donnell
the prototype of Sweeney, as some have suggested? Anyway, it
was our habit to dine together after these gymnastic afternoons,
usually at the Greek restaurant in Stuart Street, a small, dirty,
and wonderfully inexpensive establishment which was in fact
half restaurant and half pool-room; and it was here on one un-

fortunate occasion, when he had accidentally hit Steve too hard, that he turned up with a magnificent black eye, a shiner that did Steve great credit: it was really iridescent.

What did we talk about? or what didn't we? It was the first "great" era of the comic strip, of Krazy Kat, and Mutt and Jeff, and Rube Goldberg's elaborate lunacies: it was also perhaps the most creative period of American slang, and in both these departments of invention he took enormous pleasure. How delighted we were with the word "dinge" for negro! This rich native creativeness was to be reflected, of course, in his poetry, notably in *Prufrock*, just as our dear deplorable friend, Miss X, the *précieuse riducule* to end all preciosity, serving tea so exquisitely among her bric-a-brac, was to be pinned like a butterfly to a page in *Portrait of a Lady*. But more immediately it gave rise to the series of hilariously naughty *parerga* which was devoted spasmodically to that singular and sterling character known as King Bolo, not to mention King Bolo's Queen, "that airy fairy hairy-'un, who led the dance on Golder's Green with Cardinal Bessarion." These admirable stanzas, notable at times for their penetrating social criticism, were to continue for years as a sort of cynical counterpoint to the study of Sanskrit and the treatise on epistemology. Their influence on the development of a Style will no doubt come in due course to the attention of Herr Dr. Krapp of Wien.

But what did we talk about? What to write, of course, and how to write, and what to read—Charles Louis Philippe and Vildrac, fresh from Paris—but also increasingly, and perhaps more concernedly, where to live, and how. Europe? And if so London, or Paris? Could one successfully lay siege to either, and how should one go about it? A year or so later, letters of introduction took me to London, and to W. H. Davies in Little Russell Street, to Rupert Brooke in Gray's Inn, to Edward Thomas, Harold Munro, and Ezra Pound. With me also was the typescript of *Prufrock*, typed by its author with meticulous care on a Blickensderfer which produced only italics, and *La Figlia che Piange*, neither of which was I able to sell. Monro—though ten years later he was a convert, if this side idolatry—thought *Prufrock* bordered on "insanity." But Pound, serving tea not so exquisitely among his beautiful Gaudiers, recognized *Prufrock* instantly, and this was the beginning.

The beginning of the war, too: which was to wash Eliot up in London, back from Marburg, where he had just begun his studies, and myself in Boston. Where to live? The letters are full of the question. England was clearly impossible. "A people which is satisfied with such disgusting food is *not* civilized." London is at first detested. But Oxford, and Merton with its "Alexandrian verse, nuts and wine," the professors with pregnant wives and sprawling children and hideous pictures on their walls, makes him long even for London, perhaps to work in the British Museum. "Come, let us desert our wives, and fly to a land where there are no Medici prints, nothing but concubinage and conversation. Oxford is very pretty, but I don't like to be dead." Conversation, yes—but where to find it? Well, "Pound is rather intelligent as a talker: his verse is touchingly incompetent." "O Conversation, the staff of life, shall I get any at Oxford?" Then follows his *War Poem, for the $100 prize, entitled UP BOYS AND AT 'EM! Adapted to the tune of "C. Columbo lived in Spain," and within the compass of the average male or female voice,* and a new stanza of King Bolo. And he adds "I am keen on rhymes in -een."

As for more serious work, he writes: "I think you criticize my work too leniently. It still seems to me strained and intellectual." (This refers to an unfinished poem, never published, called *The Love Song of St. Sebastian.*) "I know the kind of verse I want, and I know that this isn't it, and I know why. I shan't do anything that will satisfy me (as some of my old stuff *does* satisfy me—whether it be good or not) for years. I feel it more and more. And I don't know whether I want to. Why should one worry about that? I feel that such matters take care of themselves, and have no dependence upon our planning."

I can't say that I always understand
My own meaning when I would be very fine.
But the fact is that I have nothing planned
Except perhaps to be a moment merry . . .

The prediction is uncanny: for the year is 1915.

FAULKNER, WILLIAM   (1927)

Mr. Faulkner has a sense of character; he has a sense of humor; he has a sense of style; and for his new novel, *Mosquitoes*, he has found an amusing and more or less original setting. He places his odd miscellaneous group of people—second-rate artists and second-rate hosts and a couple of Tough Guys (one male, and one female) on a yacht; and the greater part of the action (such action as there is) takes place in the week of a cruise.

To say that there is not a great deal of action is in the present instance no disparagement; for the charm of Mr. Faulkner's highly entertaining novel resides almost entirely in the astonishing lifelikeness and immediacy of his "scene"; the comings and goings, the absurd actions, the drunken conversations, of his people, recorded hour by hour, almost minute by minute.

The dialogue is as good, in its way, as Mr. Hemingway's; it is "tough talk" straight off the street and out of the dance halls; it has the unmistakable rhythm of living speech; and when Mr. Faulkner also wishes to give us "highbrow" talk—the aesthetic discussions of his novelist (for whom one guesses a living prototype)—he does so with wit and color and an intelligence that is occasionally sharp to the point of brilliance. There is a great deal of talk in the book—so much, that one finds oneself thinking that the thing might almost better have been a play; a farce-comedy. And the talk falls naturally and easily into scenes. One suspects that it would take very little pruning and shaping to turn the thing into an actable affair, with the characters just enough broadened into caricature to make them easily actable.

To mark all this, and to mark the fact that Mr. Faulkner writes well (in the main) and that he has the gift, rare enough in writers of fiction, of making scenes and people come vividly alive before us, with something of Katherine Mansfield's sense of light and texture, and a good deal of Mr. Huxley's erudition, is to define one's appreciation of *Mosquitoes* as a distinctly unusual and amusing book. It is good enough to make one wish that it were better, and to make one hope that Mr. Faulkner will outgrow certain mannerisms which now tend rather seriously to come between him and his reader. He has, distinctly, the fault of many young writers of today (and of certain others not so young); a desire to shock, a desire to see how naughty he can be, and how very, very sophisticated he can appear. This results in a good many blemishes in the book, one or two of which are both unpardonable and useless.

If these minor episodes and anecdotes and innuendoes served any valid purpose; if they threw, for example, any sort of light on a particular character, or in any way forwarded the course of the action, then one might conceivably forgive them. But there is no such justification; they appear to be a wanton self-indulgence. This is a great pity, draws the attention of the reader away from the book's true excellence, and does, further, a good deal to invalidate it. Moreover, Mr. Faulkner has an unfortunate addiction to preciosity. He has an ungoverned appetite for purple passages; and when he is purple, his purple is of the purplest. It screams. One gets heartily sick of his blanched moons, spreading their boneless hands, or their ceaseless hands, or their boneless ceaseless hands, on the boneless and ceaseless water. One positively faints when he indulges himself (as all too frequently) in romantic fantasy, usually couched in italics, as part of the interior monologue of a character who is undergoing stress of emotion. On these occasions he gets off into a mawkish and morbid world that reeks of patchouli and Beardsley and anemic Bakst and a kind of *morbidezza* that has a sickly flavor as of Baudelaire and rose water.

One resents these pseudo-poetic intrusions—they would be somewhat out of place even if well done. For the rest of the story is excellent realistic satire; pungent to the nostril, brilliant to the eye, palpable, if somewhat coarse, to the touch. Here and there, one feels that Mr. Faulkner's hand has shaken a little. One gets the impression, for example, that when he began the book, he intended to make his sculptor, Gordon, the chief character, or, at any rate, *one* of the chief characters; but Mr. Faulkner's attention was distracted, and Gordon slipped into the background, only to be rather hastily resurrected at the end. In the same way, his novelist, Fairchild, undergoes a kind of queer metamorphosis in midstream; he suddenly becomes a rather different Fairchild (and it must be admitted a more plausible one) from the Fairchild whom we encounter at the outset.

From such accidents one gathers the impression that Mr. Faulkner, having been seized by the excellent suggestion of scene and "crowd" that his setting supplied for him, gave himself up to reckless improvisation, and allowed the story to run away from him. The story has the brilliance of improvisation, but also its shapelessness.

These defects being admitted, the critic must also admit, and without a shadow of reluctance, that the book is a delightful one. And one adds Mr. Faulkner's name to the small list of those from whom one might reasonably expect, in the course of a few years, a really first-rate piece of fiction.

FAULKNER, WILLIAM   (1939)

The famous remark made to Macaulay—"Young man, the more I consider the less can I conceive where you picked up that style"—might with advantage have been saved for Mr. William Faulkner. For if one thing is more outstanding than another about Mr. Faulkner—some readers find it so outstanding, indeed, that they never get beyond it—it is the uncompromising and almost hypnotic zeal with which he insists upon having a style, and, especially of late, the very peculiar style which he insists upon having. Perhaps to that one should add that he insists *when he remembers*—he can write straightforwardly enough when he wants to; he does so often in the best of his short stories (and they are brilliant), often enough, too, in the novels. But that *style* is what he really wants to get back to; and get back to it he invariably does.

And what a style it is, to be sure! The exuberant and tropical luxuriance of sound which Jim Europe's jazz band used to exhale, like a jungle of rank creepers and ferocious blooms taking shape before one's eyes—magnificently and endlessly intervolved, glisteningly and ophidianly in motion, coil sliding over coil, and leaf and flower forever magically interchanging—was scarcely more bewildering, in its sheer inexhaustible fecundity, than Mr. Faulkner's style. Small wonder if even the most passionate of Mr. Faulkner's admirers—among whom the present writer honors himself by enlisting—must find, with each new novel, that the first fifty pages are always the hardest, that each time one must learn all over again *how* to read this strangely fluid and slippery and heavily mannered prose, and that one is even, like a kind of Laocoön, sometimes tempted to give up.

Wrestle, for example, with two very short (for Mr. Faulkner!) sentences, taken from an early page of *Absalom, Absalom!*

Meanwhile, as though in inverse ratio to the vanishing voice, the invoked ghost of the man whom she could neither forgive nor revenge herself upon began to assume a quality almost of solidity, permanence. Itself circumambient and enclosed by its effluvium of

hell, its aura of unregeneration, it mused (mused, thought, seemed
to possess sentience as if, though dispossessed of the peace—who was
impervious anyhow to fatigue—which she declined to give it, it was
still irrevocably outside the scope of her hurt or harm) with that
quality peaceful and now harmless and not even very attentive—the
ogre-shape which, as Miss Codfield's voice went on, resolved out of
itself before Quentin's eyes the two half-ogre children, the three of
them forming a shadowy background for the fourth one.

Well, it may be reasonably questioned whether, on page
thirteen of a novel, that little cordite bolus of suppressed references isn't a thumping aesthetic mistake. Returned to, when
one has finished the book, it may be as simple as daylight; but
encountered for the first time, and no matter how often reread,
it guards its enigma with the stony impassivity of the Sphinx.

Or take again from the very first page of The Wild Palms—
Mr. Faulkner's latest novel, and certainly one of his finest—
this little specimen of "exposition":

Because he had been born here, on this coast though not in this house
but in the other, the residence in town, and had lived here all his
life, including the four years at the State University's medical school
and the two years as an intern in New Orleans where (a thick man
even when young, with thick soft woman's hands, who should never
have been a doctor at all, who even after the six more or less metro-
politan years looked out from a provincial and insulated amazement
at his classmates and fellows: the lean young men swaggering in their
drill jackets on which—to him—they wore the myriad anonymous
faces of the probationer nurses with a ruthless and assured bragga-
docio like decorations, like flower trophies) he had sickened for it.

What is one to say of that—or of a sentence only a little lower
on the same page which runs for thirty-three lines? Is this, somehow perverted, the influence of the later Henry James—James
the Old Pretender?

In short, Mr. Faulkner's style, though often brilliant and always interesting, is all too frequently downright bad; and it has
inevitably offered an all-too-easy mark for the sharpshooting of
such alert critics as Mr. Wyndham Lewis. But if it is easy
enough to make fun of Mr. Faulkner's obsessions for particular
words, or his indifference and violence to them, or the parrotlike
mechanical mytacism (for it is really like a stammer) with
which he will go on endlessly repeating such favorites as "myriad, sourceless, impalpable, outrageous, risible, profound," there
is nevertheless something more to be said for his passion for
overelaborate sentence structure.

Overelaborate they certainly are, baroque and involuted in the extreme, these sentences: trailing clauses, one after another, shadowily in apposition, or perhaps not even with so much connection as that; parenthesis after parenthesis, the parenthesis itself often containing one or more parentheses—they remind one of those brightly colored Chinese eggs of one's childhood, which when opened disclosed egg after egg, each smaller and subtler than the last. It is as if Mr. Faulkner, in a sort of hurried despair, had decided to try to tell us everything, absolutely everything, every last origin or source or quality or qualification, and every possible future or permutation as well, in one terrifically concentrated effort: each sentence to be, as it were, a microcosm. And it must be admitted that the practice is annoying and distracting.

It is annoying, at the end of a sentence, to find that one does not know in the least what was the subject of the verb that dangles *in vacuo*—it is distracting to have to go back and sort out the meaning, track down the structure from clause to clause, then only to find that after all it doesn't much matter, and that the obscurity was perhaps neither subtle nor important. And to the extent that one *is* annoyed and distracted, and *does* thus go back and work it out, it may be at once added that Mr. Faulkner has defeated his own ends. One has had, of course, to emerge from the stream, and to step away from it, in order properly to see it; and as Mr. Faulkner works precisely by a process of *immersion*, of hypnotizing his reader into *remaining immersed* in his stream, this occasional blunder produces irritation and failure.

Nevertheless, despite the blunders, and despite the bad habits and the willful bad writing (and willful it obviously is), the style as a whole is extraordinarily effective; the reader *does* remain immersed, *wants* to remain immersed, and it is interesting to look into the reasons for this. And at once, if one considers these queer sentences not simply by themselves, as monsters of grammar or awkwardness, but in their relation to the book as a whole, one sees a functional reason and necessity for their being as they are. They parallel in a curious and perhaps inevitable way, and not without aesthetic justification, the whole elaborate method of *deliberately withheld meaning*, of progressive and partial and delayed disclosure, which so often gives the characteristic shape to the novels themselves. It is a persistent offering of obstacles, a calculated system of screens and obtrusions, of confusions and ambiguous interpolations and delays, with one express purpose; and that purpose is simply to keep the form—and the idea—fluid and unfinished, still in motion, as it were, and unknown, until the dropping into place of the very last syllable.

What Mr. Faulkner is after, in a sense, is a *continuum*. He wants a medium without stops or pauses, a medium which is always *of the moment,* and of which the passage from moment to moment is as fluid and undetectable as in the life itself which he is purporting to give. It is all inside and underneath, or as seen from within and below; the reader must therefore be steadily *drawn in;* he must be powerfully and unremittingly hypnotized inward and downward to that image-stream; and this suggests, perhaps, a reason not only for the length and elaborateness of the sentence structure, but for the repetitiveness as well. The repetitiveness, and the steady iterative emphasis—like a kind of chanting or invocation—on certain relatively abstract words ("sonorous, latin, *vaguely* eloquent"), has the effect at last of producing, for Mr. Faulkner, a special language, a conglomerate of his own, which he uses with an astonishing virtuosity, and which, although in detailed analysis it may look shoddy, is actually for his purpose a life stream of almost miraculous adaptability. At the one extreme it is abstract, cerebral, time-and-space-obsessed, tortured and twisted, but nevertheless always with a living *pulse* in it; and at the other it can be as overwhelming in its simple vividness, its richness in the actual, as the flood scenes in *The Wild Palms.*

Obviously, such a style, especially when allied with such a method, and such a *concern* for method, must make difficulties for the reader; and it must be admitted that Mr. Faulkner does little or nothing as a rule to make his highly complex "situation" easily available or perceptible. The reader must simply make up his mind to go to work, and in a sense to cooperate; his reward being that there *is* a situation to be given shape, a meaning to be extracted, and that half the fun is precisely in watching the queer, difficult, and often so laborious, evolution of Mr. Faulkner's idea. And not so much idea, either, as form. For, like the great predecessor whom at least in this regard he so oddly resembles, Mr. Faulkner could say with Henry James that it is practically impossible to make any real distinction between theme and form. What immoderately delights him, alike in *Sanctuary, The Sound and the Fury, As I Lay Dying, Light in August, Pylon, Absalom, Absalom!* and now again in *The Wild Palms,* and what sets him above—shall we say it firmly—all his

American contemporaries, is his continuous preoccupation with the novel *as form*, his passionate concern with it, and a degree of success with it which would clearly have commanded the interest and respect of Henry James himself. The novel as revelation, the novel as slice-of-life, the novel as mere story, do not interest him: these he would say, like James again, "are the circumstances of the interest," but not the interest itself. The interest itself will be the *use* to which these circumstances are put, the degree to which they can be organized.

From this point of view, he is not in the least to be considered as a mere "Southern" writer: the "Southernness" of his scenes and characters is of little concern to him, just as little as the question whether they are pleasant or unpleasant, true or untrue. Verisimilitude—or, at any rate, *degree* of verisimilitude— he will cheerfully abandon, where necessary, if the compensating advantages of plan or tone are a sufficient inducement. The famous scene in *Sanctuary* of Miss Reba and Uncle Bud, in which a "madam" and her cronies hold a wake for a dead gangster, while the small boy gets drunk, is quite false, taken out of its context; it is not endowed with the same *kind* of actuality which permeates the greater part of the book at all. Mr. Faulkner was cunning enough to see that a two-dimensional cartoonlike statement, at this juncture, would supply him with the effect of a chorus, and without in the least being perceived as a change in the temperature of truthfulness.

That particular kind of dilution, or adulteration, of verisimilitude, was both practiced and praised by James: as when he blandly admitted of *In the Cage* that his central character was "too ardent a focus of divination" to be quite credible. It was defensible simply because it made possible the coherence of the whole, and was itself absorbed back into the luminous texture. It was for him a device for organization, just as the careful cherishing of "viewpoint" was a device, whether simply or in counterpoint. Of Mr. Faulkner's devices, of this sort, aimed at the achievement of complex "form," the two most constant are the manipulation of viewpoint and the use of the flash-back, or sudden shift of time-scene, forward or backward.

In *Sanctuary*, where the alternation of viewpoint is a little lawless, the complexity is given, perhaps a shade disingenuously, by violent shifts in time; a deliberate disarrangement of an otherwise straightforward story. Technically, there is no doubt that the novel, despite its fame, rattles a little; and Mr. Faulkner himself takes pains to disclaim it. But, even done

with the left hand, it betrays a genius for form, quite apart from
its wonderful virtuosity in other respects. *Light in August,*
published a year after *Sanctuary,* repeats the same technique,
that of a dislocation of time, and more elaborately; the time-
shifts alternate with shifts in the viewpoint; and if the book is a
failure it is perhaps because Mr. Faulkner's tendency to what
is almost a hypertrophy of form is not here, as well as in the
other novels, matched with the characters and the theme. Neither the person nor the story of Joe Christmas is seen fiercely
enough—by its creator—to carry off that immense machinery of
narrative; it would have needed another Popeye, or another
Jiggs and Shumann, another Temple Drake, and for once
Mr. Faulkner's inexhaustible inventiveness seems to have been
at fault. Consequently what we see is an extraordinary power
for form functioning relatively *in vacuo,* and existing only to
sustain itself.

In the best of the novels, however—and it is difficult to choose
between *The Sound and the Fury* and *The Wild Palms,* with
Absalom, Absalom! a very close third—this tendency to hypertrophy of form has been sufficiently curbed; and it is interesting, too, to notice that in all these three (and in that remarkable *tour de force, As I Lay Dying,* as well) while there is still
a considerable reliance on time-shift, the effect of richness and
complexity is chiefly obtained by a very skillful fugue-like alternation of viewpoint. Fugue-like in *The Wild Palms*—and
fugue-like especially, of course, in *As I Lay Dying,* where the
shift is kaleidoscopically rapid, and where, despite an astonishing violence to plausibility (in the reflections, and *language* of
reflection, of the characters) an effect of the utmost reality and
immediateness is nevertheless produced. Fugue-like, again, in
Absalom, Absalom! where indeed one may say the form is really
circular—there is no beginning and no ending, properly speaking, and therefore no *logical* point of entrance: we must just
submit, and follow the circling of the author's interest, which
turns a light inward towards the center, but every moment from
a new angle, a new point of view. The story unfolds, therefore,
now in one color of light, now in another, with references backward and forward: those that refer forward being necessarily,
for the moment, blind. What is complete in Mr. Faulkner's pattern, *a priori,* must nevertheless remain *in*complete for us until
the very last stone is in place; what is "real," therefore, at one
stage of the unfolding, or from one point of view, turns out to be
"unreal" from another; and we find that one among other things

with which we are engaged is the fascinating sport of trying to separate truth from legend, watching the growth of legend from truth, and finally reaching the conclusion that the distinction is itself false.

Something of the same sort is true also of *The Sound and the Fury*—and this, with its massive four-part symphonic structure, is perhaps the most beautifully *wrought* of the whole series, and an indubitable masterpiece of what James loved to call the "fictive art." The joinery is flawless in its intricacy; it is a novelist's novel—a whole textbook on the craft of fiction in itself, comparable in its way to *What Maisie Knew* or *The Golden Bowl.*

But if it is important, for the moment, to emphasize Mr. Faulkner's genius for form, and his continued exploration of its possibilities, as against the usual concern with the violence and dreadfulness of his themes—though we might pause to remind carpers on this score of the fact that the best of Henry James is precisely that group of last novels which so completely concerned themselves with moral depravity—it is also well to keep in mind his genius for invention, whether of character or episode. The inventiveness is of the richest possible sort—a headlong and tumultuous abundance, an exuberant generosity and vitality, which makes most other contemporary fiction look very pale and chaste indeed. It is an unforgettable gallery of portraits, whether of character or caricature, and all of them endowed with a violent and immediate vitality.

He is at once [to quote once more from James] one of the most corrupt of writers and one of the most naif, the most mechanical and pedantic, and the fullest of *bonhomie* and natural impulse. He is one of the finest of artists and one of the coarsest. Viewed in one way, his novels are ponderous, shapeless, overloaded; his touch is graceless, violent, barbarous. Viewed in another, his tales have more color, more composition, more grasp of the reader's attention than any others. [His] style would demand a chapter apart. It is the least simple style, probably, that was ever written; it bristles, it cracks, it swells and swaggers; but it is a perfect expression of the man's genius. Like his genius, it contains a certain quantity of everything, from immaculate gold to flagrant dross. He was a very bad writer, and yet unquestionably he was a very great writer. We may say briefly, that in so far as his method was an instinct it was successful, and that in so far as it was a theory it was a failure. But both in instinct and in theory he had the aid of an immense force of conviction. His imagination warmed to its work so intensely that there was nothing his volition could not impose upon it. Hallucination settled upon him, and he believed anything that was necessary in the circumstances.

That passage, from Henry James's essay on Balzac, is almost word for word, with scarcely a reservation, applicable to Mr. Faulkner. All that is lacking is Balzac's greater *range* of understanding and tenderness, his greater freedom from special preoccupations. For this, one would hazard the guess that Mr. Faulkner has the gifts—and time is still before him.

FITZGERALD, F. SCOTT ·   (1926)

American criticism is seldom responsibly aware of contemporary figures, and for that reason one can say that the deaths of Melville, Crane, and James, in successive decades, aroused in the American consciousness little sense of loss. They were gone, it is true: but as their presence had been little felt, and their influence had been practically negligible, their departure left little awareness, as it should have done, that there were no writers of fiction to take their places. As a matter of fact, American criticism was all too cheerfully convinced that in the diagnostic inventions of Frank Norris and Mr. Upton Sinclair, in the short stories of O. Henry, and above all in the cumbersome journalistic epics of Mr. Dreiser, it possessed a quite sufficient guarantee of excellence. No criticism is so fascinated by the ephemeral as American criticism, or so careless of the past in its appraisal of the present. It is joyfully headlong in its passionate pursuit of the autochthonous, it delights to find queer geniuses in queer corners (it finds them every day), and if they aren't *too* queer, *too* complicated, it treats them all alike: with magnificent generosity. It is sufficient comment on the results of this tendency to note that in the recent abridged *Cambridge History of American Literature—A Short History of American Literature*—which purported to be an authoritative and complete survey by American critics of good standing, Melville was dismissed in four scant pages as a sea-romance ruined by metaphysics, while Crane and Emily Dickinson were not even mentioned.

But what does it matter? This shortness of memory, and this

· Also reviewed here: Ring Lardner and Anita Loos.

indiscriminateness of taste, combine to produce for American critics an illusion of perpetual novelty and inexhaustible plenty. The great realistic novelist, who reappears every ten years as a Norris, a Sinclair, a Dreiser, or a Lewis, is always perfectly and surprisingly new. Great new poets emerge, have a moment's unprecedented glory, and are swallowed up in oblivion. The American language is periodically rediscovered and employed—always, of course, for the first time. Here, for example, is its latest practitioner, Mr. Lardner, an admirable journalistic humorist, whose sketches of baseball characters have been delighting American newspaper readers for several years. Mr. Lardner writes in an amusing vernacular, and he has a satiric vein which is just good enough (if coarse, and not infrequently cheap) to carry one safely through a first reading. Further than that, one cannot go: it is impossible to agree with those critics who, perhaps a little thrilled at having discovered Mr. Lardner's striking talent on the sports page of a newspaper, suggest that he is another Mark Twain, and that his short stories "are the best ever written by an American." Mr. Lardner's gift is a small one. He has an alert understanding of one type of American—the genial, gum-chewing "roughneck": shrewd, humorous, immature, self-deceiving, pathetically gregarious and romantic: and this type he uses again and again, male or female, old or young, always with the same vernacular. The vernacular is skillfully caught, the orthography is entertaining, but Mr. Lardner relies too much upon it, and it becomes tiresome. As for the story, the plot, the psychology, the art—one has only to put the best of Mr. Lardner ("The Champion," in *How To Write Short Stories*) beside Stephen Crane's *Maggie*. In *Maggie*, one sees the same sort of material, American language and all, used by a poet for the making of a genuine and moving piece of literature. Nowhere, in Mr. Lardner's two books, is there any slightest attempt to achieve that sort of alchemy. Mr. Lardner seeks, like Mr. Will Rogers, to entertain; and in that he often delightfully succeeds.

And so does Miss Loos, whose *Gentlemen Prefer Blondes* has already become a byword. Miss Loos has one great advantage over Mr. Lardner—she has published only one book, and in this she has not attempted, with any elaborateness, to create more than one character. This character (caricature) is exactly the sort that Mr. Lardner might have conceived—the vernacular is remarkably like (so much so that one could transpose passages from *Gullible's Travels* to *Gentlemen Prefer Blondes*, and *vice versa,* without the slightest jar to contexts) and the wit moves in the same manner, a manner familiar to anyone who knows the American vaudeville stage: laconically eccentric, laconically exaggerative, laconically depreciative, laconically shocking. Miss Loos uses this manner more sharply than Mr. Lardner, and manages to say, in the course of her book, a greater number of memorably absurd things; and the European tour of her beautiful baleful blonde affords a more various scene for satire than Mr. Lardner has been able to find on the baseball diamond or at Palm Beach. Of her cynicism, all one can say is that it is an abyss. And surely there was never before, in a tale so reckless of conventional morals, a discretion so miraculous. Miss Loos' terrifying blonde, so infinitely more deadly than any of the males she encounters, employs in this regard a perfection of technique which is really beautiful in one so young and (apparently) so ingenuous. It reminds one, however, that the profession is among the most honorable and ancient.

Nevertheless, *Gentlemen Prefer Blondes,* like Mr. Lardner's *Gullible's Travels,* is an ephemerid. Is it likely that Miss Loos will do anything better, or will even experience a desire to do so? Her limitations are those of Mr. Lardner—one guesses that her vein is small, that she has no great resources (save as an entertainer) and that she would probably be a little surprised if one urged her to move up from the class of *The Young Visiters* to something better . . . And it is because he does, in this sense, try to move up, that Mr. Scott Fitzgerald deserves to be reviewed in better company than Miss Loos or Mr. Lardner afford him. Mr. Fitzgerald has enjoyed a spectacular career as a writer of short stories for American magazines; and in these, as well as in *This Side of Paradise,* his first novel, he showed (mixed with much magazine shoddy) enough ability to make one fearful lest he should allow himself to be manipulated, by his audience and by his success, as O. Henry was manipulated. In his latest collection of stories, *All The Sad Young Men,* he appears still all too manipulatable; though in one or two of the stories he also makes it evident that his conscience is not yet wholly dead. *Absolution* is an attempt at a close psychological study of hysteria which has good things in it but as a whole is somewhat forced: one feels that Mr. Fitzgerald is not speaking his own language. In this, and in *The Rich Boy,* he fails to detach, and to make clear, his effect—so much so that one suspects him of not seeing it too clearly himself.

In *The Great Gatsby,* however, Mr. Fitzgerald has written a

highly colored and brilliant little novel which, by grace of one
cardinal virtue, quite escapes the company of most contemporary American fiction—it has excellence of form. It is not great,
it is not large, it is not strikingly subtle; but it is well imagined
and shaped, it moves swiftly and neatly, its scene is admirably
seized and admirably matched with the theme, and its hard
bright tone is entirely original. Technically, it appears to owe
much to the influence of the cinema; and perhaps also something to Henry James—a peculiar conjunction, but not so peculiar if one reflects on the flash-backs and close-ups and paral-
leled themes of that "little experiment in the style of Gyp," *The
Awkward Age.* Mr. Fitzgerald's publishers call *The Great
Gatsby* a satire. This is deceptive. It is only incidentally a
satire, it is only in the *setting* that it is satirical, and in the tone
provided by the minor characters. The story itself, and the main
figure, are tragic, and it is precisely the fantastic vulgarity of
the scene which gives to the excellence of Gatsby's soul its
finest bouquet, and to his tragic fate its sharpest edge. All of Mr.
Fitzgerald's people are real—but Gatsby comes close to being
superb. He is betrayed to us slowly and skillfully, and with a
keen tenderness which in the end makes his tragedy a deeply
moving one. By so much, therefore, *The Great Gatsby* is better
than a mere satire of manners, and better than Mr. Fitzgerald's
usual sort of superficial cleverness. If only he can refrain altogether in future from the sham romanticism and sham sophistication which the magazines demand of him, and give another
turn of the screw to the care with which he writes, he may well
become a first-rate novelist. How deeply does he feel? That is
the question, a question we do not ask of Miss Loos or Mr.
Lardner.

FLETCHER, JOHN GOULD   (1921)

Balzac once remarked, "Without genius I am lost." One may
easily make the mistake of assuming that there could not conceivably be an artist who might not say of himself the same
thing. The remark applies with particular force to that sort of
artist whose work is "charged," who is at his best when his pages
have "flight," whose method, in other words, is in the nature of
half-deliberately guided improvisation. It hardly applies, if it

applies at all, to the calmer type, the builder-artist Trollope,
for example. Nor does it particularly apply to the mere orna-
mentalist, the sort of poet who learns by patience and application how to say pretty things in a pretty way, to wreathe them
into pleasantly foliate patterns. Compulsion, of a psychotic nature, is in such cases at a minimum, and the writer is free in a
sense in which the other type of artist is not. We do not expect
him to give us any phoenix of art, plumed with sheer brilliance,
certainly, but we do not expect him, either, to fall very far below the moderately good. He is a craftsman, and his craft sustains him.

More interesting by far is the sort of artist who is more creator
than craftsman. Mr. John Gould Fletcher, who continues er-
ratically to hold one of the highest places among contemporary
American poets, is as striking a case of that as we could find. If
we include his new book, *Breakers and Granite,* Mr. Fletcher
has now published ten books of verse: he is a prolific writer. To
the first five of these books Mr. Fletcher now permits only a
subterranean existence. They are not in circulation, and presumably he considers them mere juvenilia. There was little
verse in them that could be called distinguished. It was in *Irradiations* that Mr. Fletcher first found himself—something happened to him, something to which perhaps he alone, if he
wished, could give us the clue; something more, perhaps, than
a mere exposure to the influence of pre-contemporary French
poetry or the influence of Mr. Ezra Pound. A new sort of tactilism had been given to poetry by the French Symbolists, and
Mr. Fletcher was among the first to take this out of the general
air and make it a property of English verse. It was a sort of
tactilism to which he was born, but for which, in the American
literary scene, he would have starved. In Paris and London he
found it and grew upon it. *Irradiations* was the flower of it;
Goblins and Pagodas and parts of *The Tree of Life* the fruit.

It would be an error, however, to suppose that in all this Mr.
Fletcher was deliberate or orderly. He was in a sense a happy
victim: a tree pollenated by a chance air. At the outset his self-
discovery made him drunk, he committed excesses of color, and
these excesses—in *Irradiations,* in the *Symphonies,* less often in
The Tree of Life—remain perhaps his finest achievement. These
poems have, for the most part, no moral, no "meaning," no intention—they reveal no general attitude, preach no doctrine.
Those who wish poetry to embody, among other things, the
concise statement of a problem, or the formulation of an an-

swer, may pillage these poems in vain. All they will get is a color, a fragrance. For if it was to the new tactilism of Mallarmé and Laforgue and Rimbaud and Verlaine that Mr. Fletcher so richly responded, it was to the tactilism alone: to the self-analysis, half bitter, half sentimental, with which in French poetry this tactilism was usually alloyed, he remained unresponsive. He took the colorism to which it was in his case the key, and omitted the psychology, precisely as Mr. T. S. Eliot took the psychology and omitted the colorism; the former following Rimbaud and Mallarmé, the latter following Verlaine and Laforgue.

Mr. Fletcher's "genius" is therefore for coloristic vividness, primarily, and it must be remarked immediately that it is the "genius" of Balzac's comment—without it Mr. Fletcher is undone. He is at his best when his method is that of fierce improvisation. If the initial stimulus is one happily calculated to draw forth the poet's richest deposits of association, and if, moreover, those deposits have not already too often or too precisely at one point been drawn upon, then he gives us work which has the lustre of the "inspired." But one cannot go on for ever being inspired—the stimulus may not be always as strong, or it may strike at exhausted rifts. Then is one fortunate if one is craftsman as well as creator, or if one knows as well how to write with one's eyes open as with one's eyes shut, and in full possession, perhaps, of a wide knowledge, a rich consciousness of experience, a myriad sympathy. But Mr. Fletcher is not, in this regard, fortunate. When improvisation fails him, he fails altogether. Many a newspaper poet has a better "conscious" technique in verse than he; when he attempts to write in cold blood, his verse is irregular, colorless, and weak. The rhythmic and verbal richness, which is overwhelming in his best "inspired" work, at such moments escapes him wholly, and one would suppose the work to have been by a different hand. One characteristic alone remains—rhetorical speed. Great is the temptation for a poet, whom habit rather than the compulsion of a theme urges toward composition, to echo that part of his own manner which is suggestible by the word "speed." But this speed, excellent when it is the heat, the flame of the theme itself, becomes, when superimposed upon a theme, a mere trick of rhetoric—it is a simulation of excitement, irritating because we can find nothing in the theme, or rather in the poet's reaction to it, out of which the excitement might properly spring. We feel the hollowness; we feel that the poet is goading himself, that he is pretending to an intensity of feeling which he has on other occasions possessed, and would like to possess again, but to which he has lost the key.

Breakers and Granite, like *The Tree of Life,* shows Mr. Fletcher often in this predicament. There are fine things in it—notably the experiments in "polyphonic prose," such as "Clipper Ships," and "The Old South." It is well for us to be reminded that these antedated Miss Lowell's "Can Grande's Castle." But the book as a whole does not satisfy. It is true that Mr. Fletcher's attempt to summarize America, past and present, in a series of poems in verse and prose lends a solidity and a fragmentary grandeur to this book which one cannot find in his others—one's historical sense is refreshed by it, certainly; but despite one's pleasure in this and in several poems on the Mississippi and the Mexican Quarter, and in the Lincoln poem, one comes away from the book with the feeling that Mr. Fletcher has labored heroically at a theme not designed to do him justice. Without color, to paraphrase Balzac, Mr. Fletcher is lost, for he has nothing, or little, to fall back upon. He has not the self-awareness of the good psychologist, his motives remain dark to him; and yet, on the other hand, he is too egocentric to observe widely the external world. One turns from *Breakers and Granite* to the poems by Mr. Fletcher in the recently published *Miscellany of American Poetry* with relief, for in those was not only an achievement, vivid, magical, and swift, but a promise—a hint of an earth-mysticism which might conceivably prove, for Mr. Fletcher, a new well of color.

GALSWORTHY, JOHN   (1928)

Into the general characteristics and obvious virtues of Mr. Galsworthy's *Forsyte Saga* it is perhaps not necessary, at this date, to go. The book has been accepted as a "social satire of epic proportions"; as a "masterpiece of knowledge and insight"; as a "compendium of the Victorian epoch"; as a "masterpiece of form"; and as being "written with a flow and music that is found only in the work of the masters of prose." Certainly, this enormous and painstaking survey of a whole half-century of English life, the life of the propertied classes, has earned its right to a very definite place in English literature: like the Barchester series of Anthony Trollope, its sheer weight as a social document alone is almost enough to guarantee its permanence. What Trollope did for the "country family" in England in the early and middle parts of nineteenth century—taking up the theme about a generation after the point at which Jane Austen dropped it—Mr. Galsworthy has set out to do for the second half of the century, and the early years of the next. The three authors provide us, indeed, with an almost perfect *continuum*. Not only do they deal with the same scene and with the same kinds of people: they also share a common method. It is the "wholeness" of the social picture that interests them, and all three of them go about the presentation of this picture with something of the unexaggerative detachment of the sociologist. Allowing for individual differences—for the shrewder wit of Jane Austen, the generous urbanity of Trollope, the more inquisitive intellectualism of Mr. Galsworthy, and also his keener interest in the purely *dramatic* element in the architecture of fiction—the three authors are very obviously congeners.

Nevertheless, if Mr. Galsworthy resembles his two predecessors in his comprehensiveness and in his predilection for a level and cumulative realism, he has also his striking differences. He is not as "pure" a literary phenomenon as either of the others: his talent is not, like Jane Austen's or Trollope's, a single and immediately recognizable thing, but rather a kind of synthesis, whether we regard it from the point of view of style or the point of view of method. We can, and should, grant immediately his greater intellectual grasp: he assumes for his purpose a far more complex scene, and this more complex scene he handles with admirable control. Nothing is left out, everything is adequately seen and rendered. If we take the picture as a whole, we can say that it is true and rich, and that in assembling so much material on one canvas he has achieved a remarkable feat of design.

It is when we look at the thing in detail that we begin, perhaps, to be here and there a little disquieted and to feel that for all its energy his talent is not quite so fine or deep, not so individual, as that of either of his literary forbears. Writing the other day of Tolstoy, Mr. Galsworthy observed: "His style, in the narrow sense, is by no means remarkable. All his work bears the impress of a mind more concerned with the thing said than with the way to say it. But if one may add to interminable definitions: 'Style is the power in a writer to remove all barriers between himself and his reader—the triumph of style is the creation of intimacy,' then, though such a definition will put many out of court, it will leave Tolstoy a stylist; for no author, in his story-telling, produces a more intimate feeling of actual life." That is interesting, for it suggests that Mr. Galsworthy has himself, in some degree, aimed at a style of this sort, or at all events, finding himself so inclined, he has decided to make the best of it. Mr. Galsworthy, too, is more interested in the thing said than in the manner of the saying: and if, for the most part, he succeeds in producing an effect of immediacy or actuality, by being— shall we say—rather informal in his literary manners, it must be added to this that he is often downright careless. One cannot, in fact, agree with that critic, quoted above, that he writes "with a flow and music that is found only in the masters of prose." Mr. Galsworthy's prose is an adequate prose, but it is not a distinguished one. It is frequently awkward, frequently monotonous, to the point of becoming actively and obtrusively *not* a good medium for the thing said. And again, Mr. Galsworthy has always been somewhat disposed to purple passages. There are, in other words, times when he wants something a little better than his "mere medium" for the thing said; he desires to be poetic; an emotional scene or atmosphere is to be conveyed, and accordingly he attempts a prose more charged and ornate. These attempts are almost invariably failures: Mr. Galsworthy's taste fails him. What one usually feels on these occasions is that he is simply unable to express feelings delicately; and that is, perhaps, a definition of sentimentality.

One feels, therefore, that when one accepts, as one does, Mr. Galsworthy's place in English fiction, one does so with very definite reserves as to the quality of his style. And even the "wholeness" of his picture, which is his major virtue, is not without grave faults. If he gives us admirable scenes, sharp, quick, and living, and admirable portraits, like that of Soames Forsyte, or Irene Herron, or old Jolyon, he also gives us a good many scenes which we do not believe in for a minute, and more than a handful of portraits which do not belong at all in any such gallery as this, but rather in the category of the Jonsonian or Dickensian "humor." Swithin, and the Aunts Hester and Euphemia, and such minor personages as the detective, are the flimsiest of caricatures, and are quite unmistakably out of key. In these instances, and in others, Mr. Galsworthy's taste has gone wrong; his tact has betrayed him; his perceptions have not been sufficiently deep. The result is always an immediate and fatal destruction of the unity of tone.

There are times, moreover, when even his handling of the "good" characters seems to be at fault: times when it seems as if he were not entirely to be trusted as a psychologist. Now and then this is due to his desire for a strong dramatic scene—as when he despatches Bosinney under the wheels of a horse-omnibus, in a fog, with George close behind him. This, like his repeated use of coincidence, violates one's sense of the actual, and gives one the feeling that one has strayed out of the world of Trollope or Tolstoy and into the world of Wilkie Collins. And one begins to entertain a disquieting suspicion. Is it possible that Mr. Galsworthy has a kind of psychological blind-spot? Is it a perhaps tenable view that the sense of the actual he gives us is largely due to his patient accumulation of *little* scenes and actions and conversations, but that in the more important business of psychological dynamics—the business of creating characters which will function powerfully and inevitably out of their unmanageable integrities—he is sometimes helpless? One has the feeling, occasionally, that he is describing his characters rather than letting them live; that when they face a crisis, he solves it for them *intellectually:* and that again and again he fails to sound the real truth in the situations which he himself has evoked. Soames Forsyte, for example, is a real person, on the whole admirably drawn. But could Soames, granted the sensitiveness with which we see him to be endowed, possibly have lived four years with Irene in so total a blindness as to the real state of things between them? Here was a situation which could have been magnificent. A real "realism" would have luxuriated in the minute-by-minute analysis of this profound disaccord. But Mr. Galsworthy never comes to grips with it.

Something of this failure to get inside his characters shows again in *Swan Song,* the coda to the Forsyte Saga. In this charming but rather slight book, we are given the culmination of the interrupted affair of Fleur and Jon, and the death of Soames. The whole story moves toward, and is focused on, the eventual love-scene between Jon and Fleur: we look forward to it from the very beginning: but when it comes, it is quite lamentably inadequate; it is as if the author had gone into a complete psychological funk about it, and had simply not *known* how two such people would have behaved on such an occasion. This scene needed to be the realest and richest and most moving in the book; and given the sufficient actuality of the two people, it could easily have been so. Mr. Galsworthy's failure to give us here anything but a stagey little scene of rhetorical melodrama suggests anew that his gravest fault is his habit of *thinking* his way, by sheer intelligence, into situations which he has not sufficient psychological insight to *feel*.

GISSING, GEORGE   (1927)

To this collection of short stories by George Gissing, "never before issued in book form," Mr. Alfred Gissing contributes a preface, which is largely a discussion of "realism" in fiction; and in this preface Mr. Gissing moves, a little naively, to the conclusion that the author of the *Private Papers of Henry Ryecroft* was something more, or better, than a mere realist, because his stories contained a "moral," or here and there pointed to a "higher truth." At this date, it seems a little odd to encounter a critic who is still worrying about the defense of the "ugly" in art, and who finds it necessary to discover a moral or social—if not aesthetic!—justification for such a portrait as that of Mrs. Gamp. And it is odder still that Mr. Alfred Gissing can proceed, as he does, with his pointing of Gissing's "moral," after quoting a passage from a letter in which Gissing wrote: "Human life has little interest for me, on the whole, save as material for artistic presentation. I can get savage over social iniquities, but, even then, my rage at once takes the direction of planning revenge in artistic work." This could hardly be clearer. If, in his early work (*Demos,* for example) Gissing was occasionally tendentious, in his maturity he was first and last an artist. His purpose, in his descriptions of lower middle-class life, was not moral at all, but aesthetic: his problem was a problem of presentation. His novels and stories were his reports of life as he knew it; he was, in his narrower field, as honest an observer as Trollope; and if he was of far smaller stature as an artist than Chekhov, less poetically gifted, he shared with that great man a tendency to minimize "plot" and to make of his stories mere evocations of life.

In this regard, Gissing was very much ahead of his time. When one reflects that it is now almost a quarter of a century since he died, one reads this posthumous collection of his short stories with astonishment: for with only one or two exceptions these stories are strikingly, in tone and manner, like the sort of thing which, in the hands of such a writer as Katherine Mansfield, critics hailed as revolutionary. In most of these tales the "story" amounts to little or nothing. If one compares them with the contemporary work of Hardy or Meredith or Henry James, one finds a difference as deep as that which severed Chekhov from Turgenev. Here is little or nothing of Hardy's habitual use of tragic or poetic background, his intermittent reference to the backdrop of the Infinite; here is none of Meredith's brilliant, and brilliantly conscious, counterpoint of comment, with its inevitable heightening of distance between the reader and the story; none of the exquisite preparation and elaboration of James. Much more than he admitted, or realized, Gissing *was* interested in "human life"; it is above all for his uncompromising fidelity to his vision that we can still read him with pleasure and profit. He seldom shapes or heads his narrative as these others did, attaches less importance than they to dramatic climax. He is content with a bare presentation of a scene or situation.

To say that Gissing would have been liked by Chekhov is to say that he is a "modern"—he is decidedly more modern than Hardy or James. James, of course, would have disapproved of him, as he disapproved of Mr. Arnold Bennett, on the ground that he offered his reader a mere slice of life, the *donnée* without the working out. Whatever we may feel about that, and however much this sort of modernity may ultimately make Gissing appear old-fashioned, we must unquestionably accept him as an artist of the Chekhov generation, and a good one. He is not great—he lacks force, depth, range, subtlety; he has almost nothing of Chekhov's poetic profundity, only a tithe of his exquisite sensibility; by comparison with him, Gissing seems prosy, bread-and-butterish. But he is good. He can almost always be counted upon to tell his story with a clear eye and a fine gravity of spirit. There is no rhetorical nonsense about him, he is capable of no literary pyrotechnics, his style is level and undistinguished; but within his limits he is an honest and just creator of people and pictures, exaggerating nothing, never forcing a mood, and often using understatement with the most delicate skill. What could be better than the ending of his charming story, *The Fate of Humphrey Snell?* Humphrey was a queer stick—lazy, dreaming, impractical, not very strong; he had a passion for countryside; and eventually found a happy solution of his difficulties by becoming an itinerant herb-collector. He tramped the country, slept where he found himself, enjoyed this simple existence hugely. And then one day he fell in love with a girl who was no better than she should be; applied for a job as steward to a Workman's Club; and asked the girl to marry him. And this is how Gissing ends his story: "Annie, whose handwriting was decipherable only by a lover's eyes, answered his news by return of post: 'Send me money to come i shall want all i have for my things i cant tell you how delited I feal but its that sudin it taks my breth away with heeps of live and—'. . . . There followed a row of crosses, which Humphrey found it easy to interpret. A cross is frequently set upon a grave; but he did not think of that."

That is all—and it is all we need. And Gissing is just in his story of the two Cockney families who go to Brighton for their Bank Holidays, or in the story of the matrimonial failures of Miss Jewell. These tales are, in their kind, perfect. The Budges, the Rippingvilles, Miss Jewell, and the two splendid Cockney girls, Lou and Liz, are done from the life—they are as trenchantly recognizable as Mrs. Laura Knight's etchings of Cockney folk on Hampstead Heath. And if the interior of an English middle-class boarding-house, with all its heavy smells and dreary sounds, its aspidistra plant and its scrubbed white step, has ever been better done, one doesn't know where to find it.

HARDY, THOMAS •   (1924)

In *Three Philosophical Poets,* Mr. Santayana observes of the *Divine Comedy:*

This art does not smack of life, but of somnambulism. The reason is that the intellect has been hypnotized by a legendary and verbal philosophy. It has been unmanned, curiously enough, by an excess of humanism; by the fond delusion that man and his moral nature are at the center of the universe. Dante. . . . seems to be a cosmic poet, and to have escaped the anthropomorphic conceit of romanticism. But he has not escaped it. . . . He is, in a moral sense, still at the center of the universe; his ideal is the cause of everything. . . .

It would seem a long way from Dante to Mr. Hardy; but Mr. Santayana's remark is almost as illuminating of the latter as of the former. Mr. Hardy, too, at first sight, would appear to be a cosmic poet, and to have escaped the anthropomorphic error of the romantics. But, like Dante, he remains carefully at the center of the universe, viewing the world from his own moral rampart;

• Ernest Brennecke, *Thomas Hardy's Universe.*

and even when he is most assiduous in demonstrating man's unimportance in the deterministic stream of things, he exalts him by exalting the vast horror of the stage on which he acts. Cherishing a hope that eventually the "Will" may become as conscious and as compassionate as Man, he makes clear a secret belief in a debatable human superiority. Again, Mr. Hardy's work has always to some extent smacked of somnambulism. His novels have the melodramatic and unreal and fitful vividness of dreams; his characters are as often as not the hollow bright people in a nightmare, vivid, but as a whole not quite apprehensible or credible, "with dreamy conventional gestures" (to quote Mr. Hardy himself), and an air of having been hypnotized. It is reasonable, I think, to see the cause of this in Mr. Hardy's perpetual preoccupation with "ideas." His obsession with the "thing to be demonstrated" is uppermost in his mind; and it is ruthless with him. A touch here and a touch there, every so often a tiny omission or interpolation, it diminishes the real in order to round the pattern; and it is precisely in this diminishing and this rounding—which Mr. Hardy terms "truth" —that he often sacrifices the real and substitutes the phantasmagoric. What this "thing to be proved" may be Mr. Brennecke, in his essay on Hardy's "universe," seeks to make clear. He traces Hardy's intellectual growth from a belief in "crass chance," or the tyranny of "circumstance," or Fate, or Providence, to his almost complete acceptance of Schopenhauer's system with its basis of "the World as Will," and its accompaniment, in the world of phenomena, of absolute determinism. Mr. Brennecke makes an overwhelming case of it. Quoting liberally, he shows that the choruses in *The Dynasts* contain a nearly perfect abstract of Schopenhauer's metaphysical theories. This is certainly a rather surprising and interesting fact. If we quarrel with Mr. Brennecke about it, it can only be because he is prolix and repetitious in the telling of it, uses a great deal too much metaphysical jargon, and is perhaps a little too inclined to take his "fact" seriously, and to leave it at that.

Mr. Hardy, in his preface to *The Dynasts,* disclaims (as Mr. Brennecke admits) any attempt at a systematized philosophy. The doctrines of his "Intelligences," he says, "are but tentative." But Mr. Brennecke is not deterred by this disclaimer: he takes what he terms Mr. Hardy's "intellectual content" very seriously. Is it so "difficult" or "exhilarating" as he thinks "to come to grips with it": or is it especially important to do so, beyond recognizing its nature? Mr. Hardy's philosophy is not original, on the whole; and the really important questions, for criticism, are the questions which Mr. Brennecke almost wholly ignores: why has Mr. Hardy, as an artist, always been so enthralled by "ideas"; and to what aesthetic use has he put them? . . . On the latter question Mr. Brennecke does throw an incidental light when he points out the very remarkable accuracy and compactness with which Mr. Hardy, in the choruses of *The Dynasts,* retails Schopenhauer's conception of the unconscious Will. This affords one an opportunity of observing Mr. Hardy's method, of watching the characteristic vigor, and austerity, and dry economy with which he converts an idea into a feeling or an action; it lights exceptionally his habit of personifying the abstract, and of abstracting the personal; but into these matters Mr. Brennecke, unfortunately, does not see fit to go.

And this is precisely where any careful criticism of Mr. Hardy *ought* to go. Without for a moment forgetting Mr. Hardy's exceptional power of thought, and the remarkable degree and variety with which he has "caught up" nineteenth-century abstract thinking, of the more skeptical sort, into poetry, we can more fruitfully concern ourselves with the interesting fact that he evinced in his work an emotional craving for a skeptical intellectual basis long before the skeptical intellectual basis took the precise shape to which Mr. Brennecke attaches such importance. The precise shape, indeed, does not particularly matter. The half-dozen intellectual viewpoints through which Mr. Hardy has travelled are metaphysically different; but it is useful to notice that they are emotionally the same. What we see here is an emotional determinism of thought which Mr. Hardy himself would probably be the first to admit, and which clearly suggests that for Mr. Hardy it is the common factor of emotion, in these successive viewpoints, which has been most necessary. Mr. Hardy was determined—by what motives we can leave a chartered psychoanalyst to ascertain—to take a tragic view. Leaving aside, then, both the personal and the philosophic aspects of this, and restricting ourselves to the aesthetic, we find in Mr. Hardy the extraordinarily interesting case of an artist with a powerful appetite for a tragic view, who, beginning with melodrama, has gradually and laboriously sought the "rationale" which would not only permit, but actually invite, the maximum of disaster, and carry him thus from melodrama to tragedy. In *A Pair of Blue Eyes,* and in all those novels in which chance, or mere coincidence, dominates—that is, a purely external and unpredictable force—we have melodrama; but by degrees Mr.

Hardy substituted a gloomy determinism for chance, and thus greatly extended the dimensions of his tragic view, partly by increasing his plausibility (since the downfall of a protagonist could be derived from the defects of his own nature), but also by increasing the unity and aesthetic value of his "scene," which was now conceived not as chaos but as order. In this, the "philosophy" was perhaps simply derived from the appetite for disaster and pity. That it was the emotional implications in Schopenhauer's ideas which most signally attracted Mr. Hardy we can see clearly in the fact that he persistently "sentimentalizes" them, as, for example, in *The Dynasts;* where, instead of Schopenhauer's aseptic unemotionalism, we have the "Spirit of the Pities" and "Spirits Sinister and Ironic," and with admirable effect. If even here we feel that Mr. Hardy has not wholly replaced the melodramatic by the tragic or the grandiose by the poetic—and the same thing is yet truer of even the latest and best of the novels—we must suppose that it is due, as suggested earlier, to the fact that the artist does not sufficiently "command" the philosopher. Mr. Hardy's appetite for the disastrous and pitiful often outruns his inventive power, as his inventive power (especially in his prose) almost invariably outruns his sense of effect. The "idea" thus too often and too bleakly emerges in his prose, crippling or hypnotizing his characters, or reducing them to lifelessness. It is in poetry that the "idea" takes its place most naturally and effectively; and it is therefore not surprising that Mr. Hardy should have shown in poetry, most unmistakably and unintermittently, his tremendous power and individuality.

Mr. Brennecke's treatise suggests these and related problems; and it is extremely interesting and careful. Reduced to two chapters instead of six, it would make the very best of bases upon which to build an exact aesthetic and psychological study of Mr. Hardy's work. It is a pity that Mr. Brennecke should so painstakingly have left aside all the aesthetic implications which so clearly start from his notes on Mr. Hardy's metaphysical preoccupations. But even so he has given us something which will be useful. . . .

HOUSMAN, A. E.   (1936)

The *Last Poems* of Housman have now been succeeded by
More Poems, chosen from among the completed verses which he
left behind him at his death, and thus the total number of lyrics
given to the world by this most reticent and self-denying of poets
grows to the total of one hundred and fifty-three; but one can
say at once that it is an addition which does not change, that
the addition of the third volume, like the addition of the second,
extends slightly, if at all, the range, does not alter the character,
and that the three books are really one, are really *The Shropshire Lad*. It is more or less true that the third collection is very
slightly inferior to the second, just as the second was very
slightly inferior to the first. The thinnesses and barenesses are
more noticeable, the repetitions of theme and tone more staring,
the genuine felicities are certainly fewer. Nor are there whole
poems, as many of them, which attain to quite the cool completeness of the best in *The Shropshire Lad*. Nevertheless, the
best here are *almost* as good as ever, and admirers of Housman
will find much here to please them; while for those whose admiration is more temperate the slight slackening of the fiber will
itself be of interest, as so often it tends to lay bare Housman's
essential limitedness.

That he is limited, no one in his senses would deny. The
actual range, when one stops to consider it, is extraordinarily
narrow, and the perhaps too-well-disposed critic wonders
whether he is not wish-thinking in supposing that many of Housman's restrictions were self-restrictions. It is one thing—one may
say—to be limited, another to *impose* limitations on oneself;
and somehow or other the myth has grown up that Housman's
limitedness, like the smallness of his output, was the result of an
iron-discipline and restraint, a process of selection and elimination at a very high degree of tension, and that the product was
accordingly, *ipso facto*, severely and beautifully classic. Housman himself did a good deal to encourage the growth of this
notion—the twenty-six years of silence with which he followed
the tremendous success of the book which made him famous,
years during which he allowed it to be supposed that he had
turned his back on poetry forever in order to bury himself in
scholarship, calculatedly or uncalculatedly were bound to impress his admirers with the extreme *preciousness* of his work;
and to break the long silence at last with the publication of

forty-one little lyrics, rather somberly and pointedly entitled
Last Poems, as if to say "this little parcel of verses is the work of
a lifetime," was only to carry the process further.

Moreover, an idea got abroad, whether with his own impri-
matur or not, that one reason for the extreme smallness of his
output was that the intensity of the effort, as of the "inspiration,"
for even the tiniest and most fragile of his verses, was too exhausting for him, could not more than occasionally be endured,
an idea only partially offset by a sister rumor that it was really
beer which was his inspiration—the often-celebrated "pot" of
the poems. Just the same, it is permissible perhaps to question
whether the narrowness of the range and the smallness of the
output were not actually implicit in the nature of Housman's
talent, and imposed from within rather than from without; and
to question in parallel fashion whether the often-praised "classic"
perfection and severity of his style might not more justly, now
and then, be termed pseudo-classic.

And that, for better or worse, and at the risk of being considered guilty of something perilously like *lèse majesté,* the present
reviewer has always thought, and still thinks, thinks more than
ever after a rereading of the three little books. It is idle to deny
the charm, the grace, the dexterity, the neatness, whether of
form or thought, just as it is idle to deny the wistful and brave
individuality which everywhere shows in these poems; but it
seems equally idle to deny that the classic should be made of
sterner and deeper stuff than this, and that if it is not to be
profounder, then it must at least be more richly and variously
wrought.

And even taken at its best, the texture of Housman's verse
tends to be thin. Nor is this wholly a matter of choice. Simplicity is aimed at, to be sure, but there is always, also, a little
more simplicity than was aimed at, and this looks as if it arose
from the fact that Housman's sensory equipment for poetry was
definitely somewhat arid. The range of mere perception is very
narrow indeed—it is a world in which the grass is green and the
sheep are white, as simple a world as that of W. H. Davies, for
example, but with almost nothing of Davies' sudden felicities of
observation or quick aptnesses of statement. Housman conven-
tionalizes, and that would be all right if the conventionalization
were itself more interesting; but for this reader at least the
constant reliance on a pretty threadbare and perhaps deliberately anachronistic kind of martial imagery, joined with a bu-

colic imagery just as deliberately "quaint" or "homely," becomes
in the end both barren and defrauding.

That one should cease to believe might not matter, provided
the *playing* at poetry, the playing at profundity or skepticism,
were itself more richly and ingeniously managed; but this Housman only seldom achieved. The result is a charming but incomplete and essentially adolescent poetry—the questionings and
despairs and loyalties are alike adolescent, and so are the
thoughts and the bravenesses and the nostalgic gayeties; and
what makes it sometimes worse is one's suspicion that this adolescent note, this boyishness, is a cultivated thing, a calculated
falsetto. It has been pointed out that one of the longest of the
new poems—"Down the waterway of sunset drove to shore a
ship of gold"—is a little Kiplingesque. But the truth is that something very like the Kipling note is always lurking just round
the corner, in these poems, both in the tone and the text. The
slightly too dactylic dittylike use of the octosyllabic quatrains,
coupled with the characteristically too-thumping use of Universals, an attitudinizing orotundity, produce now and then an
effect perilously close to that of the *Barrack Room Ballads*.

But no, that is perhaps being too hard on a very fine poet, and
to overdo our point that at least a part of Housman's charm grew
from his very limitations. Greatness? No. Epigrammatic, lovely,
light-colored, youthfully charming above all; but to quote a typical epigrammatic quatrain by a greater poet, Emily Dickinson,
at once shows him up as a little bit thin:

Lay this laurel on the one
Too intrinsic for renown.
Laurel, veil your deathless tree;
Him you chasten, that is he.

Which is a real voice, and the real thing.

HUXLEY, ALDOUS   (1925)

Mr. Aldous Huxley has acquired a remarkable position among
the younger novelists; and there can be no question that he is—to
use advisedly a term perhaps a little invidious—a very accomplished writer. It has been freely suggested that he is brilliant; it

has been taken for granted that his position is unique. Of his three novels, and three volumes of tales, it has been urged that they witness to the evolution of an "artist" in fiction: it has even been suggested that the artist thus posited may, ultimately, prove to be great. If this attitude is a trifle solemn, nevertheless one willingly enough subscribes to a part of it. Mr. Huxley *is* exceptionally accomplished; his talent *is*, in the contemporary medley, conspicuous; and it is not for nothing that critics have so unanimously pronounced him to be ophidianly clever. The latter quality, indeed, has occasioned a particularly loud chorus of encomium. The critics, and Mr. Huxley's audience, have been pleased to dwell on something a little sinister in it, and a little naughty. It has been seen as a peculiarly delicious blend of the best and most ingenious *morbidezza* of the '90's with the very latest fashions (and modern improvements) in morals and ideas from Paris and Vienna. There is also, it is pointed out, his erudition. How astonishing his ease and copiousness of allusion! And what could be more appropriate, in this post-war world of sad, gay disillusionment and scientific luxury, than Mr. Huxley's macaronic *mélange* of the classical and the up-to-date, of Peacock and the *fin-de-siècle*, of Folengo and Freud? Mr. Huxley's affinities, in this respect, are easy to find. During the last decade there has been what one might almost call a "macaronic school"—an international school concerned with satire, with burlesque, and, in the absence of any stable convictions concerning art or morals, with the breakdown of forms and the extensive use of reference and quotation. If Mr. Huxley does not go as far as some in the direction of the *cento*, he at any rate shares in that tendency.

It is this absence of conviction that most impresses one in his work; it is in this that his cleverness, his wit, his queer, uncomfortable ingenuity of fancy seem to strike their somewhat shallow roots; and one begins to wonder, after reading his sixth book of fiction, how likely it is that a basis so insubstantial can make of Mr. Huxley the writer one would like to see him become. Mr. Huxley seems himself to be in some doubt about this. He has steered a somewhat uncertain course. He has always had a little the air of one who could not quite decide how serious he dared to be, or to what extent the act of being serious is a kind of naive confession of credulity, a lack of sophistication which might be too maliciously enjoyed in drawing-rooms. This ambiguity was pretty clear in his first book, *Limbo*. The beginning of a serious attempt at seriousness can be seen there in such stories as

"Happily Ever After" and "Richard Greenow"; but in both of these the impulse to be clever, to be sophisticated, finally triumphed, with the result that they were not successful either as satire or as credible fiction; neither very amusing nor wholly true. In *Crome Yellow*, his next book, it was natural that, taking so frankly the Peacockian model, Mr. Huxley should also take a step backward, a step further away from the actual. *Crome Yellow* is as artificial, as flimsy, and, alas, as unreadable as a clever book can be. The occasional note of sincerity, of verisimilitude, of feeling, of seriousness, which now and then almost brought his characters alive in *Limbo* has here been deliberately exorcised; and in its place Mr. Huxley abandons himself to his terrible passion, a passion positively narcissistic, for conversation. His *personæ*, totally lifeless and indistinguishable one from another, are merely ventriloquist's puppets, the device by which he can indulge himself, as often and as long as he likes, in witty talk. Has Mr. Huxley a frustrated desire to be a great conversationalist? The question is an impertinence, but it is one that it is difficult to refrain from asking; for, despite its ingenuities, *Crome Yellow* is simply an apotheosis of talk, talk in the most exasperating drawing-room style. One sees, of course, what Mr. Huxley was after—he indeed tells us himself, describing the "great Knockespotch, who delivered us from the tyranny of the realistic novel. . . . Oh, those Tales—those Tales! How shall I describe them? Fabulous characters shoot across his pages like gaily dressed performers on the trapeze. There are extraordinary adventures and still more extraordinary speculations. Intelligences and emotions, relieved of all the imbecile preoccupations of civilized life, move in intricate and subtle dances, crossing and recrossing, advancing, retreating, impinging. An immense erudition and an immense fancy go hand in hand. All the ideas of the present and of the past, on every conceivable subject, bob up among the Tales, smile gravely or grimace a caricature of themselves, then disappear to make place for something new. The verbal surface of his writing is rich and fantastically diversified. The wit is incessant." . . . There, of course, but for the grace of God, goes Mr. Huxley. He, too, has a passion for the superlatively and purely articulate, for intelligences (but not emotions) relieved of imbecile preoccupations, for immense erudition, immense fancy, incessant wit, and a verbal surface richly semined (to borrow his method) with oddities that smell of camphor. He shares, also, with the great Knockespotch, his passion for ideas. One imagines him sitting with Bartlett in one hand and

The Times in the other, compiling thus his *omnium gatherum* of
the antique and the quotidian, and turning it all into airy talk:
setting it in motion with his easy and skilful rhetoric; giving it
the accomplished twist that imparts a sparkle. One is aware that
he regards this purely as a kind of boring game; he wishes to
give the impression of employing his skill automatically, as if
without too much lending to the performance either mind or
heart; but one also perceives, as noted above, a secondary Mr.
Huxley who wants, a little timidly, to do something else.

For in *Mortal Coils, Antic Hay, Little Mexican,* and now in
Those Barren Leaves, it is perhaps not altogether fanciful to
guess a growing doubt in Mr. Huxley's mind, a doubt as to
whether the great Knockespotch is, after all, the best model. To
be incessantly frivolous, to try in every phrase to be diverting,
to round unctuously and a little smartly every sentence, to conduct with so Mozartian a grace his glassy passages of sustained
bravura from page to page—can one, by this method, achieve
the best? It is true that occasionally he manages this sort of thing
with delightful skill. *Nuns at Luncheon* could hardly be better.
It is perhaps as triumphant an example of a dexterous and
heartless *playing* with a tragic theme as one could find. Not
wholly satisfying—for the click of the spring at the end is too
sharp, too prepared, too small, and serves only to reveal the
story as an anecdote (like many of Mr. Huxley's stories) comparatively empty of beauty, of feeling, or intensity, and indeed
actuated more by a desire to toy with the theme, holding it at
arm's length, than by any deeper concern. This externalism has
a peculiar and delightful effect in this instance: an effect as of
an inverted sentimentality, a deliberate frolic in the presence of
tragedy. But the method is not one that can be used *passim;*
and, unfortunately, the habit of doing so, of trying always to remain cynically aloof, has been indulged by Mr. Huxley too long
to be easily broken. In *Antic Hay* it is obvious that he wants to
concern himself more deeply and frankly with his characters,
and invites his readers to do so; but the Mr. Huxley who enjoys
buffoonery and burlesque insists on introducing his satirical ingenuities, which are ungainly rather than diverting, and his
saffron interludes, which are pawky rather than frank. It is not,
in consequence, a satisfactory satire, since one believes in the
characters too much; it is not a satisfactory novel, since one believes in them too little.

The same difficulties must be urged against *Those Barren
Leaves*. It is Mr. Huxley's best work, and it marks, perhaps, the

sharpest single advance that he has made. It is rich, it is witty, it is admirably if ornately written. But if Mr. Huxley the buffoon is less in evidence, Mr. Huxley the non-stop conversationalist, and Mr. Huxley the cynical onlooker, are still all too tediously here. It is difficult, therefore, to judge his capacity for "seeing" a character in the round. Has he, indeed, as yet, created a single character in whom one can believe, who escapes the Huxleyan gesture and intonation, and obeys a *daimon* of his own? He comes closer to Miss Thriplow and Irene than he did to their many prototypical predecessors, with whom they share their bell-like bobbed hair, round eyes, and doll-like faces. Chelifer and Calamy and Cardan—these, too, have moments when they come alive, are perhaps a little more recognizably and dimensionally real than Gumbril, with his pneumatic breeches and false beard, or Marcaptan with his sofa. But Mr. Huxley still has his uncontrollable appetite for talk, still strives to be that "miracle of nature, breathing libraries." Scarcely has a character begun to take on the warmth of the actual, or the action to be enticing, when off he goes once more into endless discussion; the drawing-room style puts on its quotation marks; effective phrase is added to effective phrase, paragraph to paragraph, page to page, no matter who it is who happens to be speaking; the reader's will to believe is remorselessly defeated; and we are presented at last not so much with a story, or a series of character studies, as with another tremendous example of Mr. Huxley's highly cultured conversation. Chelifer, Cardan, and Calamy become interchangeable shadows, and, if all three are divinely articulate, it is not themselves they talk into existence, but their author. Chelifer's "autobiography" is indistinguishable in tone from any other part of the story. Was it—one asks after closing the book—Calamy who was the poet, and Chelifer, who, wearying of his amorous successes, became a mystic? Was it in this novel, or in *Crome Yellow*, that the dashing young lord, with his lisp and his high-powered car, flew from one house-party to another? Was it Calamy or Chelifer or Cardan who talked so well, and so perpetually and wearily fell into love and out again?

But this is ungrateful. The book is, when one has weathered the first hundred pages, extremely entertaining. The Chelifer section is managed with a technical virtuosity that any novelist must envy; and many of the interpolated discussions—notably that of Cardan on art—contain admirable criticism. If only Mr. Huxley could abjure his habit of cynical intrusion, and wear for a little, without shame, his heart on his sleeve, one feels that he might achieve something very fine indeed. Could he not also, for a time, give up these emancipated house-parties and exquisite boudoirs? We encounter them, in his pages, far too often.

JAMES, HENRY ·   (1925)

The very brief and very characteristic note on criticism, written by Whitman in the sixties or seventies, and now unearthed and published by Mr. Spingarn, is, if not exciting, sufficiently interesting to send one back to Whitman's prose again; and its appearance simultaneously with Miss Bosanquet's admirable and charming note on the later method of Henry James provokes one to renewed wonder at the scene and era which could produce two men so remarkably unlike. Whitman, Poe, Hawthorne, James, Melville, Emily Dickinson—it is an extraordinary troupe; and its heterogeneity bears witness, if witness were needed, to the fact that when we speak of American literary origins we have, even yet, scant right to generalize regarding scenes and eras. There is no such thing as the American scene—more precisely, there are as many as we have the patience to find. And every era, in America, is not one but a dozen.

Whitman and James can conveniently be placed at opposite ends of a given spectrum. One is tempted to suggest that the only thing they had in common was their perception of an American scene which was, morally, socially, and aesthetically, the same; they saw substantially the same thing; but their responses to it were another matter. Whitman, as we know, "embraced" the United States, collectively and severally; and James, after a long and earnest look, departed. What they thus perceived, and thus differently responded to, was the vulgarization (to give the word its full Latin sense) which, in its first stages, democracy was achieving for the Anglo-Saxon in America, and which the War of Secession, by thinning out the good stock, greatly accelerated. James's disillusionment with this new America was, if early, not so early as has been supposed. At the age of twenty-three we find him writing: "This democratic, liberty-loving, American populace, this stern and war-tried people, is a great civiliser. It is devoted to refinement. If it has sustained a monstrous war, and practised human nature's best in

* And Walt Whitman.

so many ways for the last five years, it is not to put up with spurious poetry afterwards." Perhaps, in this judgment of his country's devotion to refinement, the wish was father to the thought. Within five years his own devotion to refinement had transported him to Europe; and within another decade, in his study of Hawthorne, he had gone almost to the opposite extreme, and had concluded that America was both vulgar and provincial.

In this devotion to refinement, on many planes, one may excusably see a major principle of James's life and work. Miss Bosanquet throws a good deal of light on this—her account of James's anxious maternal revision of his earlier novels is delightful, and contains some excellent criticism. But it must be noted that James had not at all, in this anxiety, changed. From beginning to end his view of art was exclusively aesthetic; and his growth as an artist was not an alteration, but a heightening of consciousness, the principle which his consciousness most cherished being that a work of art must primarily deal with the supremely "workable," and must, above all, be superlatively *worked*. It is no wonder, therefore, that Whitman disgusted him. What Whitman saw and loved, in America, was exactly what he himself saw and fled from; and what Whitman "did" with this scene was the one thing which to James was wholly inexcusable —it was, in his view, a mere unselected and unarranged outpouring, made worse by the fact that it was "insincere." The remark of James which I have quoted above is from his review of *Drum Taps*—invidiously entitled, "Mr. Walt Whitman"— published in 1865. The review left, of poor Whitman, almost nothing. "It has been a melancholy task," wrote James, "to read this book; and it is a still more melancholy one to write about it. Perhaps since the days of Mr. Tupper's *Philosophy* there has been no more difficult reading of the poetic sort. It exhibits the effort of an essentially prosaic mind to lift itself, by a prolonged muscular strain, into poetry." Again: "Every tragic event collects about it a number of persons who delight to dwell upon its superficial points—of minds which are bullied by the *accidents* of the affair. The temper of such minds seems to us to be the reverse of the poetic temper; for the poet, although he incidentally masters, grasps, and uses the superficial traits of his theme, is really only a poet in so far as he extracts its latent meaning and holds it up to the common eyes." In regard to Whitman's "prosaic" form: "There is, fortunately, but one attempt at rhyme. . . . But what if, in form, it *is* prose? Very good poetry has come out of prose before this. To this we would reply that it must first have gone into it. Prose, in order to be good poetry, must first be good prose. As a general principle, we know of no circumstance more likely to impugn a writer's earnestness than the adoption of an anomalous style. He must have something very original to say if none of the old vehicles will carry his thoughts." He decides, of course, that what Whitman has to say is neither original nor edifying. It is "monstrous," because it "pretends to persuade the soul while it slights the intellect; because it pretends to gratify the feelings while it outrages the taste." "We find art, measure, grace, sense, sneered at on every page." At the end, he advises Whitman: "You must be *possessed,* and you must strive to possess your possession. If, in your striving, you break into divine eloquence, then you are a poet."

It is interesting to find that James so completely missed the flavor of Whitman; not surprising, however, if we reflect on the extent to which flavor, in Whitman's poetry, is identifiable with what James would have termed vulgarity—immersion in the quotidian mobsoul, the here-and-now, combined with a conscious disregard of traditions. Presumably, as time went on, James somewhat modified his original view. It is doubtful, however, if he could ever have gone as magnanimously far toward meeting the tenets of the "opposition" as Whitman, on *his* side, succeeded in doing. From 1860 to the end of his life Whitman steadily grew in tolerance, steadily widened and deepened his view of the aims and uses of art. It is true that he never did, and never could, abandon his belief that art has a religious or social function, and that any merely aesthetic measure of it must be fatally inadequate. "Has it never occurred to any one," he asks, "that the real test applicable to a book is entirely outside of literary tests; and that any truly original and grand production has little or nothing to do with the rules and calibres now in mode? . . . I have fancied the ocean and the daylight, the mountain and the forest, putting their spirit in an utterance— and that utterance a judgment on our books, and especially on the current poetry production of this country and Europe. I have fancied some lofty and disembodied human soul giving its judgment; and fancied emotional Humanity, in some single representative, giving its . . ." That view, allowing for the characteristic mythopoeia, is a functional one, and underlies all of Whitman's work, as the aesthetic view underlies all of James's. But Whitman could and did find a place, in his scheme, for the

"aesthetic." While he regarded it as a product of feudalism, and
could assert that "the spirit of English literature is not great . . .
is almost always material, sensual, not spiritual—almost always
congests, makes plethoric, not frees, expands, dilates—is cold,
anti-democratic, loves to be sluggish and stately . . . ," nevertheless, he increasingly emphasized the importance (for American letters) of a close study of the literature of Europe. If he
could complain that Poe's verses "without the first sign of a
moral principle . . . or the simpler affections of the heart
. . . illustrate an intense faculty for technical and abstract
beauty . . ." and "probably belong among the electric lights of
literature, brilliant and dazzling, but with no heat," he could
add that "Poe's genius has yet conquered a special recognition
for itself, and I too have come to fully admit it, and appreciate
it." And if he ridiculed the *beauty disease,* from which American
poetry then suffered (quoting aptly from Baudelaire), he could
none the less praise Tennyson highly. "Poetry here of a high
(perhaps the highest) order of verbal melody, exquisitely clean
and pure, and almost always perfumed, like the tuberose, to an
extreme of sweetness."

This, certainly, is a more complex and conscious Whitman
than the Whitman whom James saw. It makes one wonder,
amusedly, how far, had he lived, Whitman could have got with
The Golden Bowl. If one suspects that he would have done better by James than James did by him, perhaps in that we measure justly a deficiency in James. James was the *subtler* critic, in
the sense that he was immensely more perceptive and finely
analytic of the communicative aspects of art; but Whitman was
the wiser. He was a shrewd, though slipshod, judge of literature's psychological values in art, seeing more clearly the functional position of art in the human scheme. There was room,
thus, for James in Whitman's republic; but no room for Whitman in James's ivory tower.

JAMES, HENRY *

Alice James quotes Anatole France as having said *"Tout vaut
mieux que de s'écouter vivre,"* and goes on to add "which is not
to be denied surely; but if destiny, Anatole, offers you no other

* Alice James: *Her Brothers: Her Journal,* ed. Anna Robeson Burr.

opportunity, you will find that, if you lend an indulgent and imaginative ear, you may strike, even from that small keyboard, all the notes of melody, comedy, and tragedy."

Nothing could be more appropriate, to the journal of Alice James, than this quotation from France and Miss James' comment upon it; taken together, they are the truest possible description of Miss James' purpose and achievement. The business of "listening to oneself live" is an inescapable, and perhaps the most important, characteristic of that peculiar thing, the "journal mind"; and if that is true of all keepers of journals, it is particularly true of those who happen also to be invalids. Inevitably, there is an enclosed and sick-room quality about such records: the light, if bright, is feverish; the immediate is exaggerated and foreshortened, with an effect of distortion; and what one gets is in consequence a self-portrait a little larger than life-size, a little too close to the camera, a little queer. One felt this in Barbellion, and in Katherine Mansfield, one feels it again here. Miss James is as terrifyingly honest as Barbellion was, and in some respects more intelligent; but, no more than he, can she quite escape that tiny chromatic fringe of "falseness" which seems to be the penalty of a too-devoted recording of the minute-by-minute sound of one's life. A further part of the difficulty lies in the fact that the self-portrait is done, of course, with half an eye on posterity. One cannot put in everything, one must select, and with the best intentions in the world one ends by selecting what is most important, or most striking. The peaks are put in, the plateaux are left out. The wit is always a wit, the brilliant person always brilliant, the conscious person always conscious. The dullnesses and *longueurs* disappear.

This much granted, but by no means in derogation, the journal of Alice James must be accepted as one of the most remarkable specimens of its kind. No wonder that Henry James praised it so highly, in a letter here printed as a preface, nor, on the other hand, that he should have felt a natural timidity about its being published in his own life-time. It deals exclusively with the last few years of her life, which she spent in England, and therefore, unavoidably, it deals very largely with Henry and the social world to which he had introduced her. If she is generous and perceptive in her praise of Henry, she is also, and with a vengeance, his New England conscience and consciousness: his individual Englishman she may like, but of the English and the English scene she is as penetrating and destructive a critic as only a sophisticated and liberal New Englander can be. She might yield a little to her brother's gentle and eager social *arrivisme*—she loves to sprinkle her pages with titled names, and to "be in touch"; there is more than a trace of New England snobbery in her; she enjoys *patronizing* the English; but despite this, she remains undauntedly and gaily a democrat and a skeptic.

How grateful we ought to be that our excellent parents [she exclaims] had threshed out all the ignoble superstitions, and did not feel it to be their duty to fill our minds with the dry husks—leaving them *tabulae rasae* to receive whatever stamp of individual experience was to give them, so that we had not the bore of wasting our energy in raking over and sweeping out the rubbish. I used to wonder at father's fulminations against what seemed so extinct, little dreaming until I came here, what vitality the ugly things had.

In all this she remained, of course, much more keenly and essentially American than Henry, whose spiritual and intellectual loyalty to the bleak New England scene had long been an uneasy one; perhaps she held him back; she was herself something to which he *could* be loyal; certainly, after her death, his Europeanization became more rapid and complete. She was, in fact, as fine a specimen of New England individualism as one could find—as perfect in her way as Emily Dickinson, whose approximate contemporary she was, and whom she resembled—with due allowance for her social cosmopolitanism—very closely. For her, as for Emily Dickinson, as Henry put it, the Emersonian doctrine "of the supremacy of the individual to himself, of his originality and, as regards his own character, *unique* quality, must have had a great charm." It is of herself she really speaks when she says: "It is reassuring to hear the English pronouncement that Emily Dickinson is fifth-rate—they have such a capacity for missing quality; the robust evades them equally with the subtle." In the last entry of her journal, dictated two days before she died, she remarked: "I am being ground slowly on the grim grindstone of physical pain, and on two nights I had almost asked for K's lethal dose; but one steps hesitatingly along such unaccustomed ways, and endures from second to second." It is almost a paraphrase of Emily Dickinson's poem *Experience*.

Of Miss Burr's long introduction, perhaps the less said the better. Such information as it gives, chiefly about the two younger brothers of the James family, Wilky and Bob, is scarcely needed here; and in all other respects it is a melancholy aesthetic miscalculation and would much better, in future editions, be omitted. The journal is a brilliant and delightful thing, and can stand by itself.

JAMES, HENRY   (1935)

Mr. Blackmur and Messrs. Charles Scribner's Sons, between them, in making the James critical prefaces available in a single volume, have performed a service to English letters which it is difficult to overstate. The result is in some respects the most important single book of English criticism—*practical* criticism— since the time of Arnold: even some might say, since the time of Coleridge and Hazlitt. James was not a "great" critic in the sense of being a wide one: the range of his natural sympathies was too narrow for that, and too idiosyncratically refined; he had as little eye as ear for poetry (as one may see by looking at his early review of Swinburne's *Chastelard,* his essay on Baudelaire), and his feelings about the "slice of life" sort of fiction, or fiction as "revelation," are well known. But that he was a great *specialist* in criticism this collection of prefaces makes admirably clear. Never has there been, never perhaps can there be again, such a taking to pieces and such a putting together again of the whole idea and craft of the fictive art. As James was the most completely "formal" novelist who has ever written, everywhere and always passionately conscious of the smallest items of design, sequence, mass, picture, and scene, so in a sense it was inevitable that it should be he who would first think of taking himself as a critical *corpus vile* and making of his own practice a theory. Implicit in even the earliest of his work, almost glaringly *explicit* in the latest, the theory was the thing that was dearest to him; and that he should end his days by going through those extraordinary novels for a last loving analysis of his own devotion to form was the most natural thing in the world.

Of course, James loads the dice, unconsciously, in his own favor: he is concerned entirely with that sort of pure fiction, that abstract "other world" creation, of which he himself became the first practitioner and the consummate master. The novel as a mere representation of life, or as mystic penetration into it, doesn't interest him. Of those, he merely says: "These are the circumstances of the interest—we see, we see; but where is the interest itself, where and what is its center, and how are we to measure it in relation to *that?*" What he wants, above all, is organization, and it is wholly characteristic that we find him saying in one of these prefaces that he sees it as impossible to make any real distinction between theme and form. Verisimilitude, if it threatened to get in the way, was ruthlessly sacrificed, or at any rate compromised. Of *In the Cage* he observes: "My central spirit, in the anecdote, is, for verisimilitude, I grant, too ardent a focus of divination; but without this excess the phenomena detailed would have lacked their principle of cohesion." There it is, plain as a pikestaff, and very interesting too in its suggestion that to some extent, at least, James was aware of what he was doing in pushing the novel into a logical world of form in which the probabilities must often be sustained by form alone. Analogous are his remarks in the preface to the *Princess Casamassima*, where, confronted with the problem of rendering the unknown London underworld of anarchy and conspiracy, he ingeniously discovered that to be *vague*, to use hints and notes, "not of sharp particulars but of loose appearances . . . just perceptible presences and general looming possibilities," was precisely to achieve an effect of reality. The reality, for us, may not be quite convincing, and obviously, for James, it was of secondary importance—*enough* of it must be there, but it need not be dominant. But one wonders a little, also, whether he was not a trifle self-deceived in this, the method ancillary to the nature, and that superb aesthetic economy precisely compelled by the comparative poverty of experience?

And to wonder this is also to wonder whether those miraculous last novels, which so triumphantly take possession of the "other world" (a possession as complete, in a diametrically opposite way, as Dostoevsky's), were not in *some* degree a queerly uncalculated by-product of the theory and the nature, their precise beautiful quality of *logical unreality* not wholly seen by James himself: just as Dostoevsky could say: "Is not my fantastic Idiot the very dailiest truth?" Impossible to speak with any certainty, of course, one can only guess; and at all events it *is* certain that the novels are the kind of thing which James, the critic, makes enticingly clear, in these brilliant and copious prefaces, as desirable. The prefaces are not easy reading, they are often diffuse and repetitious, the late vice of the dragged-in and obligatory metaphor, for the sake of "brightness," is tiresomely overdone; but for all that they are the most fascinating critical adventure of our time, and the profoundest. Granted the aim, the theory, there is not an aspect of the fictive art which is not here dealt with brilliantly and subtly and—one is tempted to add—forever.

Mr. Blackmur contributes an excellent analytic preface, a model of its sort, which might well have been longer, particularly in its summing up. One should be grateful to him, too, for reminding readers of that extraordinary address of James on *The Novel in the Ring and the Book*—perhaps still the best single statement of James' aesthetic . . .

As a final note on a humbler level, one would like to point out that the very peculiar sentence (in the preface to *What Maisie Knew*) in which James forgot to finish a central clause is here reprinted without correction: "The passage in which her father's terms of intercourse with the insinuating but so strange and unattractive lady whom he has had the detestable levity to whisk her off to see late at night, is a signal example of the all but incalculable way in which interest may be constituted." A very fine specimen, as James himself would have called it, of the misplaced middle.

KEATS, JOHN   (1925)

It is perhaps idle to ask whether there is sufficient warrant for another life of Keats. One may question whether even for Sir Sidney Colvin's Life there was much necessity—his excellent monograph in the English Men of Letters series would be, if brought up to date in certain minor particulars, all that one needs. Miss Lowell pleads, of course, for her *John Keats,* the excuse of new material. But this new material amounts, quantitatively and qualitatively, to very little. One is glad to have the rest of the Dawlish poem for the further faint light it sheds on the "bawdy" side of Keats; one is glad of the Gripus fragment, which very slightly extends one's knowledge of his dramatic gifts; and the letter to Woodhouse is important in its bearing on the Hyperion problem, though in a sense opposite to that which Miss Lowell intends. The other things—the other few fragments of verse, the Brawne and Taylor letters—are useful, certainly, but I cannot think they excuse a biography of thirteen hundred pages. A pamphlet might have been made of them, with perhaps an essay; it would have been enough. For the fact is that in the letters of Keats—in many respects the most vivid and living of letters—we possess a portrait which no biographer, writing after the event, can match. In those letters is far the greater part of our knowledge of him—a biographer must, with embarrassing frequency, either paraphrase them or quote them. He cannot possibly create a substitute for them. At most, he can hope to supplement them with a collection of other contemporary material.

This much Miss Lowell has done with enormous industry and patience; and for this reason her life of Keats must be—at any rate until this collateral material has been put to better use—indispensable. She covers the ground of Keats's brief life extraordinarily. No scrap of information is considered too uninteresting for introduction, or too trivial as a basis for speculation; she attempts to accompany Keats like the ticking of a clock; to know of his whereabouts and preoccupations at every second. If Miss Lowell had a genius for biography the result might have justified this. But she is as far from having such a genius as she is—and this perhaps is worse—from being a good critic. Her biography becomes, therefore, a triumph of engineering, a miracle of dimensions; like the Great Wall of China, or the largest potato at the Fair. It contains a stupefying mass of information more or less co-ordinated; but the order thus given is mechanical rather than aesthetic.

To be summary, I think Miss Lowell signally fails in what might be called the "finer" departments (as against the mere collating of facts) of biography. She has little tact; her taste is uncertain; her sense of proportion is uncertain; her psychological perceptions are imprecise; her imagination is forced and hectic, not instinctively apposite. There are many admirable and graphic pages in her John Keats. She makes also many admirable points. But on the whole the effect is one of provincialism, a pervading unripeness which no amount of cocksureness and bluster can cover. Miss Lowell is unfortunate (to begin with) in her prose. If her *Tendencies in Modern American Poetry* appeared to be written by a popular lecturer to women's clubs—breezy, careless, and superficial—her *John Keats* is in this regard little better. Her style is abominable—it is scarcely a style at all. It is disheveled and inaccurate—it is monotonous and awkward. It has energy, but its energy is given little direction, little beauty of rhythm or color. It is a prose so uniformly undistinguished and so frequently amateurish as to put grievously in question the quality of the mind it expresses and the use to which that mind has been put. Let me quote a few examples, which will show in various ways what I mean.

But give Keats half a chance and he could not help learning, he learnt so fast that he outlearnt his teacher in a short time, but that is only to say that Keats was a genius and Hunt was not.

Keats was writing on September twenty-first, nine weeks before, on July eighteenth, Jane Austen had died at Winchester.

Indeed, the moment, whether through accident or design, was fortuitous, for the moon lacked but twenty-four hours of being at the full.

But Brown was unaccustomed to considering his own health, which never wanted consideration, and probably, also, he believed Keats's statement that his throat was "in a fair way of getting well," this he told Tom next day, but such indeed was not the case.

The lover's words are not what they should be, any one can see that; but Endymion suddenly finding his empty uplifted arms clasped about a naked waist is a beautiful flight of imagination, astringently absorbingly expressed.

The poem will not be denied, to refuse to write it would be a greater torture. It tears its way out of the brain, splintering and breaking its passage, and leaves that organ in the state of a jellyfish when the task is done.

What, one is moved to ask, is the state of a jelly-fish when the task is done? And how seriously can one take a writer who twice uses "fortuitous" when she means fortunate and "jejune" when she means young? This inaccuracy of speech parallels Miss Lowell's inaccuracy of thought. She has a passion for glib generalization. Her book is "exhaustive" in the sense that it marshals vividly all the available facts, but it is not exhaustive in the sense of being a judicious study of them. Her judgment is highly capricious: as a guide and interpreter she takes many unwarrantable liberties with the probabilities. Her book is full of ingenuous speculation and naive argument: argument with scant premise and speculation with little aim. She cannot be trusted—she must be watched. She is dangerous, too, because, though unreliable, she is positive, and carries herself with such bravado.

II

It would be difficult to write an uninteresting life of Keats, and in this, in spite of her stupendous prolixity, Miss Lowell has not succeeded. Even when stretched to thirteen hundred pages, Keats's brief and tragic story remains the most moving, the most harrowing of literary histories. No other poet has given to posterity so brilliant and living a self-portrait as Keats left in his letters. From his "I will be as punctual as the bee to the clover" in 1816 to his "I always made an awkward bow" in 1820—the four years of adolescent maturity which were all the life he had—we see his entrance, his agony, and his exit, with a vividness that is terrifying. This is not only because his correspondence was voluminous—others in this have surpassed him —nor only because his genius went as much into his letters as into his poetry. His genius *did* go into his letters, and in certain particulars a part of it (his speculative freedom, his critical sureness, his extravagance of humor, and his sharp sense of character) which never found much place in his poetry. But more important than this is the fact that Keats was the possessor of a devouring self-consciousness, a passionate and exquisite absorption in his own relation to things. Many of the problems— we must remember—which have occupied Keats's critics and biographers could never have arisen if the letters had never been published: for if the Keats of the letters is more "interesting" than the Keats of the poems, he is also more vulnerable. Arnold's essay is largely devoted to proving that Keats is not so entirely "unmanly" as the Brawne letters indicate; Swinburne complained of them that "even a manly sort of boy will not howl and snivel after this fashion"; Mr. William Watson reiterated the charge of Cockneyism and vulgarity, "Apollo with an unmistakable dash of 'Arry." Miss Lowell, more idolatrous or less critical, denies flatly both the unmanliness and the vulgarity. The vulgarity, she maintains (except for one phrase in Isabella) does not exist: and the unmanliness was not intrinsic, but a weakness due to ill health and misfortune.

This generosity does credit to Miss Lowell's heart, but as criticism (whether of life or letters) it is, I think, valueless. The vulgarity and unmanliness are not characteristics to be shuddered at or concealed or excused: they are highly significant features of Keats's genius and ought to be studied with every care. To begin with, it has not been pointed out that the "vulgarity" and "unmanliness" are essentially the same thing. The vulgarities of Endymion, of Isabella ("slippery blisses," "darling essence," "dainties made to still an infant's cries," "moist kisses," "creamy breast," et cetera) exactly parallel the unmanliness of the letters to Fanny Brawne (i.e., the extravagances of feeling). The fault, in both cases, is the fault of excess—the "fine excess" without the fineness; in both cases, the excess is erotic. Superficially, we may say this is due to Keats's habit of passionate and conscious abandonment to sensation. This habit we can attribute partly to the inheritance of an unusually vivid sexual nature from his mother and partly (I think we are safe in assuming this) to an unusually intense erotic relationship between the mother and son. It has been suggested that Mrs. Keats was a nymphomaniac. Allowing for exaggeration, there is sufficient evidence, on the one hand, that she was sensual, if not immoral, and on the other that John Keats was her favorite child, and was "spoiled" by her. The characteristics of the maturing Keats are precisely those we should expect of a passionate and sensitive boy who had been, in early childhood, too much fondled and excited and indulged: he is voluptuous, vain, and self-willed; he has an inordinate craving for admiration and love; his sensibility is exceptional; he expects the world to give him his way and worship him; and when thwarted, he disproportionately and uncontrollably suffers.

In conflict with a deeply-rooted habit of sensuous self-indulgence was Keats's first-rate intelligence, with its growing skepticism; and, also, a very acute sense of having taken a step upward, socially, from his parents, and a desire to square his behavior with more "refined" standards. He undoubtedly felt that his past, his origins, must be "lived down"—it is worth noting that nowhere, in all his letters, is there any mention of his childhood, and only one slight reference to his mother. That he disliked any one whom he felt to be socially superior (Shelley, for example) was noted by Haydon. That he suffered from references to his livery-stable origin was noted by Hunt. But living down his past meant also living down his mother; and in the hidden conflict over this point (and in his mother's alternating attraction and repulsion for him—it must be remembered that he was intensely loyal) I think we can detect one source of much that is weakest in him. Emotionally, he remained after Mrs. Keats's death dependent on her—he was never destined to escape. It was her influence (more than Hunt's) that led to the excesses of Endymion; and it was Fanny Brawne's inadequacy as a substitute for her that led to the abject implorings and yearnings of the love letters.

That Keats had sought an escape from this situation in sexual promiscuity is clear. He contracted syphilis, and this aspect of his life Miss Lowell discusses with candor and good sense. As regards his promiscuity, however, she is not so honest. She remarks with characteristic assurance: "We may say, with something like certainty, that we know everything he did; for which reason, it is safe to assume that what we do not know of, he did not do." To this she adds that although fond of "broad speaking," he was not personally addicted to the "making of mud-pies." The assertion that we "know everything he did" is, of course, meaningless. Up to the end of his twenty-first year, we know practically nothing either of his daily life or of his preoccupations. From that time till his death—four years—we have his letters, and the notes of his friends; but there are many gaps; and, as Miss Lowell herself says elsewhere, there is good reason to suppose that many letters were lost. We know a *little,* in other words, of the last four years of Keats's life, but it would be folly to assume that we know all.

As regards his sexual adventures, it is scarcely likely that he would have mentioned them in letters, or, if he had, that the letters would have been preserved unexpurgated. In the letters extant, however, there is enough evidence, for one who can read between the lines, that Keats and his companions were normally and joyously, even coarsely, promiscuous. In the case of Keats himself, it may indeed have been something more than this—I am inclined to think that it was an obsession. He remarked, on one occasion, that his feeling for women was not *"healthy."* He disliked and scorned them, when encountered merely socially, but nevertheless *"every bit of riband"* interested him. He was restless, incapable of finding happiness with any one woman, but nevertheless under a compulsion to seek it; and his extraordinary behavior to Fanny Brawne suggests the alternation of hate and desire we should expect, and also that, once having possessed her, he might have found her repellent. Further, if Keats was secretive in his letters about his love for Fanny Brawne, he was presumably secretive about other episodes as well. This, of course, is "negative" evidence. On the positive side, there are the two calm references to what was unquestionably syphilis in letters to Bailey and Dilke, a year apart. (This must have added greatly to the tragic conflict of his feelings for Fanny Brawne and may have had a bearing on his concealment of his engagement from his brother George and on the delay of the marriage.) Aside from this, we have the two or three "bawdy" poems (it is suggestive that the Dawlish poem has been suppressed hitherto*) and specific reference to an affair at Hastings, the very phrasing of which is illuminating; he "warmed with her" and "kissed her." He goes on to remark that this mysterious lady of Hastings, and Georgiana (his sister-in-law, to whom he is writing!) are the only women for whom he has "no libidinous thought." This is not the language of an ascetic. It is the language of the John Keats whose early poetry was full of toyings, of gentle squeezes, of the "tasting" of faces, of "Pleasure's nipple" and "milky sovereignties." It is the language of the Keats who enjoyed jokes about "More feet for little stockings," "Amo amas I loved a lass," and the frankly (and delightfully) bawdy poem of Dawlish. In short, there is no escape from the fact that Keats was highly sensual, and that he probably lived quite as uncontrolledly in this regard as in others. Haydon reports that he was once drunk for six weeks. Miss Lowell chooses to disbelieve this but admits that at one time he was in the habit of taking laudanum. The general picture is incontrovertibly that of a young man who was at the mercy of his appetites, and who lived up to his plea of "O for a life of sensations rather than thoughts!"

It may be considered that I am stressing too much these psychological and physiological factors. I think, however, it is only by keeping them very clearly in mind that we can arrive at anything like an adequate understanding of Keats. Miss Lowell follows previous biographers in attempting to attribute the "unmanliness" and allied weaknesses of Keats to "external" factors. Going further than Arnold, who merely exonerated him, she declares him to have been strong, to have had great decision of character; and his breakdown, she argues, was simply the result of an unparalleled series of misfortunes. Briefly, these misfortunes were: the death of his mother in 1810, when he was fifteen; the emigration of his brother George to America, and the death of his brother Tom, in 1818; the indifference of the public to his first book, *Poems*, in 1817, and the hostility of the critics to Endymion in 1818; financial difficulties owing to the trusteeship of his inheritance; and, finally, his breakdown with consumption, and death, while in love with Fanny Brawne, in

---

* I suggest that Keats's literary remains may have been more "edited" than we have supposed. Why, for example, has the complete memoir of Brown never been published?

1821. These misfortunes, it will be noticed, were distributed over a period of ten years. They are misfortunes, certainly, but on the whole not such as the normal young man cannot and does not meet with stoicism—it is worth remembering that Keats's sister Fanny and brother George faced similar difficulties, and apparently with equanimity. The truth is, these misfortunes are not very far from the normal human lot; and the so-called "tragedy" of Keats has been exaggerated, and indeed *became* a tragedy, largely because Keats himself helplessly exaggerated it. The departure of his brother George to America was the sort of thing which any brother expects—families do not remain together for ever. The financial difficulties did not greatly disturb Keats, or disturb him for very long at a time. He was young and confident; borrowed as cheerfully as he lent, and his publishers were extremely generous to him with advances.

Moreover, there is another side to the picture. It must not be lost sight of that Keats had in many respects a phenomenally rapid and lucky rise from social darkness to a secure position among the leading men of his time. Even before he had reached his majority, he found himself surrounded by a group of admirers, all of them mature and brilliant men. Through Leigh Hunt and Cowden Clarke he was in a position to meet practically anybody whom he cared to. At the very outset of his career he encountered, on more or less equal terms, though himself much younger, Shelley, Wordsworth, Lamb, Hazlitt, and Coleridge. Furthermore, in Reynolds, Clarke, Haydon, Dilke, Woodhouse, Bailey, and Charles Brown (not to mention Hunt, whom he partially dropped) he possessed a circle of outspoken and enthusiastic admirers who were all intelligent men, who perceived his genius, and who helped him in every possible way. They copied his poems, handed his books about, mixed excellent advice with their praise, lent him money, and evidently (seeing him to be his own worst enemy) *conspired to make him and keep him happy*. There is scarcely another poet in the history of English literature who can have been so swiftly recognized and placed, or so handsomely encouraged by those whose help was in itself a clear validation of his genius.

III

In the presence of these facts, I think any ascription of Keats's "unmanliness" to external misfortune breaks down. Is it not impossible to find, in the events of his life (unfortun .te in some

respects as it was) any "objective correlative" for his extraordinary emotional instability, his loss of self-control, his abject self-
pity and despair? The situation is analogous to that of Hamlet:
we see him peculiarly unbalanced, unbalanced to the point of
insanity; but we do not see on the surface any wholly adequate
cause. We can, and should, add to the list of his misfortunes the
fact that he acquired syphilis (a fact not usually stressed) for
this may have contributed much to the poisoning of his relationship with Fanny Brawne. But even so, the "disturbance" remains
so obviously disproportionate to apparent causes that we must
seek the real reasons not in external but in internal factors. In
short, we must say that these external factors were only able to
undo him because he was weak. A Keats with great strength of
will, great decision of character, such as Miss Lowell posits for
him, will not "work." If we assume this, we are left with an
enormous quantity of "behavior" (and the poetry may here be
included) which can only be regarded as "overdetermined."
Everywhere, in the smaller issues of Keats's life, we see that
assumption belied. The *instability* of the Keats in the letters is
striking. He is an emotional weathercock. He never knows his
own mind or feelings for more than a day at a time. We do not
need the word of Haydon for this—he tells us so himself. He is
marvelously adept at self-analysis, but it is always *of the moment*—that is, in a particular state of feeling; and his passion,
for all its sensuous circumstance (heightening the description
to the point at which it will be a direct and palpable *sensation,*
or immediate experience, for his reader), inevitably led him to
exaggerate. "I carry all matters"—he says apologizing to Bailey
for a letter which had disturbed him—"to an extreme—so that
when I have any little vexation it grows in five minutes into a
theme for Sophocles."

This is the Keats who at school was subject to paroxysms of
weeping rage; who constantly gave way to fits of luxurious and
indolent melancholy; who wrote insufferably patronizing letters
to Taylor, his publisher, demanding money, and then followed
with letters of a beautiful humility; who could frame a savagely
conceited dedication for *Endymion,* and then substitute another, penetratingly self-censorious. This is also the Keats who
could, and did, so repeatedly cry from one extreme to the other
in his relations with his mistress. He imagined and desired her
with a voluptuous obsession so consuming that he must go away
from London in order to work; having gone away to work, he
wrote her that his work had absorbed him, that he was hard-

hearted, that work left no room in his mind for her, and that if he came to town he would not see her. He passed from an insanity of jealousy, gloatingly sensual in the extreme, to an abject humility of trust. During his illness, he constantly refused to see her, in order that he might not have to part from her. When he was in Italy, dying, he never once wrote to her—he could not bear to; his own feelings came first. As regards his work, his judgment was just as capricious and immoderate. It was seldom so much a judgment as a feeling. "Here lies one whose name was writ in water," he suggested for his epitaph; but he also said, not long before, "I think I shall be among the English poets after my death."

All of this, we see, is in one picture—the picture of one bewildered "by what is false within." It was a hierarchy of profound psychic schisms which ruled him, and it is scarcely to be wondered at, in the circumstances, that his fine mind was so seldom permitted to work uninterrupted, and that he regarded the poet as a "chameleon," without identity. In this psychotic instability the half-hate half-love of his mother was the dominant feature. He wanted still, and inordinately, to be loved. Society, taking her place, was to receive him with open arms—he was to be its darling, its god. It would cherish him and fondle him. When, however, society did no such thing, or when his friends betrayed in their admiration the least ambiguity, or when his mistress (who bore the same name as his mother, and who perhaps represented, for Keats, the negative pole of his mother's character—cold, hard, and chaste) flirted harmlessly with Brown, his sense of isolation and betrayal was morbid. He had, like the spoiled child, his secret tantrum; and then, with a grimness and tragic courage as excessive as the grief from which it was the reaction, he set himself to prove how cruelly he had been underestimated.

Taylor said of him: "He does not bear the ill opinion of the world calmly." His own letters are full of an overweening pride, an assumption of greatness, which, in a character less lovable than Keats, would be repellent. The note of entire humbleness alternates with this, and completes our impression of a divided personality. A morbid feeling of inferiority fed, and fought with, his burning ambition and self-confidence. Mr. Watson is, therefore, right—without the "dash of 'Arry" Keats would not have been so much the "Apollo." The livery stable played its part, as did his mother's immorality. The fact that his mother married beneath her (his father was an ostler) was important also. . . .

It is extraordinarily interesting to note that of his two "epics" one deals with the love of a goddess for a mortal, and the other with the dethronement of the "father," Saturn. In an earlier hint of the Diana-Endymion theme, having described the nuptials of the unequal lovers, he asks, "*Was there a poet born?*" —and *Hyperion* ends with the casting of Apollo into a celestial frenzy which will make him a god; it is Mnemosyne, the goddess of memory, who arouses him to this paroxysm.

IV

The Keats whose life was a feverish search for luxury as a replacement of his mother was also, of course, the Keats whose poetry is the most completely and consciously sensuous ever written. The erotic difficulty which rendered his life unstable, unhappy, and of a febrile intensity made of his poetry the remarkable worship of sensuous delight (and linguistic substitute for it) which has been so often discussed. I have already noted the fact that the so-called vulgarities of Keats's poetry are almost invariably sexual in character. Perhaps, as this was the focal point of the disturbance, it is only what we should expect; it is natural that over these, his strongest feelings, the victory of poetic "taste" should have been longest deferred. This becomes all the more reasonable an assumption when we recall that the primary aim of Keats, in all his poetry (as indeed in his letters) was to embody a sensation so completely, with so richly organized a tactilism, as to make the poetry approximate the vividness of a direct experience. This method, at the outset, might result only in a harmless and cloying prolixity when it dealt with the natural luxuries of a summer's day: but it led, when applied to erotic themes, to "slippery blisses" and "milky sovereignties." In his maturer poetry (it was never to be wholly mature) these obsessions were still manifest enough, but the excitement they occasioned was better controlled, his taste improved; though even at the height of his powers, in "St. Agnes Eve" and "Lamia," he was subject to serious lapses. Perhaps in time he would have learned to control this perfectly, for his taste developed with extraordinary rapidity. We see in his letters that it was joined to a critical faculty, and a sense of values, exceptionally keen. Keats might have become, among other things, a great critic.

The Keats who could think, however, and the Keats who could feel remained peculiarly separate, and it is a point of great importance that the "growth" of Keats as a poet was not a growth in emotional power or thought or in any widening of view and sympathies but a growth in *taste*. His genius being primarily for *luxury* (the finding of a verbal and prosodic equivalent for luxury of feeling), it became a question of discovering the right pitch of selection and control to give most richly the effect as of immediate sensation. In *Endymion,* this was prevented by the riot of rich images, and by excess in the image itself—he was undone by his "nectarous camel-draughts." The improvement in his later work is almost entirely due to a surer sense of effect. In the "Ode to a Nightingale," he managed miraculously to present a rich constellation of sensations and feelings, only just stopping short of surfeit. It was not that his capacity to organize had particularly improved—though perhaps it had done so very slightly; it was rather that he was more jealously selective of his crowding intensities. It is possible, also, that he was helped by the fact that in his later work the top of his energy was gone, so that he lacked the superfluous gusto for his characteristic "chain of sensations." As regards his theme, or "thought," however, it must be remarked that the later work shows strikingly little development. There is scarcely an idea or attitude in *Hyperion* or the *Odes* which had not already been clearly developed in *Endymion* or the *Poems.* The ideas, indeed, are extraordinarily few—the thought is almost nil. In so far as thought is present, it is a thought apprehensible through the senses, or employed only for its value in *enhancing* the life of the senses. If we can believe Keats, a queer vague pseudo-philosophical scheme of "soul-making" (outlined in letters to Taylor and to his brother George) moves dimly and sluggishly under the flowery surface of *Endymion:* but it reduces itself to the idea that a hierarchy of sensations (with love at the top) educates the soul.

Perhaps the revised *Hyperion* would have been an attempt to define, in such a scheme, the office of the poet. But in this, and in the *Odes*, if we have any development at all, it is simply in Keats's slightly sharper sense of the material he was dealing with, material essentially unchanged. It is still "O for a life of sensations rather than thoughts"; "A thing of beauty is a joy for ever"; "Beauty is truth." Of the Odes it has been said that they most fully develop Keats's "idealism of beauty." In this connexion there are two peculiar things to be noted. The first is that the *Odes* all deal (unless we except "Autumn") with *one theme,* the antinomy of beauty and death. The "Ode on Melancholy" states this theme succinctly; the "Ode to a Nightingale" seeks escape (from the melancholy thus induced) in the thought that natural beauty is immortal; the "Ode on a Grecian Urn" seeks escape from it in the thought that beauty may be immortal in art; the "Ode to Psyche" seeks escape from it in the thought that beauty may be immortal in the consciousness of the witness—"in some untrodden region of the mind."

The second point to be noted is that the so-called idealism so restlessly sought, and in these successive forms, is not at all a convinced idealism but, on the contrary, a profound pessimism. In every case—even in "The Grecian Urn"—the *affective* burden —the melancholy of the overtone—far outweighs the *logical* burden in which Keats pretends to discover peace. A great part of the extraordinary beauty of the Odes ("the perfect simplicity of their simple perfection") results precisely from this unconscious conflict. They are all, to paraphrase and invert Wordsworth's *dictum*, tranquillity remembered in melancholy. And although Keats pretends to believe that he has transcended the senses, or found a refuge from their transience in a kind of "principle of beauty," nevertheless we must remark that this ideal is a *sensual* ideal, it is apprehensible only through the senses, and only desirable in proportion as it *is* so apprehensible. It is not essentially, therefore, an *ideal* that concerns and obsesses him, but a *permanent*. He does not really want to escape from the world of the senses, but to escape death.

This is complicated, and greatly enriched emotionally, by a peculiar obsession of Keats, traceable, I should imagine, to his central difficulty, the mother-fixation; the curious obsession with death. Death and love, death and beauty, negative and positive, are a sort of bi-polar basis seldom absent from his poetry. But the curious thing is the degree in which these terms, for Keats, were interchangeable. Death, for him, had a profoundly erotic significance—it became a symbol for consummation; and love, just as significantly, meant death. Into the precise mechanism of this it is not necessary to go. It forms the most pronounced single symptom of his disequilibration, and relates clearly enough to his love-hatred of Fanny Brawne and his mother—his desire for love and his conviction that it would kill him—and his consequent morbid instability of behavior in that regard. It also relates to the fact that everywhere in his poetry the ideas of love and death are ambivalent. His lovers are perpetually swooning; love is death; and death is both terrible and desirable. In the "Nightingale," it is "rich to die." Endymion, whenever he encounters Cynthia, faints. Porphyro melts into the dream of Madeline. The victims of La Belle Dame Sans Merci are kissed into unconsciousness. In a letter to Fanny Brawne, Keats is explicit about this obsession. "I have two luxuries to brood over in my walks," he says; "your loveliness, and the hour of my death. O that I could have possession of them both in the same minute."

The intellectual accompaniment to all this is pessimism. In his letters of the same period as the *Odes* we see Keats quite definitely standing on the verge of a gloomy mechanistic view. He sees nature red in tooth and claw, and man, like the hawk, pursuing an undeviating and instinctive way. He sees the rose in blossom, imagines it to have sensation, and then sees it deflowered by frost. He is disheartened: "The point at which man may arrive is as far as the parallel point in inanimate nature, and no farther"; man will never escape pain and death. Would this point of view have been fruitful for Keats—would his poetry have taken it over? It is possible that out of this "horrid morbidity" he would have cultivated a wisdom. But his poetry, at the time of his death, had taken not this thought to which he had so rapidly reached but the emotion that accompanied it, the excess of torture which it had occasioned. It is possible that his love-death obsession would never have allowed him more freedom, either in poetry or in speculation, than he had already found. In the *Odes,* his maturest work, the emotional side of Keats quite definitely funked the prospect. This might, or might not, have been a temporary escape-adjustment which he would quickly have outgrown.

v

Miss Lowell touches little on these psychological features of Keats's genius, and that must be my excuse for perhaps dwelling on them too much. Of the "literary" influences on his work, Miss Lowell gives an exhaustive account, not always very convincing. To *Endymion* she allots too much space, and goes a good deal too far afield in her search for influences. Diodorus Siculus, for example, is invoked to explain the "Triumph of Bacchus," but even he is not enough: for Keats's Bacchus is *plump*. A fearful difficulty! from which however the escape is triumphant. Rabelais has a Bacchus who, *inferentially* at any rate, is plump; so it is all satisfactory. But has Miss Lowell never encountered "plumpy Bacchus with pink eyne"? . . . There is too much of this sort of loose analogy in her John Keats. She strains at a gnat —when it is a rival who supplies it—but swallows her own camels very easily.

With immense gusto she purports to prove that the fragmentary "Fall of Hyperion" antedates the longer *Hyperion.* The Woodhouse letter sufficiently disposes of that speculation. If more evidence is necessary, it is perhaps worth pointing out that in a letter to Woodhouse on October 27, 1818 (*i.e.,* about the time he is supposed to have begun the poem in one form or the other) Keats mentioned "*cogitating on the characters of Saturn and Ops.*" As Ops does not appear in the "Fall," and does appear in *Hyperion,* one may assume that *Hyperion* was the first written. Again, Miss Lowell attaches tremendous importance to a blue mantle, embroidered with stars, which Cynthia wears in *Endymion.* This points conclusively to Drayton's *Endymion and Phoebe,* she argues—although the book is so rare that only one copy could have been even speculatively accessible to Keats. Keats could quite as well, however, have got the mantle from Jonson. In the *King James's Entertainment* occurs: (1) "Agrypina, in yellow, a sable mantle, seeded with waking eyes, and silver fringe"; and (2) "Irene, her attire white, semined with stars." Or he could have got it from Marston, who influenced Keats in more ways than one. In his *Entertainment,* "Cynthia was discovered ryding; her habit was blewe satten, fairely embroidered with starres and cloudes." Keats learnt much from Marston, as a careful scrutiny of this particular poem, and the dedications, will show.

But this sort of influence must be studied with extreme care, wide reading, and unerring fastidiousness of taste, and in these regards Miss Lowell is inclined to be headlong. She touches least on an influence which for Keats was of great importance— the influence of Chatterton. Chatterton, it is possible, influenced him not only in his work (the medievalism especially) but also in his life. The tragedy of Chatterton's life was then comparatively recent. It parallels in so many particulars Keats's own life that one speculates—idly perhaps—on the extent to which Keats, in his adolescence, may actually have been warped by it. His death-obsession found in Chatterton's early death a ready symbol; the temptation to romanticize that unfortunate career must have been great; and it was then only a step to the morbid assumption (peculiarly easy for Keats) that genius is *ipso facto* doomed to obloquy and premature death. Love, fame, and death were Keats's three graces. The death of a

young poet—this was almost the most tragic (and attractive!)
thing he could imagine. The death of a young poet while in
love, however, was a turn of the screw which, if he had conceived, he had certainly not discounted. When he realized that
this was to be his destiny, his imagination gave it fullest value,
and he died as passionately and uncontrolledly and *consciously*
as he had lived. He grasped death hard with all his senses and
went under the earth alive.

KEATS, JOHN

The epidemic of books on John Keats continues unabated: and
I suppose (as the upshot of it must be that we shall slowly clar-
ify and solidify our view of him) we ought to be grateful. It
was certainly time that some sort of attention should be paid to
the Keats of the "letters," who is in so many respects vividly unlike the Keats of the poems; and that an attempt should be
made to bring the two characters into, if not a harmony, at any
rate a workable relation. Until quite recently, it has been the
disposition of critics to accept Keats a little too much as his
contemporaries accepted him—that is, as a poet almost exclusively of the emotions and the senses. This, of course, was a
manifest injustice. Keats was by no means a fool, as the most
casual study of his extraordinary letters must convince any one;
he was an extremely intelligent young man, and an extremely
self-conscious one, his self-consciousness as often as not being
directed upon the nature of the poet (as he saw it in himself)
and the nature of the poet as he conceived it to be, or desired
it to be, in the social order.

It is to this side of Keats, the intellectual and analytic side,
that Mr. Murry and Mr. Thorpe, the latest champions of Keats
the "philosopher," devote their studies; and it must be admitted
that they make out (as was indeed inevitable) pretty good
cases. Unfortunately, like all zealots, they go too far. They are
both so burningly aware of the prevailing disregard of the
"mind" of Keats, so intensely conscious of the fact that they are
trying to *correct* an established opinion, and so naively delighted by the comparative wealth of their "discoveries," that
they try to prove too much. Of the two critics, Mr. Thorpe is
distinctly the more reliable. He works his case pretty hard,

with an inordinate amount of repetition: he rubs it in, he won't let us off, his recapitulations are unsparing and exhausting, and his terminology (to make it worse) is often far from precise; but it must be said for him that he never *quite* loses sight of the fact that in all this there must, naturally, be a large element of mere speculation. He is willing to admit that Keats progressed, intellectually, not in an orderly way, nor in a straight line, but by fits and starts, and with many inconsistencies. These inconsistencies he does not try to suppress or ignore—though he does, now and then, tend to minimize them or to force a convenient and somewhat strained interpretation upon them. In the end, he wants us to accept a Keats who had, before he died, formulated a pretty definite philosophic credo of his own, a semi-Platonic, semi-Hegelian idealism. Life on this planet was to be considered as a kind of experiment in "soul-making": "Intelligences" were to become "souls" by being put through a course of trials and tribulations, emerging ultimately from the inferior to the superior state by virtue of an act of imagination (or intuition) which enabled them to accept both good and evil as necessary parts of a divine harmony. When Keats speaks of "beauty"—according to Mr. Thorpe—he means not a sensuous but a supersensuous beauty: he means, in fact, precisely this profound acceptance of things as they are, the bad with the good, an intuitive penetration of the superficial veil of things, a mystic contemplation, a "sense of oneness with the infinite." This, we are told, is what Keats intended by his famous "Beauty is truth." And as a subsidiary doctrine, he held that the poet is *par excellence* the leader in this mode of apprehension, since it is primarily by imagination that this flight can be taken, and not by any orderly process of reason.

In all this, there is a good deal of talk about the soul, and even a half-hearted reference or two to the "all-soul" and the "eternal life-spirit," which the poet (I am quoting Mr. Thorpe, not Keats) captures for us, in a poem, by an act of "emotionalized intuitive perception"—stupendous and meaningless phrase.

In the main, however, Mr. Thorpe is content with a somewhat tedious and prolix canvassing of Keats's theories, critical and metaphysical; and it is left to Mr. Murry to sound more emphatically, and more distressingly, the clarion of pure mysticism. Mr. Murry goes, in this regard, the whole hog. More confessedly than Mr. Thorpe, he takes the revelationist view of art—art is for him a religion; it is our chief means of establishing a relationship with God; the poet is therefore a kind of priest; and Mr. Murry wrings, ruthlessly wrings, from the letters of Keats a conscious and elaborate thesis of this kind, and endeavors to convince us that Keats moved to this thesis by a series of rapid and orderly stages. Keats, according to Mr. Murry, identified himself, in some queer mystical fashion, with Shakespeare. Shakespeare was his presiding genius, Shakespeare gave him the clue to the doctrine (sketchily formulated in his letters) of detached and yet compassionate contemplation of the world, a sort of God's eye-view, which was to be the ideal basis for a great poetry. Mr. Murry makes far too much of this —he repeats himself *ad nauseam*, and it must be added that he has at times an extraordinarily offensive way of putting things. He has a shade too much the air of regarding himself as a sort of *vates*—he has the somewhat mawkish and narcissistic zeal of the missionary. He wants, a little too much, to be admired for his extraordinary acumen. It results from this that one pays him perhaps less attention than he deserves.

In this regard, however, both these books are failures: they renew one's heretical suspicion that in such a case as the present one (and indeed in most cases where a critical approach to an author is required) what one wants, and all one needs, is an essay, not a book. All that one can profitably say about Keats as a thinker can be said in a very few pages. To do more than that is to defeat one's aim. Certainly, it is desirable to say that Keats could think, and that he did think; but it is fundamentally impossible to make any system out of his thought, for it was entirely unsystematic, riddled with contradictions, and almost invariably presented in such metaphorical terms, or in such undefined abstractions, that interpretation is largely a matter of inspired guesswork. What right have we to assume that Keats meant "intuitions" by "sensations"? How can we be so sure that his idea of "beauty" was so wholly supersensuous? The truth is, he was as characteristically inconsistent and emotional in his thought as in behavior. It is clear enough that there were two strains in him—there was a romantic Keats, who was almost ridiculously idolatrous of poetry and the poet, and there was also a Keats who was increasingly skeptical about this as about all things. There was a Keats who believed (momentarily) in the essential goodness and harmony of life, and another Keats who was just as profoundly a nay-sayer. It remains a curious fact—to which, I think, neither Mr. Thorpe nor Mr. Murry gives sufficient attention—that this skepticism emerges,

as concept, practically not at all in Keats's poetry: he had not
reached, before he died, a point at which he could compel his
genius (or whatever) to express his whole mind, doubts and all.
The doubts betray themselves in his work only indirectly—as a
deep melancholy, a despairing feeling of the impermanence of
the life of the senses, and a horror of death. The latent burden
of despair almost invariably, even in his finest poems, outweighs the manifest burden of "acceptance": it is indeed arguable that it is precisely because of this internal conflict that
the poems achieve their extraordinary beauty. Whether Keats
would ever have solved this problem is doubtful. Might he have
become a playwright? a critic? a philosopher? The question is
metaphysical. At all events, there is much to be said for the
view of Mr. G. R. Elliott, in his *Real Tragedy of Keats,*
quoted by Mr. Thorpe, that this conflict had perhaps already
ended Keats's career as a poet. He was beginning to be disillusioned not only with the world but with poetry.

LAWRENCE, D. H.   (1924)

One cannot be indifferent to a book by Mr. Lawrence. He is
very much alive in his own very peculiar way. If he is reck-
lessly unequal, uncontrolled, one must add that even at his
worst he is interesting; and at his best, in prose, he is decidedly
the most living and "possible" of contemporary writers of English fiction. One does not guess where he will go. His novels
are never wholly satisfactory—they are not good works of art.
Almost uniformly they show a tendency to break in two, their
construction is faulty, incredibilities are indulged in, and at some
vital point in each the credulity of the reader is forever lost. It
has long been apparent that Mr. Lawrence is a man obsessed,
unable to conceal his obsession; sex-crucifixion is his iterated
theme; and he displays in all his work, verse and prose, the
sensitive fierceness, the sadistic awareness, which almost invariably accompanies this type of obsession. He is an
Erisichthon: tears wolfishly not only at his own flesh but also at
the world which, inevitably, he has created in his own image.
In his novels, at the dictation of this fever, he sublimates his
characters into types; and one watches him, over and over,
luxuriating in the last pang of ecstasy at his subjugation, so

richly arranged and so intensely pitched, of the cold tall blond "Arctic" type (which has a predilection for Alps) by the swart furry animal "Mediterranean" type (which has a predilection for underworlds and darkness). Latterly, also, one observes a somewhat disquietingly increased effort toward a rationalization of this obsessive "world"—a rationalization irrational and clumsy, a muddy psychoanalytic mysticism, full of meaningless jargon and highly "affective" logic. One sympathizes with Mr. Lawrence, and hopes that he will find his way out, solve his problem, discover peace; but one is bored and incredulous; and one prefers his solution when it is in narrative form, a parable.

One sums up one's feeling, in all this, by simply saying that Mr. Lawrence is a man of genius, but of that sort which lacks sufficient self-control and self-awareness. This fact has been as manifest in his verse as in his prose, perhaps more so; and his latest excursion into verse, in which one sees him quite perceptibly deflected by Whitman, is no exception. *Birds, Beasts and Flowers* is not a wholly successful book. Taken simply as description, some of Mr. Lawrence's birds, beasts, flowers, and prophets are, as one would expect, intensely vivid. The baby tortoise, seen as a "Tiny, fragile, half-animate bean," "Rather like a baby working its limbs"; the mother tortoise "Taking bread in her curved, gaping, toothless mouth"; the father tortoise, "tupping like a jerking leap, and oh! opening its clenched face from his (*sic*) outstretched neck and giving that fragile yell, that scream, super-audible from his pink, cleft, old-man's mouth, giving up the ghost, or screaming in Pentecost, receiving the ghost"; the mountain lioness with "her bright striped frost-face"; the snake who "sipped with his straight mouth, softly drank through his straight gums, into his slack long body, silently"; the cyclamens, "Like delicate very young greyhound bitches, half-yawning . . . folding back their soundless petalled ears"; and the "weird fig-trees, made of thick smooth silver, made of sweet untarnished silver in the seasouthern air—I say untarnished, but I mean opaque"; all these are excellent bits of descriptive prose, sharp and exact, and one could cite a good many others. But their excellence, it must be insisted, is a prose excellence, level, cumulative, explanatory; only infrequently in his book does Mr. Lawrence substitute for this method the method of poetry, with its sharp brief suggestion, its "*vox et praeterea nihil*," and its total elimination of the personal presence—everywhere else so manifest—of Mr. Lawrence; Mr. Lawrence in an old suit of clothes, affable,

informative, speculative, a little inclined to be facetious, now
and then somewhat cheap, and often dull.

And it is of this relaxed personal presence that one is, after
all, most tiresomely aware in Mr. Lawrence's book. In general
these poems are verbose; a piling up of descriptive epithets, a
stringing together, in apposition, of words curiously strained
and forced, images strained and conscious. This prolixity, now
and then brindled with vividness or mere idiosyncrasy (verbal
or affective) finally makes one wonder whether it is the display
of a kind of literary vanity. Mr. Lawrence appears to believe
that all that is necessary for him is to "spill" his consciousness.
If there is any selection or arrangement at work at all, it is not
enough in any poem here printed to make of it a work of art.
It remains simply a kind of amusing chatty comment, under
which one perceives that Mr. Lawrence's aim is simply the
assertion of his personality. Perhaps he caught this from Whitman? At all events it is a common form of aesthetic error at
present, and worth examination.

It is customary, in discussions of art, to use the terms objective and subjective. Strictly speaking, the distinction is in-
defensible, for no work of art, however "objective" in appearance, can be anything but the artist's self-portrait. But the
distinction can have a clear validity if we define it: and we
must define it as meaning that the ideal "objective" artist
is one who, in the production of his self-portrait, employs affective terms—symbolisms of theme and form—which are universally significant and intelligible; whereas the ideal "subjective" artist is one who in the production of his self-portrait
employs affective terms (of theme and form) significant and
intelligible only to himself. Of course, the ideal objective artist
is an impossibility—the ideal subjective artist a lunatic. Or one
may put it another way: that the objective artist's psychosis
corresponds at a maximum number of points with the "average"
psychosis of mankind, whereas the subjective artist's psychosis
is peculiar to himself.

Again: the objective artist, in whom a sense of reality is
relatively mature, is aware of and understands the psychotic
needs of mankind, and endeavors to be as useful to his audience
as to himself; but the subjective artist, in whom the sense of
reality remains infantile, disregards and scorns his audience,
and considers himself a god, the only true source of wisdom,
the only true center of awareness. With these relative distinctions in mind, it is easy to see that in what we are accustomed to

call the "disintegration" of the arts, during the last decade, we witness a very marked movement away from the objective (in our sense) and toward the subjective.

In Cubism, Vorticism, Expressionism, and Dadaism, the emphatic common factor is the marked increase in the solipsism of the artist, accompanied, as we should expect, by a more or less complete breaking up of established forms and symbols, and a conscious attempt for manifest intelligibility. We are assured by psychologists that this breaking up, accompanied as it curiously is by a distinct historical regression, or return to the primitive, is a good thing, and is necessary periodically if art is to remain "healthy" and to "develop." But we are also assured that the actual work produced at the moment of regression—poetry, for example, in which the holophrastic method is reverted to; sculpture which is precultural or negroid; or, in general, the reversion to a primitive ritualism—is, naturally, infantile; and is only of use as the starting-point for a renewal of growth, which would perhaps take the form of a gradual selection and refinement of *valid* symbols from amid the mass of the *in*valid. At its lowest, there can be no distinction between this art and the art of the definitely insane. It is hardly a step from the compulsive iterations of religious mania to the stammerings of Miss Gertrude Stein, or Mr. Pound's "Spring . . . Too long . . . Gongula"; and even so fine a poem as Mr. Eliot's *Waste Land* is not untainted. That the "latent" meaning may be, for the artist himself, tremendously rich, dazzlingly illuminating, and highly organized, makes no difference, if this meaning is not successfully conveyed. Dr. Pfister, in his *Expressionism in Art*, observes:

. . . there is no doubt that the expressionist often chooses his colours not on account of their character as felt by men in general, but . . . on the strength of repressed experiences and fancies of which other men cannot have any idea.

He also cites the analogous case of a youth, suffering from cryptolalia, who

felt himself compelled . . . to fill up . . . whole volumes with written characters that resembled shorthand, the Morse code, or exotic scripts. An incredible number of perfectly elaborated systems were at his disposal, but not one was intelligible. Only on closer investigation it became evident that there really existed a *system full of meaning* . . . a regular artificial language, *but inexplicable to consciousness.*

If now we keep some such reflections or speculations as these in mind; and if we keep in mind also the fact that we have no right to attribute any "absolute" badness to the ideal subjective work of art, or absolute goodness to the objective; if we reflect further that the practical test of "successful communication" compels us to accept Sir Hall Caine, Mr. Harold Bell Wright, and Mr. Robert Service as the greatest living artists; and if we add to this the often demonstrated fact that (representing subjective as a and objective as b) a work of art may be in its own generation a-2, but five or ten generations later, b-2; then we are in a position to contemplate with some freedom any such particular specimens of the contemporary disintegration, or reintegration, of poetry as these poems by Mr. Lawrence. It is clear that we must put Mr. Lawrence pretty far toward the subjective end of the scale.

We have already seen, and taken as our point of departure for speculation, the fact that the "relaxed personal presence" is one of the most striking features of these poems; a fact which clearly corresponds with the common expressionist view that unexplained confession, direct or in symbolism, is sufficient. But we can now object to this that if the mere presentation of his own personality is to satisfy us, we must insist that the personality should (1) be one of genius; (2) with a decided gift for communication; and (3) unconscious partly or wholly of the extent to which it merely communicates *itself*. The latter point is important. We enjoy, in a work of art, the overtone or aroma of personality; but the deliberate exploitation of personality, as Whitman exploited it, is apt to be otiose, if not repellent. The real "ghost" is lost in the process of elaborate dishevelment, and all that remains is a parade of irritating superficialities, and perhaps a considerable vanity. In Mr. Lawrence's case, we find this result conspicuous. And, in addition, we find him a little tiresomely idiosyncratic in a way we suggested earlier: i.e., sex-crucifixion. In this regard, too, he is well along toward the subjective maximum. He sees the world exclusively in terms of a personality which is an obsessed one, and which has in some respects remained infantile. Figs, tortoises, goats, dogs, flowers—all, to Mr. Lawrence, writhe in sex-martyrdom. Even the harmless, necessary moon is adjured in rising to burst the membrane of the stars, and

Maculate
The red macula.

Finally, as regards form, it remains to be observed that Mr. Lawrence has carried disintegration a long way back, and has only in a few instances taken a new step forward from the point of rest. For the most part his structure is casual, slipshod, and rhythmless, or, as said earlier, a prose structure. In this, too, it is to be feared that he speaks too idiosyncratic a language —his "formal" symbols are not likely to be found either widely or intensely valid, now or later. Or so, at any rate, one dares to guess.

LAWRENCE, D. H.   (1924)

Mr. Lawrence's book on American literature is perhaps even more singular than one now expects a book by Mr. Lawrence to be; and it is probably without exception the most singular book ever written on American literature. Singularity, in this day of democratic monotone and colorless competence, has its charm, has almost the air of being a virtue. Mr. Lawrence appears to know this—one suspects occasionally that he positively *cultivates* his singularity. In *Studies in Classic American Literature*—as in his latest book of verse, *Birds, Beasts, and Flowers,* and (to a lesser extent) in his psychological debauch, *Fantasia of the Unconscious*—he behaves like a man possessed, a man who has been assured by someone (perhaps an analyst) that restraint is nonsense, that nothing is of importance save a violent, unthinking outpouring of feelings and perceptions; unselected, unarranged, and expressed with a conscious disregard for personal dignity. Perhaps it is Whitman's barbaric yawp which has so disturbed him. Let us, he says in effect, get rid of these literary niceties and conventions and manners, let us be naked and unashamed. "If only people would meet in their very selves, without wanting to put some idea over one another, or some ideal. . . . Damn all ideas and all ideals. Damn all the false stress, and the pins. . . . I am I. Here am I. Where are you? . . . Ah, there you are! Now, damn the consequences, we have met." These sentences occur in Mr. Lawrence's study of Cooper. Of Franklin he remarks: "O Benjamin! O Binjum! You do NOT suck me in any longer." Of Hawthorne: "Old-fashioned Nathaniel, with his little-boy charm, he'll tell you what's what. But he'll cover it with smarm." He confides in the same essay:

"I always remember meeting the eyes of a gypsy woman, for one moment, in a crowd, in England. She knew, and I knew. What did we know? I was not able to make out. But we knew." He confides further: "'I can read him like a book,' said my first lover of me. The book is in several volumes, dear." Discussing the flogging episode in *Two Years Before the Mast*, he writes: "The poles of will are the great ganglia of the voluntary nerve system, located beside the spinal column, in the back. From the poles of will in the backbone of the captain, to the ganglia of will in the back of the sloucher Sam, runs a frazzled, jagged current, a staggering circuit of vital electricity. . . ." Of Whitman: "I AM HE THAT ACHES WITH AMOROUS LOVE. What do you make of that? I AM HE THAT ACHES. First generalization. First uncomfortable universalization. WITH AMOROUS LOVE! O, God! Better a bellyache. A bellyache is at least specific. But the ACHE OF AMOROUS LOVE! Think of having that under your skin. All that! I AM HE THAT ACHES WITH AMOROUS LOVE. Walter, leave off. . . . CHUFF! CHUFF! CHUFF! CH-CH-CH-CH-CHUFF! Reminds one of a steam engine."

These excerpts, while not perhaps the most striking that could be found, will serve to suggest Mr. Lawrence's manner. He is nothing if not colloquial, racy, and confidential. No trifle is too irrelevant for introduction. In his passion for the direct, for the naked and unashamed, he insists on drawing our attention to the very odd clothes he wears (stylistically speaking) and, not satisfied with this, flings them off in a kind of dance of the seven veils. At bottom, this is nothing but intellectual vanity. Mr. Lawrence is convinced that anything he says, no matter how he says it (and he tries perversely to make his saying of it as aggressively and *consciously* and peculiarly naked as possible), will be important. This is a great pity; for here and there, in the course of this amazing farrago of quackeries, occultisms, ganglia, and devil-women, Mr. Lawrence observes his American subjects and their American scene with quite extraordinary acuteness. His tracing of the wish-fulfillment motive in the novels of Cooper and Hawthorne would be wholly admirable if it were not so overshadowed by his alternate efforts to be funny (which are lamentable) and to be shocking (which are pathetic).

Again, one is extremely interested in his thesis that all art, but particularly and most persistently American art, springs from or accompanies the attempt of man to adjust himself to a supersensual morality. In this, he approaches (and is almost alone in approaching) an understanding of the fact that it is the functional nature of art which should pose for the critic his chief problem. Mr. Lawrence is consistently aware of this problem in every study here presented; he invites us to watch with him the drama of the struggle between man's unregenerate "unconscious" and civilization, as it works itself out in the "dream" of art. Unhappily, his awareness of the problem never leads him to define it with any care or precision. His recklessness with terms is astounding. Logic, in his hands, achieves monsters—fantastic structures grow, ascend, throng the universe, and disappear into the intense inane, in the twinkling of an eye. Unhappily again, for all the fact that he moves toward a scientific basis for criticism and delights in the exposure of shams and shibboleths, he brings with him as many shams and shibboleths as he destroys. He is as full of nostrums as a Californian. His book swarms with gods (of the "soul"), greater and lesser; he attaches a tremendous importance to something he calls the "Holy Ghost"; and to complicate the situation, he is all the time ferociously aware of the "blood" and the "ganglia."

These paraphernalia, undefined and numerous, confuse Mr. Lawrence's book and make apparent, of course, his own confusion. One comes away with a feeling that Mr. Lawrence could perceive psychological and aesthetic causes with remarkable shrewdness, but that for the most part he is prevented from a clear view by a frenzy of excitement. Life, art, and criticism of art—all, for Mr. Lawrence, have in them something feverish and sensational. He must talk about them in terms of gods, ghosts, and nether darknesses. His own affects, in other words (which are of a highly peculiar and tyrannous nature), are too immediately and uncontrolledly engaged—he loses his distance. The result, when he turns to criticism, is a kind of sensationalism—awkward, harshly jocose, violent, and often offensive—but here and there lighted with an extraordinarily fine bit of perception, beautifully given.

LAWRENCE, D. H. (1927)

Mr. D. H. Lawrence seems to be turning himself into a kind of literary Baedeker. His *Mornings in Mexico,* a loosely knit volume of descriptive essays, is one more of his attempts to rifle the soul of a landscape and its people; as in the past he has also sought to perform the same psychoanalytic office for birds, beasts, and flowers. This is a curious thing—one can call to mind no other author who has so persistently and restlessly busied himself with a desire to get under, and into, the souls of the supposedly soulless—the souls of nations, the souls of countrysides, the souls, as it were, of sticks and stones. There is something charming in this attitude, something desperate, and also something decidedly childlike. Isn't Mr. Lawrence exactly like the small boy who tears a dog-rose to pieces, or a fly, or an alarm-clock, in full expectation of discovering at last the secret not only of the particular organism, but of the world, the infinite, and God? One must admit immediately that sometimes, as in *Birds, Beasts, and Flowers,* this odd attempt has provided Mr. Lawrence's readers with delightful portraits, full of humor and insight. One will not soon forget his tortoises, or his goats.

In his *Studies in Classic American Literature,* Mr. Lawrence attempted to deal in a similar manner—a sort of inquisitorial passion—with American men of letters. In this book, one first became rather distressingly aware of Mr. Lawrence's *penchant* for a semi-mystic, semi-psychological jargon of his own, a jargon not altogether happy; and one also became aware of a concurrent change, if not deterioration, in the character of Mr. Lawrence's prose. It was as if at last this curious passion for pillaging souls, for ravishing out the innermost secrets of things, had become his sole preoccupation; his desire to see things naked has itself become increasingly naked, not to say brutal; his passion for understanding, for exposing, has become almost synonymous with a passion for destroying. If Mr. Lawrence were merely a psychologist, and if his violent probings and dissections were at all systematic, or anywhere pointed to a *donnée* of system, one would not so much mind this. But, unfortunately, one has, everywhere in this latest phase of his work, the feeling that for Mr. Lawrence the *act* of dissection is everything, the idea behind it almost nil.

At all events, it is only too apparent that with the development of this obsession for "tearing apart," Mr. Lawrence's prose has, *pari passu,* become less important to him. He has been increasingly willing to sacrifice everything stylistic to his passion. It is surely no exaggeration to say that in his *Studies in Classic American Literature* his literary "manners" are, to put it baldly, bad. Justly or unjustly, one feels, on reading these pages, that Mr. Lawrence is extremely patronizing; he has an air of knowing, and of being sure that he knows, very much more than his reader; he can hardly be bothered to make his assertions politely; he resorts to a truculent shorthand of style, and a habit of irritated reiteration, which makes it hard for his reader to admit, without grudge, the acuteness of many of his observations. Mr. Lawrence wants, for example, to tell us that he finds in Hawthorne a curious mixture of psychological profundity with superficial hypocrisy and sentimentality. But is it quite necessary for him to say "Blue-eyed Nathaniel, with his little boy charm, will tell us what's what, but he'll cover it with smarm"?

In *Mornings in Mexico*, Mr. Lawrence is in a somewhat serener mood, and is dealing with material which is less apt to lead him into such repellent outbursts as this; but once again one finds oneself regretting, and regretting deeply, that the author of *Sons and Lovers* and *Women in Love* and *The Captain's Doll* should be satisfied—if one can suppose he *is* satisfied—with a prose so slipshod and journalistic. One suspects that if this book did not bear his name, it would receive little attention. It is a fair enough piece of descriptive writing, moderately coloristic—it gives one flashes of picture, suggests with occasional vividness the heat and glow and torrid torpor of the Mexican scene—but the whole thing is done carelessly, repetitiously, in a structureless and graceless prose, as if the author were entirely indifferent whether he pleased his reader or not. When he does, occasionally, give himself more conscientiously to a passage of description, he tends merely to heap up his color-words, one upon another, till one is blind and deaf. His instinct for rhythm seems to have deserted him; and, whereas in his earlier prose he selected the one or two details which might magically imply a whole scene, drenched with scent and sound, now he is tiresomely explicit and spares us nothing. Consider this characteristic passage from the essay entitled "Corasmin and the Parrots":

I like to think of the world going pop! when the lizards had grown too unwieldy, and it was time they were taken down a peg or two. Then the little humming birds beginning to spark in the darkness, and a whole succession of birds shaking themselves clean of the dark matrix, flamingoes rising upon one leg like dawn commencing, parrots shrieking about at midday, *almost* able to talk, then peacocks unfolding at evening like the night with stars. And apart from these little, pure birds, a lot of unwieldy skinny-necked monsters bigger than

crocodiles, barging through the mosses; till it was time to put a stop
to them. When someone mysteriously touched the button, and the
sun went bang, with smithereens of birds bursting in all directions.

And then put beside it a passage from *Sons and Lovers:*

The beauty of the night made him want to shout. A half-moon, dusky
gold, was sinking behind the black sycamore at the end of the garden,
making the sky dull purple with its glow. Nearer, a dim white fence
of lilies went across the garden, and the air all round seemed to stir
with scent, as if it were alive. He went across the bed of pinks, whose
keen perfume came sharply across the rocking, heavy scent of the
lilies, and stood alongside the white barrier of flowers. They flagged
all loose, as if they were panting. The scent made him drunk. He
went down to the field to watch the moon sink under.
A corncrake in the hay-close called insistently. The moon slid
quickly downwards, growing more flushed. Behind him the great
flowers leaned as if they were calling. And then, like a shock, he
caught another perfume, something raw and coarse. Hunting round,
he found the purple iris, touched their fleshy throats and their dark,
grasping hands.

That is a vigorous and vivid prose; and if it is obviously
more formal than the colloquial *insouciance* of the later passage, it is also, just as obviously, a great deal more intimate. If
it is intimacy that Mr. Lawrence aims at in this recent manner
of his, then it is clear enough that he has miscalculated his
means. An artist of Mr. Lawrence's brilliance ought to know
that intimacy is not merely an affair of shedding one's clothes
and one's manners. A sweet disorder—yes, by all means; but
not this *farouche* condescension, this almost exhibitionistic
flaunting of the "short and simple flannels of the poor."

LAWRENCE, D. H.   (1929)

It would, perhaps, be invidious, and it would certainly be unjust, if the reviewer of Mr. Lawrence's *Collected Poems* confessed to a temptation to entitle his review (after Mr. Lawrence
himself), "Look! We Have Come Through!" For, with the
humblest feelings of admiration for Mr. Lawrence's genius,
one nevertheless has, after reaching the end of these two thick
volumes, a deep sense of relief and an extraordinarily virtuous
sense of accomplishment. The truth is that Mr. Lawrence is

not a poet to be read through at a sitting. That we know pretty much what to expect of him—having more than a decade followed his career in both prose and verse—and that we come (on the whole) prepared to admire, does little to mitigate the somewhat sharpened sense of disappointment which we bring away with us from a renewal of our acquaintance with his verse, when we are permitted to see it as a whole.

We know in advance, of course, that Mr. Lawrence will be astonishingly vivid and direct, that he will startle and shock us on almost every page, that he will deploy the English language with a violence or brutality of linguistic genius which is unique. He will not be afraid of harshnesses, whether technical or tactic; with indifferent ferocity, he will take rhetoric and wring its neck, or wring the reader's neck with rhetoric; he will be lethally monosyllabic on one page and savagely prolix on the next. Of his sense of form, too, we know enough in advance to be distrustful. We know the habit his novels have of breaking in two, and that whether in verse or prose he has remarkably little sense of when or where to stop. If his novels seldom "shape," his poems seldom "point." He is shapeless, with a kind of shining excellence of shapelessness; and if we count this a fault (as on renewal we certainly tend increasingly to count it), we at any rate see the fault as an almost inevitable accompaniment of his peculiar virtue.

His peculiar virtue is his terrific endowment of "consciousness." If we like, we can see his whole literary career as one prolonged and desperate and exhausting effort to be as conscious as possible. Everywhere, in his work, we encounter a burning fever of awareness; everywhere, we find ourselves involved in the same bloodshot tissue, a tissue positively vascular, so heavy is the raw network of veins and nerves. And this kind of consciousness, with its characteristic and almost mystic passion for all-inclusiveness, is almost in the nature of things directionless. It is not its nature to select or to focus—and in consequence it will light for us as often and as brilliantly the peripheral as the central. If one sees the world as an interwoven and vascular All, then it becomes impossible to select any particular unit of the All as more important than any other.

Mr. Lawrence's poetry is, in other words, just what we ought to expect. It has no beginning and no end; it is a kind of demoniac chaos which is everywhere vividly and terrifyingly alive. Like life itself, it is a process rather than a fulfillment—and perhaps that is tantamount to saying (if we are aesthetic purists) that it is seldom a work of art. The process is simply Mr. Lawrence's process; it is his unresting struggle to be as conscious as possible and to be conscious in terms of language. Hardly in terms of rhythm; the struggle is too urgent for that, the moment must be grasped quickly or not at all, and Mr. Lawrence is almost frantic in his clutch at the immediate. Rhythm and pattern, therefore, except for certain earlier and perhaps less characteristic poems, some of them very beautiful, must go by the board. A less formal medium must be found, and a tone less restrictive; the ungainly, the ugly, the casual, the undignified, even the ridiculous and the obscene, must be admissible, and cheerfully so; and that Mr. Lawrence should have found it necessary, eventually, to employ a kind of Whitmanese should occasion us no surprise. In this, he is freest for his "process" of consciousness; he can deliver up the immediate, however it comes to him, with the maximum of immediateness. He seizes the moment violently, and kills it outright with a powerful, and sometimes bloody, phrase.

That Mr. Lawrence is psychologically acute goes without saying. His perceptiveness, on any plane, is extraordinary—but perhaps more extraordinary on the sensory plane than on any other. One often thinks of him, in fact, as a kind of raw sensorium, which, in its passion for understanding, simply hurls itself against the world, again and again, with an almost suicidal force. His poems are the record of this remarkable process; and if they are streaked with agony and morbidity, or grotesque with too humorless and shameless abandonment to the actual, or if (as on the whole they do) they present us with a world too uniformly and perhaps gloatingly seen in terms of sex (lower case), they have also an unmatchable honesty and that sort of special splendor of the thing which is alive.

LEWIS, WYNDHAM •   (1928)

Mr. Wyndham Lewis is something of a cornac himself—he is not without curious resemblances to his admirable portrait of a showman in the story called "The Cornac and His Wife." In this story we are presented with a melancholy creature who is in a sense a victim of his own audiences. His audience *works* him,

• *The Wild Body.*

just as he, too, in turn works his audience; a queer kind of reciprocal puppetry. The public expects, demands, *extracts* from the sad cornac the kind of humor it wants. His mere presence there, in the ring, provokes the public to a particular appetite: they are unable to look at him without becoming excited; without beginning to desire to see *him* excited. And at the proper moment, when the mutual chemical or psychological influence has reached the right pitch, the cornac goes into action. He and the audience throw themselves into the ritual, which has become inevitable for them, each playing on the other. The cornac thus becomes something which is not exactly himself: a current passes through him, or a string pulls him, and he is drastically changed. He behaves to something outside himself. He is thus two people (at least): a man, and also a man whom an audience has contorted to a particular end.

In his new book Mr. Lewis is very much in that plight. He is on the one hand a very original observer of human nature, a brilliant chronicler of its small beer, with a queer, angular, muscular, awkward and sometimes ungrammatical prose at his command—a prose which despite its lapses is astonishingly effective. He strikes one as being a very independent creature: the kind of fellow who knows exactly why he prefers Latour to Lafitte, who has discovered for himself that salt is good with this and pepper with that, and who measures out the ingredients for a salad with the atomizing eye of a connoisseur. One feels also that he has the power to survey this curious world into which we are born with a very remarkable degree of detachment—a detachment so complete as almost to amount to genius in itself. There is something of the behaviorist in him: he habitually sees emotions as actions, ideas as responses to stimuli, and takes an almost sadistic delight in pursuing a character through rigidly logical sequences of cause and effect. He has, in short, a very keen mind, and a very vigorous imagination, and one can at first discover no good reason why he should not be one of the most brilliant of contemporary writers of fiction.

But there is also, on the other hand, that aspect of Mr. Lewis which makes one think of the cornac being acted upon by his public. One gradually becomes aware, as one reads these delightful and highly idiosyncratic stories, that Mr. Lewis is perpetually adopting a role: he is, in fact, being *forced* into a special part. His awareness, whether vague or definite, of an audience there in the background—an audience waiting to see whether Mr. Lewis is clever or not (and, if so, *how* clever)—is an unresting one and an uneasy one. It gives him a nervous manner, a high degree of self-consciousness; it takes away from him precisely that pure freedom of mind with which he appeared to be starting out. His detachment is swallowed up in this other reaction: he remembers that something unusually dexterous is expected of him, and in his anxiety to produce a startling effect he begins, now and then, when he suspects he is not being too closely observed, to indulge in a questionable sleight or two.

Thus, in the present book, he appears in two lights. He is a first-rate narrator of psychological short stories; and he is also, less fortunately, a theorist with an ax to grind. His ax is the theory, not especially original, of the comic; and throughout his book he is periodically taking this out and giving it a polish, and then burying it again, or simply forgetting it in the pleasure of creation or observation for its own sake. This is the clever side of Mr. Lewis, and one cheerfully enough admits that it *is* clever.

But wouldn't it be a relief to Mr. Lewis, as well as to his audience, if he were told that after all he needn't bother to try to impress us in this fashion? One needn't be a crank to be interesting—and there are moments when one sees Mr. Lewis well along the road to crankiness. There are amusing things in the essay entitled "Inferior Religions"; though one finds some difficulty in seeing it as a work of genius (*cf.* the remarks of Mr. T. S. Eliot on this subject). And one can extract a certain amount of dubious pleasure in watching Mr. Lewis's efforts to project *himself* as a kind of observing character, or recording instrument, in the first of these stories. He informs us that he is large and blond and fiercely humorous, with flashing teeth. Now and again in the later stories he remembers to remind us of this, but for the most part he forgets it. The projection doesn't quite come off. The truth is, it is not good enough. Or perhaps the trouble is that Mr. Lewis could not wholly give himself up to it. Sufficiently sophisticated to see the notion as an engaging one, and the role as amusing and original, he was also *too* sophisticated to be able to carry it out wholeheartedly or simplemindedly.

So we go back to the stories themselves. And here we are on solid ground. They are brilliant, and they show everywhere a psychological astuteness of a high order. They are at the same time actual and queer. They have that consistence in oddity for which the only convenient word is genius. If only Mr. Lewis would content himself with this admirable tale-bearing as regards the foibles of human behavior and forget for a while that he thinks he has a philosophical mission, one feels certain that he could write fiction that would make any living writer green with envy.

LEWIS, WYNDHAM   (1928)

Mr. Wyndham Lewis is a kind of jack-of-all-trades. He was one of the founders of *Blast,* that singular, and now so old-fashioned, organ of the cult known as Vorticism; for a time one associated him with Marinetti, with futurism, with concerts in which cannons were fired or guinea-pigs compelled to squeal, and with paintings which resembled rather minor and obscure explosions among bric-à-brac. That he had a vigorous and individual mind was evident enough; and that he could draw was admirably attested by occasional exhibitions of his work at the Leicester Galleries in London. Some of these—notably those drawings in which he was least doctrinaire—were characterized by a singular delicacy and purity, a quality which one might suggest by saying that it was a blending of the feminine and the mathematical. In fiction, he has now produced a novel and a book of short stories, both of them energetic and original, both of them somewhat marred by his passion for dogma, his love of controversy, or, in short, by his spleen. In the realm of controversy itself, he has been increasingly a kind of angry sharpshooter of his generation. In this regard, he has somewhat resembled Mr. Ezra Pound, with whom he was early associated; but the resemblance has been (if one may put it so) antithetical. Mr. Pound's love of new "movements," and of being in the forefront of aesthetic battle, is well known. He has been one of the most striking *entrepreneurs* of our time: a brilliant, if occasionally misguided, leader of rebellions. Mr. Lewis, on the other hand, if he has shared with Mr. Pound this passion for novelty and for positions conspicuously dangerous, has differed from him in his emotional reason for doing so. For whereas Mr. Pound has always been what he himself has described as a "broken bundle of mirrors," a sort of reflector of this and that and the other, Mr. Lewis has remained singularly and truculently himself. He has wanted to be there, in this advanced position, but for a purpose of his own. Sufficiently a prey to this herd-instinct, and to this *Zeitgeist,* to desire a part in its "show," he was nevertheless somewhat annoyed (or so one guessed) at his weakness in obeying so base a desire. He was, in short, an individualist who had, willy-nilly, been swept along with a crowd whose components he could not wholly admire.

Something of this division has shown itself in all of Mr. Lewis's work. One always feels in his criticism that he is himself a sort of exasperated victim of the very things which, with so magnificent and vivid a gusto, he attacks. He has become a professional enemy: one almost feels, indeed, that at times he merely attacks because only in attack can he become reassuringly aware (by a kind of negative assumption) of his own identity. One does not go to him for that Greek or Chinese serenity which, in his new book, he claims to admire; hating the philosophy of the dynamic, he is nevertheless typically dynamic himself; at war with chaos, he adopts the language of chaos; desiring peace and assurance, and hungering for perfect *rest,* that perfect rest which only an almost religious conviction of the permanence and value of the ego can give, he contributes, in Time and Western Man, the most violent and confused and restless and peaceless of contemporary books of philosophy.

Mr. Lewis' latest *bête noire* is the Time-doctrine of Spengler and Whitehead and Alexander, and of modern science in general. The present reviewer is not a metaphysician and cannot presume, and does not particularly desire, to follow the argument in all its massive and chaotic detail. Suffice it to say that Mr. Lewis hates the idea of flux and change and relativity; that he fears the consequences of such ideas; that he prefers the comparative calm and order which one may suck from the pure objective idealism of Berkeley (a choice with which his reviewer is cheerfully but unexcitedly in sympathy); and that he attacks this latest time-ghost with an almost unexampled ferocity. Not only does he attack it with ferocity; he also, like a man obsessed, sees it everywhere. If we are to take Mr. Lewis' word for it, this time-beast is devouring us. It animates the pages of Marcel Proust, it deadens the pages of Mr. Joyce's *Ulysses,* it prattles in the person of Miss Loos's Lorelei, it stammers in the protracted and posed and iterative *longueurs* of Miss Gertrude Stein, it even kicks its heels in the timed and timeless heels of Mr. Chaplin. This is, to say the least, a singular collocation. Is one right in suspecting that Mr. Lewis is so fixed on this notion that he has lost all sense of values? Is he merely, in this, following not so much a logical method as a method of which free association is the basis? At all events, the connexion becomes, at times, extremely attenuated; one suspects that there is no connexion at all, save in the emotional picture of our brilliant author. One is irresistibly reminded of Mr. Rank's description of the habits of thought—or feeling, to be more precise—of the dementia-praecox, or schizophrenic, type of mind: of his suggestion that such people think in terms of "quality complexes," allowing the unguided mind to flow from image to image in obedience to feeling-associations. Thus, Miss Stein is clearly enough interested in the psychological idea of time; and she also prattles, iterates, stammers, is a kind of false-naive child. We proceed, therefore, from the child-idea, and discover Miss Loos, who adopts the same pose (in the person of her heroine) and assimilate her to the Stein-complex: and *ipso facto,* Miss Loos becomes a part of our idea about "time." From Miss Loos, it is only a step, or a frolic, to Mr. Chaplin; and so on, and so on. And in the end, we have a kind of vague notion (extremely vague) that Mr. Chaplin has something to do with Mr. Spengler; which is very far from being the case.

Mr. Lewis, in other words, is not to be trusted. He is brilliant, entertaining, fertile in suggestion, full of fine phrases, and bursting with energy; in the item, he is acute to the point of incandescence; he can knock on the head a Hegel or a James or a Heraclitus with as emphatic a maul as was ever wielded; but in the end one feels that he is a man obsessed, and blind to whole patterns. One begins to wonder what it is, in this harmless preoccupation of the present with the notion of time, which so upsets him. Is he terribly afraid of something? Is he afraid of flux? Is he afraid of the unknown? Why is he so insistent that the external world should be fixed? Why must he, like the mollusc, be so determined on a retreat into the positively apprehended of the ego? And will he carry this retreat further, or will he ultimately seek satisfaction in one of those grand orthodoxies, like the Church—where he can be absolved of all responsibilities, and simply *accept* a reality? . . .

The truth is, I suppose, that Mr. Lewis is a dyed-in-the-wool romantic. He is part and parcel of his age; and while he attacks it, he is indelibly conditioned by it. Incapable of achieving the "long" view of man's place in the world, disquieted by scientific analysis, of whatever sort, horrified by the prevailing doctrine of change and flux (which is no newer than Heraclitus), and frightened by modern psychology, as much as by relativity or the quantum theory, he lashes out against everything that is not the quietism of the idealist. And, nevertheless, there is nothing of the quietist in him: nothing whatever. Here is no Platonic serenity, but the gesticulatory vehemence of the dynamists whom he would depose; he is tainted, and deeply, with the excitements, the fashions, and fads of his age; too much himself a victim of the Time-beast, he is therefore largely a reactionist to the moment; he lacks the calm independence (?) of the scientist, on the one hand, and the poet on the other.

LINDSAY, VACHEL (1923)

Mr. Vachel Lindsay, a few years ago, had a good deal to say of what he termed "the higher vaudeville." Mr. Lindsay's reputation, at that time, was at its brassiest and brightest. His recitations of "The Congo" and "The Chinese Nightingale" were famous, and everywhere, from Oxford even to Boston, audiences were eager to roar like lions for him. One cannot be certain which came first, theory or practice, but at all events it was early in the "Congo" and "General Booth" period that Mr. Lindsay began preaching his higher vaudeville doctrine; and it was at that time that one or two rude, perspicacious critics dared to suggest that Mr. Lindsay might be, as it were, digging his grave with a saxophone. By the "higher vaudeville" Mr. Lindsay meant that poetry ought, in his opinion, to be primarily an entertainment—and not only that, but a popular one. Poetry should be recited—the troubadour must be revived—and, above all, the audiences should participate. The theory was engaging, not to say startling; and defining it in practice with such brindled oddities as "Daniel," "King Solomon and the Queen of Sheba," and "The Potatoes' Dance," Mr. Lindsay easily eclipsed his sedater contemporaries. This, certainly, was a poetry which required no effort on the part of the reader; and it was deliciously, dangerously, "original." Not the least of its virtues, in the American view, was its richness in topical allusion (ranging all the way from Mary Pickford to John L. Sullivan and the Anti-Saloon League) and its patent morality—Mr. Lindsay was clearly a sort of puritan zealot, the Bryan of poetry. In the English view, Mr. Lindsay was seductive largely because he was so shining an example of the barbaric yawp. His poetry, like that of Joaquin Miller and Bret Harte, came with the proper Wild West credentials. It yelled, and it wore a sombrero.

But the rude, perspicacious critics worried Mr. Lindsay. The "high seriousness" of which they unseasonably reminded him made him a little uneasy and furtive with his saxophone, and he began keeping it out of sight. He not only dropped his doctrine of the "higher vaudeville"—he even suggested that recitation, and the writing of poetry for recitation, had not been of his own choice, but had been forced upon him by his audiences. He added, adroitly, that he was far more interested in drawing and hieroglyphics than in writing, and that in a great many instances the poem was merely a descriptive title written for, and after, a drawing. The motive beneath this singular change of heart becomes quite clear, finally, in the ambling, confidential autobiographical preface with which Mr. Lindsay now introduces his *Collected Poems*; it is a passionate, a pathetic desire for respectability. He wants to be taken seriously—he wants not only audiences, but critics too, to roar for him. At great pains, therefore, to assure us that he is not a mere "wild man," he offers evidence that his childhood was passed in an environment not innocent of culture. Before his fourteenth year he read Poe, and Woodberry's *Life of Poe*—"every inch of it." He participated, as a Cupid clad in mosquito-netting, in *Olympus*, a kind of Greek miracle-play written by his mother—the part of Venus being taken by his Methodist Sunday-school teacher. He was sent to a "breathlessly exclusive" drawing-school. "Literature was taken for granted": that is, he was drilled in reciting "choice verses" from the Bible. He read "the Brownings and the Pre-Raphaelites." He "knew and loved in infancy the lines of Keats—'Heard melodies are sweet.'" And the amount of time he spent in museums lecturing on "the Ionic and Doric elements in the evolution of the Parthenon," or drawing casts of the Elgin marbles, is astounding. I, who have done all this, he cries, "am assumed to hate the classics and champion their destruction. I, who have spent delightful years in the corridors of cool museums, am assumed to love noise and hate quiet." It is a cruel misconception. And the "Kallyope Yell," a case in point, seeming perhaps to prove that he likes noise, he defends on the ground that it is really intended to be *whispered*. In fact, he adds, "all my verses marked to be read aloud, should be whispered, however contradictory that may seem."

Well, unfortunately or fortunately, there is also the verse of

Mr. Lindsay, which is noisy or nothing. We need not take too
sagely Mr. Lindsay's petition that we judge it "for lifetime and
even hereditary thoughts and memories of painting"; nor need
we scrutinize it too passionately for "evidence of experience in
drawing from life, drawing architecture, drawing sculpture, trying to draw the Venus de Milo, and imitating the Japanese
prints and Beardsley, and trying to draw like Blake." One might
as well try to tie knots in eggs. But the verse itself, if we do not
ask too much of it, can be enjoyed—a little of it. "The Chinese
Nightingale" and the moon poems have charm and color (color
uncertainly and coarsely used), and "The Congo," "The Santa
Fé Trail," and "The Fireman's Ball" have a delightful, unre-
strained, vaudeville vigor and humor. The ragtime rhythms are
amusing, the use of sonorous vowel sounds is broad and lavish,
and in general Mr. Lindsay has gusto and what one vaguely
calls "originality." But when one has said that, one has said
everything. Mr. Lindsay has little mind, and little sensibility;
his poetry is imageless, its ideas are childish; and as verse it is
extraordinarily amateurish. One reads it, ultimately, only because Mr. Lindsay had a reputation, and because in queer corners he still has an influence. And one foresees no future for it
whatever. It is the business of the poet to delight with beauty,
or to amaze with understanding; and Mr. Lindsay does neither.

LORCA, FEDERICO GARCIA   (1940)

With each fresh addition to our knowledge of Federico Garcia
Lorca, the poet's genius becomes more impressive. That extraordinary brilliance which struck one at once, in the first few of
his poems to be translated, has turned out by no means to be an
intermittent or accidental thing—it was sustained. Brilliance
came as naturally to him, in fact, as dullness or preciosity to
others; it was simply his speech. Nothing could be more remarkable, in this new collection, *The Poet in New York*, than the apparently inexhaustible fertility of Lorca's imagination. It was
everywhere at once, it was prodigal, it was fantastic—the subjective and objective worlds rolled up and ignited in a single
ball—the quotidian married singularly to the classic, the folk-
song crossed with the baroque. To call him a surrealist is a mis-

take, for to be a surrealist is to be something else than a poet, something less than a poet: surrealism is perhaps one of many names, merely, for the substratum out of which poetry is made. Lorca devoured all the properties of surrealism, stuffed his cheeks with them, like a conjuror, blew them out of his mouth again as poems—but so he did with everything else that he fed on. The papery guitars, the ingeniously misplaced eyes, the little traplike mouths cropping out of the sides of heads, and all the rest of that slightly sinister and somehow iodine-tinctured phantasmagoria of the followers of Loplop and synesthesia, these are certainly here, in the New York poems, but they have been made into poetry.

On the whole! There are times, let us admit, when the prodigality of image does seem to be indulged in for its own sake, and when the virtuosity and rapidity become blinding: the Gongoresque multiplication of idea carries one too far, and on too wide a front: too many things are required to be embraced at once, as if one tried to organize a single wave from end to end of the Atlantic. But even so, the fault is more often ours than Lorca's—*he* knows perfectly well what he is doing, and the tiniest or queerest item of the sargasso which his wave lifts will presently yield its meaning, like something heard afterward, like an echo. Back will come the main theme, the recurring preoccupation, of this book—pain, pain and suffering, fear of death and injury, the agony of the conscious mind in the presence of universal pain:

But there is no forgetfulness or sleep:
Raw flesh. Kisses bind the mouth
In a tangle of fresh veins
And whom his grief pains it will pain forever
And who fears Death will carry her on his shoulders.

It takes a hundred forms—the earthworm singing the terror of the wheel, "those who forever watch the tracks of claw and raindrop," the little paw of the cat crushed by a car, the ocean remembering the names of all its drowned, the woman dying in childbirth, for whom every sound is a stone, every footprint a throb—and "the little tiny dead along the shore."

A little corrosive glove detains me. Stop!
I felt on my handkerchief the tinkle and crash
Of the first vein breaking.

And again:

This is the world, my friend, agony, agony.
The dead rot under the clocks of the cities
War with a million gray rats goes weeping
Rich men give their beloveds
Little illuminated corpses
And life is never noble, nor good, nor sacred.

If there is nothing in the present collection quite as good as **the** *Lament for the Death of a Bullfighter,* which was perhaps **the finest** of all Lorca's poems, there is nevertheless much that is magnificent. The "Ode to Walt Whitman"—bitter, comic, wry-mouthed, double-faced—is devastating: and so are the New York poems, "Unsleeping City," "Blind Panorama" and others. There has been no more terribly acute critic of America than this steel-conscious and death-conscious Spaniard, with his curious passion for the modernities of nickel and tinfoil and nitre, and for the eternities of the desert and the moon. He hated us, and rightly, for the right reasons. Intensely Spanish, he is best of course in Spanish, which, next to English, is the best of all poetic languages; and therefore exceedingly difficult to translate. But Mr. Humphries has done a really excellent job, and made very few mistakes.

MacLEISH, ARCHIBALD   (1927)

These are lean days for the poetry-lover—it is now a decade since that exciting time when every week or so brought us another new and brilliantly promising poet, of whose future one might dare to predict in terms both hopeful and spacious. Those hopeful futures have now, for the most part, become disappointing pasts or hopeless presents; since Mr. Eliot gave us *The Waste Land,* there has been little to inspire in us the sacred terror, unless we except an occasional poem by Mr. Stevens or Mr. Cummings or Mr. Sacheverell Sitwell, and perhaps also Mr. Ransom. Even with these, however, we are in a sense already familiar—we feel that we know what sort of thing they are likely to do. What we really desire—for we are all of us lovers of the new—is a young poet whose brilliance has progressed beyond that point at which both he and ourselves might be deceived

by a mere youthful flash, and in whose promise one can begin to see the outlines of something large.

Mr. Archibald MacLeish, who entitles his latest book (for no discoverable reason) *Streets of the Moon*, qualifies admirably for this role. One has felt of him from the beginning that he had a very exceptional talent, and that if he might once escape from the several "influences" which have in succession so deeply stained him, and succeed in discovering his own identity (most difficult of the poet's tasks), he might easily become one of the most exciting of contemporary American poets. *The Pot of Earth*, despite its "monstrous debt" to *The Waste Land*, was a very impressive piece of work: if one failed to do it justice, it was because it posed for the critic the subtlest of problems, that of assaying, in the midst of so much that was obviously derived (whether in texture of thought or texture of rhythm) the precise weight and value of the individual contribution. Might the thing have been merely wrung out of Mr. MacLeish by his reading of *The Waste Land*—or was there more to follow? And Mr. MacLeish's next book, *Nobodaddy*, a play in blank verse, helped one very little, for it was written earlier than *The Pot of Earth* and clearly belonged to a more formative and more academic period in his growth. It was good, but it was not, in the same way, exciting.

Streets of the Moon, however, sets one's doubts at rest. Influences there still are—one could enumerate three or four; but in these three groups of poems Mr. MacLeish makes it perfectly clear at last that he is very much himself, and that he has found a murex of his own. One regrets a little that in some of the shorter things he should have yielded to the contemporary taste for typographical and punctuational oddity—devices which, as he shows us himself, he can better dispense with; one regrets also a slight leaning, now and then, to the sentimental-interrogatory and sentimental-exclamatory; and one wishes that he would oftener eschew the fragmentary and asymmetrical, though he occasionally makes delightful things of them. His ability really runs the other way—it is in the full and rounded, in the richly organized, that he finds his natural expression; he writes, when he wants, magnificent blank verse; he is an Elizabethan in his love of fine phrases and in his power to grasp the metaphysical in sensuous terms; and he knows how to build toward a climax, both conceptual and prosodic, in a large and complex fashion of which most of his contemporaries seem to be sentimentally afraid. Certainly Mr. MacLeish need not **be** afraid, as his *Einstein*, in the present volume, superbly proves —a long poem which any living poet might envy, as rich in thought as it is in color and movement. If he can do this, and such exquisite smaller things as "Selene Afterwards," not to mention a dozen others, what mightn't he do next? One simply abdicates as critic, and flings one's hat in the air.

MacLEISH, ARCHIBALD ·   (1929)

There is only one thing to be said in favor of the "group review" of books of verse, especially when the group is as miscellaneous as the present one; and that is the fact that nothing can be so well calculated to sharpen anew one's sense of the predicament which any contemporary poet must face. Here are these five poets—Mr. Robinson, Mr. Jeffers, Mr. Coppard, Mr. Sandburg, and Mr. MacLeish; and their very dissimilarity, which is striking, suggests, a good deal, that the contemporary poet is in a sense a lost man. Tradition, which in other ages was precise and dictatorial, is now overwhelmingly complex. Which, of all the traditions he inherits, shall our poet obey? Or shall he endeavor to combine several of them, and of the combination to make something new?

The situation is a difficult one, at best; and one is aware of the difficulty when one reads these five volumes of verse. They are all of them good books, very much above the average. But one feels of all of them that they lack that ultimate power and directness and rootedness which seems, unfortunately, to accrue only to those works which are produced at a time when tradition is great and single and even, perhaps, *simple*. That these five poets feel the *need* of some such sustaining certainty and simplicity is at once obvious. A. E. Coppard, for example, in his *Collected Poems*, deliberately goes back to the seventeenth century for his quality, and very charmingly he does it, too. His formal lyrics are admirable: they have the genuine freshness and neatness, the dexterously naive mingling of conceptual and sensory view, which one associates with the best of Cavalier and metaphysical poetry. He has wit, too, and an engaging lustiness. But in thus retreating to an earlier period, he admits himself to

· Also reviewed here: A. E. Coppard, Edwin Arlington Robinson, Carl Sandburg, and Robinson Jeffers.

be lost; and *how* lost betrays itself in his other and more modern poems, which as a rule are loose and unsuccessful.

E. A. Robinson, whose collected *Sonnets: 1889–1927* are now presented to us, plays a little safer, chooses a tradition less remote and odd: his roots are in the nineteenth century; and perhaps his closest congener, in that era, was Meredith. He treats the sonnet formally, a little abstractly, at a low pitch of intensity; he is not much gifted on the sensuous side; there is a kind of Puritan bleakness in him, which rather fortunately blends with his intellectual irony and dry Yankee humor; and if his sonnets never glow, or become radiant, or *melt* into a sort of white-hot integrity, as one feels the best sonnets should, they are nevertheless excellent. One reads them with a genuine pleasure and with a feeling (rare enough in poetry) that one's mind is being employed; but one fails, afterward, to remember them particularly. They are just a little colorless.

Carl Sandburg is another matter. His roots, clearly enough, are in Whitman. On the technical side, in fact, he is the chief of Whitman's disciples; he endeavors to bring Whitman up to date. He has a rich feeling for slang, for the jazz rhythms of the age, a fine "voice," a splendid gusto; if he fails on the whole to satisfy us it is because his *range*—mental or spiritual or emotional, or whatever one wants to call it—is so narrow. He is too persistently sentimental, crooning, nostalgic, yearning. And while he achieves very often a charming effect by his mixture of neologism or slang and sentiment, he does so with insufficient sense of variety and selection. His poems wear out comparatively quickly— partly because they are all too much alike, too much in one key, and partly because, for all their "thickness" (in William James's sense), they contain so little "idea." Of his new book, *Good Morning, America*, one can only say that it seems to be as good as the others, and very like them.

Our two remaining poets are in a way more exciting. Robinson Jeffers is a remarkable poet: there is no dodging that fact. One may not like him; one may feel him to be uncouth, overstrained, hyperbolic, too laboriously and unintermittently violent; but of his power there can be no question. Is he, too, lost? He has evidently been at pains to transplant Sophocles to California; and the effect is a little queer. His consequent grandeurs become at times, unfortunately, a little grandiose; his tragedies lie too close to the horrible; attempting the stark and awful, he too often, like D. H. Lawrence, revels in the merely and rawly abnormal, and with a kind of cruelty; his poems are always bloodshot. But his new poem, *Cawdor,* a kind of nightmare novel in a loose prose-verse (like a semi-prose semi-verse translation from the Greek) is, for all its monstrosities and absurdities and excessive use of symbolism—his wounded eagles and shot lions—a very impressive thing. His people are vivid, psychologically true. If at the outset one feels an extraordinary unreality in the whole affair, disbelieves in these farmer folk who talk like Clytemnestra at one moment and like a Henry James or Dostoevsky character the next, one soon finds oneself being swept off one's feet by the sheer force of Mr. Jeffers's creative power. He seems to be developing something of Dostoevsky's ability to take one bodily into an unreal world so unified and consistent and apprehensible that one ends by believing it against one's will. That is a rare kind of power: if only Mr. Jeffers can hold himself down a little, be a shade less drastically and humorlessly dramatic, one feels that he might give us something pretty astonishing. Even so, *Cawdor* is a fine thing, despite its bad lapses. He is a poet to be watched enviously by his fellows.

Archibald MacLeish is perhaps the most fascinating psychological problem, among contemporary poets, which is at our disposal. On the technical side, there is no living poet to whom he need take off his hat. He has technical genius. He can say things with a cunning, a brilliance, a suppleness, a power, which any living poet might covet. But he, too, is a kind of slave of tradition: with the difference that the traditions which enslave him are contemporary ones. He seems unable to throw off the influence of T. S. Eliot, of Mr. Stevens, of various French poets of the last quarter century; an influence which is so deeply pervasive that it seems to have affected even his way of thinking and feeling. His new poem, *The Hamlet of A. MacLeish,* is again, like *Pot of Earth,* a kind of brilliant *pastiche.* It is full of beautiful things. There are passages which move one, or hurt one, deeply. But, also, the poem is so full of echoes as to be positively prismatic with them; not only prosodically and verbally but even in the very frame of the idea, the approach. Why must Mr. MacLeish keep us in such a despair about him? If he could free himself—if he could get down to the *Ding-an-sich,* the thing which is himself—if he could, make *this* discovery, which is the final discovery of any artist, and mine *this* material— one feels that the result might be dazzling. Meanwhile, one perpetually notes in his work a kind of falsity of tone, a falsity which seems to result from the fact that he is always, in a sense, playing a part, a part which is not wholly natural to him. For a passage or two, at any point, he can maintain the tone admirably; but sooner or later he is betrayed into that sort of overstatement which the parodist and the imitator equally achieve, but with a different purpose. He appears to *think* his way into attitudes which are not, unfortunately, native to him. Just why he should do this, with so tremendous an ability at his disposal, one cannot guess. Nor can one be wholly sure whether his "echoes" might not, by a future generation, be actually preferred to the things they echo.

MacLEISH, ARCHIBALD · (1934)

Mr. MacLeish is one of the best contemporary poets, and also one of the most interesting—two statements which do not mean quite the same thing: for a considerable part of one's interest, in his case, is, and has always been, in the question why he is not better than he actually is, and *more* interesting. His virtues are obvious. He is vivid, he is various, he is energetic, he is experimental. More than most poets, he has given his hand away, in the sense that he has either deliberately or accidentally invited the public to participate in his private dilemma: one need only cite the title of one of his books, *The Hamlet of A. MacLeish.* Whether accidental or deliberate, this is courageous—though more courageous if deliberate; one of the most useful of the poet's functions is just such a projection of the private world into the world at large; and this, willy-nilly, Mr. MacLeish has done. He has, in a word, made us walk with him and think with him. He has compelled us to listen, by the sheer persuasion of his voice—but not only by that, also by a suggestion that he faces a problem, that to be a modern man involves inevitably a facing of a problem, the necessity of a decision.

Unfortunately, it is at precisely this point that Mr. MacLeish lets us down. He dons the robe of the prophet, with one hand, only to doff it with the other. In *The Pot of Earth* and the *Hamlet* he seemed to be saying that life was pretty futile, a waste land (with variations) of private despair in a mechanistic world which scarcely deserved the lifting of an active hand. In *Conquistador,* on the contrary, he seemed to be saying just the opposite: that the desideratum was action; and if he said this not

· *Poems: 1924-1933.*

quite convincingly, or not quite successfully, this serves only to increase our feeling that he was not quite convinced himself, or that he perhaps shrank from the implications of his own statement. One's feeling about this is heightened by a peculiar remark in the foreword to the present selection from his poems. He says of it that it does not "purport to trace [my] development as a poet. My development as a poet is of no interest to me and of even less interest, I should think, to anyone else." Try as one will, one cannot think this is quite honest. One might as well say that one's growth as a human being, as a tree, as a world, or even as a God, is of no concern either to oneself or to another. It simply isn't true. One *is*, and profoundly, interested in one's own growth: one cannot escape it: and to deny one's interest is perhaps merely (inversely) to overstate it. Is it possible that Mr. MacLeish is *over* concerned with his development as a poet, just as we are?

There is much to be said for this possibility. For Mr. MacLeish has not developed. He has evolved, it is true, but he has evolved in a circle—revolved is the better word—always remaining, in his progress, equidistant, on the one hand, from the ego and, on the other, from the world. Is this the problem of the narcissist? He never sees either outside or in. He can only alternately imitate those who understand and those who conquer. And there is a quality in Mr. MacLeish's poetry which suggests this sort of adaptation—a kind of ventriloquism; one is thinking here of the mere tone of it, the verbal and prosodic one; he speaks now with one voice, now with another, always with a sort of approximate authenticity, because he has genius, but never quite authentically. His voice is sometimes that of the Eliot of *Gerontion*—more often that of the Pound of the *Cantos* or of *Cathay:* a solution or dilution of these: apart from either, it appears convincing: compared, it at once seems to lack force or precision. It makes one suspect that Mr. MacLeish is still "immature," unformed: as if, afraid to look prolongedly either inward or outward, but with a genius for talking, he must at least take a fashionable part.

This may appear unjust. The poet who wrote *Einstein* and *You, Andrew Marvell*, to mention only the two best, and in different sorts, needs no apologist. These are among the finest poems of our generation, and both have behind them a kind of "tough thinking" which compels us to expect better things of Mr. MacLeish than he has yet given us. Why, instead, must he go on giving us his so extraordinarily skillful pastiche of evasions? In this regard, to read over, in the present collection, *The Pot of Earth,* the *Hamlet,* the *Conquistador* and the shorter poems is simply to renew one's feeling that the technical genius which goes into these might better be directed to a more specific and more individual purpose. What this purpose might be, or what the direction, one cannot possibly presume to indicate. One cannot suggest development to one who dislikes the idea of development: at most, one can suggest a point of departure. The point of departure, one might say, is the nostalgic, the note of self-pity, the "pathos of distance," which everywhere cries and rings in these poems—so much so that one eventually thinks of them as all one repetition of the same theme. Whether it is the wind, or the weather, or the remembrance of things past, or the desire to be remembered, or the impossibility of being remembered or of remembering, it all comes to the same thing—it is like somebody speaking to himself in a mirror, listening affectionately to his own voice, watching his own expression, playing a part. Mr. MacLeish can do better than this—he has already proved it. He has the means, he only lacks the aim. Already a poet to make us all envious, if he could only break this glass and walk either inward on himself, or outward to the world, he could perhaps say what no other contemporary poet could say.

MacNEICE, LOUIS •   (1941)

"I consider," says Mr. Louis MacNeice, "that the poet is a blend of the entertainer and the critic or informer; he is not a legislator, however acknowledged, nor yet, essentially, a prophet. As informer, he is not a photographic or scientific informer, but more like the 'informer,' in the derogatory sense—he is grinding an axe or showing off, telling tales about his enemies, flattering his friends. . . . The poet does not give you a full and accurate picture of the world nor a full and accurate picture of himself, but he gives you an amalgam which, if successful, represents truthfully his own relations to the world." And Mr. MacNeice goes on to say, in the conclusion of his admirable little book, *Modern Poetry,* that the sort of poet he prefers is the ordinary fellow who likes to talk, reads the papers, knows something of

• Also reviewed here: E. E. Cummings and John Peale Bishop.

economics and is appreciative of women, and is "susceptible of physical impressions."

It is an interesting off-hand sketch of the poet's nature, whether we take it to be ideal or merely literal; as interesting for what it proposes to leave out as for what it includes. Notice that the first emphasis of all is on entertainment, the second on criticism; that although he is to be a critic, he is nevertheless not to be a legislator, and that—essentially—he need not expect to be much of a prophet: divination and the religious business are to be left out, together with the whole notion that the poet—or any artist, for that matter—has any special insight, intuition or inside view. He will merely report on his relation with the world (as in an autobiography) and if he is successful this will be true. Why —one wonders—the proviso of success? Wouldn't the report be just as true even if it were *not* successful? Even the bad poet reports, one suspects, quite truthfully on his relation with the world, the badness being a vital part of the truth. But this is only one of many questions which Mr. MacNeice's definition suggests, and for the moment not the most interesting—unless we take it to mean that Mr. MacNeice is indifferent to badness. Is he? Is he perhaps not very much interested in the *art* of poetry, and much more, at any rate, in these other matters of entertainment and criticism, or information?

But leaving aside for the moment that troublesome question of art, with its perpetual nuisance value to poets and critics alike, and leaving aside as well, if we can, all such teleological vanities as the notion that the poet is, if anything, a *vates*, a seer, a profound leader and creator, we can perhaps see the more clearly in Mr. MacNeice's poems how admirably he practices what he preaches. "We stand convicted," he says in the poem called "Men of Good Will," "votaries of the topical and transitory, we put in words what is topical and transitory, anyone can detect it." He will make a virtue of precisely that, and of allowing himself no nonsense, no romantic pretense, no vision. His own life is ineffectual and trite; he will report it so. But the entertainment, yes, that is another matter: he can at least be entertaining. And indeed he is.

For sheer readability, for speed, lightness, and easy intellectual range, Mr. MacNeice's verse is in a class by itself. Open it anywhere, whether in narrative, eclogue, or lyric, and at once you are swept away by the tireless and effortless enumerative pace, the bright rush of nominal images, the gay prodigality of scene, the so easily caught tune and mood. Yes, this is the world

we know, all right, and this too is a fellow we can like, here are
pubs and football games and Freud and the dreary economic
muddle and the confused political ideologies through which we
try to think, or feel, our way, and the sad glad conquests and
vapors of love too, the whole great blooming buzzing confusion
(to quote William James)—it's all here, bright and quick as a
river to swim in. And so, in we go; and out we come; and it is
only then that we find how little of all this has stuck to us. Not a
thing—practically not a thing. For the trouble is, it is *too* topical,
too transitory, *too* reportorial—it has that sort of merit and vividness which is good in the presence of the object, and by virtue
of the object has a kind of quick and momentary magic; but it
has, one fears, very little *residual* magic, very little of that quality of intricate and teasing wroughtness which sends one back to
a poem not for the meaning but to see how the meaning was
said.

No, Mr. MacNeice writes as he runs; he is always in a hurry;
we catch the delightful fragments of speech which he addresses
to us, as it were, over his shoulder—but we cannot help thinking
that he would be better if he could take more seriously either
the function of the poet as *genus irritabile vatum* or the virtue
of the artifact. Even the best of the lyrics—and they are very
good—such as "Meeting Point," "A Toast," with their very skillful use of vernacular refrain to dignify a sentimental theme, suffer from that sort of carelessness about the fine points of form
which indicates an essentially barbaric attitude toward art. If
only all that brilliance could be put to better use! But then, Mr.
MacNeice professes indifference to this, believes that nowadays
only a more off-hand method can be natural or true, and prefers to be merely entertaining. We must therefore leave it at that.

After Mr. MacNeice's cornucopia, the dainty devices of Mr.
Cummings and the mild eclecticism of Mr. Bishop certainly
seem a little pale. Of Mr. Cummings it has been noted—by Mr.
MacNeice among others—that there are usually two styles: ty-
pographic delirium, scrambled orthography and syntax, a kind
of linguistic battle-royal, and all to conceal the real sentimentality; and, as well, an almost sweetly "poetic" attack, archaisms
and all, which is made to look adventurous by lack of punctuation. Mr. Cummings pulls his own leg too much; he can be a
master of the "smubtle," but indulges in it too often; he is also a
master of the pure lyric, and in that he indulges us too seldom.

Mr. Bishop is very much more varied, and in thematic range,
at least, is comparable to Mr. MacNeice. He is a fastidious

writer, with a nice sense of form, when he doesn't violate it out of a feeling of obligation to modernity; he uses many colors and styles equally well; it is hard therefore to say just why one doesn't like his poems better. They are very good, and yet they seem somehow a shade *voulu*, and, though pleasing in the item, to lack that vague thing we call character, the identifying voice. An eclecticism of style can play funny tricks—witness the case of Mr. MacLeish—and perhaps Mr. Bishop has to pay, as it were, too many pipers. "Unless 'twere better to be very single, to follow some diviner monotone"—might one suggest that? To follow for a while a single line might be, for Mr. Bishop, more rewarding and more revealing.

MANN, THOMAS (1928)

The process by which one comes to know an author, or that part of him which appears in his books, is exactly the process by which one comes to know a person in the flesh. One moves from one impression to another; he is this today, and that tomorrow; at first he seems predominantly sad, later one finds that this sadness conceals an undercurrent of irony or secret glee; his face is immobile, but one discovers that his talk is full of emotional or affective overtones; or one moves forward from a first impression of copiousness to a second one of essential thinness. And by slow evolution, all these separate impressions fuse in one image. The glee is added to the sadness, the thinness to the copiousness, the mysterious hint to the impassivity. One acquires a single image, in which, if the first magic of mystery is lost, one finds a kind of definite consolation in the fact that it now quite clearly seems to belong to a category.

The present reviewer's acquaintance with Thomas Mann, or his books, has been of that sort. It has been kaleidoscopic, confused, directionless, delicious. *Buddenbrooks* created the first image—solid, distinct, forthright, almost of the Arnold Bennett order. A four-square three-decker, but with a German, or Gothic, distortion. *Death in Venice* broke this image, precisely as a dropped pebble breaks an image in a surface of water. This was something new—here was an affective overtone not experienced before. What, exactly, was this added something? As before, the story was simple and direct and naturalistic. The secondary characteristics were all, apparently of the realistic school, if one may be permitted so loose a term. But decidedly there was something else. On the surface, everything was clear and simple and distinct. The story—what there was of it—moved with no subterfuges to its tragic and quiet climax. And, nevertheless, there was this queer something else, this nameless undertone, deep and melancholy, which gave the story a different quality, and gave the author, in one's memory, a new reputation. Perhaps the easiest epithet for this added quality is "poetic." If one had felt this in the earlier work, here and there, one had forgotten it in the prevailing sense of the real, or (as Henry James preferred to call it) the actual. But in *Death in Venice* this became the dominant tone; the poetic or allegorical quality was precisely what one most remembered afterward. One remembered a tone, a haze, a vague disquieting tapestry effect, as of the smoke from autumnal burnings of leaves; an atmosphere heavy and *charged;* a feeling of that kind of poetic counterpoint which was habitual with Poe and Hawthorne. The tale was deep, melancholy, almost (in a sense) horrible. Beauty and horror were met, here, in a kind of balance.

The Magic Mountain moved one's general impression back again toward *Buddenbrooks,* but not all the way. Is one perhaps right in calling this enormous novel a kind of "secondary" masterpiece? It resembles *Buddenbrooks* in its leisure, its copiousness, its massive employment of circumstance. It differs from it in a slight dislocation toward what one might call the spiritual. This again is a three-decker: one of the finest examples of the really "exhaustive" novel which the present generation has given us. But it moves away from *Buddenbrooks* in at least one particular: one feels in it just a trace of an *arrière pensée,* a mystic or pseudo-mystic current, barely revealed, a preoccupation with ultimates and eternals. Its superlative leisure, like that of Proust's great novel, annihilates time: it is indeed, in a sense, as the prologue makes clear, preoccupied with the sense of time, or of timelessness; and it is also curiously, and perhaps naturally (given this circumstance) preoccupied with death, and with the scale of values peculiar to the man who stands on the brink of death. Here we have a sanatorium full of tuberculosis victims, all of them obsessed with death, all of them charged with that queer recklessness and detachment which supervenes in such cases, where the approach of death is gradual, and all of them sub-normal, as regards energy; the characterization is acute, detailed, profound; the hero, and Mynheer Peeperkorn, and Madame Chauchat, are magnificent; and the amount of time, for a patient and cynical review of the world, is unlimited. Except for the slight and intermittent love story, which comes to no climax, there is no plot: the novel has its excuse in its richness as a microcosm (which everywhere refers to a macrocosm) and second in its exquisiteness of tone. It is a three-decker with a deep undercurrent of poetry: a kind of *William Clissold* written by a poet who happens, also, to have a streak of morbidity.

This streak of morbidity comes out most clearly, apparently, if one may safely judge by what has thus far been translated from the German, in the latest of Thomas Mann's books, *Children and Fools*. These are short stories, of which the most recent and best is dated 1926, and the others from twenty to thirty years earlier. In all of them is this queer Gothic something-or-other which one has obscurely felt from the beginning in Mann's work—most definitely in *Death in Venice*, perhaps, but also, as just noted, in *The Magic Mountain*. Knowing little of contemporary German literature, one hesitates to say that this is a mere Germanness: and nevertheless one is constantly feeling how curiously these tales resemble—if one may speak wholly of *affects*—the German fairy stories which one read when one was a child. Here again is that blending of beauty and horror: of the mystic with the terrible: of life and the most morbid aspects of death. One feels that Mann is a victim of certain obsessions which he cannot escape. He must torture, and be tortured; he must die, and see death; he must be weak, and submit to the brutal; he must manage the scalpel which dissects an anguish, and manage it with a surgeon's scientific detachment. "Disorder and Early Sorrow" is one of the most beautiful stories the present reviewer has ever read: the story of a child's first love, and of the father's jealousy; but even in this is the note of Gothic morbidity. And in the earlier and shorter stories, which are more purely analytical, and less circumstanced—almost, indeed, clinical statements—one detects a nearly unintermittent note of morbidity. They all deal with abnormals—they all deal with psychological disaster. The difference between these and the later stories is simply that the later ones are more poetic, more sublimated. "The Path to the Cemetery," in the present volume —a story dated 1901—is a bare pathological or psychiatrical outline for what might, in 1926, have been another *Death in Venice*.

Eventually, therefore, we begin to see Thomas Mann as a very special and slightly warped figure. But he is a poet, and that is all we need.

There are, I suppose, as many views of the proper method of short-story writing as there are reviewers—a fatuous comment, which will serve, none the less, to remind us that ultimately, in the case of the extremely brilliant writer or the extremely bad one, it will not first of all be his method which attracts or repels, feeds us or starves us, but his sensibility. We may, and should, on second thought hold off at arm's length the method for a cooler inspection; but without the sort of sensibility—and by sensibility we mean pretty nearly everything!—which from the very outset "feeds" us, the unhappy author will never have persuaded us to that second thought. Of course it is possible that we shall then find ourselves somewhat tricked—we may believe ourselves to have dined more heartily than is, in fact, the case, so glittering is the array of dishes, so brilliant the silver, so aromatic the very air; our inspection of method, our cooler survey, may discover to us that our fare has been more spicey than substantial.

This is perhaps not wholly fair as a prelude to the discussion of Miss Katherine Mansfield's short stories. Miss Mansfield is brilliant—she has, more conspicuously than any contemporary writer of fiction one calls to mind, a fine, an infinitely inquisitive sensibility; a sensibility indefatigably young which finds itself in the service of a mind often cynical, sometimes cruel, and always sophisticated. One has not read a page of Miss Mansfield's book before one has said, "Chekhov": but one has not read two pages before Chekhov is forgotten. What provokes one to say "Chekhov" is the fact that almost alone among writers of fiction in England and America Miss Mansfield has followed Chekhov in choosing to regard—in being compelled to regard? —the short story "form" not as the means to the telling of a tale, and not always or wholly as the means for the "lighting" of a single human character, but rather as the means for the presentation of a "quintessence," a summation of a human life or group of lives in the single significant "scene" or situation or episode; and, by implication, the illumination, thus, against a somber background (the somberness being given by absence of values, in the objective world; absence of express concern on the part of the author) of life itself. This, one observes, is the method of

• *Bliss, and Other Stories.*

poetry: in the hands of Chekhov it becomes, according to his theme, either epic or lyric.

Miss Mansfield's range is more restricted. She takes a single treble octave of Chekhov's piano and finds in it the most exquisite of melodies. Such stories as "Escape," "Sun and Moon," "Prelude," "The Man Without a Temperament" are, of their kind, perfect. They are not Chekhov—what has happened is merely that Chekhov has revealed to Miss Mansfield her genius for a kind of short narrative poem in prose, a narrative lyric. One must emphasize the kinship with poetry, because it is clear that in Miss Mansfield's prose, when it is at its best, there are more subconscious compulsions at work, shaping and selecting and coloring, than we expect to find at the bottom of "ordinary" prose: they lend it a shimmer and iridescence, a chromatic vividness (the vividness of dream rather than the vividness of life) which apprise us that we are in the presence of work not so much "calculated" as happily, and with the deepest of intensity, improvised. Miss Mansfield has learnt of Chekhov the kind of effect to aim at; and with this and her theme in mind she has but to close her eyes and listen to the song of sensibility, a sensibility intense to the point of febrility, ecstatically aware of texture and hue, magnificently responsive, most of all, to the *sound* of life, to the rhythms, leisurely or staccato, of street-sounds and house-sounds, to the auditory rhythms, again, which constitute pattern and a hallucinated vividness in certain states of mind, and, lastly, to those minute inflections of the human voice which most reveal themselves as the unconscious overtones of emotion.

But the "compulsory" method is limiting. Can one always properly employ a "hallucinated vividness" of style? It is exquisitely appropriate in a description of the dreamlike consciousness of a child; in "Sun and Moon" and in parts of "Prelude," it gives us a sharp beauty which we can only match in "The Crushed Flower." It is appropriate, again, in a description of the feverish hyperaesthesia of a neurotic young woman —there are several such in Miss Mansfield's book. To these necessities her subconscious most richly responds. Elsewhere, where it responds less fully, Miss Mansfield resorts to cleverness, esurient humor, or even, as in the termination of "Bliss," to the trickery of surprise: the story should have ended indecisively. Here, we feel, the poetry has escaped, as also in "Feuille d' Album," and in the comparative triviality of "Psychology," or "A Dill Pickle." These stories are highly diverting, are clever;

but it is to that miraculous apocalyptical tree in "Escape" that
we turn back, as to beauty itself, and to the motionless aloe, or
the elfish medicine bottles, in "Prelude." Here we have poetry—
a magical evocation of mood, and, through mood, of character.
This is the finest of Miss Mansfield's gifts, and the one upon
which, in the future, we should most like to see her consciously
build.

MANSFIELD, KATHERINE · (1922)

Miss Katherine Mansfield's *Bliss*, a volume of short stories published a year or so ago, attracted, and deserved, a great deal of
attention. It was at once recognized that Miss Mansfield was a
short-story writer of unique sensibility—sensibility in the modern, not in the pre-Victorian sense—and exquisite deftness. If
her stories suggested the influence of Chekhov, notably in their
repeated use of what might be termed the completeness and
charm of the incomplete, the suggestion was fleeting and un-
important: method is, after all, not a copyrightable affair, and
all we have the right to ask of the borrower of a method is that
he shall not permit it to cloud his own personality, or to supplant
it. In the case of Miss Mansfield there could be no question of
this. If one thing was arresting in her work, it was the evidence,
luminous, colorful, and resonant everywhere, of a tactilism extraordinarily acute and individual. One was inclined to question,
even, whether this perpetual coruscation, this amazing sensitiveness to rhythms and sounds and almost shuddering awareness of texture, was not symptomatic of a sort of febrility which
would, sooner or later, impose on Miss Mansfield's work its very
definite limitations; limitations already quite clearly implied.
"Exquisite! yes—this song of sensibility," one might then have
commented, "this poetry of the eyes, the ears, and hands a little
feverish; but is it, ultimately, quite enough?"

It depends, of course, on what one means by enough. Clearly,
this sort of febrility, clairvoyant and clairaudient, *is* enough, if
one wants, in one's fiction, only and always an ecstatic awareness. How admirably such a tone adapts itself to the case of,
say, a neurotic young woman, Miss Mansfield has several times
triumphantly demonstrated—notably in "The Man Without a

· *The Garden Party.*

Temperament." It lends itself superbly, too, to description of the adolescent—what could possibly be better, more brilliant, than the portrait of "The Young Girl" in Miss Mansfield's new collection of stories? Equally applicable is it, again, to descriptions of children, whose minds may be said to exist wholly in their five senses—no contemporary writer has given glimpses of the bright, disintegrated, peripheral consciousness of the child as exquisitely true as those Miss Mansfield gives us in "Sun and Moon" or portions of "Prelude." But it is precisely here that one reaches a suspicion that if Miss Mansfield does these things beautifully it is because in these things she is freest to speak her own language; that her choice of these things is a dictated choice; and that her failure to step often out of this small charmed circle, and her relative failure when she does step out, are failures that we should quite expect.

What we get at is the fact that Miss Mansfield goes to the short story as the lyric poet goes to poetry—Miss Mansfield's short story is, in essence, an essentially "subjective" thing, far more subjective than one is accustomed to expect a short story to be. Of course the distinction between subjective and objective is relative. One may reasonably claim that Chekhov's short stories are "subjective" also, that they represent in the case of Chekhov a psychic compulsion just as unaccountable and uncontrollable as that indicated by Miss Mansfield's *Garden Party.* That is perfectly true, and it compels us to see that the difference between the so-called subjective method in art, and the so-called objective method, is at bottom nothing whatever but a difference in range. Chekhov's range was enormous. He was as tremendously "rooted" in life, perhaps, as Shakespeare. His sensibilities, and therefore his curiosity, were not merely of one sort, but led him everywhere, gave him joy, pain, understanding everywhere, were both sensitive and tough. The world of consciousness (and of subconsciousness) with which he was thus by experience gradually endowed, and the language of associations which he spoke, were not merely intensely individual (independent of the literary) but, by comparison with the language of associations of the average writer, infinitely various. This is what leads us to think of Chekhov as a superlatively "objective" artist, and it is the reverse of this that leads us to think of Miss Mansfield as—just as superlatively?—a "subjective" artist. For Miss Mansfield's sensibilities, if clearly individual, are remarkably limited, and the language of associations which she speaks is, if brilliant, extremely small. The awareness, the personality of the larger artist is an infinitely more divisible, and therefore infinitely less recognizable thing; but the personality of the smaller artist is recognizable everywhere.

Thus, in Miss Mansfield's short stories, as in the poems of a lyric poet, it is always Miss Mansfield's voice that we hear, it is always Miss Mansfield that we see. How it is that limitations of this sort impose themselves on an artist, in childhood or infancy, we leave psychology to discover. Why did Miss Mansfield's extraordinary sensibilities find, as it were, so little to feed on? That is the question we must ask, whether or not we answer it. Did she lack the requisite "toughness"? At all events, her awareness is a very special and limited sort of awareness; the circle of her consciousness is small and bright, and we soon know its outermost limits. Miss Mansfield's new book confirms our speculations in this regard. If one makes the reservation that "Prelude" in the earlier book is the best thing she has written, then one can say that the second volume is just as good as the first. But the limitations are here again, and now seem more striking. We are not so easily deceived a second time, and we perceive too clearly that it is all a beautiful, an exquisite, a diabolically clever masquerade, with the protean Miss Mansfield taking now the part of Beryl, now that of "The Young Girl," now that of both "Daughters of the Late Colonel," now that of Miss Brill; achieving quite extraordinary ventriloquistic feats as Mr. Neave or Mr. Hammond—though she seldom attempts the masculine; and shining out beautifully, with not even the pretence of a mask, as Kezia. Yes, these people are all Miss Mansfield, all speak with her voice, think as she thinks, are rapidly, ecstatically aware, as she is aware; share her gestures and her genius; and represent, in short, not so many people or lives, but so many projections of Miss Mansfield's mind and personality into other people's bodies and houses. How exciting to disguise oneself, for a morning, as Ma Parker, or, for an afternoon, as the singing teacher! And Miss Mansfield's dexterity in the matter is extraordinary. She almost completely deceives us, and even when she has ceased to deceive she continues to delight.

The secret of this legerdemain is simply in Miss Mansfield's mastery of local color, of twinkling circumstance, of the inflection of the moment. It is the song of a sensibility ecstatically aware of the surfaces of life. Her people are not real people, in the sense of being individual, of appearing to have, as Chekhov's characters have, whole lives, apart from the particular story, which the author does not touch on; but they give the illusion of reality; first, because Miss Mansfield endows them all with her own super-sensitive and febrile (and perhaps sentimental) awareness, and, second (which follows from the first), because, therefore, the small circumstances of mood and scene are thus given to us with the feverish vividness of objects seen under lightning. Miss Mansfield puts a kitchen before us with her mention of the gritty soap in the sink; she desolates us, when, describing the bare floors of an abandoned house, she notes the carpet-tacks with their shreds of wool. She sees everything, sees miraculously, feels textures where the less sensitive would see only a smooth surface, hears rhythms and intonations where others would only note the persistence and dullness of a sound. Yes, it is the scene, the scene as apprehended by the hungriest of sensibilities, that Miss Mansfield above all gives us. Must we content ourselves with this? For if Miss Mansfield has little skill at characterization—substituting for "character" a combination of vivid externalities and vivid mood—one must also observe that even in "mood" her range is very small. In a sense the mood *is* the scene—it is the eternal responsiveness to scene. Whether the particular state of mind to be presented is gay or melancholy, bitter or resigned, capricious or saturnine, whimsical or cruel, hardly seems to matter. For the psychological process by which her people are gay or melancholy, bitter or resigned, is always, for Miss Mansfield, the same; the content may change but never the *tempo*. Everything is staccato and exclamatory, everything is intense, even grief is somehow sibilant. If one may use a metaphor which will not bear close psychological scrutiny, but nevertheless conveys one's impression, one may say that Miss Mansfield, instead of submerging herself in her characters, submerges her characters in herself. They come up shining, certainly, and peacock-hued; they burn and glisten in the bright air, shed fine plumes of flame; but they are all just so many Mansfields.

Well, this sort of vividness is something to be profoundly thankful for. The short story created in this manner approaches the poetic in proportion as its theme is largely and emotionally significant, and the color thereby patternized. When the theme is slight, the story tends to become merely a triumph of colorism. In "Prelude," and in one or two other instances, Miss Mansfield has given us poetry; but mere cleverness—cleverness to the point of brilliance—too often betrays her into giving us a colorism which, for all its vividness and verisimilitude, is comparatively empty. The delight that many of these stories afford on the first reading is intense; it wanes a little on the second, and we notice the cleverness—fatal sign! And on the third reading —but is there a third? One cannot dine on the iridescent.

MANSFIELD, KATHERINE   (1927)

Heaven only knows what genius is: the psychologists have, thus far, failed to give us any adequate explanation of this singular and unhappy phenomenon; but, whatever it is, there can be no doubt that Katherine Mansfield had it, and that by her death, in January 1923, English literature suffered perhaps the greatest single loss which has befallen it in this century.

Taken as a whole, her short stories form the best group of short stories which have ever been written in the English language. Single stories that surpass hers, in depth or beauty or poignance, it may be possible to find; though even of this one is uncertain. But the more one considers her work, comparing it with the work of other writers of the short story in English, past or present, the more one is driven to the conclusion that she was *sui generis.*

It is true that her range, in a sense, was not very great. She tended to repeat herself—the same tones reappeared, the same types of character; one felt Katherine Mansfield herself, again and again, in the neurotic, over-intense, feverishly sensitive young women whom she so delighted to portray; one felt her, above all, in the brilliant dissociated consciousness of the children whom she so exquisitely drew; and if one compared her to her avowed master, Chekhov, one was at once aware of his immensely greater scale. But within her limits Katherine Mansfield had a genius as pure and unmistakable as one can call to mind. First and foremost, one thinks of her characteristic intensity—a kind of white heat of sensibility and awareness, for any analogy to which one instinctively turns to John Keats. How curiously like these two people were, and how strangely parallel their destinies! If Keats had written short stories, one hazards that they would have had exactly the kind of burning and prismatic nakedness, emotional and sensuous, that Katherine Mansfield's had. And if Katherine Mansfield had been a poet—?

But, in the finest sense, she *was* a poet: her nature was essentially a poetic one. Her stories were poems; they were as characteristically the products of the unconscious as any poems ever written; they have the hallucinatory vividness and swiftness, the sensory magic and kaleidoscopic verbal brilliance, of dreams. That she was an excellent critic, also, and a very witty one, is neither here nor there. Her critical faculty (and incidentally her reviews in the now defunct *Athenaeum*, when her husband was editing it, were a delight) was of enormous help to her in shaping the material with which her extraordinary unconscious kept her supplied: and one must be careful to do it full justice. But it is above all in her remarkable sensibility, and in the unconscious which it had so richly stored, that one seeks some sort of explanation for her genius.

The *Journal*, which she kept intermittently for thirteen years and which has now been published, deepens but does not alter this impression. It is a fascinating, an extraordinary, and in some respects an appalling book. And again one is reminded of Keats. For here, as in the letters of Keats, is an almost unmatched record of suffering. Like Keats, Katherine Mansfield was born with a sensibility so acute, so exposed, so raw, that it almost inevitably doomed its possessor to pain, to agony of spirit and to tragedy. Like Keats, she was excessively self-centered; like Keats, she was unintermittently and terribly and terrifyingly conscious; she was unable to live in a comfortable and easily drifting continuum of half-awake senses, as the normal human being does—every minute presented itself burningly and separately to her awareness. Every faculty, here, is alert to the extremity of alertness: her sense of humor no less than her sense of pathos and grief. And how delicious was her sense of humor! If, in this journal of hers, there is hardly a page which does not bear witness to agony of spirit, there is also hardly a page on which her indomitable sense of the ridiculous does not break forth. She could be incomparably and extravagantly funny.

Her prose is as miraculous, in this book, as ever. Whether it is a fragment of short story, or a note for a plot or scene, or an unposted letter, or a bit of recollection of her beloved New Zealand, or just a description of the weather or her mood—it doesn't matter; her eye selects the essential, her infallible instinct for language gives her the right word, the lizard-quick phrase; and we live with her as intimately as if she were present. One could rifle phrases, paragraphs, pages, quote them gloatingly—but it's no use. The book must be read. One must follow this tormented spirit from place to place in search of health, watch the growth in her mind of her curious obsession of guilt, her desire for a sort of mystic conversion—for it is, above all, the *person* who captivates us here, and not the authoress: and a phrase or two, a page or two, will not content us.

An extraordinary woman—not a woman with whom, on casual encounter, one could easily be comfortable. She was too direct, too truthful, for that: too much a creature of smoldering and violent loves and hates. Shams and polite conventions shriveled away in her presence. One discussed essentials with her, or one discussed nothing. One knew her intimately, or one knew her not at all.

MASTERS, EDGAR LEE •   (1918)

Does the critic exist who, on reading over the same book on two successive days, or in two successive months or years, will not receive from it a richly different set of impressions? If he does, he is a miracle of petrifaction: his sensibilities have been standardized to the point of dullness.

The average human should and does vary temperamentally from hour to hour, and what he admires today he may resent tomorrow. He likes things, he gets tired of them, he likes them again, in a modified form, and so on through a long spiraling cycle of evolution. For that reason a reviewer ought really to review each book several times over. The sum total of his various reactions might possibly approximate justice.

Thus, although I have just finished a review in extended order of Edgar Lee Masters's new book, I find after dipping into it again after an interval that certain things about it strike me which did not strike me before. The power and fecundity of Mr. Masters still impress me. I watch him with the fascination with which one might watch a steam shovel. I feel in his work when it is at its best a curious muscular magic, the magic of kinesthesia, of energy; and I am often delighted by its psychological richness.

I still feel, in regard to form, that whereas the form of *Spoon River* was an accident imposed from without, in his later work Mr. Masters has been painfully evolving a form (as in "Arabel," "Widow LaRue," "Saint Deseret," "In the Cage") which is more organic and controlled; and that as an artist, though perhaps

• *Towards the Gulf.*

not as a creator, he has gone farthest in these. And, of course, I still feel that the influence of Mr. Masters at the present moment, when American poetry is so given over to the far-from-harmless and frequently unnecessary poetess, is incalculably wholesome.

But, if these first impressions remain fixed, another has come to join them, and that is in the form of a question. Is Mr. Masters writing the sort of poetry which, after reading once with pleasure, one will desire to read again? Whatever my opinion may be tomorrow I am today inclined to say that he is not. It is not that he cannot be interesting. He is frequently prolix, to be sure, and in a good many of his longer things he is downright dull, but at his best he tells a story or draws a portrait with amazing celerity and power.

No, the trouble is not precisely there, though it is always true that a part of the attraction of any narrative, the element of suspense, fades largely with the first reading. The trouble is in the matter of art. It is a far from simple matter, and there are many phases of it that could not be dealt with in less than a solid chapter, but is it not in general true that one derives pleasure in rereading a poem in proportion to its perfection—and perhaps even more important, its elaborateness—as a work of art?

This combination of perfection and elaborateness is itself a combination of other qualities; of which perhaps the chief are, on the one hand, fecundity and freshness of ideas and sensations, and, on the other, beauty, ease, and intricacy of form. Most poets fall short with regard to one or more of these qualities; few command them all.

It is these few, and the few more who approximate such command, whom we can read and reread, always sure to find new delights, since in the presence of such wealth of imagination, both poetic and prosodic, it is impossible to remember more than a small part. A Burns cannot perpetually entice us back, because, despite his lyric beauty and perfection of form, his ideas are few and his sense of form far from subtle. In one reading we perceive the beauty in its entirety.

A Whitman, on the other hand, though fecund in ideas and occasionally intricate in form, is lacking in prosodic ease and beauty. He, also, fails to hold. It is to Shakespeare, Dante, Shelley, and Goethe that one must turn for lasting satisfaction. And even Goethe might be questioned.

Mr. Masters belongs, of course, to the Whitman rather than the Burns type. He is richly and variously creative; and since he

is restless and always in evolution, one looks with keen interest
to each new book. As an artist, however, he is never securely far
from failure. His sense of form is rudimentary. When he writes
metrical verse it is stiffly metrical; when he writes free verse it is
prose. His rhythms are never subtle, rarely magical. The incantations, the blandishments, the suavities, the sonorities, the
accelerations and diminuendos, the discords and resolutions
which constitute a good half of a poet's power are beyond his
reach.

Equally beyond him (with such exceptions as I have noted)
are the architectonics of larger design. He does not select or
arrange; he simply heaps up till exhausted. His method is that
of the steam shovel. He does not always plan ahead for this or
that effect, or keep in mind frrom the outset such and such a
climax. He relies instead on sheer prodigality, and sometimes he
comes out well and sometimes he does not.

It is this method that prevents one from rereading these poems
with any great renewal of pleasure. The element of surprise is
gone, and there is no beauty, or ease, or intricacy of form to lure
one forward. The poems have begun to look a little shabby.
Their power has dwindled. And yet, is it simply and solely a
matter of form—or is it possible that the magic of realism is less
enduring than the magic of beauty? Or should the two be combined? . . .

These are some of the questions which Mr. Masters brings
sharply before us. For these, as well as for the richness and
downrightness, an important influence of his work, we are grateful.

MENCKEN, H. L. •   (1934)

Mr. Mencken's excursion into ethics reminds one of the German's definition of a picnic—the longest way round to an inn. It
is an agreeable enough commonplace book, and Mr. Mencken
arms it with a preface bristling with disclaimers; but one cannot
help wondering why, if Mr. Mencken's purpose was not to write
a systematic or careful treatise on ethics, he was moved to write
about ethics at all. Moreover, in addition to eschewing a "systematic treatise," he frankly and somewhat astonishingly ad-

• *Treatise on Right and Wrong.*

mits that he avoids the labor of trying to define "such concepts as right and wrong, good and evil, moral and immoral, sin and virtue," on the ground that such labor seems to him useless. And he further adds that he has a profound repugnance for metaphysics.

The exclusions are willful and drastic, and they leave Mr. Mencken little scope save the historical. Granted that a "popular" history of ethics would be a useful thing, it must be questioned how helpful it can be if it is so careful to avoid all attempt at definition or analysis. Mr. Mencken claims to have given "more attention than is usual to the moral ideas and practices of so-called uncivilized peoples," a claim hardly borne out by his book: he does indeed give us a good deal about the early Jews and Greeks, and a few odds and ends of primitive tribes are mentioned: but this is quite obviously a very meager historical survey, and even if he had given it a greater anthropological completeness it would still fail to be good "history" because it fails to examine *causes*. The history of ethics is in a sense always contemporary, because it is a history of behavior. The interesting and essential part of it is the genetic or dynamic part—the *why* underlying the particular habit or custom of the particular time and place: the psychological principles underlying law and tabu. In this regard man is a constant; what is true of him today was always true; and the most fruitful study of his ethics must therefore be a functional and psychological one. Mr. Mencken gives us a great deal of mere "fact," some of it amusing enough, some of it pretty familiar, but in avoiding all effort at a sociopsychological study of origins he gives us in the upshot a very hollow sort of structure. Several of his side-shows are entertaining—his opinion of poets is characteristic and peculiar, his excursions into religion are always good fun, and his suggestion that the Freudians and behaviorists deal almost exclusively with "pathological states" certainly gives one pause.

It is precisely in the direction indicated by Freud and his followers that one would like to have seen Mr. Mencken go exploring; and to consider this is to recall a brilliant and much neglected book by E. B. Holt, *The Freudian Wish*. Holt works out a very neat and practical ethics on the basis of Freud's concept of the wish: in the sense that it affords the most satisfactory dynamic explanation of ethics, of its social and psychological function and mechanism, it is the completest *history* of ethics.

What is new [says Holt] is that Freud shows what in the concrete case the mental mechanism of wise dealing is. It is the establishment through discrimination of consistent and not contradictory (mutually suppressive) courses of action toward phenomena. The moral sanction lies always in facts presented by the phenomena; morality in the discrimination of the facts. . . . This is, of course, an ethic "from below." For such a view morals evolve and develop; they grow, and are a part of the general growth and evolution of the universe. . . . Much remains to be learned, but in this learning it may be that the suppression-discrimination formula for wishes, which we have been studying, will serve somewhat as a talisman.

A little invidious to Mr. Mencken, but it is hardly an exaggeration to say that in these few sentences there is more clear thinking than in the whole of Mr. Mencken's book. It is perhaps fairer to remember that Mr. Mencken's aim is neither definition nor metaphysics, but a mildly informative entertainment.

MOORE, GEORGE   (1919)

Dear Henry:
No doubt you are expecting of me, as always—now that you have sent me George Moore's new book, *Avowals*—a review sanely judicial, chaste to the point of reticence, governed from first to last by the golden proprieties. But you should have known, or at any rate I should have told you, that of all living artists George Moore is the one of whom I am least fitted to write sanely. My enthusiasms as regards living artists are, you may have observed, few and far between. Of living artists who use English prose as their medium, and who are still giving us from time to time a new book, what one can we call great? Thomas Hardy has fallen into silence; Bennett has long since ceased to deserve much of us; Wells has become more than ever a tractarian. Joseph Conrad? That is a long story which I will not go into here, partly because I am not sure how the story should end. But of George Moore, from the very first moment, the moment of my casual and inadequate introduction to him by means of *Confessions of a Young Man*, I have always felt that here is a writer who has been, is, and will always be, as

long as he continues to write, a great artist, one of the few consummate masters of English prose.

You know, as well as I do, that the usual division of opinion
on George Moore is over the question of his audacity in dealing
with sex; he is always as frank as a satyr in such matters; he
takes an innocent and wise delight in them; he knows their
importance; he will not concede anything to Parson Prim nor
deny anything to the spinster, and if he is as frank as the satyr,
let it be added that he is also as mischievous, and wags his
pagan tail in a manner prototypical of the wink. It is perhaps
this which led Austin Harrison—upright soul!—to remark of
Hail and Farewell that it was "the great work of a little man"; it
was this which induced a tolerably well known young critic in
this country to rebuke Moore for his love of writing, like a
small boy, carnal hieroglyphs on public walls. But you and I,
who are so much wiser, while we should confess delightedly
our delight in these things, base our admiration for Moore on
issues far more important. The degree to which Moore is or is
not shocking has ceased to interest us, and it is not the "dear
audacious Moore" of Walter Pater's letter to whom we turn—
however much, for his own amusement at us, Moore himself
may wish to tempt us further—but the Moore who perceives so
much more finely than any one else alive what beauties a narrative in English prose should possess; the Moore who has
himself shown us in *The Lake* and *Celibates* and *Evelyn Innes*
and *Esther Waters* and *The Brook Kerith* that these beauties
are not merely chimerical or attainable only in Russia, the
Moore who knows instinctively what shape, in a novel, and
what rhythm, in a paragraph, make for beauty, as well as he
knows what motives or behavior in an individual are significant
—that is the Moore of whom we are somewhat idolatrous.

And, above all, the Moore who writes such incomparably
beautiful English prose. It is my own feeling that not in the
history of English literature has there been a prose style so
beautiful. It is seven or eight years since I read *Evelyn Innes*
and *Esther Waters*—six, at any rate, since I read *The Lake* and
Sister Teresa and *Celibates*—and I am not prepared to say,
therefore, how the prose of these compares with the prose of the
later works, though I am sure it is beautiful, more beautiful
than any other English prose. *The Brook Kerith* is fresher in
my mind, and I can say with unhesitating insanity that I believe
it to be the finest novel in the English language, so far finer
than any other I know that there is indeed no comparison.

What Euripides in his plays did with the waning mythologies of Greece, Moore in *The Brook Kerith* did with the "waning myth of Christ." The conception was a marvelous one, not least marvelous in that it excluded utterly the element of sex, with which Moore is so commonly supposed to be obsessed. And in this story Moore's prose style seems to me to have reached its perfection. Its flexibility had been sufficiently demonstrated in *Hail and Farewell*, but its opportunities for sustained employment in one direction, or in a direction so beautiful (and the life of Christ, even discounting for the pathos of distance, seems to be a more beautiful theme than the life of Moore) were, of course, not nearly so great.

I know that Moore is often accused of carelessness in grammatical structure—he is careless; there can be no question about it, and *Avowals* is no exception. But it is a golden carelessness, usually in inessentials; and it is never that most unpardonable thing, a carelessness of thought. Nor does it in the least affect the style or rhythm; for rhythm, after all, is style. I was about to say that rhythm was even more than in most cases the secret of the beauty of Moore's style, and that is perhaps true; I qualify it, however, for one must think not only of rhythm but also of texture. As regards rhythm, Moore is a contrapuntalist, a harmonist, a weaver of verbal melodies, one superimposed on another, so skillful, so sure of the genius of the language, so delicately in tune with it, that I know of no writer of English prose, living or dead, who can favorably be compared with him. Pater's rhythms are not so instinctive, so spontaneously fluent, nor Poe's; Hearn's rhythms are sometimes as beautiful, but only momentarily; who else can be summoned to the contest? Perhaps only the authors of "The Wisdom of Solomon" and "Ecclesiasticus" in the Apocrypha. Almost equally beautiful is the texture of Moore's style—by texture I mean the characteristic feel of it, the indications that the language has been winnowed again and again by the finest of temperaments. It is a translucent style, a style which has singularly the quality of light, and in which ideas move as happily as fauns might have moved in sunlight. In the course of *Avowals* Moore gently ridicules Flaubert for having started the cult of the inevitable word; a vicious theory which it was high time some one exposed. A page of inevitable words is merely a series of unconnected explosions, each equally demanding attention, drawing the attention away from the beauty of the whole. Moore knows the value of the explosion; and he uses it when the occasion warrants. But a fine prose style must be symphonic, and in a symphony one cannot be forever using the kettledrums.

I draw to the end of my space, and I suppose I ought to say something of *Avowals,* something which will tempt your readers to read it; though, heaven knows, Moore and Liveright between them have made the price a deterrent. Let me say, however, that in *Avowals* will be found some of the most enchanting literary criticism ever written: the wake held with solemn gusto by Gosse and Moore over the lifeless body of English prose narrative; the exquisitely perceptive pages on Turgenev; the hunting down of poor sentimental Pater by means of one clew (the famous passage on the Gioconda); the cruel analysis of Kipling, the hostile notes on Henry James—all of these, or any of them, should be sufficient reasons for opening *Avowals.* Was there ever a more delicious interweaving of criticism and gossip, was there ever a tone more beautifully adapted to it? It is a conversational tone always, the inflections of Moore's voice are always engagingly clear; humorous, ironic, and not least humorous or ironic, not least fantastically so, when the humor and irony are directed at himself. With his literary opinions one need not always agree—one is none the less entertained. Do you really think, Moore, that Henry James had no understanding of human psychology, do you really believe that in the later novels nothing happens save the lighting of cigarettes, or the not lighting of them, on terraces? *** I prefer to think that this opinion is in the nature of a defense reaction—that Moore is a little frightened, in more ways than one, by *The Wings of the Dove* and *The Awkward Age* and *The Golden Bowl*—and that at bottom he perceives quite as clearly as any one the greatness of James, or would so recognize it, if he could read James again; and this time with a faith in his own so different genius not so easily to be shaken. Heaven knows there should be few enough things to shake it! But genius is as often remarkable for its modesty as for its self-worship, and George Moore, despite a superficial brashness, is at bottom full of quakings when he considers his own achievements. And this, too, in spite of his style—the never beginning, never ending delicate clear line of the Moorish arabesque! Surely Moore knows the beauty of this? Yes, he does; he couldn't write it if he didn't. Yours, c.a.

MOORE, GEORGE

(1927)

Will Mr. Moore never tire of serving up to us his earlier works in a slightly disguised and altered form—as a chef serves us the familiar dish of chicken with a new sauce—*à la crême* or *au berre* or *au jus?* This latest of his books, *Celibate Lives,* is the third—positively the third—appearance of what is roughly one book. First known as *Celibates* simply (and this remains the best title of the three) it next slipped out as *In Single Strictness* with a few changes and substitutions. And now, brought out once more (with no reference anywhere in the preface or on the jacket to the fact that the material is not wholly new), it makes an ingenuous bow as *Celibate Lives.* It is true that Mr. Moore has omitted one long story—substituting for it a section torn out of the *Story Teller's Holiday,* so that not even the new member is new. Otherwise the book is about evenly made up of *Celibates* and *In Single Strictness.* Sarah Gwynn and Wilfred Holmes were not in the original *Celibates,* nor were Priscilla and Emily Loft. Henrietta Marr was, but at that time it was entitled *Mildred Lawson.* Why has Mr. Moore gone to the trouble of changing the heroine's name, one wonders. It is very odd.

This mania for revision is a curious thing. Henry James had it, and did the most unaccountable things to his earlier works— sometimes happily, and as often not. Mr. Moore is quite as unreliable. With the best intentions in the world one cannot see that Mildred Lawson has become any more of a person, or her story in the least a more moving one, now that she has changed her name to Etta and has decided to make a suicide of it. Mr. Moore has cut out the first third of his story and has in so doing sacrificed a great deal that was good. In fact, one gets, on the whole, a good deal finer and completer portrait of the woman in the earlier version than in the later. To some extent, one sees what Mr. Moore was after. He was pursuing that will-o-the-wisp, concentration. Accordingly, he omits a great deal of the documentation, a great deal of *mise en scène,* a great deal of admirable motivation; and the Henrietta who emerges is not nearly so complete or understanding a person as was her prototype Mildred. Most of the dialogue remains untouched. And most of the characters appear as before, save that the Count, who shipwrecked Etta's hopes, was in the earlier story a mere literary man named Delacour.

The story as it stands is good—it is the best in the book. But one cannot hesitate in stating that "Mildred Lawson" was better. It is true that the present version opens more *in medias res*, is swifter, is stripped down to the essentials of narrative; but it has undoubtedly lost, and lost sanguinarily, in body. More importantly, it has lost something of subtlety and truth. For it looks as if Mr. Moore, in attempting to sharpen and focus his story, to make it more emphatic, to bring it a notch higher toward the dramatic and tragic, had somehow lost his touch. The Mildred who merely (after a succession of flirtations, to none of which had she been able to surrender—her motive being almost wholly a desire to feed her vanity) sank into an impotent despair of self-knowledge and prayed to God to send her an overmastering passion—this Mildred is a good deal more credible and moving than the Henrietta who abruptly, after her failure with the Count, takes an overdose of veronal. The later climax is bolder, yes; but as a psychological ending for the given situation it is hopelessly inferior. In fact, when one compares it with the earlier form, it looks suspiciously like bad art, the overstatement of the straining amateur.

"Wilfred Holmes" is a charming fantasy, pushed, perhaps, in the same fashion, a shade too far—but only a shade. And the other stories, too, are admirable. But in all of them one feels a certain thinness—a thinness which one is apt to think is characteristic of Moore until one turns back to "Mildred Lawson" and "Agnes Lahens." Is his creative vein running out? Is he substituting for it a teasing interest, or obsession, in style for its own sake? Here, at all events, is the familiar cursive and fluent manner, once more—the well-known Moorish arabesque —but one finds it a little too overdone. There are paragraphs which sag, falter, sag again, under the never-ending burden they carry. They are difficult, almost impossible to read aloud; one needs, if one is to manage it successfully, the longwindedness of a prima donna.

This, in its way, is such a hypertrophy of manner as Henry James grew into; though one is bound to add that it is not so fraught with snares and pitfalls for the intelligence.

In February 1914, on the eve of his departure for Palestine, George Moore wrote to his friend Edouard Dujardin: "I leave Marseilles by the *Macedonia* for Port Said, bound for the land of camels and concubines. I have ordered 50 of the first, and 500 of the others."

The remark is characteristic as it is amusing. All his life, Moore delighted in shocking his friends and acquaintances with tales—often exaggerated, occasionally obviously untrue— of his amatory prowess: so much so, in fact, that by many people, and especially in view of his habitual mendacity, he was almost totally disbelieved. Mr. Hone, in his altogether delightful and extremely witty biography, puts the matter right, along with many others. Moore's love affairs may not have totaled 500, but they were numerous, and they were actual; and Mr. Hone, wherever possible, has been specific about them. Stella, for example, really existed; and it is a comfort to know that there was *some* basis for the story that Moore, asked at a dinner party if he had known John Oliver Hobbes —Mrs. Pearl Craigie, who had died some years before—replied loudly, "Naturally. She was my mistress!" One of the stories, incidentally, which did much to give him the reputation, among the really *nice* ladies of Chelsea and Kensington, of being an "odious person."

But this, after all, is only to regard the more superficial and merely amusing implications of the camels and the concubines. What lies behind, and is both more interesting and more important, is a characteristic feature of Moore's life, and one for which the casual observer and reader is hardly prepared: namely, that Moore had the true artist's genuine and self-sacrificing devotion to his art, that he gave up his whole life to it, and that he was not afraid to endure the extremes of hardship for it. Physical courage, one would have thought off-hand, was not likely to be one of Moore's salient features, but it becomes obvious that it was. He was a fearless rider to hounds, speaks laconically of riding with a boot full of blood, and it turns out to be all of a piece with his character that at the age of sixty-two he should set out alone on a journey to Palestine, where he spent whole days in the saddle, noting the landscape and all that might be of use to him for *The Brook Kerith*. He would leave nothing to chance, nothing to inspired

improvisation, he must know the facts, must document himself
with the utmost of care; not necessarily from books, for, as
Frank Harris noted, "Moore will not study, and cannot read
authorities; yet he is industrious in his own way. His method of
writing is laborious in the extreme. Before beginning he makes
a scenario, divided into chapters, then he writes the book hastily
chapter by chapter, putting in all his chief ideas; finally he
goes over the whole book, rewriting it as carefully as he can."
And what he could or would not look up for himself, he set
his friends, or other qualified experts, to doing for him; so that
there should be no howlers, for example, about the habits of the
clergy in 1200, as reported in *Héloise and Abelard;* nor about
seventeenth-century music and modern opera as repeatedly
evoked and described in *Evelyn Innes.* As Mr. Hone justly
remarks, "*Evelyn Innes,* his later musical novel, is convincing
as few musical novels by non-musicians have ever been. It is
not only the almost complete absence of slips which is remarkable, for Moore always took enormous pains over the background of his stories and was adept at picking the brains of
others; but there are many passages which persuade the reader
that he really understood something of the subject." And this
despite the fact that there is considerable evidence that Moore
had no ear at all, and that his interest in music was mainly
"literary."

Inexhaustible patience, endless hard work, plenty of courage
—but these qualities would have done little for Moore had he
not also had the *sine qua non* of the artist, a profound and true
humility, with a searching self-critical eye and a passionate
absorption in learning and *willingness* to learn. Wilde, whose
quip about Moore's excited successive discoveries of grammar,
the sentence, and the paragraph, is well known, also once remarked of him that "He conducts his education in public."
Which caused Robert Ross to reply—"Well, the public pays for
it. They have a right to know how he is getting on!" Amusing
enough, and Moore's mistakes were sometimes very funny, but
the important thing is that he was not *afraid* to make mistakes,
nor to correct them. He had made it his business to learn how
to write, and nothing was to be allowed to stand in the way—
friends, money, social position, nothing. Not even his own
vanity. One can have little but admiration for the man who
could write, as Moore did to his brother Maurice in 1890: "I
do not think I shall do anything of real value. The others
delude themselves, they confuse temporary reputations with the

real reputation that time grants slowly but always with inflexible justice. The fools quarrel as [to] whom they should sit next to at the author's dinner. I see over the heads of such possible vanity, I have the sentiment of great work but I cannot produce it. *Voilà ma confession,* what I strictly believe to be true." Perhaps he underestimated himself—it is too soon to say. He may live only, or largely, by the autobiography—which Austin Harrison once described invidiously as "the great work of a little man"—but one suspects that he will do better than that. Profound he may not have been, but he was a wonderful observer, and a witty and civilized one; he was not afraid to bring back poetry into the novel—*genuine* poetry— nor genuine bawdry either; nor a sense of style; nor a sense of form. And, apart from his existence as an artist, one must read Mr. Hone's extremely engaging biography to realize what a naughty and mean and selfish but essentially single-minded and *delightful* person Moore must have been.

MURASAKI, LADY   (1928)

The Tale of Genji, by Lady Murasaki—which has now, apparently, been completed with the publication of the fourth volume, *Blue Trousers*—takes a place with the great "stories" of the world. One says "stories" more or less advisedly. For it is primarily as a story that one reads it: it falls, in a sense, somewhere between the epic and the novel: somewhere between the mere collection of episodes (loosely surrounding the history of one particular hero) and the careful delineation and charting of a character: but it is obviously nearer to the *Odyssey,* or the *Arabian Nights,* than to *Swann's Way.* It is really a compilation of stories, a compilation managed with an extraordinary skill. If Prince Genji is the principal character, and is more often on the stage than off it, there are also (especially in the later chapters of the book) almost as many episodes which do not concern him at all, or only very obliquely. Of at least half a dozen people we get the more or less complete life history. A half century of time is covered, roughly, and in the course of it we are given an astonishingly complete survey of the entire "court" life of the period. The country, of course, is Japan, although no names are mentioned. And incidentally, but importantly, we are presented with as complete a view of Japanese civilization, in the year 1000, as the *Odyssey* and *Iliad* give us of early Greece, or *Beowulf* of early Britain.

This, apart from the story, will be the feature of this remarkable book which will most impress, one imagines, the majority of readers. At a time when our English forbears were just emerging from savagery, two thirds of a century before the Norman conquest brought Latin refinement to England, Lady Murasaki, in Japan, wrote a masterpiece of fiction in which one of the most striking things is the sophistication and culture of the *milieu* described. Of superstition there is a certain amount of evidence: ghosts, or fox-spirits, figure importantly in several of the death scenes, for example, and it appears that Lady Murasaki subscribes to the current belief that hate may actually be a destroyer of human life. But of barbarism, unless one is very niggling with one's definitions, there will scarcely be found a trace. This is an extraordinarily civilized society. It is as rich in conventions as the court life of France from 1650 to 1790; and far richer in aesthetic conventions than the only parallel in European culture which one easily thinks of—the period of the troubadours. Every courtier was, if one wants to put it invidiously, an aesthete. Every man or woman who belonged to the privileged stratum of society had to be an expert in the "forms" of social behavior. Social life was simply a long series of ceremonies, and of the most elaborate description. Every occasion demanded its special form, whether of dress or decorum; and for every encounter, even of the most casual description, the individual was expected to be prompt with a poem improvised for the moment, a poem packed with reference and cross-reference. It is no exaggeration to say that everyone who in the least participated in court life, or who belonged in the remotest degree to the upper classes, had to be an accomplished poet.

In short, one is compelled to accept the Japan of the year 1000 as representing one of the high-water marks of human civilization. It was one of those moments when the genius of a race comes to flower. That very few "great" works of art were produced in Japan in this period—comparable for example to Chinese art in the Sung or Tang dynasties, or to Greek art in the age of Socrates—does not materially alter this fact. It seems simply to have happened that Japanese genius went for the most part into an elaboration of life itself, an elaboration almost to the point of ritual. Was there ever a people so conscious, for instance, of the beauty of nature, so steeped in it or so close to it? One doubts it. The whole racial attitude to life was a poetic one: sentimental, perhaps, but none the less exquisite and imaginative in the highest degree.

It is this background that Lady Murasaki gives us for her *Tale of Genji*. And one could not have conceived an author better fitted for her task. It is clear, in Mr. Arthur Waley's admirable translation, that she had a poetic genius of the finest order: for the whole of this enormous four-volume novel is simply soaked, simply opalescent, with poetic beauty. One suspects that in no other single literary work in the world could one find so marvelous and delicate and various an interpretation of every mood of nature. In this world of plum-blossom and dewfall, of frost on the grass-blade and moonlight on the pine-needles, this world in which the peculiar beauty of every season received intimate reverence, Lady Murasaki sets her tale in motion. It has been compared to the *Arabian Nights*—and in sheer inventive power it is indeed not far behind it. The scene is a crowded one, an extraordinary number of people are deployed for us, the complications are endless: but the author keeps complete control of her complex narrative and manages even the time-element with consummate skill. Not only this, but also, as Mr. Waley points out in his excellent preface to the third volume, *A Wreath of Cloud*, Lady Murasaki has employed contrast, between chapter and chapter or section and section, with a nicety in sense of value for any parallel to which one must go to music. Humor follows and sharpens pathos, the most poignant and searching of realisms alternates with farce, the succinct and graphic gives way to the leisurely reflective or the idyllic. Everything is in its place, nothing is disproportionate, the intricate narrative moves forward as harmoniously as a tone-poem. And gradually we become aware that in addition to the fascination of the tale itself, with all its by-paths and retrogressions and momentary cul-de-sacs of intrigue, we are also in the presence of a series of psychological portraits which are as astonishingly modern as they are unforgettable.

There has, apparently, been some disagreement among the critics as to this matter of Lady Murasaki's "psychology." One critic has maintained that there is more than a mere surface resemblance between Murasaki's compendium and Proust's great "autobiography." Other critics have challenged this assertion, and have felt, rather, that Lady Murasaki gives us a keen psychological perception of "moments," but not of that other and profounder affair which we might vaguely call the "dynamics of character." On the latter point we are accustomed to hearing a great deal of cant: the textbooks on the novel are full of it. For example, we are assured again and again that no "character" is worth the name if he doesn't "evolve" under our eyes. We must see him emerge from the chrysalis of some complex, and then, in accordance with the laws of that complex, take a predetermined and inevitable course of development. This strikes the present critic as a very limited view—or, at the very least, as a view which may lead to serious misunderstandings of the matter. Why should we object to the presentation of a character *a priori*, a character who does *not* especially change or evolve, a character who in a sense remains fixed, except for those minor deviations or modulations which are sufficiently explainable and natural in *any* human being? Why, indeed, so long as this character is made vivid and recognizable and identifiably individual for us? And this, precisely, is what Lady Murasaki has done for us. Her "Murasaki" of the novel, Genji's chief concubine, is a patient Griselda of flesh and blood. She is an extraordinarily moving figure, she behaves exactly as we expect her to behave, she dies as we expect her to die. She is a tragic figure as convincing as she is beautiful. Her death, and its effect on Prince Genji, is one of the half dozen great things in the book. Aoi, Genji's first wife, is another figure almost as good; and so is Yugao. These women do not, in any useful sense, "evolve": they are stationary; but they are none the less real for that. We know them and believe in them.

That Murasaki should have made vivid her female characters for us is perhaps not so surprising, however, as that she should have given us, in Prince Genji himself, perhaps the most sympathetic and humane and, *ipso facto,* the wisest, portrait of a Don Juan that can be found in literature. Genji is, without exaggeration, one of the great figures given to the world by the art of letters. That a woman should have succeeded in understanding a man of this type is surprising enough; but one would rather naturally have expected such a portrait to be somewhat contemptuous, or grudging, or bitter. Of these things, however, there is here not a trace. Murasaki is in love with Genji, as indeed she is in love with life itself. Never minimizing his weaknesses, making fun of them deliciously, she nevertheless *sees* him perfectly, with the maximum of poetic divination; and she ends by achieving through her creation of him that enhancement of our valuation of the world which is the gift of only the greatest artists.

Of *Blue Trousers,* the final volume of this novel, it is only necessary to say that it is as good as the other three. With the death of Genji's Murasaki (not to be confused with the authoress) and his impending retirement to a monastery, it brings the story to a close on precisely the right note. A life, with all its complexities, has ended. And with its ending we are made to feel, as only the best elements in art or religion can make us feel, that life is incommensurable.

O'NEILL, EUGENE   (1928)

If we are arriving, as we seem to be, at a point where the American stage is ready to accept experiment in form, this changed attitude is almost wholly to the credit of Mr. O'Neill. More than any other contemporary American dramatist, he has made his career one long series of experiments with stage-craft; he has never for long remained contentedly in one position; he has moved restlessly from out-and-out realism (as he saw realism to be—which, it must be confessed, is a thing peculiar to Mr. O'Neill) to poetic melodrama, from poetic melodrama to poetic monologue, from monologue to something very like opera (*Lazarus Laughed*), and, finally, in the latest and finest of his experiments, which has been awarded the Pulitzer prize, to something very like a stream-of-consciousness novel for the stage.

This last development need not surprise us. Mr. O'Neill has always been much preoccupied, as indeed any dramatist worth his salt ought to be, with the secret dynamics of the mind or psyche. One has always thought of him as a kind of desperate, even despairing, epistemologist of the soul. One sees him perpetually as in pursuit of this elusive and complex ephemerid, stalking it with a net, lying in wait for it with a microscope, trying, as it were, to conjure it with verbal incantations; even, at times, when his subtlety has seemed to fail him, assaulting it with a sort of intellectual hammer. The pursuit has been earnest, passionate, gloomy, relentless. There have been moments when his intensity has become so humorless and—let us

admit it—obtuse as to seem grotesque, even comic. And, nevertheless, one has always, despite these occasional miscarriages of
effect, enormously respected his honesty and zeal. If he has
now and then appeared to be existing in some remote blue
backwater of his own—a world logical indeed but grandiose
to the point of unreality—one has forgiven him, one has even
tried to follow him into this half-phantasmagoric world, partly
enticed by his extraordinary dramatic instinct, partly enticed
by a never quite abandoned hope that at last he was going to
swerve right to the heart of things. Has he not always worn,
a little, the air of a prophet? One has somewhat distrusted
the prophet in him—he has indeed worn the air and the robes,
but somehow the prophecy, like those at Delphi, has usually
been disappointingly ambiguous; one has almost suspected that
at times it was meaningless.

In *Strange Interlude* he is still wearing the robes of the
prophet; he appears to be suggesting to us that he is getting at
something very secret and esoteric; we are going to be told
something extremely important about life, and miraculously
new. And precisely what this message is we never find out.

But, fortunately, there is much more than this. The play is
really a novel for the stage—a novel (thanks largely to the use
of the asides) pitched in the key of the interior monologue.
We can, if we like, observe in this regard that the use of the
aside is merely a return to the freer and larger liberalism of
(for example) the Elizabethan stage—an outpouring, unchecked
by niggling stage traditions, of life's prodigal and artless abundance. If the novelist may be permitted to sit, like a signalman
in a trainyard signal box, somewhere behind the hero's frontal
bone, watching the arrival and departure of every image or
effect, why should not the dramatist be allowed a similar freedom? Shakespeare was not inhibited by the convention that
we cannot know what a man is thinking—his Hamlets and
Gertrudes and Claudiuses unpack their hearts with words to
excellent effect. There is no good reason why Mr. O'Neill should
not do likewise. The device seems new only because it has
not recently been used and because he uses it wholesale.

Whether Mr. O'Neill uses it with entire success is another
question. If one regards it simply as a technical device, then
one may say that on the whole he does. Mr. O'Neill's instinct
for the stage has always been almost uncannily sound, and the
present instance is no exception. Many of the asides in the

present play make pretty tough reading but prove actable to an astonishing degree. Asides which on the printed page sound flat or empty or grandiose or over-intense or maudlin megaphone over the footlights with instant effect. And there are many scenes in which the queer and delicious counterpoint provided by the contrast between two or more streams of consciousness, simultaneously going their own ways, is productive of the finest kind of dramatic value.

But on the psychological side, a side which is clearly just as important for Mr. O'Neill as it is for us, one is not quite so sure. If one takes *Strange Interlude* simply as a story and chiefly the life history of Nina, certainly one can extract an almost unflagging pleasure from it. But the minute one begins to analyze the characters who compose this story and to put together or take apart the psychological motives which supply the *donnée* of the action, one becomes slightly uneasy. One has always felt, a little, that Mr. O'Neill's sense of character was oddly deficient. He sees a shape, a guise, a color, an emotional tone, a *direction* (if one may apply such vague terms to the sense of character), but somehow or other he very nearly always just misses the last quintessence of what one calls individuality. One cannot wholly, in this play, believe that Nina would have done what she did. Not that her actions are in any way impossible, but that she isn't, by Mr. O'Neill, quite made for us the sort of creature of whom we would have expected them. In the same way, Marsden remains unconvincing throughout, and so does Darrell, and so does Evans. They think, in their asides, the things which the *situation* would naturally and inevitably demand of them, but they do not think the things exactly, or richly, which their own inner *identities* would demand of them: they have not, in other words, that ultimate surplusage of sheer *being*, in their own rights, which a Shakespeare would have given us. One feels, rather, that Mr. O'Neill has come to them from outside, has made for us a set of admirably lifelike puppets and has urged them into a series of admirably plausible actions, but that there are very few moments when any of these people become subtly or powerfully or aromatically *themselves* and, *ipso facto*, run away with the scene as a first-rate character creation ought to do.

And it is precisely in the asides that Mr. O'Neill had, of course, his golden opportunity to bring this about. Here, one would suppose, Nina or Evans could have come before us with naked and terrifying reality. But one has, on the whole, the feeling that Mr. O'Neill's poetic divination has not been quite equal to the task.

Perhaps, in *Strange Interlude*, he comes closer to this kind of divination than he has ever come before? . . . That is hard to say. One still feels a kind of hollow and melodramatic unreality in Mr. O'Neill's realism: an operatic largeness which is not quite life itself. And, nevertheless, it would be ungracious and dishonest not to admit that this play seemed to the present reviewer the finest play by an American which he ever saw on the stage—and the most moving.

PEGUY, CHARLES   (1943)

It is a curious pair that is now brought out together, the German poet Stefan George and the French poet Charles Péguy—in a way, a curious pair of literary casualties. During the First World War, and the two decades that followed, George had a tremendous following in Germany. His fame comparable to that of Rilke, but more carefully cultivated by himself and his disciples, nevertheless he has never, then or since, acquired much export value, and this despite his long and intimate association with French and Belgian poets and painters, and even with such English figures as Cyril Scott and Ernest Dowson. And similarly, Péguy, who died in action in the Battle of the Marne—"*Heureux ceux qui sont morts dans les grandes batailles*"—left to his country a handful of great poetry, and a name which has seemed steadily to grow in importance, and yet has had to wait thirty years for his first adequate appearance in English.

Perhaps in neither case was the delay wholly accidental; and in neither case, one ventures to think, will the transplantation be very successful. For the two poets, dissimilar as they are in most respects—if not indeed in all—are both primarily poets of the *word*, poets of the genius of language itself; and of all poetry this "pure" poetry is the most difficult to translate, the most unrewarding; the luster disappears, and with it, somehow, the very life-blood of the meaning; it seems to require of the translator a genius comparable to that of the poet himself. The luster *is* the poetry. And where, as in the intensely religious and Catholic poems of Péguy, the language is reduced to an almost monosyllabic simplicity, and a vernacular simplicity at that, with endless ingenuities of liturgical repetition, there are no "right" English equivalents to be found. "Blessed are they that died in great battles"—is this the same thing at all? No, it would have to be reinvented by an English or American poet who felt profoundly the beauty of Péguy's diction and the oldness and purity of the French rhythm, worn, smooth, with its deceptive clarity, its limpid ambiguities, and always the little quarreling overtones and undertones, like ghosts, of Latin and the Catholic Church.

This is where the French *song* is, its individual magic, and of this Péguy was a master, and it is this, primarily, that makes him a poet, and not his Catholicism or his socialism. His passionate belief, after his conversion, and his extraordinary love of his fellow man, the poor, the sick—*"Et qui les aime tant les ayant connus"*—gave him the same singleness and saintliness that we see in Van Gogh: his poems, like Van Gogh's paintings, always say simply, "I love this." And much of this, in the translations of Ann and Julian Green, comes through; but not enough, it tends to become a mere bare statement; one has to go back to the French. The "Vision de Prière" is surely one of the greatest of religious poems—if not so profound or rich as Thompson's "Anthem of Earth" nor so spectacular as *The Hound of Heaven*, it is tenderer than either, homelier, sweeter. And "L'Innocence et l'Expérience" and "La Passion de Notre Dame" are very nearly as fine. We must be grateful for this excellent edition of Péguy's verse and prose, with both French and English texts, and for Julian Green's perceptive and sympathetic introduction.

The difficulties with Stefan George's poetry are analogous, but greater. George may indeed have been, as his translators claim for him, an inventor of language, a recreator of language, and for this very reason he would of course be particularly hard to translate—we face again that invisible barrier, the genius of German here (to give the devil his due), as there the genius of French. But nothing of this genius appears in the present English version, nothing whatever. Is this partly because the translators have tried too elaborately to keep to George's forms? At all events, it would be difficult to imagine anything much lamer than these singular verses: crammed with tasteless archaisms, grotesque neologisms, inversions, they are in fact a lesson in how not to do it. And this is all the more curious and baffling, for Mr. Morwitz, one of the translators, was many years ago one of George's disciples, and in common with others makes tremendous claims for his hero, both fatidical and poetic—"a world of poetry and thought that is as significant for cultural development as that of Goethe and Nietzsche." It may be so, but the evidence is certainly not here. For in these poems we discover a kind of German romanticism, and a decadent romanticism, with which we have long been familiar: how well we know that pastel-pink paganism, with its temples, fauns, flutes, and the blond gods all too white in an all too Teutonic Hellas! Here again, too, is the typical German war-worship and youth-worship, and all the customary laborious unwholesome wholesomeness. No harm in it, to be sure, nor even, perhaps, in the quasi-candid overtones of homosexuality —George's group quite openly worshiped, and deified, a handsome young poet, Maximilian Kronberger, who died at sixteen. The homosexuality may have been quite unconscious and innocent, indeed, a pseudo-Platonic idealism. But does all this add up, thematically, to a "great" poetic content, or to anything remotely like it? Rather, it makes one think of some of the lesser French Decadents, and of the still lesser English echoes of these—Earnest Dowson, Arthur Symons, Oscar Wilde. Just as it also makes one think of the decorative *morbidezza,* the corrupted classicism, of the Viennese artist Von Bayros.

It may be, of course, that George's genius for language some-how managed to give life to this somewhat operatic world— we must take it on trust, until some better version of his work appears. In the meanwhile, we can only say that, compared to Rilke, whose wonderful sustained allegorical images came whole and clean through the process of translation, even in prose, this looks like pretty trumpery stuff.

PERSE, ST. JOHN · (1945)

To many poets, or even writers of prose, sooner or later comes the discovery that there are two methods of procedure which are open to the poet; and which may become, one or the other, or both together, habitual to him. The first of these

• And Robert Frost.

might be called the procedure by *whole meaning:* like Mr. Eliot, the poet finds his beginning in his end: his idea or theme or meaning lies complete before him, complete even to the overtones and undertones, in advance of his putting a single word on paper. What remains for him to do is to explore the logical implications of the theme, and the feeling-tone with which or from which it starts; and this is of course the actual writing of the poem. During this, with its unforeseeable adventures to right or left, he maintains a strict liaison with the strong outline of the theme, and, only in closest accordance with that, rejects or selects from among the insistent offerings of conscious and unconscious alike. The other method of procedure, and on the whole the commoner, because easier, might be called the procedure by "doodle" meaning: the idea or theme or, more often, the image-plus-feeling, with which the poet starts, is the opposite of complete, for it is without beginning or end, offers no dynamic frame. Perhaps it could, with a little thought, be given one; but for whatever reasons, the poet takes the line of least resistance, and, like a chain-smoker, proceeds from one associational smoke-ring to another. It is a sort of poetic recital of the alphabet: the poem goes straight onward and outward, always farther from its starting point, and must depend entirely for its effect on its incidental brilliance; for even if brought round on itself at the end by some artifice, it remains a string of brightly colored but barely connected a's and b's. The unity is superficial.

This is of course improvisation, and if it can on occasion do quite miraculous things, it must be obvious too that on the whole it can hardly hope to make up in speed for what it lacks in direction. That is why those poets are most fortunate who learn to combine the two methods in one. Under the control of "whole meaning," the sluices of free association can safely be opened, with the result that to the arid power of the one method may be added the more reckless riches of the other. And no finer example of exactly this combination of methods could be found than St. John Perse's *Pluies,* which now comes to us with an English translation by Denis Devlin. For in this magnificent poem, which is at once a kind of litany, or litany of litanies, and an allegorical history of mankind, a history in terms of metaphor, the poet drives his tandem of methods with complete mastery. The *whole meaning,* the history of man in terms of rain, or the interpretation of him in terms of rain—rain as the fertilizer, rain as the purifier, even as the principle itself of life and change—gives a majestic centripetal design to the poem, and a tremendous sense of controlled richness, but it is also of such a nature, even more so than in the case of *Anabase,* as to make the utmost possible use of incidental, but directed, improvisation. With the beginning of each of his nine canticles the poet can return, as it were, to his base, his central theme, only then to allow himself, in the long, rich, flexible triads, the dispersed exfoliation of imaginative reference, the sheaves of image and metaphor, which so wonderfully evoke a sense of the many-corridored, many-layered, many-echoed and many-faceted past of man. Here too the use of highly affective language, and what at moments seems an almost "blind" symbolism, is precisely what contributes most to the poem's remarkable projection of the racial unconscious: it isn't *about,* it becomes and is, our sad rich dreadful glorious disastrous foul and beautiful history. We emerge with it, shedding and altering; and at the end, after a prayer to rain, it is as if by a ritualistic achieving of self-knowledge we had released ourselves from what is binding or shameful and were now free to go forward again. Surely this is one of the finest poems of the century. Mr. Devlin's translation is on the whole very effective in keeping M. Perse's freshness and vividness of language, and a good deal of the immense variety of movement. Just now and then, however, he appears to have fumbled the meaning a little —excusable enough in translating so dense a symbolism—and now and again a simpler and plainer statement would better have served his purpose.

Robert Frost's new long poem, *A Masque of Reason,* is another example of "whole-meaning" method. Here too the poet has begun with his end, has known in advance every move on the board; but although Mr. Frost starts us off with one of his very happiest openings, and takes us with dexterity to one of his most amusingly inconclusive conclusions, one cannot help feeling that through a good deal of the poem the "whole meaning" goes, unfortunately, a little bare. Dare one whisper, of a poet to whom one so gratefully owes so much, that a little more affectionate and affective care with his blank verse might have prevented its becoming *quite* so—and frequently— unrewardingly blank? It's all great fun, of course, and not too dangerously unorthodox; but there are times when the cracker-barrel wisecrack grates a little, and when the texture and text alike become too thin. Mr. Frost himself once reminded us that good fences made good neighbors—but he himself doesn't much

like a wall. Far indeed from the art that conceals art, is this
(if we may say it without impertinence) the artlessness that
conceals artlessness? But Mr. Frost is no doubt laughing up
his sleeve at us, and this remains a most engaging little *jeu
d'esprit*, and is not intended, like Hardy's "God's Funeral,"
to give us a real pause.

POUND, EZRA   (1927)

If Mr. Ezra Pound has, on the whole, received far less attention
from contemporary criticism than he deserves, that is partly his
own fault: he has been so extraordinarily mercurial a figure, has
successively presented for inspection so many facets, that one
has never been quite sure where to have him. One imagines
him, at the outset of his career, to have been a pretty romantic
young man—a romantic rebel (which to a considerable extent
he still is) with nostalgic longings for something a good deal
more distant, both in time and space, than the United States.
Perhaps it was for this reason that the first literary influence
to which he heavily succumbed was that of Hovey and Carman
and the *Songs from Vagabondia*. Has he ever recovered from
that influence? One wonders. The Vagabondia motif shines
continuously through all of his career: in space, it has led him
to London, to Paris, to Avignon, to Rapallo; in time, it has led
him to Propertius and Catullus and Li Po and Rihaku and the
Provençal poets. He has, always, the air of a man on the point
of departure. His hat is in his hand, and he is off to some
place remoter still; he has acquired a smattering of odd and
colorful phrases, in a strange tongue, which will find him his
way about that far country; he assures us that this time he will
at last discover the golden secret, the wisdom of wisdoms; but
we know that this new country will only serve as the threshold
to the next.

This is perhaps a clumsy way of saying that the work of Mr.
Pound, now collected, strikes one as being curiously without a
center. Who and what and where, is this extraordinarily able and
diversified volume of verse, is Mr. Pound? What is his identity?
What is his own peculiar attitude toward this terrifying world?
He seems, indeed, to have none; and one cannot help feeling
that the lack is very serious. Perhaps not, however: for Mr.

Pound seems to tell us, obliquely, that after all there is nothing easier than this affair of an "attitude toward the world," that no new one of any importance is at all possible, and that therefore it is better to play, idly and ironically, with the attitudes of others. Apart from a handful of satirical poems, in which he makes amusing fun of contemporary manners, he has nothing to say of his own day and age; he prefers to try on, one after another, the styles of the ancients; and it must be admitted that he often does this very spiritedly. Can one not— he says in effect—make a poetry of poetry, a literature of literature? If one's consciousness, nowadays, is so much (granted that one is literary) a consciousness of the literature of the past, shouldn't *this*, then, this grab-bag of literary smatterings, be precisely one's own unique attitude—an attitude of attitudes? Well, why not? Mr. Pound makes an extremely entertaining, and often beautiful, though almost always artificial, thing of it. He is a good craftsman—Mr. Eliot goes so far as to call him *"il miglior fabbro";* he turns things with a coldly conscious nicety; and yet at the end one feels cheated, one feels that Mr. Pound has withheld the one thing that one above all wants. Isn't literature, after all, something more than this mere playing of a game, this sciolistic juggling with odds and oddments of erudition? One is amused, no doubt, by such curiosities of poetry as the Empress Athenais's attempt to narrate the life of Christ wholly in terms of quotations from the *Iliad:* and what Mr. Eliot could do in this *cento* form we have seen and admired in *The Waste Land.* But Mr. Eliot gave us the something more, whether or not he intended to do so: he betrayed, perhaps unconsciously, an attitude of his own; and this, in Mr. Pound's collected poems, as also in his cantos, we miss.

Nevertheless, Mr. Pound's verse remains extraordinarily interesting to anyone for whom poetic technique is interesting. Unable to achieve a perfect poem or to give us, identifiably, himself, he has none the less been one of the most suggestive and influential of contemporary poets. It is his misfortune that his many discoveries and inventions, in tone and color and rhythm, have been more useful to his rivals and successors than to himself. Mr. Waley went him several better in his translations of Chinese poetry, the Imagists despoiled him of his imagism and outstripped him, and Mr. Eliot, adapting the *cento* to his own needs, made something far finer of it than Mr. Pound has succeeded in doing. Mr. Pound, however, has always been generous: and one imagines that this will not distress him in the least. He probably has something else up his sleeve. Just as we have successfully labeled him—domesticated him in Vagabondia—he will perhaps surprise us by again moving on. Who knows? He may even come home.

POUND, EZRA   (1934)

It is no good being angry with a man because he is angry, or annoyed with him because he is annoyed; and especially in the case of so prolonged and chronic an anger and annoyance as that of Mr. Pound it is more profitable simply to consider its causes and effects. The effects, to consider them first, have been important; Mr. Pound's arrogance and truculence, in combination with his geographical remoteness, and with a real enough though limited originality and skill, have given him for the past twenty years a power and influence, particularly over young radicals and young snobs, out of all proportion to any definitely assayable wisdom either in what he has had to say or in his manner of saying it. Granted that experiment is desirable, that change and growth are healthy, that all the arts are perpetually being refreshed by the discovery of new psychological or social *données* and by the exploration of new techniques with which to unfold them, need the poet or the critic be distressed or disturbed if such explorations do not always proceed in one direction, or if now and then they appear to come to rest, or even if occasionally a movement occurs which seems positively a retrogression?

The good critic is a man of good nature; criticism becomes excellent or pure *pari passu* with its shedding of rancor; gentleness and perhaps also humility are among the marks of wisdom. If a critic shows heat in his judgments, one must suspect that his analysis has not been disinterested, that his tastes are in some respect limited and emotionally "impure," that his education (to use the word in its deepest sense, as a sound psychological "placing" of the self in the world) remains incomplete. Some private problem has remained unsolved, a private appetite has not been wholly appeased, and for such a critic the work of art to be judged is not someone else's work but his *own* work, in some mysterious fashion adulterated or *manqué*. In short, the critic is that partial sort of critic which we call a propagandist.

Mr. Pound is a propagandist, an unswerving and formidable one. He has been extremely useful in stimulating and releasing in his contemporaries and successors certain Pound-like qualities which are clear enough; he has been a good "enemy" of much that deserved enmity; but the virtues of a propagandist, as they spring from limitations, are also his defects as a poet and as a critic. A poet who wants all other poets to be like himself is a poet who is unsure of himself: he is afraid of the poetic provinces which lie to right and left of his own province, he cannot accept them as they are or try to learn their language; he must either subjugate or exterminate them. In retrospect, we can see that this has been Mr. Pound's unconscious aim from the very beginning. He has tried—and has often, alas, succeeded—to frighten us out of our *own* wits and into becoming little Ezra Pounds.

No better example of his technique in accomplishing this could be found than his *Active Anthology*. The book purports to be a selection from the work of writers in whose verse a "development" still appears to be taking place. But what is it actually? It is a "broken bundle of mirrors," arranged and selected with the uncanny ingenuity of narcissism to reflect at every angle the image of the compiler. If we except the poems of Mr. Williams and Miss Moore (which are respectively, pretty good Williams and Moore, but which do not, I think, suggest any recent "development") practically all the work in this volume might have been written by Mr. Pound. It has his accent, his vocabulary, his attitude, his compass. It is the typical Pound of the *Cantos, Lustra, Quia Pauper Amavi, Cathay:* the same wholesale use of the *cento* form, the copious grab-bag of the erudite and the vulgar, of classical quotation and racy quotidian: above all, the characteristic trick of shock by juxtaposition, the cheek-by-jowling of the quick poetic flash with the ironic matter-of-factness of the vulgate. It's a good trick, the technique is effective as it is infectious, but after twenty years it becomes a little tiresome, and surely it is somewhat anachronistic to see in it any sign of development? Real development, one might reasonably maintain, would now lie precisely in a departure from a device so stereotyped and restricted; a return to a tradition *farther back,* at such a moment, would be tantamount to a step forward. At all events, one wants more freedom, one wants the freedom—among other things—of a greater severity, a harder outline; and also a deeper synthesis of emotional and conceptual attitudes. We can't go on forever talking in the loose language of 1917, which Mr. Pound appears to desire; times have changed.

The poems themselves call for little comment. The most re-markable exhibit is that of Basil Bunting. Mr. Bunting may exist as a person, but he also, obviously, exists as a *persona*, a mask—a mask of Pound: the resemblance is so striking as to be embarrassing. Mr. Eliot's *Fragment of a Prologue* is here— why? Presumably, once again, because at this point Eliot drew closest to Pound—certainly not because it in any way indicates a "new line" for Eliot. For that, one would suggest, instead, *Marina*, or *Triumphal March*, or even *Ash Wednesday*. But these are in another country, and one, no doubt, which Mr. Pound views with alarm.

POWYS, JOHN COWPER   (1929)

Mr. John Cowper Powys's impressive new novel is so many things, and so many different kinds of things, as to make a de-tached critical approach to it exceedingly difficult. In point of sheer size—it is in two volumes and runs to nearly a thousand pages—it is quite obviously in the category of the old-fashioned three-decker. It is leisurely, copious, enormous; it covers an immense amount of ground; it affords Mr. Powys ample room for a sort of genial philosophical expansiveness, and for an endless amount of rumination and comment; and in conse-quence it becomes the kind of novel which we describe habitually as embodying a "view of life." In this sense, it reminds one a little of *Jude the Obscure* or, perhaps, also a little of Mr. Somerset Maugham's *Of Human Bondage*. It builds itself up by the method of accretion and chronicle rather than by any such arbitrary dramatic arrangement as Henry James would have considered necessary to a "work of art": it is (in no un-complimentary sense) rather the result of a process of growth than of a process of shaping.

But it is not quite so simple as this—for the fact must also be noted that Mr. Powys is not unaware, in the literary firmament, of such stars as Mr. Joyce and Marcel Proust. The course of his three-decker is subtly changed by these influences —Mr. Powys is too good a psychologist for the result to be otherwise. Accordingly, he adopts and maintains a single point of view, and to this extent gives his novel that sort of interior psychological movement which has been described as the method of "interior monologue." He has given himself a desirable advantage in this by choosing as his hero a young man of exceptional imaginative and intellectual endowment: and in consequence we are presented with a rather remarkable, and technically highly interesting, fusion of two types of novel. It is a "slice of life" (or so Henry James would have called it), forthright, cumulative, massive, crammed with excellent detail of every sort; but it is also a slice of life as recorded by a particular and highly individual sensorium. In short, it is a study of consciousness, or the problem of individual identity, in terms of action.

And, on the whole, it is brilliantly and persuasively done. Mr. Powys makes admirably vivid his hero, Wolf Solent, and through him makes admirably vivid also the two women whom he loves, and his mother. All three are first-class pieces of portraiture; one wonders whether Solent himself isn't a good deal finer specimen of character-creation than his prototype, Jude. Moreover, the psychological development of his relations with the three women (or four) with whom his life is bound up is practically flawless, as rich as it is subtle. Solent's gradual evolution from introverted idealism to disillusioned realism is beautifully managed, and with the finest of inevitableness.

It is only when one comes to the minor personages of the scene that one feels at all uneasy. Here one begins to suspect another, and, perhaps not quite so fortunate, influence—that of Mr. Powys's brother, Mr. T. F. Powys. These minor figures —Mr. Malakite, Mr. Urquhart, Mr. Valley, and Jason Otter— all verge on caricature; their abnormalities are a shade overdrawn; and, while one eventually surrenders to them, simply because the whole milieu which surrounds them becomes gradually so copious and persuasive and sustaining, one resents them a little as being definitely out of key. One or two of them might possibly have passed; but taken together they exhale a brimstone odor which belongs rather in *Black Bryony* or one of Goya's *caprichos* than here. They introduce a sort of stage moonlight atmosphere which ill accords with the level forthrightness of the novel as a whole.

Nevertheless, *Wolf Solent* is a brilliant book. If now and then Mr. Powys overwrites a little, or tends to become a shade too exclamatory, these minor faults are far more than compensated for by the sharpness of the dialogue, the astonishing vividness which lights scene after scene, the ease and fullness of the story itself. And Mr. Powys's Dorset—with all its sights and sounds and smells and grass blades—is a delight in itself.

RICHARDSON, DOROTHY   (1928)

With *Oberland,* Miss Dorothy Richardson gives us the tenth volume of a serial novel, which is the closest parallel to Proust's masterpiece discoverable in the English language. This is not to say that Miss Richardson has the genius of Proust: nothing of the sort. But she shares many qualities with that great artist; she is as much a pioneer as he was; she has as much, or even more, influenced her own contemporaries, both in her own country and in America; and she is practically the first woman novelist to make an exhaustive serial study of a single female character, and with entire, or almost entire, detachment and honesty. This is a considerable claim to distinction. If one took a roll call of the novelists of the present day who owed a debt in technique and tone to Miss Richardson, it would include some impressive names. Among them would be Mr. Joyce, Mrs. Woolf, Miss Sinclair, Mr. Ford. She is in many respects the first careful or complete practitioner of the so-called stream-of-consciousness novel in English. And she is also still the only English novelist of the moment who has done this and nothing else.

This alone will secure for Miss Richardson, one would suppose, as precise and permanent a place in the history of literature as it is ever possible to predict for a living author. And yet, Miss Richardson is curiously little known. Her books have never been best sellers—they have scarcely ever gone into a second printing. It is very greatly to the credit of Mr. Knopf that he has continued to make these books available to an American audience. Just why they should not have been more popular it is hard to say. There is, of couse, as Miss Sinclair laments on the jacket of the present volume, "no drama, no situation, no set scene," in this series; it is "just life going on and on. It is Miriam Henderson's stream of consciousness going on and on." There are readers, of course, who don't like that, who want action or set scene or situation: who become bored with this minute recording, this almost seismographic charting, of sensations and moods and appetites and velleities; and again there are others who would be prepared to accept cheerfully enough this method as applied to the mind of a man, but who weary of it as applied to the mind of a woman.

Perhaps this distinction is invidious? Invidious or not, there is a little something to be said for it. For if one takes one's seat in the balcony, say, of such a mind as that of Stephen Dedalus, or even of Leopold Blum, it is obvious enough to any merely *male* reader that the variety of entertainment is going to be strikingly greater and richer and deeper. I am afraid Miss Richardson herself would be annoyed by this suggestion: for one of the curious features of her portrait of Miriam Henderson is her insistence on the superiority of her heroine's mind—on its (precisely) richness and power and depth, as compared (frequently) with the minds of the men whom she meets.

There is something a little pinched and sour and old-maid-ish in this. One begins pretty soon to resent this attitude of the heroine and to suspect that it is also the author's. It is, of course, a feminist attitude, one which became only too familiar in England during the days of the fight for woman suffrage. But it is also an attitude which, rightly or wrongly, the mere male feels to be the natural withering of the spinster. The air of challenge which marks the behavior of such a woman is dictated by a sense of inferiority; it colors her whole thought, her whole approach to the other sex; it urges her insensibly toward a kind of dry intellectual hypertrophy, an intellectualism which is curiously thin and bloodless.

This is a quality which is sometimes annoyingly characteristic of Miriam Henderson. If Miss Richardson has detachedly projected this, then one can only praise her skill in creation; but one feels a sneaking suspicion that the character lies pretty close to home; and all the more, therefore, one begins to resent this provincialism and smallness, just as one resents the rather ridiculous attitude toward America and Americans. And Miss Richardson is distressingly unaware, at times, of her complete failure to sound the real note of the masculine. When she wants her heroine to behave like a man of the world, for example, and to indulge in genial smoke talks with the assembled males after dinner, the result is lamentable. Miriam's efforts at breezy masculine free-and-easy laconicism, the hands-in-pockets ease of reference, etc., are pitiful in the extreme; they positively make the male reader blush with discomfort; just as the male reacts, in fact, when he encounters such a woman in the flesh. Poor Miriam! She thinks she knows so very much and, alas, she knows so extraordinarily little. The whole dark, strange, horrible, fascinating, masculine mind remains an absolutely closed book to her.

This is the greatest single defect in Miss Richardson's series: a defect in the charm of her heroine. One has to forgive or overlook this. And then one is rewarded. For the skill and delicacy with which she evokes minor moods and despairs and happinesses, all the shoes and sealing-wax aspects of life, and the dissection of personal relationships, particularly those between one woman and another, are among the best things of the kind in this century. The present volume is slighter than its predecessors; one wonders a little whether the theme is wearing out. But it is a charming light interlude in Miss Richardson's scheme and should introduce many new readers to a work of importance.

RILKE, RAINER MARIA   (1942)

At bottom, one seeks in everything new (country or person or thing) only an expression, that helps some personal confession to greater power and maturity. In fact all things are there in order that they may in some sort become images for us. And they do not suffer thereby, while they express us ever more clearly, our soul broods in the same measure over them. . . .

And still, even to have memories is not sufficient. If there are many of them one must be able to forget them, and one must have the great patience to wait till they return. For the memories themselves are not yet what is required. Only if they become blood within us, sight and gesture, nameless and no longer distinguishable from ourselves, only then is it possible, in some very rare hour, for the first word of a verse to arise in their midst and to proceed from them.

In these two passages, one from a letter and the other from Malte Laurids Brigge, and in many other similar passages as

well, Rilke makes it clear that more conspicuously and searchingly than any other poet of the century he was aware always of
the roots and causes of his poetry; that for him the root, and
the process from root to flower, and the flower itself, were all of
perhaps equal importance. Elsewhere, he remarks that a poem
is not so much a feeling as an experience: and here too one feels
that what he means is really that the poem is simply a part of
what is an indivisible *whole* of experience, and itself no more
an "end-product" of anything than it is the "beginning" of
anything. To Rilke everything was to be accepted, nothing denied. All things were to be seen, loved, filtered into the unconscious, there to be turned magically into names: and then the
poetry *is* the naming. And the naming must in a sense be beyond
love, even, lest it carry with it an implied partiality or judgment—one must simply *say*. "One painted: I love this; instead
of painting: here it is." This was his dismissal of the Impres-
sionists.

It is no wonder that Rilke is the most difficult of contemporary poets, and no surprise that he is ultimately the most rewarding. Is he perhaps the first great poet of the unconscious?
Freely and dangerously, with immense courage, but also
with miraculous judgment, he dared to accept the dark, fluid,
"private world"—the private world with all its idiosyncratic
secrets; and, with a kind of instantaneous ordering of the
chaos, turned the inside out, projected the dream back again
into the world as a new object. No poet before him had been
brave enough to accept the *whole* of that private world, as if
it were unquestionably valid and potentially universal. There
is no compromise in Rilke. Must not every dream, every fragment of dream, each smallest item of literal or affective meaning, even those that seem to transcend, in some degree, common
sense, be true? He made this assumption, at all events; and in
speaking so richly out of so richly stored an unconscious—let us
not forget the long discipline in the storing—he succeeded in
stretching language, poetry, meaning itself, into the realm of
the ineffable, with a new kind of inner sensibility on the one
hand, a new kind of comprehension on the other. Of course, only
a great poet can do this sort of thing safely—in weaker hands,
what is merely affective is too loosely indulged, obeys no sovereign order of imagination or belief, and ends, as it begins, in
the realm of associational nonsense. Rilke's power was his
ability to carry that perishable, affective gleam so swiftly across
the border of consciousness and into so strong a constellation

of design, where mysticism and a genius for prosody meet, that the gleam survives and the nonsense is summarily translated.

Sometimes, it is true, we hardly know into what—his process is too quick for us, the references too blind altogether. When this occurs no amount of explanation serves much purpose. But even here there is a "poetic" meaning which is sufficient: the tone, the implication, the music, is enough. And what in a lesser poet might be condemned as obscure is accepted with a quickening belief simply because Rilke's breadth of command is everywhere so manifest. There is a sense in which we can say that poets are ultimately ranked in accordance with what might be termed their intellectual *play-content:* not, that is, according to *what* they think, but for the range, richness, ease and delight with which they manage a maximum amount of reference to thought, and thought of the best order. No other poetry of this century vibrates with so much of this *reference*. To think of Yeats or Eliot is to think of neater and smaller worlds altogether, worlds that give themselves more readily, and perhaps even more vividly, but that nevertheless are sooner traveled. Rilke's is a world which to some extent remains permanently unexplored.

The *Sonnets to Orpheus,* a sequence written in 1922, is, with the *Elegies,* Rilke's finest work—the two books really belong together, shine the better for each other's presence, and should some day be published in one volume. And as of the *Elegies,* one wants a better translation than as yet exists. The present one is at best adequate, in the barest sense of the word—a mere literal transcription—which is all it pretends to be, and for which we are grateful. But even this is now and then definitely misleading, where Rilke's summary procedure is too exactly followed. The task is one for a poet. And the opportunity a great one.

ROBINSON, EDWIN ARLINGTON   (1921)

Of his story, *The Altar of the Dead,* Henry James observed that it was on a theme which had been bothering him for years, but of which the artistic legitimacy was suspect; he had to write it, but he knew it to be pitched in a richly sentimental key which, under the hands of another, he might have condemned. His story, *The Turn of the Screw*, surely one of the finest ghost stories in any language, he frankly derided as a potboiler, making no reservations for its brilliance. He was, of course, right in both of these opinions: he was a better judge of Henry James than any other critic has been, he knew his parerga when he saw them, he could afford to wave them blandly aside. We should think, perhaps, a little less of him, as we are tempted to do of any artist, if he had taken his parerga too seriously—if he had appeared to see only dimly, or not at all, any distinction between these things, which were carved from stones flawed at the outset, and those others, which no flaw rebukes.

Thus, toward Mr. Edwin Arlington Robinson, whom we are accustomed to think of as the most unfailing artist among our contemporary poets, one looks with the barest shade of suspicion after reading his latest book, *Avon's Harvest*. One has, of course, with the critic's habitual baseless arrogance, no hesitation in placing it—it fits, in Mr. Robinson's list, in so far as it fits at all, very much as *The Turn of the Screw* fits in the completed monument of Henry James. One is not disposed, that is, to take it with too great a seriousness. More precisely, the degree of our seriousness will depend on the degree of Mr. Robinson's seriousness; if we had any reason to suppose that Mr. Robinson regards *Avon's Harvest* as he regards *Merlin* or *Lancelot* or *The Man Against the Sky*, then we should accept it with concern. For, clearly, it is not as good as these, and the most cursory inquiry into the reasons for its comparative unimportance will disclose its defects as not merely those of technique but, more gravely, those of material—as in the case of *The Altar of the Dead*. We must grant, at this point, that to every artist come moments when he delights in abandoning for an interim the plane of high seriousness, to allow play to lesser and lighter motives: when Keats dons the "Cap and Bells," the critic, smiling, doffs robe and wig. This is both legitimate and desirable. By all means let the poet have his *scherzo!* We shall be the richer for it, we shall have, as audience, a scrap the more of the poet's singular soliloquy. But it is imperative that the poet, if his *scherzo* be abruptly introduced, and amid the graver echo of graver music, should accompany it with an appropriate twinkle of eye. Otherwise his audience may do him the dishonor of supposing that he has nothing more to say.

We prefer to believe, then, that Mr. Robinson does not

himself intend *Avon's Harvest* as weightily as many of his
other things. It is a ghost story, and a fairly good one. That Mr.
Robinson should deal with an out-and-out ghost is not surprising, for ghosts have figured in his work from the very outset—ghosts, that is, as the symbols of human fears or loves,
ghosts as the plausible and tangible personifications of those
varieties of self-tyranny which nowadays we call psychotic. For
this sort of ghost there need be no justification, no more than for
the ghost of Banquo. If Mr. Robinson had been content with
this, if his ghost in *Avon's Harvest* had been simply this—as it
might well have been—we should have less cause to quarrel
with him. As it is, we are bound to observe that he has *not* been
content with this, that he has yielded to the temptation, which
an unfailing realist would have resisted, of heightening the
effect of the supernatural for its own sake. The knife, with
which in a fulminous nightmare the ghost assails Avon, must
later be re-introduced by Avon as a knife of ponderable enough
reality, which the ghost, in evaporating, left behind. The
actuality of the knife's presence there, after the admirable nightmare, might indeed have been explained by another mechanism than that of the supernatural; but no such explanation
is hinted at, or, for that matter, can be hinted at, since Avon
is himself the narrator. This is a grave defect; but a graver one
is that which again calls to mind *The Altar of the Dead* as a
fine thing made of flawed material—the psychological weakness
with which the theme is conceived. If Mr. Robinson wished to
give us, in Avon, a case of incipient insanity, with a pronounced
persecutional mania, then he should have given us, for this
aspect, a better lighting. Either we should have been made,
therefore, before Avon uttered the first word of his story, more
dubious of the man's soundness of mind; or else there should
have been, in the story itself, more light upon Avon's character
as a thing easily shaken and destroyed—ready, in short, for
the very insignificant provocation which was to turn out as
sufficient to make a ruin of it. But we are assisted in neither
of these ways, and in consequence the provocative action can
not help striking us as disproportionately and incredibly slight:
we accept it, as necessary to the story, very much as we often
accept a ridiculous element in the plot of a photo-play—accept
because acceptance conditions pleasure, not because we believe. We waive our incredulity for the moment; but it returns
upon us at the end with the greater weight.

One wonders, in this light, whether it would be unjust,

after our provisos for the artist's right to the *scherzo*, to see in *Avon's Harvest*, as one often sees in an artist's less successful work, a clearer indication of Mr. Robinson's faults and virtues than might elsewhere be palpable. The poem is extravagantly characteristic of its author—there is perhaps no other poet, with the exception of Mr. Thomas Hardy, who so persistently and recognizably saturates every poem with his personality. We have again, as so many times before, the story told by the retrospective friend of the protagonist—apologetic, humorous, tartly sympathetic, maintaining from beginning to end a note about midway between the elegiac and the ironic. This is the angle of approach which has been made familiar to us in how many of the short ballad-like narratives of Mr. Robinson, of which the characteristics were almost as definite and mature in the first volume as in the last: "John Evereldown," "Richard Cory," "Luke Havergal," "Reuben Bright," in that volume, and after them a crowd of others; and then, with the same approach again, but in long form, "Captain Craig," and "Ben Jonson Entertains a Man from Stratford," and "Isaac and Archibald." What we see here, in short, is an instinctive and strong preference for that approach which will most enable the poet to adopt, toward his *personae*, an informal and colloquial tone, a tone which easily permits, even invites, that happy postulation of intimacy which at the very outset carries to the reader a conviction that the particular *persona* under dissection is a person seen and known. The note, we should keep in mind, is the ballad note—best when it is swiftest and most concise. If, as we observed above, the elegiac also figures, it is as a contrapuntal device (by "device" one does not mean to suggest, however, a thing deliberated upon), with a clear enough melodic line of its own. To narrative speed much else is ruthlessly sacrificed. Should we admit also, in our effort to place this very individual note, an element suggestive of the rapid lyrical summary, cryptically explanatory, a little subdued and brooding, as under a giant shadow—of the choruses in the tragedies of Aeschylus and Sophocles? In one respect Mr. Robinson's briefer narratives appear closer to these than to the English ballad—the action is so consistently a thing known rather than a thing seen. The action is indeed, in the vast majority of cases, an off-stage affair, the precise shape and speed of which we are permitted only to know in dark hints and sinister gleams.

The dark hint and sinister gleam have by many critics been considered the chief characteristics of this poet's style; and it is useful to keep them in mind as we consider, in a workshop light, his technique and mode of thought. Technique, for our purpose, we cannot regard as a mere matter of iambics and caesuras; it is perhaps merely a more inquisitive term for "style," by which, again, I suppose we mean the explicit manifestation of an individual mode of thought. At all events, technique and mode of thought are inseparable, are two aspects of one thing, and it is impossible to discuss any artist's technique without being insensibly and inevitably led into a discussion of his mode of thought. Thus it is permissible, in the matter of the dark hint and the sinister gleam, to isolate them either as tricks of technique or as characteristics of a particular way of thinking: and it does not greatly matter which way we choose.

If we examine Mr. Robinson's early work, in *The Children of the Night* or *The Town Down the River*, in search of the prototype of the "hint" and "gleam" which he has made—or found—so characteristic of himself, we discover them as already conspicuous enough. But it is interesting to observe that at this stage of his growth as an artist this characteristic revealed itself as a technical neatness more precisely than as a neatness of thought, and might thus have been considered as giving warning of a slow increase in subservience of thought to form. The "subtlety"—inevitable term in discussing the gleaming terseness of this style—was not infrequently to be suspected of speciousness. In "Atherton's Gambit," and other poems, we cannot help feeling that the gleam is rather one of manner than of matter: what we suspect is that a poet of immense technical dexterity, dexterity of a dry, laconic kind, is altering and directing his theme, even inviting it, to suit his convictions in regard to style. Shall we presume to term this padding? Padding of a sort it certainly is; but Mr. Robinson's padding was peculiar to himself, and it is remarkable that precisely out of this peculiar method of padding was to grow a most characteristic excellence of his mature manner. For this padding (the word is far too severe) took shape at the outset as the employment, when rhyme-pattern or stanza dictated, of the "vague phrase," the phrase which gave, to the idea conveyed, an odd and somewhat pleasing abstractness. Here began Mr. Robinson's preference, at such moments, for the Latin as against the English word, since the Latin, with its roots in a remoter tongue, and its original tactilism therefore less apparent, permits a larger and looser comprehensiveness; and for such English words as have, for us, the dimmest of contacts with sensory reality. However, it must be remarked that, for the most part, in the first three volumes, the terse "comprehensiveness" thus repeatedly indulged in was often more apparent than real: one suspects that behind the veil of dimness, thus again and again flourished before us by the engaging magician, there is comparatively little for analysis to fasten upon. The round and unctuous neatness of the poems in these volumes has about it just that superfluity which inevitably suggests the hollow. This is not to imply that there are not exceptions, and brilliant ones —"Isaac and Archibald" is a wholly satisfying piece of portraiture, and "Captain Craig" has surely its fine moments. But for the development of this characteristic into something definitely good one must turn to the volume called *The Man Against the Sky* and to the others that followed it. Here we see the employment of the "vague phrase" made, indeed, the keynote of the style—the "vague phrase," no longer specious, but genuinely suggestive, and accurately indicative of a background left dim not because the author is only dimly aware of it, but because dimness serves to make it seem the more gigantic. That, if true of the background, a strange, bare, stark world, flowerless, odorless, and colorless, perpetually under a threat of storm, is no less true of the protagonists. These, if their world is colorless, are themselves bodiless: we see them again and again as nothing on earth but haunted souls, stripped, as it were, of everything but one most characteristic gesture. If they are shadowy they seem larger for it, since what shadow they have is of the right shape to "lead" the eye; if their habiliments of flesh, gesture and facial expression are few, we see them the more clearly for it and remember them the better. This is the style at its best, but if we move on once more to the last volume, *The Three Taverns*, and *Avon's Harvest*, even perhaps to some things in *Lancelot* (though here there are other inimical factors to be considered), we shall see a deterioration of this style, and in a way which, had we been intelligent, we might have expected. For here the "vague phrase" has become a habitual gesture, otiose precisely in proportion as it has become habitual. The "vague phrase" has lost its fine precision of vagueness, the background has lost its reality in a dimness which is the dimness, too often, of the author's conception, and the one gesture of the protagonist is apt to be inconsiderable and unconvincing. We savor here a barren technical neatness. The conjuror more than ever cultivates a fine air of mystery; but nothing answers the too-determined wand.

In connection with this characteristic vague phrase, with its freight of hint and gleam, it is useful to notice, as an additional source of light, Mr. Robinson's vocabulary. We can not move in it for long without feeling that it indicates either a comparative poverty of "sensibility" or something closely akin to it; either a lack of sensibility, in the tactile sense, or a fear of surrendering to it. We have already noted, in another guise, the lack of color; we must note also the lack of sense of texture, sense of shape. As concerns his meter these lacks manifest themselves in a tendency to monotony of rhythm, to a "tumbling" sort of verse frequently out of key with the thought. It is an iron world that Mr. Robinson provides for us: if roses are offered they are singularly the abstractions of roses, not at all the sort of thing for the senses to grow drunk on. He gives us not things, but the ideas of things. We must be careful not to impute to him a total lack of sensory responsiveness, for, as we shall see in *The Man Against the Sky* and *Merlin*, this element in his style reaches its proportional maximum and betrays a latent Mr. Robinson, a romanticist, who, if he uses color sparingly, uses it with exquisite effect.

In general, however, Mr. Robinson's eye is rather that of the dramatist than of the poet—it is perceptive not so much of the beautiful as of significant actions; and the beautiful, when it figures here at all, figures merely as something appropriate to the action. In this regard he is more akin to Browning than any other modern poet has been, if we except Mr. Thomas Hardy. Like Browning, he is a comparative failure when he is an out-and-out playwright; but he is at his most characteristic best when he has, for his poetic framework, a "situation" to present, a situation out of which, from moment to moment, the specifically poetic may flower. This flowering, we are inclined to think, is more conspicuous and more fragrant in *The Man Against the Sky* and *Merlin* than elsewhere, most fragrant of all in *Merlin*. Differences there are to be noted—"Ben Jonson Entertains a Man from Stratford" represents the perfection of Mr. Robinson's sense of scene and portraiture, sees and renders the actual, the human, with extraordinary richness. In *Merlin*, however, where Mr. Robinson's romantic *alter ego*, so long frustrated, at last speaks out, we cannot for long doubt that he reaches his zenith as a poet. The sense of scene and portraiture are as acute here, certainly, but the fine actuality with which they are rendered is, as in the best poetry, synonymous with the beautiful; and the poem, though long, is admirably, and beyond any other American narrative poem, sustained. The "vague phrase" here swims with color, or yields to the precise; the irony (Mr. Robinson's habitual mode of "heightening," so characteristically by means of ornate understatement) is in tone elusively lyrical. Merlin and Vivien move before us exquisitely known and seen, as none of the people whom Tennyson took from Malory ever did. It is one of the finest love stories in English verse.

It is not easy to explain why Mr. Robinson should thus so superlatively succeed once, and not again. Shall we say that, if intellectually and ironically acute, he nevertheless lacks "energy"? There is no Chaucerian or Shakespearean breadth here; it is the closer and narrower view in which Mr. Robinson excels, and it may well be this, and the lack of energy (aspects of one thing?) which have in the main led him to a modern modification of the ballad form, in which simplification and the "hint and gleam" may take the place of the richly extensive. These are not the virtues on which to build in long form: they are stumbling-blocks in a long narrative poem, since if they are allowed free rein they must render it fragmentary and episodic. These stumbling-blocks Mr. Robinson amazingly surmounted in *Merlin,* thanks largely, as we have said, to the fact that here at last a long-suppressed lyric romanticist found his opportunity for unintermittent beauty. But in *Lancelot,* fine as much of it is, failure may be noted almost exactly in proportion as Mr. Robinson's theme has compelled him to "broaden" his narrative stream. Of the soliloquy he can be a master, and even, as in *Merlin,* of the duet; but when the stage fills and the necessity is for a franker, larger, more robustious and changeable complex of action, as in *Lancelot,* poetic energy fails him, he resorts to the factitious, and is often merely melodramatic or strained. We grant the nobility of theme, the austerity of treatment, and, of the latter half especially, the beauty. But the poem as a unit is not a success.

When we have considered *Merlin* and *The Man Against the Sky,* it becomes unjust to consider again *The Three Taverns* or *Avon's Harvest.* We feel a technical and temperamental slackening in these, a cyclic return to the comparatively illusory "depth" of the earlier work. They are parerga which we must hope do not indicate an end.

The usual succession of best-seller novels, diagnostic novels, and volumes of spicy or grisly short stories—each of them attended in turn by the fatuous illiterate little clamor which, in America, ascends on these occasions as if it were the essential voice of criticism—cannot conceal the fact that the most important book published during the winter was the *Collected Poems* of Mr. Edwin Arlington Robinson. No great clamor went up, as far as I am aware, over this: if Mr. Robinson has for some time been accepted as the "best" of contemporary American poets, the acceptance has been more tacit than express, and, when confessed, more remarkable for a vague bright generosity (pitched in a lower key than the usual generosity of American criticism —one supposes because American criticism has lost that part of its apparatus which deals with the fine as opposed to the large) than for a sure perceptiveness. It is difficult to imagine Mr. Mencken, for example, dealing at length and subtly with Mr. Robinson—Mr. Robinson would be for Mr. Mencken, one feels, merely the most provokingly fugitive and impalpable of ghosts. Nor, on the other hand, has there been much unanimity among the craftsman-critics. The poets of the Poetry Society applaud Mr. Robinson, but their applause is largely manual, and almost wholly unintelligent: what they applaud is something they vaguely think is Mr. Robinson's aesthetic orthodoxy. The poets outside the Poetry Society seldom applaud him at all. By some few of these latter he is contemptuously referred to as a kind of American Georgian. But there is none like him among the Georgians.

Nor is it particularly easy to find anywhere, in English or American poetry, clear affinities for Mr. Robinson, or obvious prototypes. Crabbe, Wordsworth, and Browning have all, for this purpose, been invoked, but without much success. Traces, yes: Mr. Robinson has written a few brilliant dramatic monologues, notably *Ben Jonson Entertains a Man from Stratford;* a few meditative poems which might claim relationship with *Intimations of Immortality—The Man Against the Sky*, perhaps; and a good many small concise narrative portraits which suggest comparison with the carved oak of Crabbe. But beyond that, nothing—nothing, that is, unless we abandon the search for precursive signals in the poetry of the past, and look rather for Mr. Robinson's blood-relations among contemporary novelists. It is

natural to think of Mr. Hardy's poetry as somewhat akin to
Mr. Robinson's—Mr. Robinson has the same predilection for the
narrative lyric, the stringent compression of the actual, the
ballad tone, the sharp dramatic gesture. But if Mr. Robinson
shares these predilections with Mr. Hardy, he shares them only
partially, and he shares as much, or more, with Henry James. It
is, in fact, impossible to read the poetry of Mr. Robinson without thinking of Henry James. If, more than Henry James, Mr.
Robinson chooses the succinct, and if his narrative, whether
short or long, is less complex, it springs, none the less, from the
same sources, reveals a temperament strikingly analogous. It
is, like the narrative of Henry James, an affair pre-eminently of
relations: a narrative, it would be more exact to say, of relations
and contacts (between character and character) always extraordinarily *conscious*. If it is permissible to conceive the individual human being as standing, like a lighthouse, at the center of
his small bright circle of consciousness; and if we think of another such individual as coming so near to the first that at one
point the two bright circles overlap, sharing a small segment in
common; and if we then conceive our two individuals as staring, fascinated, at that small segment, with its double light, and
as approaching each other, or withdrawing from each other, to
watch, in that segment, the permutations of shape and light—
living, so to speak, almost wholly in their awareness of the consciousness shared, and having little awareness apart from that;
in some such manner we may conceive how it is that Henry
James regarded his *dramatis personae*, and moved them, and
was moved by them. His interest, like theirs, lay in the varyingly
luminous contact, and in the influences thus shed; in the alteration or corruption of character by character. And something of
the sort is true of Mr. Robinson. His *Merlin* and his *Lancelot*
give us a Malory as Henry James might have rewritten and en-
larged it, had Henry James been a poet. I am not sure that the
Lancelot is altogether successful—in so far as it calls for breadth
of narrative stream, for a crowded and noisy stage, Mr. Robinson, clearly, has not the necessary vigor. In the "crowded" scenes
of the first parts, one feels a thinness, a straining, a hint of hollow
melodrama; but the instant that the poem becomes a dialogue,
with none but Lancelot and Guinevere on the stage, Mr. Robinson makes a clear beauty of it. And of his *Merlin* what is it
possible to say but that it is one of the most exquisite love
stories ever told in verse? Merlin and Vivien have here all the
dim subtleties and delicate mutual awarenesses of the people,

let us say, in *The Wings of the Dove*. The story, the poetry, is precisely in these hoverings and perturbations, these pauses and approaches and flights. Everything is hint and gleam. Flat, outrageous statement is nowhere. The express is at a minimum, the implications are vast. The batlike flittings and pipistrelline sensitiveness are, of course, Mr. Robinson's own, as they might have been Henry James's. The thought, seen to be moving in gleams and hints, and the language and prosody, reticent and dimly suggestive, are one indivisible thing. There is nothing showy or ornate, no splashing in purple: the language verges often on the coldly abstract, betraying only the most attenuated of tactilisms; the verse is often monotonous, seldom rich, and achieves its effect with a spare simplicity that is classic.

In all this one traces the affinity between Mr. Robinson and Henry James—in either case one may hazard that the fastidiousness, the love of the veiled, the luxuriation in half-lights, constitute a sort of defense mechanism, the protective cunning of souls whom Mr. Shaw would describe as "on the shrink." This, certainly, should serve as an indication of the "texture" of Mr. Robinson's poetry. We can see it, if we like, as we can see the subtle texture of Henry James, or of Hawthorne, as a product peculiarly American—the over-sensitiveness of the sensitive soul in an environment where sensitiveness is rare. But this need not blind us to the fact that Mr. Robinson can be dramatic, or mordantly ironical, or exquisitely lyrical, or even, on occasion (as in the Shakespeare poem), robust. His range is sufficient, his thought is richly and bitterly his own. It amounts pretty nearly to a disgrace that in England he still remains unpublished, almost unknown; and that he can be referred to, as he was referred to the other day in an English weekly, as "one of the dullest poets" now alive. If the notion needs refuting, I quote one of the smallest of Mr. Robinson's lyrics as refutation. It is called "For a Dead Lady" and appeared in 1910 in the volume entitled *The Town Down the River*.

No more with overflowing light
Shall fill the eyes that now are faded,
Nor shall another's fringe with night
Their woman-hidden world as they did.
No more shall quiver down the days
The flowing wonder of her ways,
Whereof no language may requite
The shifting and the many-shaded.

The grace, divine, definitive,
Clings only as a faint forestalling;
The laugh that love could not forgive
Is hushed, and answers to no calling;
The forehead and the little ears
Have gone where Saturn keeps the years;
The breast where roses could not live
Has done with rising and with falling.

The beauty, shattered by the laws
That have creation in their keeping,
No longer trembles at applause,
Or over children that are sleeping;
And we who delve in beauty's lore
Know all that we have known before
Of what inexorable cause
Makes Time so vicious in his reaping.

ROBINSON, EDWIN ARLINGTON   (1927)

To his two preceding poems dealing with themes from the Arthurian cycle, Mr. Robinson now adds a third, this time courageously venturing on a new treatment of the Tristram and
Isolt story: courageously, because more than any other tale from
Malory has this been drawn upon by poets. Wagner, Swinburne,
and Arthur Symons have all had their turn at it; and it is to
Mr. Robinson's credit that, despite the crystallization, or conventionalization, of the theme, which has inevitably resulted
from this repeated handling, he has again, as in *Merlin* and
Lancelot, made the thing remarkably his own. Whatever his
merits or defects as a narrative poet, Mr. Robinson never fails
to saturate his theme with his own character. Like Miss T., of
whom Mr. De la Mare writes that "whatever Miss T. eats turns
into Miss T.," Mr. Robinson turns his Arthurian heroes and heroines and brooding villains into such figures as could not conceivably exist anywhere else. They are as signally and idiosyncratically stamped, as invariably and unalterably Robinsonian,
as the characters of Henry James are Jamesian. These Merlins
and Tristrams and Isolts and Lancelots are modern and highly
self-conscious folk; they move in a world of moral and emotional subtlety which is decidedly more redolent of the age of

Proust than of the age of Malory; they take on a psychological reality and intensity which would have astonished, and might have shocked, either Tennyson or William Morris—whose aim, in dealing with the same material, was so largely decorative.

Mr. Robinson's method lies halfway between the tapestry effect of Morris and the melodrama of Wagner. Its chief excellence is an excellence of portraiture. And, again like James—of whom he is in many respects curiously a poetic counterpart—he particularly excels in his portraits of women. Merlin was not so good as Vivien, nor Lancelot as Guinevere; and in *Tristram* it is again true that the heroines are much more sharply and sympathetically realized than the hero. For the full-length portraits of the two Isolts—Isolt of Ireland and Isolt of the White Hands—one can have only the highest praise; both of them are as admirable and subtle as they can be; and in Isolt of the White Hands especially, Mr. Robinson has created a figure of extraordinary loveliness and pathos, as deeply moving, in its way, as the figure of Milly Theale.

To realize, beside these, the comparative failure of Mr. Robinson with his *Tristram*, is to realize also his chief weakness as a narrative poet; and, in particular, his weakness as an adapter of Malory. For he is curiously unable to deal with a hero as "man of action." Mr. Robinson's heroes think and feel—they think and feel almost inordinately; but they do not act. Every one of them is a kind of helpless introspective Hamlet; and not only that, but a Hamlet shorn of all masculine force. One cannot much respect this melancholy Tristram—one even feels that he is rather a namby-pamby creature; and without a forceful hero, how can one possibly have an altogether forceful poem? Mr. Robinson avoids "action" as he would avoid the plague. Such action as takes place in the present poem at all takes place off-stage, soundlessly and briefly. This contributes to one's feeling that the poem is too long—perhaps twice as long as it needed to be; but there are other factors as well. One cannot safely, in a poem two hundred-odd pages long, restrict oneself wholly to analytic dialogue and romantic description, with interlardings of lyricism. The lyricism is sometimes very beautiful, though perhaps not as beautiful as certain passages in *Merlin;* the analytic dialogue is often acute; but there is a great deal too much of both.

With this diffuseness in the narrative itself goes a corresponding diffuseness in the verse. Mr. Robinson's habit of ironic elaboration has grown upon him. An excellence in the short poems, where it was kept within bounds, it has now become, or is at any rate becoming, a dangerous mannerism. In the dialogue, especially, Mr. Robinson too often gives himself up to a sort of overwrought verbalistic *playing* with an idea: as if he were bent on saying the same thing three times over, each time more complicatedly and abstractedly and involutely than before. Sometimes these tortuous passages conceal a subtlety worth the pain of extraction—and sometimes they do not. On at least one occasion, Mr. Robinson becomes so involved in his own involutions that he forgets to finish his sentence—losing himself, as now and then Henry James did, in a maze of inversions and parentheses. This elaborate obscurity, with its accompanying absence of tactile qualities in the language and of ruggedness in the blank verse, too frequently makes these pages hard and unrewarding reading. It is the more regrettable as Mr. Robinson has given to his poem great beauty of design. And that it contains many pages of extraordinary loveliness and tragic force goes without saying.

ROMAINS, JULES (1925)

It has been, I think, a little too often and too lightly said in the last few years that the novel as a literary form is about to be, or ought to be, or has been, exploded. When Mr. Joyce's *Ulysses* appeared there was a particularly loud chorus of this sort. "What now," cried the joyful critics, "is left of the novel? What now is left of naturalism?" It was suggested that no realistic novelist in his senses would presume, after a careful scrutiny of giant Leopold, to try his hand again at any mere painting of a full-length portrait. Well, giant Leopold is an astounding phenomenon, and *Ulysses* is a magnificent book; but I do not see why or how this should interdict the writing of novels. Is it urged that we must all (if indeed henceforth we use prose narrative at all) write satirical epics four hundred thousand words long, and that no other "form" can be, for the modern consciousness, adequate?

The view is a little extreme. It is one thing to note a contemporary disposition to experiment with the form and aim of prose narrative; and quite another to pronounce the novel dead. To those young critics who are always in such an Elizabethan hurry to make corpses and rush them off the stage, it might well be observed that the novel can with difficulty be called dead till we know what it is. What is it that *Ulysses* has slain? Is it *The Old Wives' Tale* or *Sons and Lovers?* or *The Death of a Nobody?* or *L'Ile des Pingouins?* or *Lord Jim?* or *The Brook Kerith?* Perhaps our young critic had something less recent in mind. Perhaps he was thinking of such outworn and unpopular books as *The Wings of the Dove* or *The Awkward Age?* Or was it the old-fashioned works of Dostoevsky? But perhaps none of these are quite what he meant by the novel. It may have been Thackeray or Dickens or Trollope; it may have been Fielding. Who knows? It may even have been *Oroonoko* or *Don Quixote* or *The Golden Ass.*

The truth is, the term novel is practically useless as a *definition*—it marks no limits. The works just mentioned are all novels in the sense that they all, to some degree, purport to tell a story about fictitious persons; but beyond that, the likeness becomes faint. There are no canons for the novel. The novelist, so long as he remains interesting, can do what he likes. How much he can dispense, for example, with mere story, or narrative speed, *Tristram Shandy* and *Ulysses* equally and diversely testify. He can choose the orderly, precise, detached synthesis of *Madame Bovary*, or the "other world" beauty, the absolute music, of *The Golden Bowl* and *The Idiot.* Whatever mode he chooses he will impregnate deeply, if he is successful, with his own character. The novel is the novelist's inordinate and copious lyric: he explores himself, and sings while he explores, like the gravedigger. And what we get at, in all this, is simply the fact that at any given moment a hundred novels might be written, each of them in its way as individual as *Ulysses*, each as much a departure from the common denominator, and each therefore a "fatal blow" to the "novel." Why not? Here, for example, is M. Romains' *Lucienne*. It goes its own way, quite unruffled. It is not a great novel—it is not aimed at greatness. It is deliberately kept small, minor, and exquisite. Except for references to "interior monologue," one would not guess that it was written in the shadow of so large a natural object as Leopold Bloom. Mr. Waldo Frank, in the excellent preface to his excellent (but sometimes too mannered) translation, remarks that it belongs to the French "mystic" tradition; but this is pretty vague; and for the most part *Lucienne* shows no striking affinities with any particular tradition; its affinities are too general and dispersed. It does not date, like M. Romains' *Death of a Nobody.* The latter, with its slightly conscious exploitation of certain very modern scientific or pseudo-scientific ideas about crowd behavior, belongs to its decade. It is also a more obviously original variation on, or departure from, the "story" tradition of the novel. *Lucienne* deviates less from—let us say loosely—the Turgenev tradition; it is, in essentials, an orderly and simple love story. But it is as good an example as one could find of the fact that no tradition can ever be dead.

Mr. Frank speaks of the "terror and mystery" of M. Romains' "vision," and of his doctrine of *unanimisme;* the latter he calls a "mystical monism," and declares to be "one of the truly great triumphs of modern literary art." Can a doctrine be said to be a triumph of literary art? This is not very precise, and I think also that Mr. Frank takes *unanimisme* a shade too seriously. The French are very fond of selecting one little corner of a familiar truth, giving it a new name with a scientific tinge, and thus starting a "new movement." A few good works may result from this naked application of an idea (like a recipe) and *The Death of a Nobody* is an exception of that sort. But I suspect that *unanimisme* is little more than a trade-mark. One regrets that so able a writer as M. Romains should find necessary that kind of mythopoeia. In *Lucienne*, at all events, the *unanimisme*, or the "terror and mystery" of the "mystical monism," amount simply to the fact that M. Romains tells a love story skillfully and directly, with a very exceptional degree of poetic insight and intensity. He is a first-rate psychologist; and his analysis, or synthesis, of mood, his awareness of all the fleeting sensory phenomena that precede or accompany it, as well as the hidden counterpoint of association, is often quite extraordinary. Without once stepping outside of Lucienne's mind, or once permitting Lucienne herself to be explicitly conscious on the point, he gives us a young woman who is in that ecstatic state of passage from introversion to extroversion which marks (though in the absence of an object) the condition of "being about to fall in love." This is done with great beauty, and so is the account of Lucienne's slow interfusion with the Barbelenet family: the difference of impact is, with each personality, subtly and exquisitely discovered. The description of the first meeting is, indeed, masterly. Looking back on that scene, after one has finished the book, one would swear that it consisted entirely of dialogue, so distinctly does one hear the echo of voices and see the whole shape and color of the family discourse. Nevertheless, there are only two brief speeches in the scene. M. Romains does the thing simply by going *under* the dialogue, and giving the successive affective responses of his heroine.

It will be said, rightly, that there is nothing new in this. The point to be emphasized is that M. Romains makes this traditional method peculiarly his own. The moments, the scenes—or what James called the "joints"—of his story are very few, very simple. They are not calculated for any largeness of effect. They are sufficient, because M. Romains brings to each of them an absorbed and exquisite consciousness. He occupies every corner of his heroine's awareness—and if he endows her sometimes with an awareness that amounts to genius, nevertheless he never makes her monologue improbable. The real beauty of the story is precisely in this flowing consciousness. Its quality is peculiarly *exciting;* it is intense and simple, it is at the same time deep and lucid; one is astonished that in a narrative stream so limpid, so much should be *given.* One has the sensation, now and then, of falling through plane below plane of reality, and of discovering new subliminal hierarchies in the order of things. The first meeting with the Barbelenets is a fine example of this quality of imagination, but even finer are the descriptions of the first music lesson and the playing of the duet. These passages, in sheer poetic intensity and immersion in the actual, are the best in the book, and rival, if they do not surpass, the scene in the diligence in *The Death of a Nobody.* The character, the life, of Marthe's hands is found with a prescience that makes one almost uncomfortable. And the subterranean mingling of the two personalities playing the duet is of that sharpness and richness in analysis of mood and sensation that gives one the illusion of having discovered a new mode of apprehension.

That, of course, is a quality for which one goes to poetry. M. Romains is above all a poet, and it is primarily for his lyric intensity of consciousness that one enjoys him. And we can also be grateful to him for reminding us that the "novel" is far from dead when the simplest of stories can thus, by a very slight alteration in the angle of light, become a new experience.

SANDBURG, CARL (1926)

It is presumable that Miss Rebecca West's selection of Mr. Sandburg's poems was intended rather for English than for American publication, and was aimed primarily at securing for

Mr. Sandburg an English as well as an American audience. This fact has its interest: English preferences in American art are always instructive; and if they are also provoking, that only gives the instruction a finer edge. Of contemporary American poets, Mr. Vachel Lindsay is the only one (unless we except Mr. Eliot, who makes his residence in England) who has had much of a following in England. Mr. Frost, though he was first published in England (a fact partly owing to the circumstance that he too was then a resident), ran him a poor second; and the majority of other American poets have found English publication a difficult and infrequent affair. What England likes, in American art—but now perhaps relinquishingly likes—is something with a definite and strong American flavor. In the eighties, when there were still real cowboys who wore real sombreros, and no hotel lobby was without its "spit-box," England found it easier to recognize Artemus Ward and Joaquin Miller as genuine products of this peculiar scene than Howells or James, who were not quite so vividly identifiable. And nowadays the English critic, still hopeful of something intriguingly alien in American art, finds it a good deal easier to "see" Mr. Lindsay than—shall we say—Mr. Wallace Stevens.

And Mr. Sandburg, from this point of view, makes an excellent export product. As Miss West observes in her very interesting preface, Mr. Sandburg is nothing if not American—and by American she means all that is comprised in the term Middle West. She finds that Mr. Sandburg uses a language that in many essentials differs from the English language as spoken and written in England. The rhythms are richer, slower, longer: and they contrive, she thinks, to express all sorts of psychological intangibles peculiar to the naive self-analytic creature who inhabits the region of the Great Lakes. In this regard, Miss West makes an interesting point. She notes that, while the typical American is almost totally incapable of giving an exact report of any objective fact or experience, he is extraordinarily expert, instinctively expert, in conveying his feelings. He does this, she thinks, largely by unconscious manipulations of the rhythms he uses—ironic, laconic, or sardonic—and in so doing charges familiar words with new effects. This is perhaps partially true—but one should be careful not to make too much of it. If Miss West is right in taking Mr. Sandburg as pre-eminently the American poet who has taken over and developed this American characteristic, she is perhaps on ground not quite so firm in rejecting "all his objective nature poems because they strike the English reader as intolerably loose statements of fact." She prefers him, that is, when he is describing "the inner life of the eager little girls who leave those small towns and come to Chicago, but still find no world that makes use of their sweetness": and the "inner life of the strong young men." But is this dichotomy, in Mr. Sandburg's work, quite so easy?

One suspects, at this point, that Miss West is seriously handicapped by the difficulties which any foreigner must encounter in his survey of the American scene. He is a good enough judge of the landscape, but can he possibly know, without prolonged immersion, enough of the "inner life" of these eager little girls and strong young men to judge of a poet's accuracy in describing them? The truth is that to the American eye Mr. Sandburg is just as apt to be intolerably loose in his analysis—if one can use the term—of the inner life of these folk as in his descriptions of nature. One cannot possibly make so broad a distinction. He is not good at one sort of thing and bad at the other—rather, he is mixedly bad and good at both. His virtues are conspicuous: he uses, better than anyone else in America today, the rich idiomatic journalistic American idiom, the idiom of the streets and barber-shops and smoking-cars; he has an extraordinary vitality and saltiness; he is a lover of the plural; and he conveys his rich sense of the "here and now" in long expatiative rhythms which are often beautiful. But if one goes behind and under these things, if one looks for the accuracy of notation in the matter of inner life, does one not find a comparative poverty?

The truth is that Mr. Sandburg is a sentimentalist. He is sentimental about his factory chimneys and sweaty crowds and stevedores and hunkies and eager young girls in exactly the way that other poets are sentimental about sunsets or broken hearts. He has a passion for the quotidian, he looks at it longingly and wistfully, he has an exceedingly quick eye for its changing colors, and he is "terribly glad" (to quote his own phrase) "to be selling fish." He is genuinely in love with the scene in which he finds himself, and his love for it is frequently infectious. He is genuinely unhappy, also, to find that impermanence and tragedy and frustration move like a groundswell through this beautiful pluralism of things: and this feeling, too, he often successfully communicates. But he does not go deeper than this; and one cannot feel that he ever strikes profoundly into the "inner life" of any of his working-folk. He can give us a good charcoal drawing—we see his Chick Lorimer, the physical Chick Lorimer, vividly enough; we even share his wistful feeling for her; but we also feel a fundamental falsity in his attitude toward her. He does not, in fact, give us Chick Lorimer at all— he gives us instead his rather cloudy sentimental identification of himself with a young woman who has unaccountably disappeared. That is all. One feels that she was a wistful young woman, and that she is gone. The quotidian was beautiful, and it is gone. But would one know her from any other of a thousand young women or young men or withering stalks of goldenrod? Has she the slightest inner reality or intensity of the sort that Miss West thinks she has? One cannot think so.

No, one feels that Miss West's distinction is a false one. Mr. Sandburg is no better, and no worse, in his descriptions of people and feelings than in his descriptions of nature. One must take him as he is—he works in a large, loose medium, inextricably mixing the vivid with the false. He is essentially a lover of surfaces. Like Mr. Lindsay, he does not very well endure the test of repeated rereading, for he is simple; a surface revisited is not so sustaining as a surface seen, and seen vividly, for the first time. And while his rhythms are often delightful, and for the American reader rich in the indigenous, they lack the sort of complexity of outline or shape which can renew one's pleasure on the third or fourth reading. The design, like the feeling, is comparatively cloudy. For this reason, among others, Mr. Sandburg's poetry is a poetry to be taken en masse, not in detail. Very few of his poems will stand well by themselves. One finds him vaguely impressive as a whole, one likes his flavor, but one is decidedly uncertain as to whether there is enough at the core to guarantee his preservation.

SANTAYANA, GEORGE   (1936)

It is surely a choice piece of irony that *The Last Puritan*, the most nearly satisfactory analysis, in fiction, of the New England character, should have been written by a Catholic and a Latin. But, perhaps, just the same, there is nothing surprising in it—perhaps Santayana's unique opportunity for a vision that should be at once detached and kindly, lay precisely in these accidents of difference. If the American has the advantage over the European that he can *become* European, the European has—and more often uses!—the same advantage over the American. During his years at Harvard, first as undergraduate and then as a professor of Philosophy, it is now obvious that Santayana "became" a New Englander, in the sense of realizing what it was to *be* one, more accurately and consciously than any other novelist of New England manners one can think of. James touched on this ground repeatedly, it is true, and saw it as itself a theme of the first importance, notably in some of the short stories: but he never got around to working it exhaustively. Santayana has worked it exhaustively—the thing is done, for good and all. *The Last Puritan* is as complete, in its way, as that New England autobiography of which it is the perfect companion-piece: *The Education of Henry Adams*.

Adams described New Englanders as "sane and steady men, well balanced, educated, and free from meanness or intrigue —men whom one liked to act with, and who, whether graduates or not, bore the stamp of Harvard College . . . as a rule, the New Englander's strength was his poise, which almost amounted to a defeat. He offered no more target for love than for hate; he attracted as little as he repelled; even as a machine, his motion seemed never accelerated." It is this sort of New Englander whom, with a miracle of tenderness, Santayana proceeds to destroy. His little twentieth-century Henry Adams, a bundle of inhibitions, an incarnated sense of duty, a skeptical awareness of which perhaps the first principle is an inherited fatigue, combined with that strangest of all paradoxes, a democratic sense of *noblesse oblige*—this unhappy creature serves only too admirably as the personification of the principles—or should we say obsessions—which Santayana so urbanely and cunningly attacked in his *Skepticism and Animal Faith:* the esurient negativism, the denial of life itself, implicit in any complete transcendentalism. It is as if he said, "This kind of self-destructive soul-searching and skepticism and conscientiousness can only grow in a moral atmosphere such as this, and from a thin soil like this." And it is as if he added, "It is a kind of uprooted refinement of which the inevitable ends are sterility and death." His Oliver Alden, born tired, child of a loveless and joyless marriage, austere, self-controlled, beautifully schooled and regimented, was doomed to remain a mere spectator in life, incapable of contact or immersion, incapable of animal faith. He might, and did, *will* a contact or immersion: but only to perceive at once, with tragic clearness, that this was by no means the same thing. "He convinced himself, on puritan grounds, that it was wrong to be a puritan. . . . Thought it his clear duty to give puritanism up, but couldn't." Once dedicated to the vision, there was somehow no surrendering it, no possibility of finding any adequate substitute.

It may be objected that Santayana has a little unnecessarily loaded the dice against his tragic young man, made his inheritance, the congenital predicament, too complete. One hardly needs, in order to account for Oliver, the opium-fiend neurasthenic father, and perhaps the whole background is a shade overdrawn. But to this the answer is that Santayana has made the father, like every other character in the book, astonishingly and delightfully real. The process is leisurely, little or nothing happens, as in life itself things seldom seem to arrange themselves in scenes or dramatic actions; but if it is all placid and uneventful it is also everywhere vivid and rich and true. Unashamedly old-fashioned in its method, and in its quiet thoroughness, *The Last Puritan* makes the average contemporary novel, even the best, look two-dimensional by contrast. It has the solidity of a *Tom Jones* or *Clarissa Harlowe*, does for the New England scene, or a part of it, what those novels did for eighteenth-century England, and with the same air of easy classic completeness. Nor is it quite fair, either, to call it old-fashioned: for Santayana's employment of a kind of soliloquy-dialogue is an extremely interesting invention technically, and very skillfully done.

But the whole book is a delight, so richly packed with perceptions and wisdoms and humors, not to mention poetry, that it can be read and reread for its texture alone. It might be of himself that Santayana speaks when he says: "The odds and ends of learning stuck pleasantly in his mind, like the adventures of a Gil Blas or a Casanova; it was the little events, the glimpses of old life, like the cadences of old poetry, that had the savor of truth. Perhaps there were no great events: a great event was a name for our ignorance of the little events which composed it." Or again: "To him the little episodes painted in the corners were often the best of the picture: they revealed the true tastes of the artist and the unspoken parts of life." *The Last Puritan* is full of such intriguing corners —perhaps inevitably, since it is the work of the kindliest of living philosophers.

SCHWARTZ, DELMORE · (1940)

"Emerson," said Baudelaire, "forgot Voltaire in his *Representative Men*. He could have made a fine chapter entitled Voltaire or the Antipoet, the king of boobies, the prince of the shallow, the anti-artist." And a little later he adds, *"Always to be a poet, even in prose!"*

Admirable sentiments, as pointed and pertinent now as when they were written; for to survey English and American poetry of the past year or so, *en masse*, in an effort to detect new drifts or directions, is to come away from it at first a little saddened. And it is all the more comforting and reassuring, in one's dismay at finding the "antipoetic" everywhere so prevalent, to recall these remarks of Baudelaire's, and to consider that it may not, therefore, be one's own fault, or a mere and private lapse of taste, or a failure to "keep up," simply—if the feeling has been experienced before, and by Baudelaire, of all people, may we not presume to feel it too? At all events, the thing is there, inescapably there. And if one is in the least concerned for poetry, for poetry as an art, then one must be very much concerned indeed.

Everywhere, in the poetry of these young poets (and some of them no longer so very young, either!) is what appears to be a studied preoccupation with the relaxed, the casual, the offhand, the essentially artless. This is not the occasion for a historical research into all the reasons for so curious a development: yet it is perhaps worth noticing that in the work of the four oldest and most established poets in the group under survey—in the *Collected Poems* of Robert Frost, Robert Graves, Laura Riding, and the *Selected Poetry* of Robinson Jeffers—we can see that this cult of artlessness is by no means new. Otherwise the work of these four need not here detain us: Mr. Frost has of late added few birch-logs to his neat New England wood-pile, and Mr. Jeffers no bones to his ossuary; Mr. Graves, reviewed, seems to have shrunk, and to be at his mild best when most mildly Georgian; and Miss Riding—most readable, and occasionally even charming, in her earliest poems—seems, in her "mature" work, to have become the victim of a sort of

---

· Also reviewed here: Robert Frost, Robert Graves, Laura Riding, Robinson Jeffers, W. H. Auden, Muriel Rukeyser, Merrill Moore, Louis MacNeice, Edna St. Vincent Millay, Lloyd Frankenberg, Ben Bellitt, Kenneth Patchen, and Dylan Thomas.

high-class intellectual self-deception: only when she has a narrative to guide her, or a "form" of some sort to sustain, does she succeed in giving any point or color to her garrulity. A song without words can of course be charming, but words without song—! No, not when there are so many of them; and in this as in other regards Miss Riding is more nearly a forerunner of the vogue of artlessness than any other of her generation, unless we except William Carlos Williams.

That it *is* a kind of vogue, this cult of the offhand and artless, this affectation of a sort of shirtsleeve poetry, no one can doubt who observes it carefully—it even shows signs of developing a critique and critics of its own. It shows, too, as much in the work of the more "formal" of the younger poets as in the freer: as much, again, in English poetry as in American. In fact, the unanimity with which this fashionable flatness is being pursued is impressive, if it weren't also so disconcerting. Rhymeless, rhythmless, cadenceless, colorless lines—seldom, indeed, can they be called verse—fill page after page and book after book: there seems to be no reason why they should ever end; and not much, either, why they should ever have begun. And if the metrics are artless or totally absent, there is a neglect just as willful and complete of any care whatever for the sensory properties of language. There is little or no concern for tone, for verbal magic: little or no concern for that *modulation* of tone without which there can be no variety of effect. This neglect, or ignorance, of language, parallels the neglect or ignorance of form: if, in fact, it doesn't arise from it.

And—just to be downright—can poetry exist without form? or at its best? And isn't it about time that we raised anew this whole question of form? And tried, just for fun, to see what could be done with it? This so characteristic American distrust of form and forms—perhaps it's time, for a change, that we distrusted *that*. Elaborate form—let us make no bones about it—is beautiful. It need not in the least be stereotyped, or deadening, or artificial—there is nothing in it to be afraid of. Form plus intensity—form *formed* intensely—it is this, above all, that the typical American poet misses, perhaps has always missed. Poetic impulse in plenty: but selection, and control, almost nil. What is needed is a long and intense training in form, so that when the poetic impulse arises it will find the means for elaborate articulation already at its disposal. Even so, it will have to struggle with this, struggle *against* it: struggle against form for its identity; *but* it is exactly in the violent issue from this violent struggle, between the necessity for elaborate form, on the one hand, and intense statement, on the other (the two to be managed simultaneously), that the finest poetry emerges. Anything else is merely the *stuff* of poetry: second-rate impulse or second-rate statement. In short, a kind of "low-frequency" poetry. . . .

And one can clearly see these principles at work—or not at work—in the poets we have under review, no matter of what camp or country. They are as true of Mr. Auden as of Miss Rukeyser: as parallel in Mr. Merrill Moore's lazy sonnets as in Mr. MacNeice's slipshod *Journal*. Observe Miss Rukeyser, for example, in her earnest and intelligent piece-by-piece portraiture, as of Willard Gibbs (deference, a shade self-conscious, to the American "myth"), or Mr. Auden, in his comparable portrait of Melville: tone and method are exactly alike. In an extremely desiccated blank verse, and so boneless and toneless as to rob it of all but the last shreds of structure, proceeds the laborious style of flat explanatory statement: it is expatiative, it is analytic, it is rational—in fact, it is precisely the procedure of prose. And in both poets—if we press the point, it is because both in this regard are so typical—we encounter the now familiar "catalogue" technique, at the level (emotionally) of prose: the repetitive, appositional attack, whether by noun or adjective, idea or qualification of idea. It is an all-too-characteristic part of a seemingly deliberate unselectedness: it is essentially, however, a fumble, an uncertainty: and it is therefore almost inevitable that the final effect should be *approximate* only, and in consequence should make a constant and exhausting demand on the good will of the reader. Surely no poet can be so naive as to hope that a wholesale series of mere bald statements, a simple dumping of "facts," will somehow be evocative!

The evocative, in fact, is something very different. It is precisely a substitution of the one for the many, the iridescent fraction for the whole: a knowledge of the conditioned reflexes of meaning which can be touched off by the affective values of language and prosody. This knowledge—based on a mere primitive gift of the gab—can and must be acquired, for without it no poetry can be. It is the gift of the gab—organized. But where, among our so carefully antipoetic, anti-eloquent, tone-deaf and time-deaf poets is any gift of the gab—much less any organization of it? There is perhaps a remnant of it, a worn remnant, in Miss Millay's now somewhat soiled romanticism;

and there, perhaps, it was from the outset a little hollow. Of
the younger poets, Mr. Lloyd Frankenberg shows in flashes
that he knows what it is, and convincingly at least once, in
the poem called "The Sea"; and Mr. Ben Belitt has it, when
he is not too self-consciously neat or lapidary. Mr. Kenneth
Patchen has it more than either—his book is a sort of uncontrolled uproar of exhibitionism: violent, sentimental, self-
pitying, too mixedly personal and impersonal, but powerful
none the less: with more control and direction, a steadier view,
this looks like the real thing; and his book is not to be missed.
He uses language as it should be used, with gusto.

But the two most completely satisfactory poets of the moment, and those who as well appear primarily to be concerned
with just these poetic juices and essences that we need, are Mr.
Dylan Thomas and Mr. Delmore Schwartz. Mr. Thomas is an
absolutely first-class magician. If at times his meanings are so
nearly pure *aff*ect as to be practically nonsense, it doesn't matter: the thing is alive and beautiful, it hums, sings, whizzes,
and in short it's poetry. What a relief for a change to read someone who is *aware* of language! It reminds one only too vividly
of the miserable extent of our starvation for it. And Mr.
Schwartz, if a good deal drier, both linguistically and prosodically—at times almost imageless—is in his different way just as
brilliant. His plain statements are not so plain, by any means, as
they look—they are cunningly weighed and weighted, there are
degrees in his dryness, and his psychological procedure is impeccable. He can even be lyrical, when he wants to. And surely
his *Coriolanus and His Mother* is altogether the finest and profoundest long poem, narrative poem, which has come into English literature for a very long time. It is beautifully designed,
rich in detail—magnificent.

SHAPIRO, KARL   (1944)

Whatever else one may conclude about the merits or demerits
of Mr. Karl Shapiro's remarkable tour de force, *Essay on Rime*,
and perhaps all the more because it is certain to be violently
liked or disliked for an immense variety of reasons, whether
aesthetic, psychological, sociological, or philosophic, one feels
assured of one thing: this little book is destined to become a

kind of literary watershed. In the very act of taking such a
theme, and taking it with deliberate high seriousness, Mr. Shapiro made that almost inevitable. The poem itself might not
wholly come off, for no poem does; the details of view or
taste might be here and there at fault, or the proportions seem
idiosyncratic; but the idea was itself of the first order, and could
do nothing but succeed. To write a treatise on poetry, and to
write it in verse, and with this to combine a critical commentary
on the evolutions and revolutions of the poetry of the past half-
century—this, for a young poet, was a quite astonishing notion,
and one of which the sheer boldness was perhaps merely the
obverse of the poet's ability to carry it into execution. Mr. Shapiro has done it, at all events, and it needs less than half a
poetic eye to see at once that in thus offering himself up as a
catalyst and crystallizer of the period, he has quite startlingly
changed everything. The whole poetic scene, whether one
looks at it with the inertia of the one-or-two-generations-past
or the tendentiousness of the generation-to-come, is subtly
reorganized, and for good.

How useful this will be we can guess at once, even if we cannot
measure it, and even, too, if each of us, in his own degree or
kind, would have preferred some other order than that which
Mr. Shapiro imposes. The point is that we now *have* an order,
where before we had little or none, and if we want to oppose it,
then it can only be with another sort of order of our own. Thus,
for the present reviewer, Mr. Shapiro's poetic constellations
seem at times a little arbitrary and exclusive, and more especially as we are taken back near the turn of the century. In a
poem of two thousand lines not everything can be included,
naturally, and Mr. Shapiro himself makes an apologetic note of
this; and, as he also points out, he has had perforce to limit
himself somewhat to such poets as afford him examples of
those faults which he wants to list and analyze. Just the same,
his preoccupations and predilections must necessarily become
apparent, and with these a gradual if not always wholly explicit sense of his values. In this implied hierarchy Hart Crane
looks decidedly too large, and so perhaps do Spender, Mac-
Neice, Barker, MacLeish, and Williams. Is it presumptuous to
suggest that, with the exception of the last-mentioned, this
largeness might be, for Mr. Shapiro, a part of the mere accident
of their nearness to him in time? Mr. Shapiro was born in 1913,
the year before the famous but now forgotten *Blast* dinner, and
Vortex, and the Imagists: Amy Lowell was about to descend on

the Poetry Bookshop in London, to frighten the wits out of
Harold Monro and Rupert Brooke and the Georgians; W. H.
Davies was shortly to buy and read two newspapers a day, in
order to follow the war, despite their being, as he put it, "so
dreadfully literal"; *The Love Song of J. Alfred Prufrock* had
been carried by the present reviewer to London, there to be refused with outspoken horror by Monro, for *Poetry and Drama*,
and Austin Harrison, for the *English Review*, and then to be
given an official stamp of delighted approval by Ezra Pound;
Frost's first two books were being published in England, so that
he too, like Eliot, was being given an English visa for travel in
America; and, in America, Robinson was about to write *The
Man Against the Sky*, Vachel Lindsay *The Congo*, and Masters
The Spoon River Anthology. The battle between *vers libre*
and "formal" poetry was fiercely under way, with a threshing
out of perceptions and values which has influenced everything
written since: the battle itself won by neither *vers libre* nor
formalism, and ending, not with a bang but with a whimper,
in *Prufrock* and *Gerontion,* and, a little later, in Wallace Stevens' *Harmonium*. Of all this one gathers practically nothing at
all from Mr. Shapiro, except in an aside, when, speaking of
Yeats's statement that the last half century had produced more
fine poetry than any other generation since 1630, he dismisses
the suggestion as palpably untrue. And, in fact, this is really his
theme—he has set himself to show that the poetry of our time is,
with a few momentary exceptions, artless, decadent, and confused: without belief, without vision or imagination, and without any trained sense of form.

Well, many of these things are incidentally true, and
Mr. Shapiro's analysis of corrupting tendencies, and his critical
examinations of individual poets, are always interesting and
sometimes acute; but one begins to wonder whether his taste is
as catholic as it should be, and whether he doesn't too often
miss the wood for the trees. The truth is that these forty years
have provided a quite extraordinary rankness and richness and
variety of poetic invention, with an immense range—perhaps
as great as any to be found in English poetry—of temper, form,
and diction. It would have to be, of course, an almost unimagi-
nably catholic critic who could like it all—or would like it?—but
also it would seem impossible not to be astonished and delighted by its profusion and brilliance. Mr. Shapiro is perhaps
too near his own end of it to see it as a fantastically enmeshed
organic whole, too much himself an end-product of the machine

to see it quite without *parti pris*. It seems a little limiting and
limited and pedantic to accept only Joyce and Eliot as first-
rate prosodists of our time—this, and other remarks, make one
wonder just how sensitive and perceptive a judge of prosody
Mr. Shapiro may be. And what of the omissions? It is refreshing to see justice done to Bridges, but where is that real giant,
Thomas Hardy? And even if Mr. Shapiro does apologize for
their absence, Frost, and more especially Stevens, the most
neglected great poet of our time, together constitute a gap that
comes close to discrediting Mr. Shapiro's sense of proportion
entirely. Similarly, too, it strikes one as very odd indeed that if
Saintsbury and Lanier are mentioned and discussed, there
should be no reference whatever to I. A. Richards's *Principles of
Literary Criticism*—a book which is itself one of the critical
watersheds of the century.

But these are objections which can only, as it were, begin by
positing the excellence and logical completeness and in general
the thoroughness of Mr. Shapiro's poem. His "attack" is, one
dares to use the word, masterly. As for the poem itself, and the
prosody, if one finds it sometimes *too* near the prose level, and
certainly oftener pedestrian than equestrian, and if it far too
seldom delights the ear, nevertheless it is very cunningly calculated for its purpose: and it is questionable whether, by
tightening and formalizing it further, more might not have been
lost than gained. Let us be properly grateful to Mr. Shapiro. He
has put himself in an enviable and dangerous position, at the
head of his generation.

SHAPIRO, KARL •   (1945)

I think it can be said that poetry resembles the dream in at
least one very important sense: the latent content, or meaning,
is not necessarily identical with the manifest content, or meaning; and indeed one may question whether it is not precisely
when the two kinds of meaning are most at variance that the
poetry becomes most rewardingly alive. The poet may believe,
for example, in a given poem, that he is praising life, all life,
with all the profundity and richness of which he is capable:

• Also reviewed here: Robert Lowell and Rolf Humphries.

such praise, and searchingly, is his theme: and the praise is in fact there. But also there, and to a great extent unknown to the poet, may be just such a selection of images, phrases, rhythms, chosen in spite of himself out of old habits and preoccupations, as will undo the praise entirely, and lend to it the unmistakable accents of despair. And it is at these moments, when the poet is unconsciously driving a tandem of meanings in such a way that he is himself drawn to the right or left of his preconceived path, that poetry is most recognizably and beautifully itself. The poetry is precisely in that harmonization of two conflicting voices: it is in the shimmer between two values: the oracle is ambiguous, but in its very ambiguity we find a new kind of statement. The "praise," in the above instance, is tragic. And similarly, a satire might be resonant with praise.

If something of this sort is true, then we have a rough-and-ready way of classifying varieties of poetic statement which might, on occasion, be useful. This varying ratio of latent to manifest meaning, might it not eventually be discovered to correspond in some degree to the old counters of "romantic" and "classic"? And with the helpful addition of a workable psychological principle. At the one extreme, we would find a maximum of manifest statement or content, and the latent content at the barest perceptible minimum: whether or not it was in verse, this work would be very close to prose. At the other extreme, where latent meaning was overwhelmingly disproportionate to manifest, we would find ourselves in the realm of "pure" poetry, poetry all affect, the poetry of nonsense and hallucination: the highly romantic and disequilibrated poetry of those poets who profess to dispense with meaning altogether, or to offer as a substitute for it simply a form or an image, or a constellation of images. And midway between, where the equivocation was controlled and pure, the two meanings inextricably compounded into a third, lies the possibility of the sort of perfection which we call classic. Abundance seems the richer for being restrained with the lightest of hands: feeling and thought fall lucidly into one pattern, each complementing the other.

The exciting thing about the poetry of Karl Shapiro is that at its best, and even when it is not at its best, it is perhaps the only poetry we have had in a generation, or even in two, which continually approaches this kind of balanced excellence. It is a more masculine poetry than any we have lately been accustomed to: its range is remarkable, all the way from the savagely satirical, as in "The Fly," a masterpiece of moral horror and intellectual disgust, to the rich and tender love poem which is the title poem of his new book, or the triumphant calm precision of the "Elegy for a Dead Soldier." Any one of these would suffice to make the reputation of a poet: but so would "The Christmas Tree," or "Interlude," or "D. H. L.," or "The Saint," in this book, or "The Twins," or "The Poet," in *Person, Place, and Thing.* And the unmistakable and assured power that creates and animates all these, lies, I think, in the fact that Mr. Shapiro drives such a *tandem* of meanings as we have just been discussing above. He can be as purely "poetic" as anyone else, when he likes—witness the pyrotechnics of "Nigger" or "Fireworks"— just as he can also on occasion be purely satirical; but his real domain lies between, the controlled poetic abundance brought into the magnetic realm of an idea. He thinks with his feelings, thinks with his imagination, and the result is a curious and delightful poetic analysis, or criticism, of the given theme. Nothing could be subtler than his symbolic dissection and synthesis of D. H. Lawrence. Into a short poem, he can pack a whole ethnological and sociological treatise on the island predicament of the Australians. And "The Twins" is a little piece of pure psychological magic. One metrical fault one finds here and there—a tendency to fall into a loose and slightly rackety anapaestic or dactylic movement, which tumbles a little too much. A small enough complaint: for this book is no promise, it is an achievement.

To go from Mr. Shapiro to Robert Lowell, a newcomer, is to go back three hundred years, and in more senses than one. For not only is Mr. Lowell a formalist, whose models and congeners are such seventeenth-century formalists as Drayton and Crashaw, Vaughan and Traherne, but he is also, as Allen Tate remarks in his Introduction, "consciously a Catholic poet"; and it would be idle to pretend that one does not find this predilection intellectually embarrassing and retrogressive. It may be true that the poetry is the thing, and not the belief it rests upon, as F. O. Matthiessen very persuasively argued in his study of Eliot; but I think it is also unanswerably true that in the *last* analysis, as between two poets of equal poetic merit, that one will be the greater, the more wholly sustaining, whose range of reference is wider than any orthodoxy could endow, freer than it would permit: intellectual limitations, there is no gainsaying, are crippling, even if they are only implicit, and, as it were, offstage. Mr. Tate is right when he says that Mr. Low-

ell's style is bold and powerful. It is. His angry and violent use
of Catholic symbolism is often—as in the fine "On the Eve of
the Feast of the Immaculate Conception"—extraordinarily
effective. Here and elsewhere in his book Mr. Lowell's undercurrent of fierce satire contributes an immense vigor and gusto,
just as it does for Mr. Shapiro: is it perhaps an element of doubt
that thus rears its angry and creative head? When this slack-
ens, however, the verse tends to become either turgid and
strained or merely heraldic, and the thematic limitations more
manifest. There are enough good things of a nonreligious sort
here—"In Memory of Arthur Winslow," "The Drunken Fish-
erman"—to give one hope that Mr. Lowell will expand his
range. He already has the power.

Rolfe Humphries's new book seems pretty slight by comparison with such essentially masculine work as Mr. Shapiro's
or Mr. Lowell's. This is engaging enough occasional verse, for
the most part; and on the whole, but not in a derogatory
sense, it is nearer perhaps to *vers de société* than to poetry.
The internal pressure is low, one misses here almost entirely
the sense of two-voicedness that enriches and makes vascular
the work of the two other poets. But, like Austin Dobson, that
forgotten master of light verse, Mr. Humphries can turn a nice
lyric, as in "Aria," or "They Talk About the Weather"; and he
has the honest virtue, rare enough, of never overreaching himself.

STEIN, GERTRUDE   (1934)

In an article in the January *Atlantic Monthly* Mr. B. F. Skinner
contributes an analysis of Miss Gertrude Stein's work—or,
rather, of that part of it which has made her famous, the
Gertrude Stein of *Tender Buttons, Geography,* and *The Making
of Americans*—which, one suspects, Miss Stein must find somewhat embarrassing. Following down a reference in *The Autobiography of Alice B. Toklas,* Mr. Skinner has unearthed an
undergraduate paper in psychology (published in *The Harvard
Psychological Review*) in which, describing experiments in
"spontaneous automatic writing," Miss Stein quotes specimens
of such writing: and these specimens are startlingly like the
"style" which was to be her great gift to the world a decade or

so later. Miss Stein herself, in the *Autobiography*, refers to these as a "method of writing" to be afterwards developed in *Three Lives* and *The Making of Americans*; but she is also at pains to assert that she "never had subconscious reactions, nor was she a successful subject for automatic writing." Mr. Skinner points out the obvious inconsistency. The early treatise proves quite completely that she *had* had subconscious reactions, and *had* been successful in automatic writing: and the resemblance of the later style to the earlier suggests pretty convincingly that in *Tender Buttons* and *The Making of Americans* she was "developing" it only in the sense of—to use her own favorite word—"repeating."

Mr. Skinner very tactfully concludes that when Miss Stein began, about 1912, to make a principle of what had really been an accident, she had simply forgotten, or chosen to forget, the origins of the thing. Whether we agree with him or not, the discovery is certainly an awkward one. For nearly twenty years we have been sedulously taught, by the highbrow critics, the literary left-wingers, and all the masters of the subtler schools that in Miss Stein's work we were witnessing a bold and intricate and revolutionary and always *consciously* radical experiment in style, of which the results were to be of incalculable importance for English literature. Like the splitting of the atom, or the theory of relativity, Miss Stein's destruction of meaning was inevitably going to' change, if not the world, at any rate the word. By a systematic dislocation of "affects," we were to get a revivification of word, rhythm, style and meaning. From the Paris laboratory came breathless rumors of the work in progress. Distinguished authors attended the experiments and came away impressed: the influence began to spread: Mr. Van Vechten praised, Mr. Anderson and Mr. Hemingway imitated, the Sitwells took notes. Mr. Joyce was attentive—even the cautious Mr. Eliot opened the pages of *The Criterion* to this new phenomenon, though he as quickly closed them again. In short, the thing was the very finest sort of literary Inside Tip. Not to believe was simply not to belong.

In the light of which, Mr. Skinner's article makes of the whole thing a very cruel joke. What becomes of all this precise and detached and scientific experimentation with rhythm and meaning if, after all, it has been nothing on earth but automatic writing? Is it merely one more instance of the emperor's new clothes? Have we been duped, and has Miss Stein herself, perhaps, been duped? It looks very like it—though of course it is not impossible that Miss Stein has been pulling our legs. That she can write well, even brilliantly, when she wants to, she has amply proved. *Melanctha,* an early story, is a little masterpiece, but perfectly orthodox. The *Autobiography* is a witty and delightful book, again perfectly orthodox—which makes one speculate slyly as to why, at this late date, in giving us her self-portrait, she should thus abruptly abandon the subtler communicativeness of her mature "style" for a method simpler and—shall we say—more effective. Is it a concession? Is it a confession?

There remains, however, the unpleasant little problem of the more purely "automatic" books, of which *The Making of Americans* is a very good example. M. Bernard Faÿ contributes a magnificently eulogistic preface—he could hardly say more if he were prefacing the collected works of Shakespeare. Scarcely less favorable in her opinion is Miss Stein herself, who, in the *Autobiography,* refers to it as that "monumental work which was the beginning, really the beginning, of modern writing." Reassuring, also, is Miss Stein's graceful acknowledgment of Henry James as her only real forerunner. But despite a considerable charm in the opening pages (which were written when Miss Stein was an undergraduate, and for a course in composition), and a clear enough emergence, here and there, of scene and character (notably the two dressmakers), the book can only be described as a fantastic sort of disaster. If there is a maximum in unreadability, *The Making of Americans* falls short of it only by the several hundred pages which, apparently, M. Faÿ has omitted from this abridged edition. In an attempt to restrict herself to the use of only the simplest words (for no matter how complicated a psychological statement), Miss Stein falls into a tireless and inert repetitiveness which becomes as stupefying as it is unintelligible. The famous "subtlety of rhythm" simply is not there: one could better find it in a tom-tom. The phrasing is almost completely unsensory, flat and colorless—or, as Mr. Skinner admirably puts it, cold. The abuse of the present participle, in a direct but perhaps simple-minded assault on "presentness," amounts in the end to linguistic murder.

In short, the book is a complete aesthetic miscalculation: it is dull; and although what it seeks to communicate is interesting, the cumbersomeness of the method defeats its own end. The analysis of human types is sometimes exceedingly acute—if one has the patience to worry it out—but as here presented it sounds as if someone had attempted to paraphrase Jung's *Psychological Types* in basic English. The attempt sometimes leads Miss Stein into unintentional comedy. She is presumably making merely a *psychological* statement when she says, "She had very little bottom to her, she had a little sensitive bottom to her enough to give a pleasant sweetness to her."

It remains to say that the book is a miracle of proofreading. How the compositor could keep his eye on the right word, the right phrase, in the gradually mounting whirlwind of repetition, or the proofreader keep accurate count of the interminable series of identical statements, without falling asleep, or, on waking, find his way to the bright particular word again, transcends understanding. Merely to think of it is almost to die of exhaustion.

STEVENSON, ROBERT LOUIS (1928)

There is a kind of temporal Limbo to which, when a famous author dies, he must sooner or later descend; posthumously, he begins all over again the dreary business of acquiring, or attempting to acquire, a reputation. Immediately after his death, there is likely to be a fanfare of eulogy. But this is succeeded, usually, by cat-calls from the gallery; and thereafter comes a lively alternation of choruses, some hostile and some friendly. The question of his permanence or impermanence, his importance or unimportance, is, according to the circumstances, languidly or vigorously debated. And eventually the patient ghost is permitted to fare forward to the slopes of Helicon, or downward to Lethe and a comfortable oblivion.

Robert Louis Stevenson is still in Limbo. His rather romantic career, the myth of his heroism (not unfounded), his brilliance, his oddity, his adventurous expedition (like Gauguin's, but for a different reason) to the South Sea Islands—all these factors, together with his books, contrived to magnify, while he was alive, his presence, and, after his death, his absence. There was an enormous curiosity about him, a queer public affection for him; it was, therefore, the most natural thing in the world that ultimately he should become a target for detraction.

Mr. Chesterton, in his new biography, undertakes the defense. In the strict sense, this is not a biography at all. It is rather a comment on preceding biographies, and particularly on those for which the motive has largely been the explosion of the Stevenson "myth." Mr. Chesterton mentions no names; but it is easy enough to recognize Mr. Steuart's book as the chief of these; and also to identify, in the earlier pages of the present work, a literary essay on Stevenson (referred to by Mr. Chesterton) as that by Mr. John Freeman, published a few years ago in the *London Mercury*. This essay has especially distressed Mr. Chesterton. It was the most formidable of recent attempts to see Stevenson afresh, and to find a place for him. Mr. Freeman felt that Stevenson had been very much over-rated. He saw him, in fact, as a distinctly minor artist; as being, in a sense, a lineal descendant of Poe, in that his preoccupation as a story-teller was with the strange and remote and exciting rather than with the human; but as being inferior to Poe in depth and power. Mr. Chesterton will have none of this. He declines to see Stevenson as a maker of "wax flowers." In fact, he sees Stevenson as the antithesis of this: as a purveyor of the sharp, the sane, the healthy, the courageous; as being almost alone among the writers of the Dreary Eighties and Purple Nineties in seeking relief from the prevailing pessimism and spiritual bankruptcy *via* a return to the doctrine of courage, on the one hand—a sort of I-am-the-master-of-my-fate Henleyism —and a return to the doctrine of "beauty as revealed to the child" on the other. In short, he sees Stevenson as a kind of evangel of Hope and Will.

There is, of course, a good deal to be said for this view. And Mr. Chesterton says it admirably. He is sympathetic in his treatment of Stevenson—almost too sympathetic. He recognizes the forces which compelled his hero to move in the queer orbit which he found for himself; he admits cheerfully enough that Stevenson, in a sense, never grew up, and made of his literary work a kind of enforced return to boyhood; he eschews Freud, but none the less does sufficient justice to the psychological factors here at work. And when he comes to a critical appraisal of Stevenson, he says a great many excellent things. He acknowledges, as an undercurrent to the doctrine of sanity and courage, the "swaggering cult of fear." Of the poems, he admits that they are "more effective in their phraseology than in their poetry." And when he discusses the novels and short stories, he grants the thinness; "he is so very thrifty that his characters are almost thin." He attempts, it is true, to justify this on the ground that it was produced by Stevenson's "instinct for hard simplification"; an apology which does not quite convince. Stevenson himself was aware of his shortcomings in this regard. In a letter to Henry James he remarked: "How to get over, how to escape from, the besotted *particularity* of fiction. 'Roland approached the house: it had green doors and window blinds; and there was a scraper on the upper step'. . . . To hell with Roland and the scraper! . . ." It is just exactly in Stevenson's horror of particularity that he failed of first-rateness as a novelist. In effect, he was a minor poet who attempted, and with considerable success, to become a writer of fiction. He could manage the salient detail, the one sharp image, the brilliant superficial description of a character or scene, the easy transitions and technical arrangements of material; but when it came to the purely cumulative factor in fiction, the slow amassing of overwhelming evidence, the patient accretion of circumstance which gradually gives to a character his real body and psychological force, he was just as conspicuously a failure. None of his people is anything but a vivid pictorial image; we see them for a flash, and they are gone. We do not know them, as we know Anna Karenina, or Milly Theale.

Mr. Chesterton does not ignore this feature of Stevenson's work; but he is perhaps a little inclined to minimize its importance. Stevenson was an admirable writer of tales: and in *Dr. Jekyll and Mr. Hyde* he took, just once, a plunge into a darker world. Had he gone on in that direction—had he worked this particular mine—we should perhaps now be saying other things about him. Mr. Chesterton somewhat deplores this particular vein. It smells, to him, of escaping gas; very much as D'Annunzio's work smelt, to Henry James, of bad drains. But it was more than that: it was a real sounding of psychological mystery. As Stevenson remarked in a letter: "The gnome is interesting, I think, and he came out of a deep mine, where he guards the fountain of tears. It is not always the time to rejoice."

Language is a living thing, and it won't down: suppress it as you will, starve or stifle it no matter for how long, mutilate or amputate it as brutally as you like, it will nevertheless, eventually, in some new and unexpected spokesman, vividly and violently revenge itself. For the roots of language are sensory and sensuous. Without that rich and basic and sensitive tactilism, it is not properly itself, nor properly our speech: and if for the little moment of a generation it may submit, apparently, to the artifices of too severe or narrow a culture, or permit a merely "social" selection of its resources, enduring a regimentation of whatever sort, this will invariably prove to be temporary. Sooner or later will come again those fellows who love language for itself because they live it. Not for these the paler and drier and more abstract of its virtues, useful as these too may be—rather, the full tumult of it at its animal and sensual best, language at its most vascular and vital. The creative chaos of perceptions and feelings is come again. And the conventual excellences die, as it were, in sunlight.

Mr. Dylan Thomas is a restorer and re-creator of this sort, and the more welcome for being so overdue. For nearly twenty years, poetry has been increasingly the victim of a kind of monkish snobbism: at the mercy of intellectual and aesthetic dandies on the one hand—effeminates, castrates, and theorists —and of hysterical social fanatics on the other, it is no wonder that it has become itself a sort of *castrato*. Eliot and Pound were good poets, but devastating influences. Themselves "on the shrink," and acidly defensive, they were predestined shrivelers and wizeners of others; there was precious little of tolerance or generosity in them; nor can it be said that the generation which succeded them a decade ago did much to improve matters. Here again was the acid defense—a shade more dilute, but essentially the same thing. The acid defense, with a note of amused self-deprecation and apology added—in fact, poetry ashamed to be poetry. . . . And Mr. Thomas, a born language-lover and language-juggler, a poet with an unmistakable genius for the affective values of language and prosody, who has the air, like a necromancer, of keeping a thousand words on the wing at once, undoes all this sterile mischief as if

• *The World I Breathe.*

it were simplicity itself. Rhetoric, and eloquence—? Of course, and why not? And all the rest of the poet's bag of tricks. He says right off, and emphatically, and unashamedly—

Now stamp the Lord's prayer on a grain of rice,
A Bible-leaved of all the written words
Strip to this tree: a rocking alphabet,
Genesis in the root, the scarecrow word,
And one light's language in the book of trees;
Doom on deniers at the wind-turned statement.

And he proceeds to pour out such a glitter of magic—magic by itself and for its own sake—as we have not seen since Wallace Stevens published *Harmonium.* It is the answer, and the right answer, to all the jejune precisionism, and dreary ironic defeatism, of the past generation: it is the return of the gift of the gab, and let us celebrate it. If Mr. Thomas does nothing else—difficult as that may be to believe—he has already given us something priceless by breaking open this door. And by offering us, as if it were the most natural thing in the world, another murex.

THOMAS, DYLAN ·   (1944)

One of the most interesting things to watch, in the perpetual backwards-and-forwards evolution of poetry, is the emergence and development, during any given period, of a new fashion —and by fashion one doesn't mean fashion in form so much as fashion in tone. The form no doubt changes too, as it must, when tone changes. But it is the tone which changes first, which is to say the voice, which is again to say the language. We remember how distinct and strange was Mr. Eliot's voice, in 1911, and yet how wholly natural, with his "evening, lights, and tea, children and cats in the alley," "short square fingers stuffing pipes," "an English countess goes upon the stage," and all the other properties of shabby twilight suburbia, so instantly recognized as universal, but till then so entirely ignored. It was all of a piece, all skillfully in one key: the deadly commonplace as the bait in the mouse-trap, but the spring itself of classic design and infallible precision, Bleistein and his

· *New Poems.*

cigar as certainly followed by defunctive music under sea as
Sweeney by the cry of Agamemnon. The effect of this on
contemporary diction was astringent in the extreme, if not
indeed disinfectant. Its influence can be traced through Pound
on Yeats, and of the two poetic movements of the period,
Imagism and the Georgians, neither could hope to stand up
against it. Mr. Eliot's voice remains the most *characteristic* voice
of the period from 1916 to 1930.

If it was the individual problem which fed and concerned
Mr. Eliot, and notably his own, with his sometimes almost
comical anxiety about *why* Mr. Eliot thinks what Mr. Eliot
thinks when he thinks it, or his taste in ties ("rich but modest")
and words ("exact without vulgarity"), or his worry over "concentration without elimination," Mr. Auden changed the tune
and tone in the early thirties by the simple device of social
multiplication. Like the sociologists and politicians of the time,
Mr. Auden thought in numbers, in plurals; and by objectify-
ing in his verse this preoccupation with classes, groups, units,
currents of economic and social change and currents of idea,
Mr. Auden found a "voice" which was almost as influential and
as readily *received* as Mr. Eliot's. Valedictory, valetudinarian,
statistical, latinate, neatly abstract and generalized, its abandoned workings and rusty tramlines began to turn up everywhere, together with the ruined boys, the unnecessary work-
shops, guides in shorts pursuing flowers, and the short-haired,
mad executives. Yes, it was something we all knew about, all
right, and Mr. Auden did it brilliantly; but although the influence was useful, in that it expanded the objective of poetry,
as against Mr. Eliot's increasing contraction of it (unless we
except here *The Waste Land*), the method, as imitated by
others and even by himself, became at last somewhat de-
hydrating. The fashion had gone too far and outlived itself, the
dry bones were chirping again, the jejune needed a corrective.
And the corrective turned out to be, what surely no one had
expected, a kind of up-to-date euphuism.

Mr. Dylan Thomas started it: with a natural and strong love
of language and of words for their own sake, and of English
roots as against Latin, he reacted violently, perhaps too violently, from the fashionable desiccation of diction; and the
consequence has been a spate of poetic purple, on all sides,
which still shows no signs of abatement. Mr. Thomas's style
and speech, nevertheless, like those of his two predecessors,
was very much his own, *sui generis:* a fast-moving tide of

images, nouns and noun-clusters, free-associational in its direction, but the association that of an imagination with enormous relish and gusto, and sense of color and, kinesthetically, of thrust and texture as well. The question was, however, and remains, whether a method so wholly devoted to the voice and the word, so deliberately given up to sound and fury, or good Elizabethan ranting (for which there is a great deal to be said), can ultimately be directable to more than one kind of poetic effect. Word-magic as a *quality* of poetry is one thing, but poetry as *nothing* but magic—one sees the limitations, as of the snake that swallowed itself and vanished, or the poet who, as Mr. Santayana puts it, merely swam about in a sea of sensibility.

The hero's head lies scraped of every legend,
Comes love's anatomist with sun-gloved hand
Who picks the live heart on a diamond.

This passage from "The Map of Love" is not an extreme instance, by any means, but it is very typical of the style, and it made one wonder where Mr. Thomas could go next. Could one do anything with this but repeat it, or repeat it with variations? The euphuism was already showing signs of self-destruction, both in Mr. Thomas's hands and in those of his many imitators; and his own new book is certainly in this regard disappointing. There are good things in it, but they aren't better, as they might be, despite the slackening of the fever and a discernible tendency to more conscious control.

TURGENEV, IVAN

(1927)

It is a curious fact that one who was called by Henry James (writing in the late seventies) "the foremost novelist of his day," and who, by general consent, has taken a place with Tolstoy and Dostoevski as one of the three greatest of Russian writers of fiction, should have had to wait till the present moment, forty-three years after his death, for his first biography, and that now, when at last it appears, it should be written in English. Where, one wonders, have the Russians been? For Turgenev does not at all belong to that class of writers whose popularity is immense but ephemeral: he has taken his place as a classic; and if his place seems, as time passes, to become a little smaller, and if a modern Russian can say of him that he has become a shade "old-fashioned," his place and his claim are nevertheless as secure as such things can be. If all of Turgenev's works had somehow disappeared, one would still have to remember him as a writer who was extravagantly admired by his greatest contemporaries: by Flaubert, Tolstoy, Dostoevski, Chekhov, and James. James was fond of calling him "the beautiful genius." Dostoevski, who was fanatically jealous of Turgenev, and who hated him as only Dostoevski knew how to hate, was none the less intensely flattered when he was told, by one of his correspondents, that the characters in *The Possessed* were Turgenev's characters "grown old." And Chekhov, despite the great gulf of time and fashion which lay between him and his elder, could write of him: "My God! What a glorious thing *Fathers and Children* is! It is positively terrifying. Bazarov's illness is so powerfully done that I felt ill and had a sensation as though I had caught the infection from him. And the end of Bazarov? And the old men? And Kukshina? It's beyond words. It's simply a work of genius."

It is high time, therefore, that our "friendly curiosity" (as James with characteristic decorum phrased it) concerning "the private personality of M. Turgenieff" should be satisfied; and this Mr. Yarmolinsky has done, and done admirably. His biography is almost everything that a biography should be. He has not only documented himself with extreme care; he has also exercised the gift, rare enough in biographers, of making his hero come to life before us. The result, in some respects, is surprising. Certainly it would have surprised, and a little shocked, poor James. For this Turgenev, with his innumerable, really innumerable, love affairs, his sundry illegitimate children (toward whom he was a little casual), his *passades*, and his one lifelong devotion to the singer, Mme. Viardot, is obviously not quite the sort of beautiful genius with whom James could have been socially at ease. This is not to say that Turgenev was merely a sensualist: he was also a sentimentalist; and to this part of his nature James could have responded—and did, in the novels, respond—with enthusiasm. Turgenev was, indeed, as profoundly sentimental, or nostalgic, in his attitude toward women, as he was in his attitude toward the country of his birth; to neither could he be anything but intermittently faithful. Incapable of living in Russia, on his family estate, he was also incapable of living happily anywhere

else. His whole life, whether in Paris or Baden, was a kind
of sentimental exile. Proud as he was of being a "good European," and much as he urged his fellow countrymen to follow
him thus westward, nevertheless he kept his eyes turned toward the East, and his returns to Russia, though always brief,
were almost annual. Rightly or wrongly, he felt that Russia and
the Russians were the only themes of which he could write.
Furthermore, he felt a deep sense of *obligation*, moral and
social, to make these his themes. And his periodic visits were
in the nature of a "touching of earth," a renewed immersion,
in order that his grasp of the scene might not become insecure
or ·inaccurate. What he no longer clearly understood or remembered, he returned to with a note-book. And it was, of
course, precisely his sense of having unfilially betrayed his
native land that forced him to write of nothing else. His conscience troubled him, and he was never capable, as James was
in a similar predicament, of taking the next step, and finding
an adequate theme in the international limbo to which his
passion for a more civilized life than the Russian had driven
him.

It was perhaps to this curious fixation, this inability to overcome a sentimental obsession, which is the peculiar fate of
exiles, that the obvious defects of his novels are traceable.
Turgenev was not at all by nature a sociological novelist: it
was only a series of accidental and (in a sense) external forces
that compelled him, time after time, to take for his theme the
struggles of the young Russian liberals to move feudal Russia
in the direction of democracy. He disapproved of serfdom,
he sympathized with the peasants, and he fell, while a young
man, under the influence of certain radicals—under that influence producing the most effective (socially) of his books,
A Sportsman's Sketches. But no one can read any of his books
today without realizing that neither his heart nor his talent lay
in this direction. We do not need to know that, in his private
dealings with his contemporaries, he showed himself to be
as convictionless as a weathercock, quite as eager to run with
the hare as to hunt with the hounds; it is distressingly clear
in "On the Eve," "Smoke," and "Virgin Soil" that he only dealt
with his country's social problems out of a sense of duty. One
does not believe in his romantic radicals, or his caricatured
radicals either, for a minute; and his handling of the whole
political scene is superficial, amateurish, and unconvincing.

What Turgenev *could* do, and what he did do intermittently, was to write exquisite poetic-naturalistic love stories about exquisite but highly romanticized and perfumed young ladies. It is true that Chekhov found these scented young ladies quite intolerable—as he remarked, "all Turgenev's girls and women are insufferable in their artificiality, and—forgive my saying it—falsity. Liza and Elena are not Russian girls, but some sort of Pythian prophetesses, full of extravagant pretensions. . . . When one thinks of Tolstoy's Anna Karenina, all these young ladies of Turgenev's, with their seductive shoulders, fade away into nothing." That is perhaps a little severe; for Chekhov, with his aim to "paint life as it is, but beyond that—nothing at all," stood too far from Turgenev to be able to do him entire justice. Nevertheless, the stricture is valuable in its suggestion that the usual view of Turgenev as a great "realist" is not quite sound. More exactly, he was a psychological poet, a romantic and sentimentalist, who used prose narrative as his medium, and who, as he notably lacked inventive power, had recourse to copious and detailed documentation both as regards character and incident. The result is a very peculiar and charming blend of romance and realism, and an alternation, not so charming, of characterization (often extremely fine) with the flimsiest of caricature. And his lack of robust inventive power was compensated for by (if it did not actually induce) an economy which occasionally resulted in an exquisiteness of form almost unmatched in fiction.

One wishes a little that Mr. Yarmolinsky had sought, somewhat more than he does, the psychological roots of Turgenev's work in his life. Might he not, in this connection, have given us a few more of Turgenev's really admirable letters? And then there is Turgenev's mother, of whom we are given an astonishing portrait—a powerful Tartar of a woman, passionately and tyrannously devoted to her wayward son, barbaric, cruel, affectionate, terrifyingly intelligent, and endowed with an extraordinarily acute sense of character. This woman, one feels, had a lot to answer for in her son's attitude toward his country and toward his art. One almost feels, indeed, that she had a sort of greatness which her more gifted son only once or twice echoed—notably in his magnificent *Lear of the Steppes*. It is a remarkable woman who could address her son as "*ma chère fille, ma Jeannette*," who could call herself his "most tender father and friend," and who could write to him, while he was staying in Berne: "Your uncle is afraid that while in Berne you may commit *de l'inceste*. When he stayed in Berne

he was very friendly with the girls there, and that was sixteen
years ago."

WALEY, ARTHUR   (1919)

When, a little over a year ago, translations of Chinese poetry
began to appear over the signature of Arthur Waley, the
literary supplement of the London *Times* devoted a leader to
a panegyric of them and, among other things, predicted that
the whole course of occidental poetry might well and for
that matter might profitably be changed by this spiritual in-
vasion from the East. The writer in the *Times* was most struck
by the total absence, in Chinese poetry, of the literary artifices
which, for the last twenty-five centuries at any rate, have made
occidental poetry what it is. He was moved, as others have been,
by the bare simplicity of it, its stalwart and rugged adherence
to the homelier facts and truths, its contemplative naïveté, its
honesty, and its singularly charming blend of the implicit and
the explicit. These are, indeed, the conclusions which nine out of
ten readers of Mr. Waley's collection, *One Hundred and Seventy Chinese Poems*, might justifiably reach. Mr. Waley has
employed as his translation-medium, for the most part, a
free verse in which, despite his preface (he appears to consider
that he has kept the rhythm of the original), there is hardly a
trace of any sort of rhythm other than that of a well-felt prose.
But this is a fact which (after a few lines) one has completely
forgotten; for Mr. Waley has produced a book which, strictly
regarded as a piece of English literature, has a remarkable
beauty. As poetry one has little but praise for it. It is a clear
enough, and precious enough, addition to our English gamut.
If one has any quarrel with it at all, one quarrels with it as a
translation.

And here, I believe, there is some ground for thinking Mr.
Waley's book misleading. For, as noticed above in the case of
the writer in the London *Times*, most people will instantly
conclude, after reading these deliciously candid and straightforward free-verse poems, that Chinese poetry is a far simpler
and far less artificial affair than ours; and many who already
incline toward the less formal of poetic methods will employ
this as the final *coup de grace* in their argument against an art

of delicate elaboration. Their argument, of course, gains force with the publication of any successful book of free verse; but of the historical argument which Mr. Waley's book seems so completely to afford them they must be deprived. For Chinese poetry is not a poetry even remotely akin to free verse; and it is far from being artless.

As a matter of fact, little as one would gather it from Mr. Waley's preface, or from Judith Gautier's preface to *Chinese Lyrics from the Book of Jade,* or from Mr. Cranmer-Byng's preface to *A Lute of Jade*—all of which are in almost equal measure informative and confusing—Chinese poetry is perhaps more elaborately and studiously artificial (as distinguished from artless) than any other. The literary traditions are so powerful and inflexible as to be almost ritualistic. The forms are few and exactly prescribed, the rules many. When it is re-called that the Chinese language is entirely monosyllabic; that the variety of rhymes is small; that all words are, for the purposes of poetry, inflected as either flats or sharps (the in-flection for each word being fixed); and that Chinese poetry employs not only rhyme, and an exact number of syllables in each line, but that these syllables must follow a precise pat-tern in accordance with inflection (equivalent, in a degree, to our ictus), one begins to see how complex an art it is. A typical four-line stanza, for example, with seven words to a line, the caesura falling unalterably after the fourth word, and rhyming perhaps *a, a, b, a,* is as follows:

Flat flat sharp sharp	flat flat sharp
Sharp sharp flat flat	sharp sharp flat
Sharp sharp flat flat	flat sharp sharp
Flat flat sharp sharp	flat flat sharp

Almost all Chinese poetry of the great periods is stanzaic, and almost all of it is short, the quatrain and the poem of eight or twelve lines being the most common lengths. A few poets have essayed longer poems, some of them narrative—notably Po Chü I—but these are exceptions.

It is therefore with all these facts in mind that one should read the translations of Mr. Waley, or Mr. Cranmer-Byng; or Mr. Whitall's translations of the French versions by Judith Gautier. Of the three books, Mr. Waley's is distinctly the most comprehensive and from the literary point of view the most successful. The other two are usefully supplementary, however, for the reason that the Cranmer-Byng versions are for the

most part metrical and in rhyme, and serve somewhat to correct
one's impression that Chinese poetry is non-literary; and that
the Whitall book consists largely of love poems, the element in
which the other books are weakest. From the three volumes,
taken together, emerges the fact that Chinese poetry is among
the most beautiful that man has written. Artificial and elaborate
it may be as regards the mold into which it is cast; but, at
any rate as represented to us in Arthur Waley's book, it seems,
by contrast with most occidental poetry, poignantly simple
and human. How much of this we must credit to Mr. Waley we
cannot, of course, tell. We must remember that it is above all
else a poet's *art* which the Chinese set store by. A part of the
charm of this poetry, stripped of its art for us who are occidental, must inevitably be simply due to its combination
of the strange with the familiar, of the remote with the com-
prehensible. But one is tempted to go farther and to say that
Chinese poetry seems more than any other a cry from the bewildered heart of humanity. Sorrow is the most persistent note
in it—sorrow, or sorrowful resignation; sorrow for the inevitable partings of friends, sorrow for the home remembered
in exile, for the departure of youth, the futility of a great career,
the injustice of man, the loneliness of old age. The Freudians
will have something to explain in the remarkable infrequency
with which it deals with love between the sexes; it is friend-
ship which is most honored. And perhaps one is wrong in saying that these poems, even as given in the limpid free verse of
Mr. Waley, in delicately colloquial prose-rhythms, are altogether artless. The rhythm of ideas is clear; and that sort of dim
counterpoint which may be manifest in the thought itself is
not less apparent. Simple and homely as appear the details by
which these poets evoke a mood, simple and homely and prosaic as the mood itself may appear, it is when one attempts
retrospectively to reconstruct the steps by which any such
mood-poem was completed that one perceives how exquisitely
selective was the poet, with what patient fastidiousness he
searched for the clear qualities of things, and with what a
magical precision he found just that tone of restraint, almost of
matter-of-factness, which fairly whizzed with overtones. A popular form of Chinese poetry is the four-line poem called the
stop-short, in which the sense is supposed to continue after
the poem has stopped. But even in the longer poems that is almost universally the method. It is the hum of reverberations,
after the poem has been read, that is sought for. And even

such a narrative poem as Po Chü I's *Everlasting Wrong*, one of the famous "long" poems of the language (though it runs only to a few pages), is constructed in accordance with this instinct, and is, therefore, really a sequence of lyrics.

Does all this mean that Chinese poetry is profoundly unlike our own? Perhaps not, in theory. Restraint and understatement have always been characteristic of Anglo-Saxon poetry, though not to the same extent. It is in the sort of theme chosen that one feels the most profound divergence. Our own themes are apt to be sublimated and "literary," to some degree conventionalized, no matter how simple and colloquial may be the treatment. The themes of the Chinese poets are highly conventionalized—the same themes used over and over again—but they are essentially simple. *Sunt rerum lacrimae*—it is the pathos in things that the Chinese poets play upon, century after century; the inanimate things, the things of humble human use, the small utilities which we associate with lives simply lived, supply the medium through which Li Po or Po Chü I or T'ao Ch'ien pierce our hearts. One is struck by the childlike candor of this poetry: no detail is forbidden—as it would be in our poetry, perhaps—because it seems too prosaic; the sole question raised is as to its emotional appropriateness. Is it a comb, a fan, a torn dress, a curtain, a bed, an empty ricebin? It hardly seems to matter. The Chinese poet makes a heart-breaking poetry out of these quite as naturally as Keats did out of the song of a nightingale heard in a spring garden. It is rarely dithyrambic, rarely high-pitched: part of its charm is in its tranquillity, its self-control. And the humblest reads it with as much emotion as the most learned. . . . Was the writer in the London *Times* right, therefore, in thinking that this poetry might be a wholesome influence for our own? If it can teach our poets warmth and humanness—qualities in which American poets are singularly lacking—the answer must be an unqualified yes.

WILLIAMS, WILLIAM CARLOS   (1934)

It was high time Williams gave us some sort of *omnium gatherum;* and the volume now published by The Objectivist Press does a good deal, though not everything, to fill the gap—

it is a good collection, but not, I think, the best possible; and if it is enough to give the flavor of his delightful and peculiar genius (and to send the reader to the separate earlier books), nevertheless it does not, perhaps, give us his work at its finest and sharpest. That is a pity. One cannot but admire the cheerful integrity with which Williams has persistently and helpfully thrown in his lot with the "little" magazines, avoiding the organized ballyhoo of Big Time publishing; but this perverse honesty has had the unfortunate effect of restricting both his reputation and his influence. Too few people have read *Al Que Quiere* or *Kora in Hell*—they were obscurely published and poorly circulated; they are the best of Williams, and ought to be read; and their omission from the present collection, possibly owing to copyright difficulties, is much to be regretted. Perhaps, however, these early books will now be "discovered."

What strikes one afresh, in reading the *Collected Poems* (the work of the past decade) and in rereading the earlier books, is Williams' extraordinary consistency: from the outset he knew what he was about, knew what he wanted to do, and *why*. Like Eliot (who is in other respects his antithesis), he seems to have developed, simultaneously, a very individual style and a formidable critical awareness with which to defend it. Wallace Stevens, in a delightful preface to the present volume, analyzes something of this—he suggests slyly that Williams, despite his concern for the "antipoetic" and the real, is essentially a romantic—"the hermit who dwells alone with the sun and moon, but insists on taking a rotten newspaper." The sentimental underlies the antipoetic: the unreal underlies the real: the struggle, the energy, arises from the opposition. There is a good deal of truth in this. One has always the feeling about Williams that he *wants* to be more "poetic" than he is. With an extraordinary sense of the actual—whether tactile, olfactory, or visual—and a passionate love for it, in all its humblest quotidian forms, nevertheless he is forever checking himself in mid-praise—he suddenly remembers that he must not say too much, but "be mostly silent"; the color must come out, the image must be bare, the rhythm be reduced almost to that of prose. What remains is certainly the "opacity" which Pound said to Williams "saves your work." But there is also a conscious avoidance of *completeness*, whether of statement or of form—and this is a very important part of William's theory—which looks like an inverted sentimentalism; and which certainly sometimes defeats his purpose.

About the theory, Williams is pretty explicit. In *Kora in Hell* —a book which contains some of the keenest and most delightful of *aperçus* on contemporary aesthetic theory and practice—he observed acridly, fifteen years ago:

It is to the inventive imagination that we look for deliverance from every other misfortune as from the desolation of a flat Hellenic perfection of style. . . . The true value is that peculiarly which gives an object a character by itself. . . . The imagination goes from one thing to another. Given many things of nearly totally divergent natures, but possessing one-thousandth part of a quality in common, provided that be new, distinguished, these things belong in an imaginative category and not in a gross natural array. To me this is the gist of the whole matter. . . . But the thing that stands eternally in the way of really good writing is always one: the virtual impossibility of lifting to the imagination those things which lie under the direct scrutiny of the senses, close to the nose.

By the brokenness of his composition the poet makes himself master of a certain weapon which he could possess himself of in no other way. The speed of the emotions is sometimes such that . . . many matters are touched but not held, more often broken by the contact. . . . Thus a poem is tough by no quality it borrows from a logical recital of events nor from the events themselves but solely from that attenuated power which draws perhaps many broken things into a dance giving them thus full being.

Notice the *"flat Hellenic perfection of style"*—it is no wonder that Stevens said, "What strikes me most about the poems themselves is their casual character," or that he disliked their air as of a perpetual *beginningness!*

What Williams has been after, in short, is a rapid succession of images (things immediately apprehended by the senses) presented in naked succession, and in broken rhythm; with no strict or ordered development, nor luxurious elaboration at any given point; least of all, any literary "calculation." This was the theory: but actually, in practice, he has repeatedly, and happily, departed from it. In "History" and "The Wanderer" (*Al Que Quiere*) there is every evidence of firm elaboration of form, and rich associational thinking, though both are long poems: as a result of which they are perhaps the best things Williams has done, and certainly among the best poems of our time. (*En passant*, it is interesting to speculate on the influence of the very subtle rhythms of "History" on the poetry of its period.)

But there are also many shorter things almost as good—for the truth is, Williams is a poet in spite of himself. The rhythms won't be suppressed; nor will the color; nor will the fine animal gusto that everywhere vitalizes his work. He is frightfully and joyfully alive. And if he perhaps overdoes his "beginningness," his fear of classic statement or finish, and too much restricts his emotions to the "feeling" plane (or to what can be animally or behavioristically said), so that one must always think of his work rather in the aggregate than in the item, his dogged theory has at least one great merit: it keeps him young; and he is still, at the age of fifty, a promising poet—which is more than can be said of most of us.

WILLIAMS, WILLIAM CARLOS   (1951)

What a rich, sprawling, shirt-sleeved, or surgeon-jacketed, *omnium gatherum* of a man, or book, this is! And to say that it is precisely what one expected isn't, however, to say the half of it. For Williams has given us in this informal autobiography a book that must become indispensable to anyone interested in twentieth-century American poetry and especially in the earlier and yeastier period—say, up to 1925; but it is also, thanks to Williams's long intimacy with painting, and his intelligent concern about it, almost as valuable for those who are interested in American art—it flings a wider net than the merely literary. Add to this that it is the autobiography of a doctor, a pediatrician, and crammed, therefore, with the kindly but unshrinking observations of a devoted servant of the people, and what you get is a triple-threat *explicatio* which makes fascinating reading and raises a multitude of questions, many more than can be touched on in a review, much less answered. Is it, for example, a "good" autobiography, whether in the sense that it successfully performs the requisite office of *explicatio*, or that it has form, or style? A recent leader in *The Times Literary Supplement*, discussing the history of autobiography, reminds us that the Socratic "know thyself" was a command in which the difficulty was implicit; that truth is practically indefinable, in personal terms; and that the personal terms, moreover, are inextricably involved in those of the particular *Zeitgeist*. "The *Zeitgeist* offers a choice from one of a few conceptions of personality that are in the air; a man may realize one of them if he can. Education may make a Spartan, fashion turns out a Romantic, and the *enfant du siècle* may have a leaning for suicide or social justice without quite knowing why." Perhaps Williams fits best in the last of these categories. Definitely a child of the times, he wants social justice—it emerges importantly in his long poem, *Paterson,* even to the extent of echoing Pound in his animadversions on usury; but he wants, just as clearly, poetic justice, too.

And, of course, it is in his concern for poetic justice, both abstractly and for himself, that most of us will be primarily concerned. For Williams has had a unique position in America, and still has: he has gone his own way, and played his own game, in his lifelong battle against the "poetic," on the one hand, and against what he believes to be the deadening effect of tradition, on the other; he has come to a late flowering and eminence, and an influence, too, that must be a source of great satisfaction to him, and the more so as it is deserved. But here it is that those of us who are involved in the next development, and health, of poetry, step up to ask our questions as to the why and the how, and to see what answers we can find in this immensely crowded, if somewhat rambling and disproportioned, book. How did he get that way? How is it that he can describe the publication of *The Waste Land* as "the great catastrophe to our letters"? Why must he so persistently attack the universities, as inimical, and as breeders of a stultifying mortmain of traditionalism?

Well, the answers come slowly and confusedly, and, as it were, by osmosis, out of these discontinuous notes and recollections and observations—as they come, too, in a sense, out of the no doubt calculated homespunness and naturalness, the conversational style, of the book itself. Is there a fear, here, of the tremendous force of European literary tradition, and of the English tradition more particularly? And is this fear reinforced by his own—as he repeatedly admits—comparative lack of background, the lack of literary "education," for which, as he says, Pound has often reproached him? Together, these would make an ideal culture for the growth of an excessive individualism, or breaking of forms, on the one hand, and an excessive preoccupation with localism, and American localism, on the other. But although Williams discusses these matters at intervals, and sometimes at length, in his book, and provocatively—as in his comments on "objectivist" poetry, for instance, or "projective" verse—he is nowhere wholly, in an intellectual sense, convincing: his enthusiasms may be infectious, his destructions and dismissals hard-hitting and downright, as in his excommunication of the poor old sonnet: but he nowhere offers an aesthetic, or a poetic, that is inherently and satisfactorily *raisonnée*, to replace the traditional one that he attempts to destroy. We must go back, he says, to the "line": first the syllable, then the "line"; and what is the line? It is the breath, corresponds to the breath of the one who writes, of the man in the act of writing. This is an *affirmation mystique* with a vengeance: and isn't it, *tout court*, a prescription for anarchy, for formlessness, for a complete individualist "let-go"? For one man's breath is by no means another's; there will be no common measure here, and therefore no identifiable line; without a norm, comparison and value become chimerical: the doctor has thrown out the baby with the placenta. Nothing said, either, about effective values, or sound values, as transmitted through the eye from the page to the ear; only the placing of the "image on the page." Nothing about mnemonic values, again, which, arising through the sound effects, or sound affects, are of crucial importance and just as objective as any image. And while one may grant that poetry needs *sometimes* to be unmnemonic, and to glide, as it were, almost undetected, past eye and ear, in order that elsewhere the emphasis may be arresting, and at the right point in the poem; mustn't this point of arrest be brought about by exactly the sort of tension between meaning, form, and sound, a sudden white-hot integration of artifact—the meaning struggling to overcome the form, which has already been established as *there*, and as in a sense hostile—that will achieve the mnemonic quality which is the mark of true poetry? And wouldn't a poetry quite without mnemonic qualities be a contradiction in terms?

No, Williams fails to be altogether satisfactory about this, just as he fails to be satisfactory about that bothersome little question of the poet's need to employ the "local," his own *ambiente*, or backyard, and out of these to make his constructs of the universal. He seems, here, to miss the essential point, that the poet must perceive and select what *is* universal in the local, using only this, and not merely drag in the local for its own sweet, or sour, sake. He has himself, as we know, dedicated himself to a passionate use of the local, from his fine early poem, "The Wanderer," the ur-Paterson, to *Paterson* itself; and sometimes with triumph, but often with more inclusiveness than circumspection. It is his art that fails him: he doesn't know what to leave out; or, if he must put it in, as with the prose documentation of *Paterson*, how to anneal it into the fabric, or make it move with the theme: it remains there, insoluble, in indigestible lumps, extraneous to the often beautiful lyric movements that lie between. A fault analogous to that of *The Waste Land*, with its so unhappily externalized verbiform appendix.

But what saves him, what makes it good, is the love, the comprehensive, warm, animal, perhaps all-too-inclusive love, such as breathes in this new book: and not the formal pattern, whether in long-form or lyric notation, which too often suffers from an excess of this very virtue, that insatiable love of his that wants to get everything in. Isn't it perhaps just here that he gives away his secret reason for his dismay at Eliot's poem, and its "academics"? For here is an explosive concentrate of statement which was only made possible by the fact that Eliot, while a literary "sport," genetically speaking, was nevertheless inseparably linked with tradition, his genius at war with it, but compelled to speak in its terms; and it is out of such violent conflicts *within the tradition* that new forms, and new works of art, arise. *Paterson*, for instance, despite its nobility of aim and its undeniable richness, not to mention the value that lies in its perfect indigenousness, seems, by comparison, diffuse and uncompressed. As in Crane's *Bridge*, the conceptual cables are neither strong enough nor evident enough to hold up, or keep in line, so much that is no doubt locally or personally relevant, and therefore ultimately explicable, but that, lacking such support and direction, tends to appear casual or meaningless, and to fall into separate, if beautiful, parts. Here, had Williams not fled from it so far into the American wilderness, tradition might have saved him.

Or may we be wrong? And will this turn out to be his Columbiad, his landfall? Whatever the answer to that, this autobiography is an invaluable document for any attempt to understand and appraise his work, and the work of his contemporaries; and it is a treasure if only as a contribution to Americana. The sections on Paris, in that great make-heyday, are an admirable extension of Cowley's notes on the subject. And the description of childhood is alone worth the price of admission, one of the best ever.

When Jonson remarked, of Shakespeare's never having blotted a line, that he wished to God he had blotted a thousand, he was indicating, perhaps deliberately, the two archetypes of poet, the two sorts of poet who, between them, have divided the realm of man's consciousness from the childhood of the race down to the present day. He must have been aware, too, that in his great rival and himself the two types were almost perfectly embodied. Not quite: one could easily enough, for another purpose, summon up the exceptions. But mainly it is true: for Jonson is the craftsman, the artist, the expert manipulator, the lapidary, the man of good sense, the carver and maker, the worker from outside in; whereas Shakespeare, working rather from the inside out, reckless, prodigal, uncontrolled, was a kind of magnificent debauchee of poetry, as much ridden by his *daimon* as riding it. Not for the artist the "first fine *careless* rapture"—that one word careless is enough, for him, to condemn it. No, the mark of the artist, or the would-be artist, is always precisely to be seen in his constant care, not to say his caution. The *curiosa felicitas* is of course what he aims at—the *careful* felicity; it is a kind of excellent coolness, the argentine soberly preferred to the aureate; there must not be too much heat; and, instead, a satisfying suggestion as of an everywhere extending and always reasoned control.

Admirable aims, without any question; and it can be said flatly that it is the poets of this line who keep poetry in order. These—like Matthew and Waldo, in Mr. Eliot's poem—are the army of unalterable law. But just the same, along with all this excellent control and this muscular and sustaining discipline (qualities too little esteemed by Americans) often goes too a perhaps depressing sense of limits, and no less limiting and limited because deliberate. Particularly is this true of the scholar-poet—Matthew Arnold is of course the best example—for here the limits are precise and express. The discipline, whether of form or idea, is obvious enough, and it is good as far as it goes; at its best, it produces a sort of negative purity, a mild decorousness: it is thoughtful, and it tries to be exact. The trouble with it is that it cannot understand or accept exuberance, either in image or word, that it is morally afraid of *sound*, with all its prosodic and linguistic implications, and that above all it dares not try for intensity or simplicity because it im-

agines these to be sentimental. In fact, it really tends to avoid
the properly "poetic" field, which it considers a little too vulgar
and easy, and to employ rather the method of the essay, the
critical essay. Statement, analysis, conclusion—the method, it
will be seen, is anti-orgastic in the extreme. The poet is wholly
safe, he runs no risk of embarrassment.

And Mr. Yvor Winters is a good specimen of this kind of
poet, all complete, too, with his defensive argument. In the
notes to his poems, explicitly and perhaps a shade preten-
tiously, he makes it quite clear that he avoids and dislikes that
quality in poetry which most people would call magic. That is
not what Mr. Winters calls it—he prefers to call it "de-intellec-
tualized sensibility." How, exactly, does one de-intellectualize
sensibility? And can the process be reversed? One wonders!
Mr. Winters describes one of his poems, "Nocturne," as "another example of material cohering by virtue of feeling and
rhythmic structure, and very little by virtue of intelligible theme.
If a poem of this sort were to be regarded as a true portrait
of a state of mind, it would indicate madness on the part of
the author; it is of course a literary method by means of which
certain elements of consciousness are isolated arbitrarily, as by
a sieve. Unfortunately, as a spiritual exercise, this sort of thing
can hardly lead toward intelligence . . ." and so on.

Well, the truth is one hardly likes to think of poetry as a
spiritual "exercise," nor does one much wonder, when reading
a poem, whether it will lead toward intelligence, though indeed
in some instances it may. The whole attitude here strikes one
as fundamentally wrong, and as conceptually withering, if only
because it begins with so airy an exorcism of the very *voice*
of poetry. "Nocturne," the little poem of which Mr. Winters
disapproves, is in point of fact not a particularly good poem,
since it lacks form; but it is poetic, because it has plenty of
feeling-tone, or affect; and it is certainly not noticeably inferior
to those later poems which Mr. Winters prefers because they
have an "idea." What are these precious ideas? Without explanatory notes, they do not emerge: with them, they seem a
little arbitrary and of no great significance. When these later
poems are effective—as, for instance, "Sonnet to the Moon,"
"A Vision," "The Journey," "Sir Gawaine and the Green Night"
—they are effective because they have *poetic* meaning, not because on chemical analysis they render up some little surd of
a concept. And no amount of concept, no amount of scholarly
care or caution, can replace that sort of poetic meaning which

is the genius of language and the genius of awareness in creative synthesis. This kind of meaning embraces all others.

WOOLF, VIRGINIA   (1927)

Among contemporary writers of fiction, Mrs. Woolf is a curious and anomalous figure. In some respects, she is as "modern," as radical, as Mr. Joyce or Miss Richardson or M. Jules
Romains; she is a highly self-conscious examiner of consciousness, a bold and original experimenter with the technique of
novel-writing; but she is also, and just as strikingly, in other
respects "old-fashioned." This anomaly does not defy analysis.
The aroma of "old-fashionedness" that rises from these highly
original and modern novels—from the pages of *Jacob's Room,
Mrs. Dalloway,* and now again from those of *To the Lighthouse*—is a quality of attitude; a quality, to use a word which
is itself nowadays old-fashioned, but none the less fragrant, of
spirit. For in this regard, Mrs. Woolf is no more modern than
Jane Austen: she breathes the same air of gentility, of sequestration, of tradition; of life and people and things all brought,
by the slow polish of centuries of tradition and use, to a pervasive refinement in which discrimination, on every conceivable
plane, has become as instinctive and easy as the beat of a wing.
Her people are "gentle" people; her houses are the houses of
gentlefolk; and the consciousness that informs both is a consciousness of well-being and culture, of the richness and luster
and dignity of tradition; a disciplined consciousness, in which
emotions and feelings find their appropriate attitudes as easily
and naturally—as *habitually,* one is tempted to say—as a skilled
writer finds words.

It is this tightly circumscribed choice of scene—to use "scene"
in a social sense—that gives to Mrs. Woolf's novels, despite
her modernity of technique and insight, their odd and delicious
air of parochialism, as of some small village-world, as bright
and vivid and perfect in its tininess as a miniature: a small
complete world which time has somehow missed. Going into
these houses, one would almost expect to find antimacassars
on the chair-backs and daguerreotype albums on the tables.
For these people—these Clarissa Dalloways and Mrs. Ram-
says and Lily Briscoes—all are vibrantly and saturatedly con-

scious of background. And they all have the curious innocence that accompanies that sort of awareness. They are the creatures of seclusion, the creatures of shelter; they are exquisite beings, so perfectly and elaborately adapted to their environment that they have taken on something of the roundness and perfection of works of art. Their life, in a sense, is a sea-pool life; unruffled and secret: almost, if we can share the cool illusion of the sea-pool's occupants, inviolable. They hear rumors of the sea itself, that vast and terrifying force that lies somewhere beyond them, or around them, but they cherish a sublime faith that it will not disturb them; and if it does, at last, break in upon them with cataclysmic force, a chaos of disorder and undisciplined violence, they can find no language for the disaster: they are simply bewildered.

But if, choosing such people and such a *mise en scène* for her material, Mrs. Woolf inevitably makes her readers think of *Pride and Prejudice* and *Mansfield Park*, she compels us just as sharply, by her method of evoking them, to think of *Pilgrimage* and *Ulysses* and *The Death of a Nobody*. Mrs. Woolf is an excellent critic, an extremely conscious and brilliant craftsman in prose; she is intensely interested in the technique of fiction; and one has at times wondered, so vividly from her prose has arisen a kind of *self-consciousness* of adroitness, whether she might not lose her way and give us a mere series of virtuosities or *tours de force*. It is easy to understand why Katherine Mansfield distrusted "Mr. Bennett and Mrs. Brown." She felt a kind of sterility in this dexterous holding of the raw stuff of life at arm's length, this playing with it as if it were a toy. Why not be more immediate—why not surrender to it? And one did indeed feel a rather baffling aloofness in this attitude: it was as if Mrs. Woolf were a little afraid to come to grips with anything so coarse, preferred to see it through a safe thickness of plate-glass. It was as if she could not be quite at ease with life until she had stilled it, reduced it to the mobile immobility of art—reduced it, even, to such comfortable proportions and orderliness as would not disturb the drawing-room. In *Jacob's Room*, however, and *Mrs. Dalloway*, Mrs. Woolf began to make it clear that this tendency to sterile dexterity, though pronounced, might not be fatal; and now, in her new novel, *To the Lighthouse*, she relieves one's doubts, on this score, almost entirely.

For, if one still feels, during the first part of this novel almost depressingly, and intermittently thereafter, Mrs. Woolf's irritat-

ing air as of carrying an enormous technical burden: her air of
saying "See how easily I do this!" or "This is incomparably
complex and difficult, yet I have the brains for it": nevertheless,
one's irritation is soon lost in the growing sense that Mrs. Woolf
has at last found a complexity and force of theme which is
commensurate with the elaborateness and self-consciousness of
her technical "pattern." By degrees, one forgets the manner in
the matter. One resists the manner, petulantly objects to it,
in vain: the moment comes when at last one ceases to be aware
of something persistently artificial in this highly feminine style,
and finds oneself simply immersed in the vividness and actuality of this world of Mrs. Woolf's—believing in it, in fact,
with the utmost intensity, and feeling it with that completeness
of surrender with which one feels the most moving of poetry.
It is not easy to say whether this abdication of "distance" on
the reader's part indicates that Mrs. Woolf has now achieved a
depth of poetic understanding, a vitality, which was somehow
just lacking in the earlier novels, or whether it merely indicates
a final triumph of technique. Can one profitably try to make
a distinction between work that is manufactured, bitterly and
strenuously, by sheer *will* to imagination, and work that is
born of imagination all complete—assuming that the former is,
in the upshot, just as convincing as the latter? Certainly one
feels everywhere in Mrs. Woolf's work this will to imagine,
this canvassing of possibilities by a restless and searching and
brilliant mind: one feels this mind at work, matching and
selecting, rejecting this color and accepting that, saying, "It is
this that the heroine would say, it is this that she would think";
and nevertheless Mrs. Woolf's step is so sure, her choice is so
nearly invariably right, and her imagination, even if deliberately willed, is so imaginative, that in the end she makes a
beautiful success of it. She makes her Mrs. Ramsay—by giving
us her stream of consciousness—amazingly alive; and she sup-
plements this just sufficiently, from *outside*, as it were, by
giving us also, intermittently, the streams of consciousness of
her husband, of her friend Lily Briscoe, of her children: so
that we are documented, as to Mrs. Ramsey, from every
quarter and arrive at a solid vision of her by a process of
triangulation. The richness and copiousness and ease, with
which this is done, are a delight. These people are astoundingly
real: they belong to a special "class," as Mrs. Woolf's characters nearly always do, and exhale a Jane-Austenish aroma of
smallness and lostness and incompleteness: but they are mag-

nificently real. We live in that delicious house with them—we
feel the minute textures of their lives with their own vivid
senses—we imagine with their extraordinary imaginations, are
self-conscious with their self-consciousness—and ultimately we
know them as well, as terribly, as we know ourselves.

Thus, curiously, Mrs. Woolf has rounded the circle. Apparently, at the outset of her work, avoiding any attempt to present
life "immediately," as Chekhov and Katherine Mansfield preferred to do; and choosing instead a medium more sophisticated and conscious, as if she never for a moment wished us
to forget the *frame* of the picture, and the fact that the picture
was a picture; she has finally brought this method to such
perfection, or so perfectly allowed it to flower of itself, that
the artificial has become natural, the mediate has become immediate. The technical brilliance glows, melts, falls away; and
there remains a poetic apprehension of life of extraordinary
loveliness. Nothing happens, in this houseful of odd nice people,
and yet all of life happens. The tragic futility, the absurdity,
the pathetic beauty, of life—we experience all of this in our
sharing of seven hours of Mrs. Ramsay's wasted or not wasted
existence. We have seen, through her, the world.

WOOLF, VIRGINIA (1929)

That Mrs. Woolf is a highly ingenious writer has been made
glitteringly obvious for us in *Mrs. Dalloway* and *To the Lighthouse:* which is not in the least to minimize the fact that those
two novels also contained a great deal of beauty. That she is,
and has perhaps always been, in danger of carrying ingenuity
too far, is suggested, among other things, by her new novel,
or "biography," *Orlando*. Whatever else one thinks about this
book, one is bound to admit that it is exceedingly, not to say
disconcertingly, clever. In England as well as in America it
has set the critics by the ears. They have not known quite how
to take it—whether to regard it as a biography, or a satire on
biography; as a history, or as a satire on history; as a novel,
or as an allegory. And it is at once clear, when one reads
Orlando, why this confusion should have arisen; for the tone
of the book, from the very first pages, is a tone of mockery.
Mrs. Woolf has expanded a *jeu d'esprit* to the length of a novel.

One might almost say, in fact—when one notes in the index that there are precisely seven references to "The Oak" (a poem which plays an important part in the story—and which in a sense is almost its ghostly protagonist) and when one re-calls that Knole, a famous English house, is at Sevenoaks (clearly the house described in the novel)—that *Orlando* is a kind of colossal pun. More exactly, one might compare it with *Alice in Wonderland;* for if the latter is an inspired dream, organized with a logic almost insanely unswerving, so the former is a kind of inspired joke, a joke charged with meanings, in which the logic, if not quite so meticulous, is at any rate press-ing.

There is thus an important element of "spoof" in *Orlando:* Mrs. Woolf apparently wants us to know that she does not her-self take the thing with the least seriousness—that she is pulling legs, keeping her tongue in her cheek, and winking, now and then, a quite shameless and enormous wink. With all this, which she accomplishes with a skill positively equestrian, she is obliged, perforce, to fall into a style which one cannot help feeling is a little unfortunate. It is a style which makes fun of style: it is glibly rhetorical, glibly sententious, glibly poetic, glibly analytical, glibly austere, by turns—deliberately so; and, while this might be, and is, extraordinarily diverting for a chapter or two, or for something like the length of a short story, one finds it a little fatiguing in a full-length book. Of course, Mrs. Woolf's theme, with its smug annihilation of time, may be said to have demanded, if the whole question of credibility was to be begged, a tone quite frankly and elabo-rately artificial. Just the same, it is perhaps questionable whether she has not been *too* icily and wreathedly elaborate in this, and taken her *Orlando* in consequence a shade too far toward an arid and ingenuous convention. Granted that what she wanted to tell us was a fable, or allegory: that she wanted to trace the aesthetic evolution of a family (and by implication that of a country) over a period of three hundred years: and that she had hit upon the really first-rate idea of embodying this racial evolution in one undying person: need she quite so much have presumed on our incredulity? One suspects that in such a situation an ounce of ingenuousness might be worth ten times its weight in ingenuity; and that a little more of the direct and deep sincerity of the last few pages, which are really beautiful and really moving, might have made *Orlando* a minor masterpiece.

As it is, it is an extremely amusing and brilliant *tour de force*. It is as packed with reference, almost, as *The Waste Land*. Some of the references, it is true, are too esoteric—for one not in the enchanted circle—to be universally valid; and this may or may not be thought a mistake. One's private jokes and innuendos are pretty apt to become meaningless with the passage of time and the disappearance of the *milieu* which gave them point. This, again, is of a piece with Mrs. Woolf's general air of high spirits; of having a lark; of going, as it were, on an intellectual spree; and that there is far too little of this spirit in contemporary literature we can cheerfully admit. But here too one feels inclined to enter a protest. For the idea, as has been said, is first-rate, an idea from which a poet might have evoked a profusion of beauty as easily as the djinn was released from his bottle. Mrs. Woolf does indeed give us a profusion of beauty and wisdom: but it is beauty and wisdom of a very special sort. Her roses are cloth roses, her scenes are scenes from a tapestry, her "wisdom" (that is, her shrewd and very feminine comments on men and things) has about it an air of florid and cynical frigidity, a weariness wrought into form; as if—to change the image—she were stringing for her own entertainment a necklace of beautifully polished platitudes. If only—one thinks—she could have brought an Elizabethan freshness to this admirable theme—if she could have worked her mine a little deeper, a little more honestly, a little less for diversion's sake, and a little more for poetry's; and if, finally, she were not quite so civilized, in the Kensington Gardens sense of the word, or so burdened with sophistication, or could admit now and then, if only for a moment, a glimpse into the sheer horror of things, the chaos that yawns under Bloomsbury—but then this book would not have been the charming *jeu d'esprit* that it is; it would have been something else.

CHECKLIST OF CONRAD AIKEN'S
CRITICAL WRITINGS

Note: Asterisks (*) are placed before pieces that were reprinted in
Scepticisms (1919), and squares (■) before those appearing in the
present collection. (Not all, in either case, were reprinted in full.) I
have omitted Conrad Aiken's undergraduate contributions to the
Harvard Advocate, his "London Letters" in the *New Yorker* that do
not bear on literature, and the prefaces and notes to his own books
of poetry. The checklist by R. W. Stallman in *Wake 11* (1952) has
been useful to me, as has the information supplied by George M.
Hall, Margaret Southworth, and of course Mr. Aiken himself. The
list, finally, aspires to, but does not claim, infallibility.

R. A. B.

1915

"The Place of Imagism," *New Republic*, 3 (22 May), 75-76.

"Limits to Imagism," *New Republic*, 3 (26 June), 204-205.

"Imagism or Myopia" (*Some Imagist Poets;* John Gould Fletcher,
Irradiations), *Poetry Journal*, 3 (July), 233-241.

"Fertilizing Poetry" (editorial), *Poetry Journal*, 4 (September),
31-34.

"Prizes and Anthologies" (William Stanley Braithwaite and Harriet
Monroe), *Poetry Journal*, 4 (November), 95-100.

"Rupert Brooke" (*Collected Poems*), *Poetry Journal*, 4 (December),
169-171.

1916

"Looking Pegasus in the Mouth" (William Stanley Braithwaite and
Amy Lowell), *Poetry Journal*, 5 (February), 20-28.

"The Declining Masefield" (John Masefield, *Good Friday and Other
Poems*), *Poetry Journal*, 5 (March), 74-77.

■ "Esoteric Catholicity" (Ezra Pound, ed., *Catholic Anthology*),
Poetry Journal, 5 (April), 127-129.

"Illusory Freedom in Poetry," *Poetry Journal*, 5 (May), 184-191.

"The Impersonal Poet," *Poetry Journal*, 6 (December), 63-66.

1917

* "Poetic Realism" (Carl Sandburg, *Chicago Poems*), *Poetry Journal*,
6 (January), 117-121.

■ "Schisophrenia" (Conrad Aiken, *Nocturne of Remembered Spring*),
Chicago News, 23 January, p. 10.

(Henry B. Fuller, *Lines Long and Short*), *Chicago News*, 21 February, p. 11.

* "Poetry in America" (William Stanley Braithwaite, ed., *Anthology
of Magazine Verse, 1916*), *Dial*, 62 (8 March), 179-182.

(Wilfred W. Gibson, *Livelihood: Dramatic Reviews*), *Chicago News*, 14 March, p. 9.

* (Alan Seeger, *Poems*), *Chicago News*, 28 March, p. 11.

(Louis Untermeyer, *Poems of Heine* (trans.) and *These Times*), *Chicago News*, 11 April, p. 11.

"Forslin and Freud," *Reedy's Mirror*, 26 (20 April), 273.

"Uninspired Echolalia" (Odell Shepard, *A Lonely Flute*), *Chicago News*, 25 April, p. 11.

"The Monroe Doctrine in Poetry" (Alice Corbin Henderson and Harriet Monroe, eds., *The New Poetry: An Anthology*), *Dial*, 62 (3 May), 389-390.

(*Some Imagist Poets, 1917*), *Chicago News*, 30 May, p. 4.

"Poetry Without Magic" (Alice Brown, *The Road to Castaly;* Orrick Johns, *Asphalt and Other Poems;* E. A. Mackintosh, *A Highland Regiment;* Odell Shepard, *A Lonely Flute;* J. C. Squire, *Twelve Poems;* Clement Wood, *Glad of Earth;* Louis Untermeyer, *These Times;* "X," *War Poems*), *Dial*, 63 (31 May), 475-477.

* "A Protean Muse" (John Curtis, *War Flames;* Samuel Hoffenstein, *Life Sings a Song;* John Masefield, *Lollingdon Downs;* George Woodberry, *Ideal Passion*), *Dial*, 63 (19 July), 55-57.

* "Three English Poets" (Walter de la Mare, *Peacock Pie;* Ralph Hodgson, *Poems;* Harold Monro, *Strange Meetings*), *Dial*, 63 (30 August), 150-152.

* "Poetry as Supernaturalism" (William Stanley Braithwaite, ed., *The Poetic Year for 1916: A Critical Anthology*), *Dial*, 63 (13 September), 202-203.

"The Female Cry" (Sara Teasdale, ed., *Love Lyrics: 100 Love Poems by Women*), *Chicago News*, 10 October, p. 13.

* "Divers Realists" (William Aspenwall Bradley, *Old Christmas;* T. S. Eliot, *Prufrock and Other Observations;* John Erskine, *The Shadowed Hour;* Wilfred W. Gibson, *Collected Poems*), *Dial*, 63 (8 November), 453-455. Page on Eliot reprinted in *T. S. Eliot: A Selected Critique,* ed. Leonard Unger, New York, Rinehart, 1948, p. 3.

* "Nightingales and Mocking Birds" (Vachel Lindsay, *The Chinese Nightingale and Other Poems*), *Chicago News*, 14 November, p. 12.

* "Confectionary and Caviar" (Theodosia Garrison, *The Dreamers and Other Poems;* Joyce Kilmer, *Main Street and Other Poems;* John Cowper Powys, *Mandragora;* Edward Bliss Reed, *Sea-Moods;* William Carlos Williams, *Al Que Quiere*), *Dial*, 63 (22 November), 513-515.

* (Amy Lowell, *Tendencies in Modern American Poetry*), *Chicago News*, 28 November, p. 13.

* ■ "The Mechanism of Poetic Inspiration" (Nicolas Kostyleff, *Le Mécanisme Cérébrale de la Pensée*), *North American Review*, 206 (December), 917-924.

1918

* ■ "The New Curiosity Shop—and a Poet" (Alfred Kreymborg, ed., *Others: An Anthology of the New Verse;* Jean de Boschère, *The Closed Door*, trans. F. S. Flint), *Dial*, 64 (31 January), 111-113.

"Yet Once More, O Ye Laurels!" (William Stanley Braithwaite, ed., *Anthology of Magazine Verse: 1917*), *Dial* 64 (28 February), 195-197.

"A Note on Blurbs" (Christopher Morley, *Songs for a Little House*), *Chicago Tribune*, 23 March, p. 8.

* "Poets as Reporters" (George Herbert Clark, ed., *A Treasury of War Poetry;* Richard Butler Glaenzer, *Beggar and King;* Christopher Morley, *Songs for a Little House;* W. R. Wheeler, ed., *A Book of Verse of the Great War;* Edith Wyatt, *The Wind in the Corn*), *Dial*, 64 (11 April), 351-353.

■ "Our Steamshovel Poet" (Edgar Lee Masters, *Towards the Gulf*), *Chicago Tribune*, 13 April, p. 10.

"The Deterioration of Poets" (Wilfred W. Gibson, *Hill Tracks;* Ralph Hodgson, *The Last Blackbird;* Alice Meynell, *A Father of Women;* Max Plowman, *A Lap Full of Seed;* Siegfried Sassoon, *The Old Huntsman;* J. C. Squire, *The Lily of Malud;* Edward Thomas, *Poems*), *Dial*, 64 (25 April), 403-405.

* "The Two Magics" (Edgar Lee Masters, *Towards the Gulf*), *Dial*, 64 (9 May), 447-449.

* "Narrative Poetry and the Vestigial Lyric" (Francis Carlin, *My Ireland;* James Joyce, *Chamber Music;* Frederic Manning, *Eidola;* John Masefield, *Rosas;* Robert Nichols, *Ardours and Endurances;* Algernon Charles Swinburne, *Posthumous Poems*), *Dial*, 65 (18 July), 70-71.

* "The Return of Romanticism" (William Rose Benét, *The Burglar of the Zodiac;* Walter de la Mare, *Motley;* John Gould Fletcher, *Japanese Prints*), *Dial*, 65 (5 September), 165-167.

* "The Mortality of Magic" (Robert Graves, *Fairies and Fusiliers;* Roy Helton, *Outcasts in Beulah Land*), *Dial*, 65 (19 September), 214-215.

* "A Pointless Pointillist" (Ezra Pound, *Pavannes and Divisions*), *Dial*, 65 (19 October), 306-307.

* "The Technique of Polyphonic Prose" (Amy Lowell, *Can Grande's Castle*), *Dial*, 65 (2 November), 346-348.

* "The Function of Rhythm" (Ford Madox Hueffer, *On Heaven*), *Dial*, 65 (16 November), 417-418.

■ "A Poet's Dream" (Conrad Aiken), *Chicago News*, 4 December, p. 12.

1919

"Baedecker Descries Parnassus" (William Lyon Phelps, *The Advance of English Poetry in the Twentieth Century*), *New Republic*, 17 (25 January), 379-380.

* "The Literary Abbozzo" (Lola Ridge, *The Ghetto*), *Dial*, 66 (25 January), 83-84.

(William Lyon Phelps, *The Advance of English Poetry in the Twentieth Century*), *Chicago News*, 19 February, p. 12.

* "Possessor and Possessed" (John Gould Fletcher, *The Tree of Life*), *Dial*, 66 (22 February), 189-191.

* "Vox—et Praeterea?" (Maxwell Bodenheim, *Minna and Myself*), *Dial*, 66 (5 April), 356-357.

(Arthur Symons, *The Symbolist Movement in Literature*), *Chicago News*, 30 April, p. 12.

* "The Ivory Tower—I" (Louis Untermeyer, *The New Era in American Poetry*), *New Republic*, 19 (10 May), 58-60.

"Dam Up Your Libido! Be a Poet!" (Albert Mordell, *The Erotic Motive in Literature*), *Chicago News*, 14 May, p. 12.

■ "Counterpoint and Implication" (Conrad Aiken, *The Charnel Rose*), *Poetry*, 14 (June), 152-159. Reprinted in *Conrad Aiken: Collected Poems*, New York, Oxford, 1953, pp. 873-877.

* ■ "Sunt Rerum Lacrymae" (Arthur Waley, trans., *One Hundred and Seventy Chinese Lyrics*), *Dial*, 67 (12 July), 23-24.

"Who's Who" (Conrad Aiken), *Chicago Tribune*, 19 July, p. 9.

* "The Melodic Line" (D. H. Lawrence, *Look! We Have Come Through!*), *Dial*, 67 (9 August), 97-100.

* "Letters from America. I. Philosophy for the Flute" (Alfred Kreymborg, *Plays for Poem-Mimes*), *Athenaeum*, 10 October, pp. 1003-1004.

"Miss Lowell Abides Our Question" (Amy Lowell, *Pictures of the Floating World*), *Dial*, 67 (18 October), 331-333.

■ "The Moorish Arabesque" (George Moore, *Avowals*), *Chicago News*, 22 October, p. 13.

(Answer to James Oppenheim on "Miss Lowell Abides Our Question"), *Dial*, 67 (15 November), 447-448.

■ "Letters from America. II. Two American Novelists" (James Branch Cabell, *Jurgen;* Joseph Hergesheimer, *Linda Condon*), *Athenaeum*, 12 December, pp. 1339-1340.

"Foreword" to *Two Wessex Tales by Thomas Hardy*, Boston, Four Seas Company, pp. 7-9.

Scepticisms: Notes on Contemporary Poetry, New York, Alfred A. Knopf.

1920

"Two Views of Contemporary Poetry" (John Livingston Lowes, *Convention and Revolt in Poetry;* Louis Untermeyer, *The New Era in American Poetry*), *Yale Review*, 8 (January), 413-416.

■ "Letters from America. III. The Lucifer Brothers in Starlight" (Brooks Adams, *The Emancipation of Massachusetts;* Henry Adams, *The Degradation of the Democratic Dogma*), *Athenaeum*, 20 February, pp. 243-244.

"Body and Raiment" (Eunice Tietjens, *Body and Raiment* and *Profiles from China*), *Poetry*, 15 (February), 272-277.

"Idiosyncrasy and Tradition" (Francis Ledwidge, *Complete Poems*), *Dial*, 68 (March), 376-380.

"American Poetry" (John Gould Fletcher, *The Monthly Chapbook*, May, 1920: *Some Contemporary American Poets*), *Athenaeum*, 9 July, p. 47.

1921

■ "The Scientific Critic" (T. S. Eliot, *The Sacred Wood*), *Freeman*, 2 (2 March), 593-594.

■ "A Poet of the Actual" (Anton Chekhov, *The Schoolmistress, and Other Stories*), *Freeman*, 3 (6 April), 90-92.

■ "The Short Story as Poetry" (Katherine Mansfield, *Bliss, and Other Stories*), *Freeman*, 3 (11 May), 210-211.

"A Letter from America" (on the state of modern American poetry), *London Mercury*, 4 (June), 197-199.

■ "Colourism in Poetry" (John Gould Fletcher, *Breakers and Granite*), *Freeman*, 3 (6 July), 405-406.

■ "A Letter from America" (Henry James and American Criticism), *London Mercury*, 4 (September), 530-531.

■ "The Poetry of Mr. E. A. Robinson" (*Avon's Harvest*), *Freeman*, 4 (21 September), 43-46.

■ "Symphonies in the Psychotic" (Feodor Dostoevsky, *The Friend of the Family*), *Freeman*, 4 (28 December), 378-379.

1922

"A Letter from America" (Harold E. Stearns, ed., *Civilization in the United States*), *London Mercury*, 5 (February), 416-418.

"The New Elizabethans" (W. H. Davies, *The Captive Lion*; John Masefield, *King Cole*; Edgar Lee Masters, *The Open Sea*; Charlotte Mew, *Saturday Market*; Edna St. Vincent Millay, *Second April*; Edwin Arlington Robinson, *Collected Poems*; Anna Wickham, *The Contemplative Quarry*; Elinor Wylie, *Nets to Catch the Wind*), *Yale Review*, 11 (April), 632-636.

■ "A Letter from America" (Edwin Arlington Robinson), *London Mercury*, 6 (June), 196-198.

■ "The Short Story as Colour" (Katherine Mansfield, *The Garden Party*), *Freeman*, 5 (21 June), 357-358.

■ "The Analysis of Poetry" (Frederick Clarke Prescott, *The Poetic Mind*), *New Republic*, 31 (19 July), 222-224.

"Sludgery" (Robert Graves, *On English Poetry*), *New Republic*, 32 (22 November), 340-341.

"Poetry," in *Civilization in the United States*, ed. Harold E. Stearns, New York, Harcourt, pp. 215-226.

"Preface," *Modern American Poets*, selected by Conrad Aiken, London, Martin Secker, pp. v-viii. Reprinted (with small changes) in *Modern American Poets*, New York, 1927.

1923

■ "An Anatomy of Melancholy" (T. S. Eliot, *The Waste Land*), *New Republic*, 33 (7 February), 294-295. Reprinted in *Wake 11* ("Conrad Aiken Number"), New York, Wake Editions, 1952, pp. 20-25.
■ "A Basis for Criticism," *New Republic*, 34 (11 April, Spring Book Section), 1-6.
"The Dostoevsky Myth" (*Dostoevsky: Letters and Reminiscences,* trans. S. S. Koteliansky and J. Middleton Murry), *Spectator*, 23 June, pp. 1045-1046. (Unsigned.)
"The Short Story as Confession" (Katherine Mansfield, *The Dove's Nest, and Other Stories*), *Nation & Athenaeum*, 33 (14 July), 490. Same review in *New Republic*, 35 (8 August), 307, 309.
"Dostoevsky and the Downfall of Europe" (Hermann Hesse, *In Sight of Chaos*, trans. Stephen Hudson), *Spectator*, 11 August, p. 196.
■ "The Higher Vaudeville" (Vachel Lindsay, *Collected Poems*), *Nation & Athenaeum*, 33 (15 September), 747.

1924

■ "American Literature and American Critics" (*A Short History of American Literature*, ed. William P. Trent, John Erskine, Stuart P. Sherman, and Carl Van Doren), *Nation & Athenaeum*, 34 (22 March), 891.
■ "Emily Dickinson," *Dial*, 76 (April), 301-308. Reprinted as "Preface" to *Selected Poems of Emily Dickinson*, ed. Conrad Aiken, London, Jonathan Cape, pp. 5-22.
■ "Mr. Hardy's 'Philosophy' " (Ernest Brennecke, *Thomas Hardy's Universe*), *Nation & Athenaeum*, 35 (24 May), 264.
■ "Disintegration in Modern Poetry" (D. H. Lawrence, *Birds, Beasts, and Flowers*), *Dial*, 76 (June), 535-540.
(Sacheverell Sitwell, *Southern Baroque Art*), *Criterion*, 2 (July), 486-489.
■ "Mr. Lawrence: Sensationalist" (D. H. Lawrence, *Studies in Classic American Literature*), *Nation & Athenaeum*, 35 (12 July), 482.
(Gilbert Seldes, *The Seven Lively Arts*), *Criterion*, 3 (October), 148-150.
(Osbert Sitwell, *Triple Fugue*), *Criterion*, 3 (October), 141-144.
■ "Metaphysics and Art" (Benedetto Croce, *European Literature in the Nineteenth Century*), *Nation & Athenaeum*, 36 (11 October), 56. Same review in *New Republic*, 40 (19 November), 301-302.

1925

■ "A Scientific Approach to Criticism" (I. A. Richards, *Principles of Literary Criticism*), *Nation & Athenaeum*, 36 (24 January), 585-586. Same review in *New Republic*, 42 (18 March), 102-103.

"It Is In Truth a Pretty Toy" (Sara Teasdale, *Love Songs, Flame and Shadow*, and *Rivers to the Sea*), *Dial*, 78 (February), 107-114.

■ (Theodora Bosanquet, *Henry James at Work;* Walt Whitman, *Criticism: An Unpublished Essay*), *Criterion*, 3 (April), 465-468.

■ (Aldous Huxley, *Those Barren Leaves*), *Criterion*, 3 (April), 449-453.

■ "John Keats" (Amy Lowell, *John Keats*), *Dial*, 78 (June), 475-490.

■ "The Dead 'Novel' " (Jules Romains, *Lucienne*, trans. Waldo Frank), *Dial*, 79 (July), 60-63.

"The Idea of Great Poetry" (Lascelles Abercrombie, *The Idea of Great Poetry;* Lytton Strachey, *Pope*), *Nation & Athenaeum*, 37 (25 July), 517.

1926

■ (F. Scott Fitzgerald, *All the Sad Young Men* and *The Great Gatsby;* Ring Lardner, *Gullible's Travels* and *How to Write Short Stories;* Anita Loos, *Gentlemen Prefer Blondes*), *New Criterion*, 4 (October), 773-776.

"An Outline of the Modern Mind" (H. G. Wells, *The World of William Clissold*), *Dial*, 81 (December), 503-506.

■ "Sentiment of the Quotidian" (*Selected Poems of Carl Sandburg*, ed. Rebecca West), *New Republic*, 49 (8 December), 86-87.

1927

■ "Palimpsest" (H. D., *Palimpsest*), *New Republic*, 49 (2 February), 309.

■ "Another Murex" (Archibald MacLeish, *Streets of the Moon*), *New Republic*, 49 (9 February), 337.

"A Portrayer of Sprightly Empresses of Byzantium" (Charles Diehl, *Byzantine Portraits*), *New York Post*, 5 March, Sec. III, pp. 1, 10.

"Wanted: A Biography of the Literary Instinct" (Pelham Edgar, *Henry James: Man and Author;* Aylmer Maude, ed., *Family Views of Tolstoy;* Michael Sadleir, *Anthony Trollope: A Commentary*), *Independent*, 12 March, p. 295.

■ "The Beautiful Genius" (Avrahm Yarmolinsky, *Turgenev: The Man, His Art, and His Age*), *New Republic*, 50 (11 May), 349-350.

■ "Tristram" (Edwin Arlington Robinson, *Tristram*), *New Republic*, 51 (25 May), 22.

■ "The Poetic Dilemma" (A. E. Coppard, *Pelagea and Other Poems;* Ralph Cheever Dunning, *Rococo;* T. S. Eliot, *Poems*), *Dial*, 82 (May), 420-423.

"Candidly Speaking" (Maxwell Bodenheim, *Returning to Emotion*), *New Republic*, 51 (1 June), 53.

■ (William Faulkner, *Mosquitoes*), *New York Post*, 11 June, Sec. III, p. 7.

■ "Vagabondia" (*The Collected Poems of Ezra Pound*), *New Republic*, 51 (22 June), 131-132.

"Speak As You Must" (S. Foster Damon, *Astrolabe;* George O'Neill, *The White Rooster;* Lola Ridge, *Red Flag*), *Dial,* 83 (July), 63-65.

■ "Novel as Work of Art" (Virginia Woolf, *To the Lighthouse*), *Dial,* 83 (July), 41-44.

■ (Sherwood Anderson, *A New Testament*), *New York Post,* 9 July, Sec. III, p. 8.

"Starting a Poet Behind Scratch" (Humbert Wolfe, *Kensington Gardens* and *Lampoons*), *New York Post,* 23 July, Sec. III, p. 9.

■ "John Keats" (J. Middleton Murry, *Keats and Shakespeare;* Clarence Dewitt Thorpe, *The Mind of John Keats*), *Dial,* 83 (August), 161-164.

(Jacob Wassermann, *The Triumph of Youth*), *New York Post,* 6 August, Sec. III, p. 9.

(Marcel Prevost, *His Mistress and I*), *New York Post,* 13 August, Sec. III, p. 8.

(Harvey Fergusson, *Wolf Song*), *New York Post,* 20 August, Sec. III, p. 8.

(Martin Armstrong, *Sir Pompey and Madame Juno*), *New York Post,* 27 August, Sec. III, p. 8.

■ (*Journal of Katherine Mansfield*), *New York Post,* 17 September, Sec. III, p. 10.

■ (George Moore, *Celibate Lives*), *New York Post,* 24 September, Sec. III, p. 10.

(Jean Rhys, *The Left Bank, and Other Stories*), *New York Post,* 1 October, Sec. III, p. 10.

(Paul Busson, *The Man Who Was Born Again*), *New York Post,* 8 October, Sec. III, p. 10.

■ "Mr. Lawrence's Prose" (D. H. Lawrence, *Mornings in Mexico*), *Dial,* 83 (October), 343-346.

(Elizabeth Madox Roberts, *My Heart and My Flesh*), *New York Post,* 12 November, Sec. III, p. 10.

■ "George Gissing" (*A Victim of Circumstance*), *Dial,* 83 (December), 512-514.

(E. E. Cummings, *Him;* Eugene O'Neill, *Lazarus Laughed*), *New York Post,* 24 December, Sec. III, p. 12.

"Preface," *Modern American Poets,* selected by Conrad Aiken, New York, Modern Library, pp. v-ix.

1928

■ (Arnold Bennett, *The Vanguard*), *New York Post,* 14 January, Sec. III, p. 12.

"The Intellectual Spotlight" (Laura Riding, *Voltaire*), *New Republic,* 54 (22 February), 23.

■ "Lost Boy" (G. K. Chesterton, *Robert Louis Stevenson*), *New Republic,* 54 (21 March), 169.

"Magnifying the Moment" (James Wood, *New World Vistas*), *Dial,* 84 (April), 329-331.

"Wisdom of the Blood?" (Robert Clairmont, *Quintillions;* Osbert Sitwell, *England Reclaimed*), *New Republic,* 54 (11 April), 252-253.

■ (Wyndham Lewis, *The Wild Body*), *New York Post,* 14 April, Sec. III, p. 14.

(Joseph Moncure March, *The Wild Party*), *New York Post,* 28 April, Sec. III, p. 13.

"Those Unknown Singers" (Carl Sandburg, *The American Songbag*), *Dial,* 84 (May), 425-427.

■ (Dorothy Richardson, *Oberland*), *New York Post,* 12 May, Sec. III, p. 9.

(J. C. Squire *et al., Contemporary American Authors*), *New York Post,* 26 May, Sec. III, p. 9.

■ "Dissecting Anguish" (Thomas Mann, *Children and Fools,* trans. Herman George Scheffauer), *Dial,* 85 (July), 59-61.

■ (Eugene O'Neill, *Strange Interlude*), *New York Post,* 21 July, Sec. III, p. 5.

■ "Mr. Lewis and the Time-Beast" (Wyndham Lewis, *Time and Western Man*), *Dial,* 85 (August), 168-171.

" 'Credos' of America's Leading Authors" (Conrad Aiken), *Bookman,* 68 (October), 204.

■ "The Last of the Forsytes" (John Galsworthy, *Swan Song*), *New Republic,* 56 (10 October), 221-222.

"Underworldling" (Julius Meier-Graefe, *Dostoevsky: The Man and His Work*), *Dial,* 85 (December), 517-519.

■ "Flower of Old Japan" (Lady Murasaki, *The Tale of Genji*), *Bookman,* 68 (December), 477-479.

1929

■ "Unpacking Hearts With Words" (A. E. Coppard, *Collected Poems;* Robinson Jeffers, *Cawdor;* Archibald MacLeish, *The Hamlet of A. MacLeish;* Edwin Arlington Robinson, *Sonnets: 1889-1927;* Carl Sandburg, *Good Morning, America*), *Bookman,* 68 (January), 576-577.

■ "Orlando" (Virginia Woolf, *Orlando*), *Dial,* 86 (February), 147-149.

(Herbert Agar and Eleanor C. Chilton, *The Garment of Praise: The Necessity for Poetry*), *New York Post,* 23 February, Sec. III, p. M11.

(Herbert Read, *Phases of English Poetry*), *Bookman,* 69 (March), 104.

(*Further Poems of Emily Dickinson,* ed. Martha Dickinson Bianchi), *New York Post,* 16 March, Sec. III, p. M11.

(Herbert Read, *English Prose Style*), *Bookman,* 69 (April), 211.

(Rebecca West, *The Strange Necessity*), *Bookman,* 69 (April), 211-212.

(Arthur Davison Ficke, *Mountain Against Mountain;* Helene Mullins, *Earthbound, and Other Poems;* Henry Morton Robinson, *Buck*

Fever; Humbert Wolfe, *This Blind Rose*), *Bookman,* 69 (April), 214-215.

(Chauncey B. Tinker, *The Good Estate of Poetry*), *New York Post,* 20 April, Sec. III, p. M11.

"New England" (Jonathan Leonard, *Back to Stay*), *Dial,* 86 (May), 432-434.

(Edgar Lee Masters, *The Fate of the Jury;* Charles Norman, *Poems;* Edwin Arlington Robinson, *Cavender's House;* Elinor Wylie, *Angels and Earthly Creatures*), *Bookman,* 69 (May), 322-323.

■ (John Cowper Powys, *Wolf Solent*), *New York Post,* 18 May, Sec. III, p. 9M.

"Emily Dickinson and Her Editors" (*Further Poems of Emily Dickinson,* ed. Martha Dickinson Bianchi and Alfred L. Hampson), *Yale Review,* 18 (June), 796-798.

■ "Retreat" (T. S. Eliot, *For Lancelot Andrews, Essays on Style and Order*), *Dial,* 86 (July), 628-630.

(Gerald Bullett, *The History of Egg Pandervil*), *New York Post,* 6 July, Sec. III, p. 6M.

(*The Collected Poems of D. H. Lawrence*), *New York Post,* 20 July, Sec. III, p. 6M.

"Preface," *American Poetry, 1671-1928: A Comprehensive Anthology,* ed. Conrad Aiken, New York, Modern Library, pp. v-vii. Reprinted (and expanded) in *A Comprehensive Anthology of American Poetry,* New York, 1944; and in *An Anthology of Famous English and American Poetry,* New York, 1945.

1930

■ "Prose and Music" (Robert Bridges, *The Testament of Beauty*), *New Republic,* 62 (26 March), 164-166.

"Anthologies, Good and 'Bad'" (*Imagist Anthology: 1930,* with Preface by Ford Madox Ford; *The Stuffed Owl, an Anthology of Bad Verse,* ed. D. B. Wyndham Lewis and Charles Lee), *New Republic,* 62 (7 May), 333-334.

"Edith Sitwell's 'Pope'" (Edith Sitwell, *Alexander Pope*), *New Republic,* 62 (14 May), 358-359.

"The Dickinson Myth" (MacGregor Jenkins, *Emily Dickinson: Friend and Neighbor;* Josephine Pollitt, *Emily Dickinson: The Human Background of her Poetry;* Genevieve Taggard, *The Life and Mind of Emily Dickinson*), *Yale Review,* 20 (December), 393-396.

1931

"Why Poets Leave Home," *Scribner's,* 89 (January), 84-86.

■ "The Future of Poetry," *New Freeman,* 3 (29 April), 154-156. Reprinted in part as "The Poets are Waiting," *Publishers' Weekly,* 6 February 1954, pp. 776-777.

" 'The Jig of Forslin' " (correspondence), *New Republic,* 68 (11 November), 355.

1932

"A Letter from Vachel Lindsay," *Bookman*, 74 (March), 598-601.

"What I Believe," *Nation*, 135 (27 July), 79-80.

1934

■ "Development of a Poet" (Archibald MacLeish, *Poems: 1924-1933*), *New Republic*, 77 (17 January), 287-288.

■ "The Use of Poetry" (T. S. Eliot, *The Use of Poetry and the Use of Criticism;* John Sparrow, *Sense and Poetry*), *Yale Review*, 23 (March), 643-646.

■ "We Ask for Bread" (Gertrude Stein, *The Making of Americans*), *New Republic*, 78 (4 April), 219.

(Letter quoted by Malcolm Cowley on Franz Kafka, *The Castle*), *New Republic*, 78 (18 April), 283.

■ "The Well Worn Spirit" (William Carlos Williams, *Collected Poems: 1921-1931*. Preface by Wallace Stevens), *New Republic*, 78 (18 April), 289-291.

■ "Personae" (Ezra Pound, ed., *Active Anthology*), *Poetry*, 44 (August), 276-279.

"Death of an Imagist" (*The Poems of Richard Aldington*), *New Republic*, 79 (18 July), 272-273.

■ "Mencken on Morals" (H. L. Mencken, *Treatise on Right and Wrong*), *New Republic*, 80 (22 August), 54.

■ "After Ash Wednesday" (T. S. Eliot, *The Rock* and *After Strange Gods*), *Poetry*, 45 (December), 161-165.

(Answers to questions about the poetic process), *New Verse*, 11, 13.

1935

■ (*Alice James: Her Brothers: Her Journal*, ed. Anna Robeson Burr), *Criterion*, 14 (January), 313-315.

(Una Pope-Hennessy, *Edgar Allan Poe: A Critical Biography*), *Criterion*, 14 (April), 501-504.

■ (Henry James, *The Art of the Novel: Critical Prefaces*, ed. Richard P. Blackmur), *Criterion*, 14 (July), 667-669.

■ "London Letter" (T. S. Eliot, *Murder in the Cathedral*), *New Yorker*, 13 July, pp. 53-55.

"London Letter" (epitaph for the Poetry Book Shop), *New Yorker*, 10 August, pp. 37-39.

"London Letter" (T. E. Lawrence), *New Yorker*, 24 August, pp. 51-52, 55.

"A Plea for Anonymity," *New Republic*, 84 (18 September), 155-157.

1936

■ "The New England Animal" (George Santayana, *The Last Puritan*), *New Republic*, 85 (5 February), 372.

"London Letter" (the death of George V and Kipling), *New Yorker*, 8 February, pp. 46-47.

"London Letter" (the literary scene), *New Yorker*, 18 April, pp. 76-78.

"London Letter" (Surrealist show), *New Yorker*, 25 July, pp. 48-50.

"Was Harvard Worth While?" (John R. Tunis, *Was College Worth While?*), *New Republic*, 88 (30 September), p. 231.

■ "Mr. Eliot in the Wilderness" (T. S. Eliot, *Essays Ancient and Modern*), *New Republic*, 88 (21 October) 326-327.

■ "A. E. Housman" (*More Poems*), *New Republic*, 89 (11 November), 51-52.

1937

"The Gentlemanly Essayist" (Henry Seidel Canby, *Seven Years' Harvest;* Bernard DeVoto, *Forays and Rebuttals*), *New Republic*, 89 (20 January), 364.

■ "The Training of the Artist" (Joseph Hone, *The Life of George Moore;* Edgar Lee Masters, *Across Spoon River*), *New Republic*, 90 (17 February), 52.

"The Dubliner" (Oliver St. John Gogarty, *As I Was Walking Down Sackville Street*), *New Republic*, 91 (26 May), 79.

■ "Literature," in *Massachusetts: A Guide to Its Places and People*, written and compiled by the Federal Writers' Project of the Works Progress Administration for the State of Massachusetts, Boston, Houghton Mifflin, 1937, pp. 89-99.

1938

(Notes on poems by Conrad Aiken), *Oxford Anthology of American Poetry*, ed. William Rose Benét and Norman Holmes Pearson, New York, Oxford, pp. 1333-1340.

1939

■ "William Faulkner: The Novel as Form," *Atlantic*, 164 (November), 650-654. Reprinted in *Harvard Advocate*, 135 (November, 1951), 13, 24-26; and in *William Faulkner: Two Decades of Criticism*, ed. Frederick J. Hoffman and Olga W. Vickery, East Lansing, Michigan State, 1951.

1940

■ "Poetry: 1940 Model" *New Republic*, 102 (22 April), 540-541.

■ "A Rocking Alphabet" (Dylan Thomas, *The World I Breathe*), *Poetry*, 56 (June), 159-161.

■ "Back to Poetry," *Atlantic*, 166 (August), 217-223.

■ "After All, I Am a Poet" (F. García Lorca, *The Poet in New York and Other Poems*, trans. Rolfe Humphries), *New Republic*, 103 (2 September), 309.

1941

■ "The Careful Rapture" (Yvor Winters, *Poems*), *New Republic*, 104 (21 April), 539-540.

"Poetry: What Direction?" (*Five Young American Poets* [Barnard, Berryman, Jarrell, Moses, and O'Donnell]; Howard Nutt, *Special Laughter*), *New Republic*, 104 (12 May), 670-671.
■ "Poetry as Entertainment" (John Peale Bishop, *Selected Poems;* E. E. Cummings, *50 Poems;* Louis MacNeice, *Poems: 1925-40*), *New Republic*, 104 (16 June), 830-832.
"Dream and Project" (Horace Gregory, *Poems: 1930-1940;* Marya Zaturenska, *The Listening Landscape*), *New Republic*, 105 (15 September), 346-347.

1942

■ "American Writers Come of Age," *Atlantic*, 169 (April), 476-481.
"That Minor Art" (Rolfe Humphries, *Out of the Jewel*), *New Republic*, 106 (15 June), 836-837.
■ "Rilke's Greatness" (Rainer Maria Rilke, *Sonnets to Orpheus*, trans. M. D. Herter Norton), *New Republic*, 107 (19 October), 521-522.

1943

■ "The Untranslatable Message" (Stefan George, *Poems*, trans. C. N. Valhope and Ernest Morwitz; Charles Péguy, *Basic Verities*, trans. Ann and Julian Green), *New Republic*, 108 (14 June), 804-805.

1944

■ "The New Euphuism" *New Republic*, 110 (3 January), 26-27.
■ "Varieties of Poetic Statement" (Rolfe Humphries, *The Summer Landscape;* Robert Lowell, *Land of Unlikeness;* Karl Shapiro, *V-Letter and Other Poems*), *New Republic*, 111 (23 October), 528, 530.
"Introduction," *A Comprehensive Anthology of American Poetry*, ed. Conrad Aiken, New York, Modern Library, pp. ix-xii.
"Preface," *Twentieth-Century American Poetry*, ed. Conrad Aiken, New York, Modern Library, pp. xix-xx.

1945

■ "Theme With Variations" (John Malcolm Brinnin, *No Arch, No Triumph;* Richard Eberhart, *Poems: New and Selected;* Ralph Gustafson, *Flight Into Darkness;* Kenneth Rexroth, *The Phoenix and the Tortoise*), *New Republic*, 112 (2 April), 451-453.
■ "Whole Meaning or Doodle" (Robert Frost, *A Masque of Reason;* John Lehmann, *The Sphere of Glass;* St. John Perse, *Rains [Pluies]*, with translation by Denis Devlin; Herbert Read, *A World Within a War;* Oscar Williams, *That's All That Matters*), *New Republic*, 112 (16 April), 512, 514.
"The Dickinson Scandal" (Millicent Todd Bingham, *Ancestor's Brocades: The Literary Debut of Emily Dickinson; Bolts of Melody: New Poems of Emily Dickinson*, ed. Mabel Loomis Todd and Millicent Todd Bingham), *New Republic*, 113 (2 July) 25-26.

■ "Watershed" (Karl Shapiro, *Essay on Rime*), *New Republic*, 113 (3 December), 752, 754.

"Introduction" (to American Poetry), *An Anthology of Famous English and American Poetry*, ed., with Introductions, by William Rose Benét and Conrad Aiken, New York, Modern Library, pp. 513-516.

1947

"The Great Audience is Ready," *Saturday Review of Literature*, 30 (20 September), 7-8.

1948

"The 'Irresponsible' Critic" (exchange with Randall Jarrell), *Nation*, 166 (12 June), 670-672.

1949

■ "The Classic Influence" (*Collected Poems of John Peale Bishop* and *Collected Essays of John Peale Bishop*, ed.), *New Republic*, 120 (21 February), 24-25.

■ "King Bolo and Others," in *T. S. Eliot: A Symposium*, ed. Richard March and Tambimuttu, Chicago, Henry Regnery, pp. 20-23.

1951

■ "William Carlos Williams' Rich, Sprawling Memoirs" (*The Autobiography of William Carlos Williams*), *New York Herald Tribune Book Review*, 16 September, p. 1.

1954

"The Poets are Waiting," *Publishers' Weekly*, 6 February, pp. 776-777.

1955

"Edwin Arlington Robinson" (letter), (London) *Times Literary Supplement*, 14 October, p. 605. Reprinted in *Colby Library Quarterly*, Series IV, No. 5 (February, 1956), 95-97.

Index of Authors Reviewed

INDEX OF AUTHORS REVIEWED

Adams, Brooks, 115–120
Adams, Henry, 115–120
Aiken, Conrad, 120–130
Anderson, Sherwood, 130–132
Auden, W. H., 357

Bellitt, Ben, 358
Bennett, Arnold, 133–134
Bishop, John Peale, 134–136, 287–288
Bosanquet, Theodora, 230–233
Bosschère, Jean de, 136–141
Brennecke, Ernest, 219–223
Bridges, Robert, 141–143
Brinnin, John Malcolm, 170–171
Brooks, Van Wyck, 107–111

Cabell, James Branch, 143–148
Cargill, Oscar, 107–111
Chekhov, Anton, 148–152
Chesterton, G. K., 367–369
Coppard, A. E., 280–281
Croce, Benedetto, 71–74
Cummings, E. E., 287

Dickinson, Emily, 156–163
Doolittle, Hilda (H. D.), 153–155
Dostoevsky, Feodor, 163–167

Eberhart, Richard, 168
Eliot, T. S., 136–138, 171–197

Faulkner, William, 197–207
Fitzgerald, F. Scott, 207–210
Fletcher, John Gould, 210–213
Frankenberg, Lloyd, 358
Frost, Robert, 322–323, 355

Galsworthy, John, 213–217
George, Stefan, 318–320
Gissing, George, 217–219
Graves, Robert, 355
Gustafson, Ralph, 170

Hardy, Thomas, 219–222
Hergesheimer, Joseph, 144–146
Hone, Joseph, 309–311
Housman, A. E., 223–225
Humphries, Rolfe, 364
Huxley, Aldous, 225–230

James, Alice, 233–236
James, Henry, 230–238
Jeffers, Robinson, 280–282, 355

Keats, John, 238–256
Kostyleff, Nicolas, 35–41
Kreymborg, Alfred, 123–126

Lardner, Ring, 208–210
Lawrence, D. H., 256–268
Lewis, Wyndham, 268–274
Lindsay, Vachel, 274–276
Loos, Anita, 208–210
Lorca, Federico García, 276–278
Lowell, Amy, 238–253
Lowell, Robert, 363–364

MacLeish, Archibald, 278–285
MacNeice, Louis, 285–287, 357
Mann, Thomas, 288–290
Mansfield, Katherine, 291–299
Masters, Edgar Lee, 299–301
Mencken, H. L., 301–303
Millay, Edna St. Vincent, 357–358
Moore, George, 303–311
Moore, Merrill, 357
Murasaki, Lady, 311–315
Murry, John Middleton, 253–256

O'Neill, Eugene, 315–318

Patchen, Kenneth, 358
Péguy, Charles, 318–320
Perse, St. John, 320–322
Pound, Ezra, 171–172, 323–327
Powys, John Cowper, 327–329
Prescott, Frederick Clarke, 49–53

Rexroth, Kenneth, 169–170
Richards, I. A., 75–78
Richardson, Dorothy, 329–331
Riding, Laura, 355
Rilke, Rainer Maria, 331–333
Robinson, Edwin Arlington, 280–281, 333–346
Romains, Jules, 346–349
Rukeyser, Muriel, 357

Sandburg, Carl, 280–281, 349–352
Santayana, George, 352–354
Schwartz, Delmore, 355–358
Shapiro, Karl, 358–364
Stein, Gertrude, 364–367
Stevenson, Robert Louis, 367–369

414 *Index*

Thomas, Dylan, 358, 370–373
Thorpe, Clarence Dewitt, 253–256
Turgenev, Ivan, 373–377

Waley, Arthur, 377–380
Whitman, Walt, 230–233
Williams, William Carlos, 380–386
Winters, Yvor, 387–389
Woolf, Virginia, 389–394

Yarmolinsky, Avrahm, 373–377

$\dfrac{1212}{865}$

Opict
arang ar Ph